D1524662

Philosophical Perspectives, 14, Action and Freedom, 2000

Previously Published Volumes
Volume 1, Metaphysics, 1987
Volume 2, Epistemology, 1988
Volume 3, Philosophy of Mind and Action Theory, 1989
Volume 4, Action Theory and Philosophy of Mind, 1990
Volume 5, Philosophy of Religion, 1991
Volume 6, Ethics, 1992
Volume 7, Language and Logic, 1993
Volume 8, Logic and Language, 1994
Volume 9, AI, Connectionism, and Philosophical Psychology, 1995
Volume 10, Metaphysics, 1996
Volume 11, Mind, Causation, and World , 1997
Volume 12, Language, Mind, and Ontology, 1998
Volume 13, Epistemology, 1999

Volumes 1 through 9 are available from Ridgeview Publishing Company,
    Box 686, Atascadero, CA 93423.
Volumes 10 through 13 are available from Blackwell Publishers, 350 Main Street,
    Malden, MA 02148.

Additional titles to be announced.

Philosophical Perspectives, 14, Action and Freedom, 2000

Edited by
JAMES E. TOMBERLIN

Blackwell Publishers, Inc.
350 Main Street
Malden, MA 02148 USA

Blackwell Publishers, Ltd.
108 Cowley Road
Oxford OX4 1JF
United Kingdom

Library of Congress Cataloging-in-Publication Data

Action and freedom, 2000 / edited by James E. Tomberlin.
    p. cm. —. (Philosophical perspectives, ISSN 0029-4624 ; 14)
    Includes bibliographical references.
    ISBN 0-631-21825-4 (case : alk. paper) — ISBN 0-631-21826-2 (pbk. : alk. paper)
    1. Free will and determinism. 2. Act (Philosophy) 3. Ethics. I. Tomberlin, James E.,
1942-II. Series.

BJ1461 .A28 2000
123'.5—dc21   00-059394

ISBN 0-631-21825-4
ISBN 0-631-21826-2 (P)
ISSN 0029-4624

Contents

James E. Tomberlin is Professor of
Philosophy at California State University,
Northridge, where he has taught since
completing graduate study at Wayne State
University in 1969. He has published more
than eighty essays and reviews in action
theory, deontic logic, metaphysics, philosophy
of language, mind, religion, and the theory of
knowledge. He is a co-editor of *Noûs*; and in
addition to the editorship of the present series,
he has edited *Agent, Language, and the
Structure of the World* (Hackett, 1983),
Hector-Neri Castaneda, Profiles (D. Reidel,
1986) and he co-edited *Alvin Plantinga,
Profiles* (D. Reidel, 1985).

Philosophical Perspectives, 14, Action and Freedom, 2000

FREE WILL REMAINS A MYSTERY

The Eighth *Philosophical Perspectives* Lecture

Peter van Inwagen
The University of Notre Dame

This paper has two parts. In the first part, I concede an error in an argument I have given for the incompatibility of free will and determinism. I go on to show how to modify my argument so as to avoid this error, and conclude that the thesis that free will and determinism are compatible continues to be—to say the least—implausible. But if free will is incompatible with determinism, we are faced with a mystery, for free will undeniably exists, and it also seems to be incompatible with *in*determinism. That is to say: we are faced with a mystery if free will *is* incompatible with indeterminism. Perhaps it is not. The arguments for the incompatibility of free will and indeterminism are plausible and suggestive, but not watertight. And many philosophers are convinced that the theory of "agent causation" (or some specific development of it) shows that acts that are undetermined by past states of affairs can be free acts. But the philosophical enemies of the idea of agent causation are numerous and articulate. Opposition to the idea of agent causation has been based on one or the other of two convictions: that the concept of agent causation is incoherent, or that the reality of agent causation would be inconsistent with "naturalism" or "a scientific world-view." In the second part of this paper, I will defend the conclusion that the concept of agent causation is of no use to the philosopher who wants to maintain that free will and indeterminism are compatible. But I will not try to show that the concept of agent causation is incoherent or that the real existence of agent causation should be rejected for scientific reasons. I will assume—for the sake of argument—that agent causation is possible, and that it in fact exists. I will, however, present an argument for the conclusion that free will and indeterminism are incompatible even if our acts or their causal antecedents are products of agent causation. I see no way to respond to this argument. I conclude that free will remains a mystery—that is, that free will

undeniably exists and that there is a strong and unanswered *prima facie* case
for its impossibility.

I

I have offered the following argument for the incompatibility of free will
and determinism.[1] Let us read 'Np' as 'p and no one has or ever had any choice
about whether p'. We employ the following two inference rules

α $\Box p \vdash Np$
β $Np, N(p \supset q) \vdash Nq.$

(The box, of course, represents necessity or truth in all possible worlds.) Let
'L' represent the conjunction of the laws of nature into a single proposition. Let
'P_0' represent the proposition that describes the state of the world at some time
in the remote past. Let 'P' represent any true proposition. The following statement, proposition (1), is a consequence of determinism:

(1) $\Box((P_0 \& L) \supset P).$

We now argue,

(2)	$\Box((P_0 \supset (L \supset P))$	1, standard logic
(3)	$N((P_0 \supset (L \supset P))$	2, α
(4)	NP_0	Premise
(5)	$N(L \supset P)$	3, 4, β
(6)	NL	Premise
(7)	NP	5, 6, β.

Since the two premises are obviously true—no one has any choice about the
past; no one has any choice about the laws of nature—, (7) follows from (1) if
the two rules of inference are valid.[2] And from this it follows that if determinism is true, no one has any choice about anything.

Are the two rules of inference valid? Rule α obviously is, whatever Descartes would have us believe about God. The question of the soundness of the
argument comes down to the question whether β is valid. And, although β does
not, perhaps, share the "luminous evidence" of α, it nevertheless seems pretty
plausible. One way to appreciate its plausibility is to think in terms of regions
of logical space. By logical space, I mean a space whose points are possible
worlds. (Distances between points correspond to the "distances" that figure in
a Lewis-Stalnaker semantics for counterfactual conditionals; areas or volumes
represent probabilities[3].) Consider Figure 1.

Suppose Alice is inside p and has no choice about that; suppose she is also
inside the region that corresponds to the material conditional whose antecedent

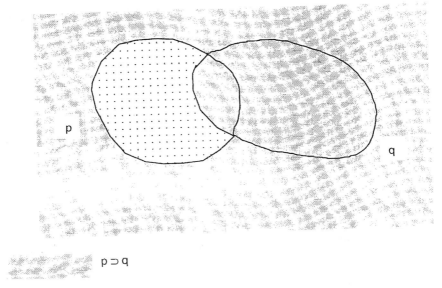

p

q

p ⊃ q

Figure 1.

is p and whose consequent is q (the heavily shaded region)—and has no choice about *that*. Alice will, of course, be inside the intersection of p and q, and hence inside q.[4] Has she any choice about that? It would seem not. As an aid to our intuitions, let us think of the regions displayed in the diagram as physical regions. Examination of the diagram shows that any way out of q—any escape route from q, so to speak—will either take Alice out of p or out of the shaded region. Therefore, *because* Alice has no way out of p and no way out of the shaded region ($p \supset q$), she has no way out of q. To be inside a region and to have no way out of it is to be inside that region and to have no choice about whether one is inside it. Rule β, therefore, would seem to be valid. This intuitive, diagrammatic argument is very plausible, and at one time I found it, or something very like it, cogent. Unfortunately, as any student of geometry knows, figures can be misleading, since a figure may have unintended special features that correspond to unwarranted assumptions. And this must be so in the present case, owing to the fact that McKay and Johnson have discovered what is undeniably a counterexample to β.[5]

McKay and Johnson begin by noting that α and β together imply the rule of inference that Michael Slote has called Agglomeration:

$\mathrm{N}p, \mathrm{N}q \vdash \mathrm{N}(p \ \& \ q).$

(To show this, assume $\mathrm{N}p$ and $\mathrm{N}q$. The next line of the proof is '$\Box(p \supset (q \supset (p \ \& \ q)))$'. The proof proceeds by obvious applications of α and β.) Rule α is obviously correct. To show β invalid, therefore, it suffices to produce a counterexample to Agglomeration. McKay and Johnson's counterexample to Agglomeration is as follows.

> Suppose I have a coin that was not tossed yesterday. Suppose, however, that I was able to toss it yesterday and that no one else was. Suppose that if I had tossed it, it might have landed "heads" and it might have landed "tails" and it would have landed in one way or the other (it's false that it might have landed on edge, it's false that a bird might have plucked it out of the air...), but I should have had no choice about which face it would have displayed. It seems that
>
> > N The coin did not land "heads" yesterday
> > N The coin did not land "tails" yesterday
>
> are both true—for if I had tossed the coin, I should have had no choice about whether the tossed coin satisfied the description 'did not land "heads"', and I should have had no choice about whether the tossed coin satisfied the description 'did not land "tails".' But
>
> > N (The coin did not land "heads" yesterday & the coin did not land "tails" yesterday)
>
> is false—for I did have a choice about the truth value of the (in fact true) conjunctive proposition *The coin did not land "heads" yesterday and the coin did not land "tails" yesterday*, since I was able to toss the coin and, if I had exercised this ability, this conjunctive proposition would have been false.

The case imagined is, as I said, undeniably a counterexample to Agglomeration. Agglomeration is therefore invalid, and the invalidity of β follows from the invalidity of Agglomeration. Our diagrammatic argument for the validity of β therefore misled us. But what is wrong with it?

We may note that a similar intuitive, diagrammatic argument could have been adduced in support of Agglomeration. Imagine two intersecting regions, p and q. Their region of overlap is, of course, their conjunction. Suppose one is inside p and has no way out of p; and imagine that one is inside q and has no way out of q. One will then be inside p & q; but does it follow that one has no way out of p & q? Inspection of the simple diagram that represents this situation shows that any way out of p & q must either be a way out of p or a way out of q. What is wrong with *this* argument?

To answer this question, we must examine the concept of "having a way out of a region of logical space." Suppose we know what is meant by "having access to" a region of logical space. (A region of logical space corresponds to a proposition, or to a set containing a proposition and all and only those propositions necessarily equivalent to it. To have access to a region of logical space is to be able to ensure the truth of the proposition that corresponds to that region, or to be able to ensure that that region contains the actual world. If one is inside a region one *ipso facto* has access to that region. If one has access to *p*, one *ipso facto* has access to the regions of which *p* is a subset—to the "super-regions" of *p*.) To have a way out of a region *p* of logical space that one is inside is then defined as follows: to have access to some region that does not overlap *p*—or to have the ability to ensure that the proposition that corresponds to *p* is false. Now consider Figure 2.

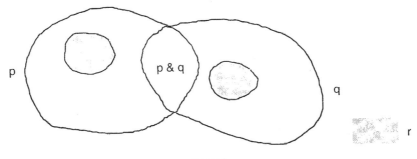

Figure 2.

Suppose I am "inside" the region *p & q*. Suppose I have access to and only to the following regions: (a) *p & q* and the other regions I am inside, and (b) *r* and the superregions of *r*. ("But what about the subregions of *r*?" From the fact that one has access to a certain region of logical space, it does not follow that one has access to any of its proper subregions. I may, for example, be able to ensure that the dart hit the board, but unable to ensure with respect to any proper part of the board that it hit that proper part.) It follows from these suppositions that I am inside *p* and have no way out of *p*—for every region to which I have access overlaps *p*. (And, of course, the same holds for *q*: every region to which I have access overlaps *q*.) But I do have a way out of *p & q*, for I have access to a region—*r*—that does not overlap *p & q*. (It is not essential to the example that *r* be a non-connected region. It might have been "horseshoe-shaped" or a "ring." What is essential is that *r* overlap *p* and overlap *q* and not overlap *p & q*.)

If one thinks about the issues raised by McKay and Johnson's counterexample in terms of diagrams of logical space, it is easy enough to construct a counterexample to β itself (at least in the sense in which Figure 2 represents a counterexample to Agglomeration).[6] Here is a simple counterexample to β. Consider three regions of logical space, related to one another as in Figure 3:

Suppose I am inside *p* and inside *p ⊃ q*. (Or, what is the same thing, suppose I am inside *p & q*.) Suppose I have access to and only to the following regions: (a) the regions I am inside, and (b) *r* and its superregions. Then I have no way out of *p* (every region to which I have access overlaps *p*) and no way out of *p ⊃ q* (every region to which I have access overlaps *p ⊃ q*), but I have a way out of *q*, for I have access to a region—*r*—that does not overlap *q*.

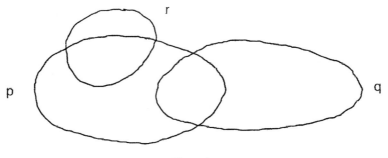

Figure 3.

How did Figure 1 and the intuitive argument based on it mislead us? The answer is simple. The informal argument invited us to think of "having a way out of a region" as something like having available a path or line leading from a particular point inside that region *to a particular point* outside that region. (Recall our use of the term "escape route.") That, after all, is what it is normally like to have a way out of a region of physical space, and our intuitive grasp of any sort of space is mainly by way of analogy with physical space. But if we exercise our imaginations, we can think of ways in which one might have an ability to change one's position in physical space that is entirely different from the ability to follow a path that leads to a given point. We might for example suppose that one can bring it about that one changes one's position in space without moving—by magic, perhaps—, and that when one changes one's position by this means, one might arrive at *any* of the points that make up some extended region.

Now consider once more Alice and Figure 1 (but add to Figure 1 a region r that is related to p and q just as r is related to p and q in Figure 3). Our intuitive argument for the conclusion that a way out of q must either be a way out of p or a way out of $p \supset q$ (the shaded region) was this:

> As an aid to our intuitions, let us think of the regions displayed in the diagram as physical regions. Any way out of q—any escape route from q, so to speak—will either take Alice out of p or out of the shaded region.

As long as Alice moves by following a continuous path through space (an "escape route"), this is correct: any continuous path that leaves both p and the shaded region must leave q. But suppose that although Alice has no way of crossing any of the boundaries shown in the diagram by following a continuous path through space, she has a single magical resource: a magical lamp such that if she rubs it, the Slave of the Lamp will instantaneously translate her to a randomly chosen point inside the region r. Has Alice a way out of p? Has she a way out of $p \supset q$? The answers to these questions, perhaps, depend on how one defines 'a way out'. But if we define 'a way out' in a way parallel to our definition of 'a way out of a region of logical space', i.e.,

> If one is inside a region of space *r*, one has a way out of *r* just in the case that one is able to ensure that one is inside a region that does not overlap *r*,

the answer to both questions is No: she has no "way out" of either of these regions. But Alice *does* have a way out of *q*: rubbing the lamp constitutes a way out of *q*, for rubbing the lamp will ensure that she is not in *q*. Our intuitions about physical space therefore misled us. As the world is, the only way to leave a region of physical space is to follow a continuous path out of that region, and our intuitions reflect this fact. Our diagrams of logical space are, of course, drawn in physical space and the diagrams therefore invite us to think of one's having access to a region *r* of logical space (a false proposition, a region not containing the actual world) in terms of one's ability to move along a line drawn from the point in the diagram that represents the actual world to some point inside the section of the diagram that represents *r*. Our "diagrammatic" argument misled us into thinking that there could be no counterexample to β (or to Agglomeration) because nothing in the concept of "access to a region of logical space" corresponds to the "continuous path" requirement that the real world imposes on our intuitions about "access to a region of physical space." A continuous path through physical space terminates in a single point, not in an extended region. To "have access" to an extended region of physical space is therefore (normally) to have access to one or more of the points that make up that region. To have access to a region of logical space, however, is in no possible case to have access to a point in logical space (a single possible world): Since one's power to direct the course of events is limited, from the fact that one is able to ensure that *some* possible world in which, say, the coin is tossed is actual it does not follow that one is able to ensure with respect to any given world in which the coin is tossed that *that* world is actual. And of course, one never is able to ensure this; if one were one would not only be able to ensure that a tossed coin land on one particular face, but one would be able to determine the truth-value of every contingent proposition.

Our definition of '*Np*' was '*p* and no one has or ever had any choice about whether *p*'. The definiens is equivalent to

> *p* and every region of logical space to which anyone has, or ever had, access overlaps *p*.

Why? Well, suppose that *p*, and that I did not do but was able to do X (and was able to do nothing else that was relevant to the truth-value of *p*), and that if I had done X, *p* might have been true and might have been false. It seems wrong in that case to say that I had a choice about the truth-value of *p*. If, for example, the coin was untossed and I was able to toss it, and if I had tossed it, it might have fallen "heads" and might not have fallen "heads," it is wrong to say that I had a choice about the truth value of the (true) proposition that the coin did not land "heads." (This point is the essence of the McKay-Johnson counterexample to Agglomeration.) Now if it were important that the coin have landed "heads" (if someone's life depended on its landing "heads," say), there would be something wrong with my defending my failure to toss the coin by saying, "Look, the coin *didn't* land heads, and I didn't have any choice about that." And it is perhaps intuitively plausible to suppose that if p and if I had no choice about whether p, then I cannot properly be held morally responsible for p. But I don't think that this consideration has any tendency to show that I had a choice about how the coin fell. If I did offer the imagined lame excuse, the proper response would not be, "You did too have a choice about whether the coin landed 'heads'"; it would rather be, "You had a choice about whether the coin was tossed, and if you had tossed it, it might have landed 'heads.' What you are to blame for is not doing your best to bring it about that the coin landed 'heads.'" In sum, if p is true proposition, having a choice about the truth-value of p implies being able to *ensure* that p is false.[7] And, as we have seen, the following is possible: p is true and no one is able to ensure that p is false; the conditional whose antecedent is p and whose consequent is q is true, and no one is able to ensure that that conditional is false; someone is able to ensure that q is false.

McKay and Johnson are therefore right. Rule β is invalid, and my argument for the incompatibility of free will and determinism is invalid.

This, of course, does not imply that free will and determinism are compatible, or that there is no plausible argument for the incompatibility of free will and determinism. I think, in fact, that the above argument for the incompatibility of free will and determinism can be turned into a valid argument by a minor modification of Rule β.[8] Suppose that, instead of defining 'Np' as 'p and no one has, or ever had, any choice about p'—that is, as 'p and every region to which anyone has, or ever had, access overlaps p'—, we were to define 'Np' as follows:

'p and every region to which anyone has, or ever had, *exact* access *is a sub-region of p*'.

One has *exact* access to a region if one has access to it *and to none of its proper subregions*. Intuitively, one has exact access to p if one can ensure the truth of p but of nothing "more definite." The properties of the "exact access" relation differ from those of the "access" relation in several important ways. If I am inside a region, I do not in general have exact access to that region. (This is an understatement: the only region I am inside and have exact access to is the actual world.[9]) If I have exact access to a region, then, by definition, I have exact access to none of its (proper) superregions.[10] If I have exact access to the region of logical space in which Hillary Clinton proves Goldbach's Conjecture, it follows that I do *not* have exact access to the region in which *someone* proves Goldbach's Conjecture—although it follows that I *do* have *access* to that region. It is, unfortunately, impossible to give a plausible example of a non-actual region to which I have exact access. Suppose that, although I do not throw the dart, it is within my power to ensure that it hit the board—*and* that, for no proper part of the board is it within my power to ensure that the dart hit that part. Do I have exact access to a region in which the dart hits the board? Presumably not, for presumably I have access to a region in which the dart hits the board *and* I exclaim, "Ah!" For one to have exact access to the non-actual region *p* it must be the case that one can ensure the actuality of *p* but not the joint actuality of *p* and any logically independent region. If one could ensure the actuality of some non-actual *world*, one would have exact access to that world, of course, but obviously no one can do that—or no one but God. Still, it seems evident that there must be regions of logical space to which any given human being has exact access, simply because a human being's ability to ensure the truth of things, to "fine tune" his actions and their consequences, must come to an end somewhere.

Consider now our operator 'N', redefined as I have suggested. I think that this is what I was trying to capture when I defined 'N*p*' as '*p* and no one has, or ever had, any choice about *p*'. What McKay and Johnson's counterexample shows is that the concept 'not having a choice about' has the wrong logical properties to capture the idea I wanted to capture—the idea of the *sheer inescapability* of a state of affairs. But if 'N' is redefined in the way I have proposed, the redefined 'N' does capture this idea. If every region to which I have access overlaps *p*, it may nevertheless be true that there is some action I can perform such that, if I did, then *p* *might* be false. But if every region to which I have *exact* access *is a subregion of p*, every action I can perform is such that, if I did perform it, *p* would be true: it is not the case that *p* might be false.

Now if 'N' is re-defined as I have suggested, Rule β is valid—for the simple reason that every set that is a subset of both *p* and *p* $\supset$ *q* (that is, of *p* & *q*) is a subset of *q*. Thus, if every region of logical space to which anyone has exact access is within both *p* and *p* $\supset$ *q*, every region of logical space to which anyone has exact access is within *q*. (And, of course, Rule α is valid: every region of logical space to which anyone has exact access is a region of logical space.)

What about the two premises of the argument for the incompatibility of free will and determinism? These both seem true—or at least the reasons for thinking them true are no worse than they were on the "no choice" understanding of 'N'. Every region of logical space to which anyone has exact access will be a subregion of P_0; every region of logical space to which anyone has exact access will be a subregion of L. (The compatibilist will disagree. The compatibilist will define 'is able' in some way—will no doubt employ some version of the "conditional analysis of ability"—that will have the consequence that each of us is *able* to perform various acts, such that, if he or she did perform them, then the conjunction of P_0 and L would be false. Thus, the compatibilist will argue, we do have exact access to regions that are not subregions of both P_0 and L. But this is an old dispute, and I have nothing new to say about it. I will say only this—and this is nothing new. The compatibilist's "move" is contrived and ad hoc; it is "engineered" to achieve the compatibility of free will and determinism; it *seems* that our freedom can only be the freedom to add to the actual past[11]; it *seems* that our freedom can only be the freedom to act in accordance with the laws of nature.)

It seems, therefore, that I now have what I thought I had when I thought Rule β was valid on the "no choice" understanding of 'N': a valid argument for the incompatibility of free will and determinism whose premises seem to be true. And this, *mutatis mutandis*, is all that can be asked of any philosophical argument. At any rate, no more can be said for any known philosophical argument than this: it is valid and its premises seem to be true.

II

Free will, then, seems to be incompatible with determinism. But, as many philosophers have noted, it also seems to be incompatible with *in*determinism. The standard argument for this conclusion (which I have called the *Mind* Argument because it has appeared so frequently in the pages of *Mind*) goes something like this:

> If indeterminism is to be relevant to the question whether a given agent has free will, it must be because the acts of that agent cannot be free unless they (or perhaps their immediate causal antecedents) are undetermined. But if an agent's acts are undetermined, then *how* the agent acts on a given occasion is a matter of chance. And if how an agent acts is a matter of chance, the agent can hardly be said to have free will. If, on some occasion, I had to decide whether to lie or to tell the truth, and if, after much painful deliberation, I lied, my lie could hardly have been an act of free will if whether I lied or told the truth was a matter of chance. To choose to lie rather than tell the truth is a *free* choice only if, immediately before the choice was made, it was up to the agent whether he lied or told the truth. That is to say, before the choice was made, the agent must have been able to lie and able to tell the truth. And if an agent is faced with a choice between lying and telling the truth, and if it is a *mere matter of chance* which of these things the agent does, then it cannot be up to the agent which of them he does.

(At any rate, this is one way to formulate the *Mind* Argument. Other statements of the argument are available, including some that do not appeal to the concept of chance. I will presently return to this point.) In *An Essay on Free Will*, I tried to show that the *Mind* Argument depended on the "unrevised" version of

Rule β. If this is correct, then, since "unrevised β" is invalid, the *Mind* Argument is invalid. But perhaps I was wrong to think that the *Mind* Argument depended on "unrevised β," at least in any essential way. Perhaps the *Mind* Argument depends only on the employment of some rule of inference *of the same general sort* as "unrevised β." Perhaps, indeed, the Mind Argument could be re-written so as to depend only on "revised β." I will not consider these possibilities. I will not try to answer the question whether the *Mind* Argument is in fact valid. I have a different project. I wish to consider the *Mind* Argument in a very informal, intuitive form, to contend that in this intuitive form the argument has a great deal of plausibility, and to use this contention as the basis of an argument for the conclusion that the concept of *agent causation* is entirely irrelevant to the problem of free will. This is no trivial conclusion. Most philosophers who have thought carefully about the problem of free will maintain that the concept of agent causation is incoherent—and perhaps also maintain that if, *per impossibile*, this concept were coherent, it would be contrary to naturalism or to some other important philosophical commitment to suppose that it applied to anything in the real world. A sizable and respectable minority of the philosophers who have thought carefully about the problem of free will maintain that the concept of agent causation is coherent and, moreover, that agent causation is real and figures in an essential way in the acts of free agents. But almost everyone seems to think that if there really *were* such a thing as agent causation, its reality would constitute a solution to the problem of free will. I am going to try to show that even if agent causation exists, even if it is an element in the acts of free agents, the problem of free will is just as puzzling as it would have been if no one had ever thought of the idea of agent causation. I am going to try to show that even if agent causation is a coherent concept and a real phenomenon, and we know this, this piece of knowledge will be of no help to the philosopher who is trying to decide what to say about free will.

I begin my argument by characterizing the problem of free will and the concept of agent causation.

The problem of free will in its broadest outlines is this. Free will seems to be incompatible both with determinism and indeterminism. Free will seems, therefore, to be impossible. But free will also seems to exist. The impossible therefore seems to exist. A solution to the problem of free will would be a way to resolve this apparent contradiction. There would seem to be three forms a solution could take, three ways in which one might try to resolve the apparent contradiction. One might try to show, as the compatibilists do, that—despite appearances—free will is compatible with determinism. Or one might try to show, as many incompatibilists do, that—despite appearances—free will is compatible with indeterminism. Or one might try to show, as many "hard determinists" do, that the apparent reality of free will is mere appearance. (To be reasonably plausible, a solution of the third type would probably have to incorporate some sort of argument for the conclusion that moral responsibility does not, as it appears to, require free will—or else an argument for the conclusion that a belief in the reality of moral responsibility is not, as it appears to be, an indispensable component of our moral and legal and political thought.) This is the problem to which, in my view, agent causation is irrelevant. (Perhaps there is some *other* problem that could reasonably be called 'the problem of free will' and to which agent causation *is* relevant. I can only say that if there is such a problem, I don't know what it is.)

Agent causation is, or is supposed to be, a relation that agents—thinking or rational *substances*—bear to events. Agent causation is opposed to *event* causation, a relation that events bear to events. The friends of agent causation hold that the causes of some events are not (or are only partially) earlier events. They are rather substances—not *changes* in substances, which are of course events, but "the substances themselves." Thus, they say, Thomas Reid caused the movements of his fingers when he wrote the sentence, "There is no greater impediment to the advancement of knowledge than the ambiguity of words." These movements, they insist, were caused simply by *Reid*, and not by any change in Reid. Or, speaking more carefully, since they are aware on empirical grounds that these movements were in fact caused by changes in Reid's hand and arm and spinal cord and brain, they will say that there were *some* events, events that occurred no more than a few seconds before these movements and were among their causal antecedents, events that presumably occurred within the motor centers of Reid's brain, that were caused by Reid and not by any prior events. Speaking even more carefully, they may say that at any rate there were causal antecedents of the movements of Reid's fingers to whose occurrence Reid, Reid himself, the thinking substance, *contributed causally*—thus allowing the possibility that earlier events in Reid's brain *also* contributed causally to the occurrence of these events.

Let this suffice for a characterization of the problem of free will and the concept of agent causation. Now how is the concept supposed to figure in a solution of the problem? In this wise, I believe: the reality of agent causation is supposed to entail that free will and indeterminism are compatible. The idea is something like this. A certain event happens in Reid's brain, an event that, through various intermediate causes, eventually produces a bodily movement that constitutes some voluntary action of Reid's—say, his writing the sentence, "There is no greater impediment to the advancement of knowledge than the ambiguity of words." (Perhaps we need not attempt to explain the notion of a bodily movement's "constituting" a voluntary action. The idea is illustrated by this example: certain movements of Reid's arm and hand and fingers constitute his writing the sentence, "There is no greater impediment, *etc.*") And Reid is, let us suppose, the agent-cause of the aforementioned brain-event that was a causal antecedent of his writing this sentence—or at any rate he contributes agent-causally to its occurrence. (From this point on, I will neglect the distinction between agent-causing an event and contributing agent-causally to its occurrence.) The action, or the event that is Reid's performing it, is not determined by the state of the universe at any time before the antecedent brain-event occurred. (And why not? Well, because the event that was his agent-causing the antecedent brain-event was not determined to occur by any prior state of the universe. And if that event—his agent-causing the antecedent brain-event—had not occurred, his hand and fingers would not have moved and he would not have written the sentence.) And yet it is as obviously true as anything could be that he is responsible for this event, for he was its cause: it occurred because *he* caused it to occur. It was therefore an act of free will, and free will is therefore consistent with indeterminism.

In the sequel, I will take it for granted that the relevance of the concept of agent causation to the problem of free will is supposed to be found in the supposed fact that the reality of agent causation entails that free will is compatible with indeterminism. And I will take it for granted that the argument of the preceding paragraph is a fair representation of the argument that is supposed to establish this compatibility. If there is some other reason agent causation is supposed to be relevant to the problem of free will, or if the argument of the preceding paragraph is a poor or incomplete representation of the reasons for supposing that the concept of agent causation can be used to establish the compatibility of free will and indeterminism, then the argument of the remainder of this essay will be at best incomplete and at worst entirely beside the point.

In my view, this argument does not succeed in showing that the reality of agent causation entails the compatibility of free will and indeterminism. Its weak point, I believe, is the reasoning contained in its last two sentences: "And yet it is as obviously true as anything could be that [Reid] is responsible for [the antecedent brain-event], for he was its cause: it occurred because *he* caused it to occur. It was therefore an act of free will, and free will is therefore consistent with indeterminism." It is not my plan to make anything of the fact that Reid knew even less than I about what goes on in the motor centers of human brains—or of the fact that other agents, agents who act freely if anyone does, do not even know that they *have* brains. Any doubts about the argument that might be based on these facts have to my mind been adequately answered by Chisholm, and I shall not bother about them.[12] Nor shall I raise questions about the cause of the event "its coming to pass that Reid is the agent-cause of the antecedent brain-event."[13] Again, I think Chisholm has seen what the friends of agent causation should say about the cause of this event, to wit, that Reid was its agent-cause—and was, moreover, the agent-cause of the event "its coming to pass that Reid is the agent-cause of the event 'its coming to pass that Reid is the agent-cause of the antecedent brain-event'," and so *ad infinitum*.[14] Some may object to the thesis that, as an indispensable component of his writing a certain sentence, Reid, without being aware of it, became the agent cause of an infinite number of events; I don't.

In order to see what I *do* object to in the argument, let us return to the question why some have thought that free will was incompatible with indeterminism. Let us, that is, return to the "mere matter of chance" argument. Let us try to state this argument more carefully. (In *An Essay on Free Will*, I had a very short way with any attempt to state the *Mind* argument in terms of an undetermined act's being a random or chance occurrence.[15] I argued there that the words 'random' and 'chance' most naturally applied to *patterns* or *sequences* of events, and that it was therefore not clear what these words could mean if they were applied to single events. It will be evident from what follows that I no longer regard this argument as having any merit.) Let us suppose undetermined free acts occur. Suppose, for example, that in some difficult situation Alice was faced with a choice between lying and telling the truth and that she freely chose to tell the truth—or, what is the same thing, she seriously considered telling the truth, seriously considering lying, told the truth, and was able to tell the lie she had been contemplating. And let us assume that free will is incompatible with determinism, and that Alice's telling the truth, being a free act, was therefore undetermined. Now suppose that immediately after Alice told the truth, God caused the universe to revert to precisely its state one minute before Alice told the truth (let us call the first moment the universe was in this state 't_1' and the second moment the universe was in this state 't_2'), and then let things "go forward again." What would have happened the second time? What would have happened after t_2? Would she have lied or would she have told the truth? Since Alice's "original" decision, her decision to tell the truth, was undetermined—since it was undetermined whether she would lie or tell the truth—, her "second" decision would also be undetermined, and this question can therefore have no answer; or it can have no answer but, "Well, although she would either have told the truth or lied, it's not the case that she would have told the truth and it's not the case that she would have lied; lying is not what she would have done, and telling the truth is not what she would have done. One can say only that she *might* have lied and she *might* have told the truth."

Now let us suppose that God *a thousand times* caused the universe to revert to exactly the state it was in at t_1 (and let us suppose that we are somehow suitably placed, metaphysically speaking, to observe the whole sequence of "replays"). What would have happened? What should we expect to observe? Well, again, we can't say what would have happened, but we can say what would *probably* have happened: sometimes Alice would have lied and sometimes she would have told the truth. As the number of "replays" increases, we observers shall—almost certainly—observe the ratio of the outcome "truth" to the outcome "lie" settling down to, converging on, some value.[16] We may, for example, observe that, after a fairly large number of replays, Alice lies in thirty percent of the replays and tells the truth in seventy percent of them—and that the figures 'thirty percent' and 'seventy percent' become more and more accurate as the number of replays increases. But let us imagine the simplest case: we observe that Alice tells the truth in about half the replays and lies in about half the replays. If, after one hundred replays, Alice has told the truth fifty-three times and has lied forty-eight times,[17] we'd begin strongly to suspect that the figures after a thousand replays would look something like this: Alice has told the truth four hundred and ninety-three times and has lied five hundred and eight times. Let us suppose that these are indeed the figures after a thousand replays. Is it not true that as we watch the number of replays increase, we shall become convinced that what will happen in the *next* replay is a matter of chance? (The compulsive gamblers among us might find themselves offering bets about what Alice would do in the next replay.) If we have watched seven hundred and twenty-six replays, we shall be faced with the inescapable impression that what happens in the seven-hundred-and-twenty-seventh replay will be due simply to chance. Is there any reason we should resist this impression? Well, we certainly know that there is nothing we could learn about the situation that could undermine the impression, for we already know everything that is relevant to evaluating it: we know that the outcome of the seven-hundred-and-twenty-seventh replay will not be determined by its initial state (the common initial state of all the replays) and the laws of nature. Each time God places the universe in this state, both "truth" and "lie" are consistent with the universe's being in this state and the laws of nature. A sheaf of possible futures (possible in the sense of being consistent with the laws) leads "away" from this state, and, if the sheaf is assigned a measure of 1, surely, we must assign a measure of 0.5 to the largest sub-sheaf in all of whose members Alice tells the truth and the same measure to the largest sub-sheaf in all of whose members she lies. We must make this assignment because it is the only reasonable explanation of the observed approximate equality of the "truth" and "lie" outcomes in the series of replays. And if we accept this general conclusion, what other conclusion can we accept about the seven-hundred-and-twenty-seventh replay (which is about to commence) than this: each of the two possible outcomes of this replay has an objective, "ground-floor" probability of 0.5—and there's nothing more to be said? And this, surely, means that, in the strictest sense imaginable, the outcome of the replay will be a matter of chance.

Now, obviously, what holds for the seven-hundred-and-twenty-seventh replay holds for all of them, including the one that wasn't strictly a *re*play, the initial sequence of events. But this result concerning the "initial replay", the "play," so to speak, should hold whether or not God bothers to produce any replays. And if He does not—well, that's just the actual situation. Therefore, an undetermined action is simply a matter of chance: if it was undetermined in the one, actual case whether Alice lied or told the truth, it was a mere matter of chance whether she lied or told the truth. If we knew beforehand that the objective, "ground-floor" probabilities of Alice's telling the truth and Alice's lying were both 0.5, then (supposing our welfare depended on her telling the truth) we could only regard ourselves as *fortunate* when, in the event, she told the truth. But then how can we say that Alice's telling the truth was a free act? If she was faced with telling the truth and lying, and it was a mere matter of chance which of these things she did, how can we say that—and this is essential to the act's being free—she was *able* to tell the truth and *able* to lie? How could anyone be able to determine the outcome of a process whose outcome is a matter of objective, ground-floor chance?

This is the plausible, intuitive version of the *Mind* Argument that I have promised to discuss. What I must do now is show that the concept of agent causation cannot be used to undermine the intuitive plausibility of this argument.

Let us suppose that when Alice told the truth, she agent-caused certain brain-events that, in due course, resulted in those movements of her lips and tongue that constituted her telling the truth. And let us again suppose that God has caused the universe to revert to precisely its state at t_1, and that this time Alice has lied. I do not see how to avoid supposing that in this "first replay," Alice *freely* lied—for if one has to choose between telling the truth and lying, and if one freely chooses to tell the truth, then it must be the case that if one had chosen instead to lie, the choice to lie would have been a free act. (One cannot say that an agent faces exactly two continuations of the present, in one of which he tells the truth but was able to lie and in the other of which he lies and was *un*able to tell the truth.) Now if Alice's lie in the first replay was a free act, she must—according to the friends of agent causation—have been the agent-cause of some among the causal antecedents of the bodily movements that constituted her lying. And so, of course, it will be, *mutatis mutandis*, in each successive replay. If God produces one thousand replays, and if (as I have tacitly been assuming) the state of the universe at t_1—the common initial state of all the replays—determines that Alice will *either* tell the truth or lie, then, in each replay, Alice will *either* agent-cause cerebral events that, a second or so later, will result in bodily movements that constitute her telling the truth or agent-cause cerebral events that, a second or so later, will result in bodily movements that constitute her lying. She will, perhaps, agent-cause events of the "truth antecedent" sort five hundred and eight times and events of the "lie antecedent" sort four hundred and ninety-three times. Let us suppose once more that we are somehow in a position to observe the sequence of replays. We may again ask the question, "Is it not true that as we watch the number of replays increase, we shall become convinced that what will happen in the *next* replay is a matter of chance?" I do not see why we should not become convinced of this. And what might we learn, what is *there* for us to learn, that should undermine this conviction? What should lead us to say that the outcome of the next replay, the seven hundred and twenty-seventh, will not be a matter of chance? What should lead us to say that it is anything other than a matter of chance whether Alice will agent-cause truth-antecedent cerebral events or lie-antecedent cerebral events in the about-to-occur seven-hundred-and-twenty-seventh replay? Well, one might say this: If it turns out that Alice agent-causes truth-antecedent cerebral events, this will not be a matter of chance because it will be she, *Alice*, who is the cause of the event "its coming to pass that Alice agent-causes truth-antecedent cerebral events." But have we not got every reason to regard the occurrence of *this* event—that is, the occurrence of "its coming to pass that

Alice agent-causes the event 'its coming to pass that Alice agent-causes truth-antecedent cerebral events'"—as a matter of chance? If the three events "the truth-antecedent cerebral events"/ "its coming to pass that Alice agent-causes the truth-antecedent cerebral events"/ "its coming to pass that Alice agent-causes the event 'its coming to pass that Alice agent-causes truth-antecedent cerebral events'" are the first three terms of an infinite series of agent-caused events, is not the simultaneous occurrence of all the events in this sequence (as opposed to the simultaneous occurrence of all the events in an infinite sequence of agent-caused events whose first member is "lie-antecedent cerebral events") a mere matter of chance?

Nothing we could possibly learn, nothing God knows, it would seem, should lead us to distrust our initial inclination to say that the outcome of the next replay will be a matter of chance. If this much is granted, the argument proceeds as before, in serene indifference to the fact that we are now supposing Alice to be the agent-cause of various sets of cerebral events that are antecedents of the bodily movements that constitute her acts. And the argument proceeds to this conclusion: if it is undetermined whether Alice will tell the truth or lie, then—*whether or not* Alice's acts are the results of agent-causation—it is a mere matter of chance whether she will tell the truth or lie. And if it is a mere matter of chance whether she will tell the truth or lie, where is Alice's free will with respect to telling the truth and lying? If one confronts a choice between A and B and it is a matter of chance whether one will choose A or B, how can it be that one is *able* to choose A?

I close with an example designed to convince you of this.

You are a candidate for public office, and I, your best friend, know some discreditable fact about your past that, if made public, would—and should—cost you the election. I am pulled two ways, one way by the claims of citizenship and the other by the claims of friendship. You know about my situation and beg me not to "tell." I know (perhaps God has told me this) that there exist exactly two possible continuations of the present—the actual present, which includes your begging me not to tell and the emotional effect your appeal has had on me—, in one of which I tell all to the press and in the other of which I keep silent; and I know that the objective, "ground-floor" probability of my "telling" is 0.43 and that the objective, "ground-floor" probability of my keeping silent is 0.57. Am I in a position to promise you that I will keep silent?—knowing, as I do, that if there were a million perfect duplicates of me, each placed in a perfect duplicate of my present situation, forty-three percent of them would tell all and fifty-seven percent of them would hold their tongues? I do not see how, in good conscience, I could make this promise. I do not see how I could be in a position to make it. But if I believe that I am able to keep silent, I should, it would seem, regard myself as being in a position to make this promise. What more do I need to regard myself as being in a position to promise to do X than a belief that I am *able* to do X? Therefore, in this situation, I should not regard myself as being able to keep silent. (And I cannot see on what grounds third-person observers of my situation could dispute this first-person judgment.) Now suppose God vouchsafes me a further revelation: "Whichever thing you do, whether you go to the press or keep silent, you will be the agent-cause of events in your brain that will result in the bodily movements that constitute your act." Why should this revelation lead me to conclude that I am in a position to promise to keep silent—and therefore that I am able to keep silent? Its content simply doesn't seem to be relevant to the above argument for the conclusion that it is false that I am able to keep silent. I confess I believe there *is* something wrong with this argument. (I expect I believe this because I fervently *hope* that there is something wrong with it.) But it seems clear to me that if there is, as I hope and believe, something wrong with the argument, its flaw is not that it overlooks the possibility that my actions have their root in agent-causation.[18]

Notes

1. See Peter van Inwagen, *An Essay on Free Will* (Oxford: at the Clarendon Press, 1983), pp. 93–104.
2. Or this will do as a first approximation to the truth. But the statement in the text is not literally true, since at least one of the two premises is a contingent truth. ('P_0' is a contingent truth, and 'NP_0', which has 'P_0' as a conjunct, is therefore a contingent truth. 'L' is *probably* a contingent truth, and 'NL' is therefore probably a contingent truth.) Here is a more careful statement. If the two rules of inference are valid, then an argument identical in appearance with the argument in the text can be constructed in any possible world and premises (4) and (6) of any of these arguments will be true in the possible world in which it is constructed if 'P_0' expresses a proposition that describes the state of the world (= 'universe') in that possible world before there were any human beings, and 'L' expresses the proposition that is the conjunction of all propositions that are laws of nature in that possible world. Thus it can be shown (if the two rules of inference are valid) with respect to each possible world that if determinism is true in that world, then none of its inhabitants has any choice about anything. And if this can be shown with respect to each possible world, then free will is incompatible with determinism.
3. That is, if a region of logical space occupies 23.37 percent of the whole of logical space, the probability of its being actual (containing the actual world) is 0.2337: the "intrinsic probability" of a proposition that is true in just that region of logical space is 0.2337. See my "Probability and Evil," in *The Possibility of Resurrection and Other Essays in Christian Apologetics* (Boulder: Westview Press, 1997), pp. 69–87.
4. In this paper, the symbols 'p' and 'q' and so on will sometimes be schematic letters representing sentences and sometimes variables ranging over propositions or regions of logical space. Although I normally deprecate this sort of logical sloppiness, it does have its stylistic advantages, and it is easily eliminable at the cost of a little verbal clutter. Similar remarks apply to '&' and '⊃'.
5. Thomas McKay and David Johnson, "A Reconsideration of an Argument against Compatibilism," *Philosophical Topics* 24 (1996), pp. 113–122.

6. The McKay/Johnson counterexample to Agglomeration is not a counterexample to β—although, since, since the validity of β entails the validity of Agglomeration, the existence of a counterexample to Agglomeration entails the existence of counterexamples to β.

7. It implies more than this. It implies something about knowledge, generally knowledge of cause and effect. If p is true, and if p would be false if I did X (which I was able to do), for me to have a choice about the truth-value of p, I must have known (or at least be such that I *should* have known) that doing X would result in the falsity of p.

8. Other ways to repair the argument have been suggested. One of these ways—it is similar to my own proposal—has been suggested by McKay and Johnson themselves. See "A Reconsideration of an Argument against Compatibilism," pp. 118–121. For a different suggestion, see Alicia Finch and Ted A. Warfield, "The *Mind* Argument and Libertarianism," *Mind* 107 (1998), pp. 515–528.

9. This statement assumes that no non-actual world is as close to the actual world as the actual world is to itself. Without this assumption, we should have to say: the only region I am inside and have exact access to is the set of worlds that are as close to the actual world as it is to itself.

10. Suppose I have exact access to r. Then I have access to r. Let R be any (proper) superregion of r. If I have exact access to R, I have exact access to a region and to one of its proper subregions (r)—which is contrary to the definition of exact access.

11. *Cf.* Carl Ginet, *On Action* (Cambridge, Cambridge University Press, 1990), pp. 102–103.

12. "Freedom and Action," in Keith Lehrer, ed., *Freedom and Determinism* (New York: Random House, 1966), pp. 11–44. See pp. 20–21.

13. The event "its coming to pass that Reid is the agent-cause of the antecedent brain-event" is the same event as "Reid's acquiring the property *being the agent-cause of the antecedent brain event*." Presumably, there is a moment of time before which Reid has not agent-caused the antecedent brain-event and after which he has, and that is the moment at which this event occurs.

14. At any rate, I *believe* that Chisholm has considered this problem and has defended the "and so *ad infinitum*" solution. But I have been unable to find this solution in his writings.

15. Pp. 128–29.

16. "Almost certainly" because it is *possible* that the ratio not converge. Possible but most unlikely: as the number of replays increases, the probability of "no convergence" tends to 0.

17. After one hundred replays, Alice has told the truth or lied one hundred and one times.

18. I am grateful to Ted A. Warfield (*il miglior fabbro*) for reading Part I of this paper and for offering valuable criticisms. I hope I have made good use of them.

Philosophical Perspectives, 14, Action and Freedom, 2000

MODEST LIBERTARIANISM

Randolph Clarke
University of Georgia

1. Introduction

I shall use the term 'libertarian' here to refer to accounts of what free will might be if it is not compatible with determinism, whether it actually exists or not. My focus will be on libertarian accounts that avoid extravagant metaphysical commitments.

Consider initially the following version of such a view. In order for a decision to be made freely, it says, the agent must have certain psychological capacities, and he must, on the occasion of making that decision, be able to exercise those capacities.[1] He must, for example, be able to regard some considerations as *reasons* for action, and he must have and be able to exercise at least something close to an ordinary capacity to engage in practical reasoning and govern his behavior by his appreciation of practical reasons. It might also be required that the reasons he possesses not have been produced in certain rationality-undermining ways, such as via brainwashing. These requirements the view will share with attractive compatibilist accounts. It will share as well the allowance that the process by which the decision is produced be a causal process; indeed, I think that both should require this. When a decision is made freely, it is made for reasons, and its being made for reasons consists partly in its being caused in a characteristic way by the agent's having those reasons. The libertarian view will differ in that it will hold that at some point (or points) in this causal process, the causation must not be deterministic; it will have to be nondeterministic or probabilistic causation. For the time being, let us suppose that the indeterminism is required in the direct causation of the decision itself. When a decision is freely made, the account will say, there remained until the making of that decision a genuine chance that the agent would not make that decision. This may have been a chance that he would instead make an alternative decision, for different reasons, or it may just have been a chance that he would make no decision at all right then. The actual decision will have been nondeterministically caused by its immediate antecedents, by the agent's having certain reasons for action and by his having an intention to make up his mind right then.

This type of libertarian account is modest in two respects. It is modest in its metaphysical commitments, appealing to nothing more than what many compatibilist accounts appeal to plus nondeterministic event causation. There may be doubts about whether causation can be nondeterministic, but those who take contemporary physics seriously tend not to harbor them, and there are several interesting accounts of probabilistic causation.[2] Certainly the doubts here are not as daunting as those that attach to such notions as the noumenal self or agent causation.

The second respect in which this type of view must be modest is in what it promises. For it hardly offers a kind of freedom that, it seems, proponents of more extravagant libertarian accounts aim to characterize. One could hardly claim that, if this modest account is correct, "then we have a prerogative which some would attribute only to God: each of us, when we act, is a prime mover unmoved" (Chisholm 1966, 23).

This second point brings us to an obvious objection, one frequently raised against this modest sort of libertarian account. The gist of the objection is that the view offers *nothing* better than what is available with a compatibilist competitor—an account that resembles it in every way except in the requirement of indeterminism. Consider a decision that meets the requirements of the modest libertarian account. There was a chance of the agent's not making that decision. But what is wanted from an account of free will is an account of an agent's *control* over which decisions he makes and which actions he performs, and the mere chance of not making a certain decision may appear not to enhance the agent's control at all. The factors that constitute the agent's control in making the decision that we are considering, it may be said, are just those factors that are shared by the modest libertarian account and a compatibilist competitor: the agent's having and being able to exercise a capacity for rational self-governance, his decision's being caused by his having certain reasons, and so forth. A decision that meets the requirements of the modest libertarian view, it may be objected, is actually made with no greater control than is a comparable decision meeting the requirements of the competing compatibilist account. There is, then, according to this objection, nothing to be gained from this modest libertarian account. If free will cannot be given an adequate compatibilist account, then this modest libertarian view is not adequate either. And if the modest libertarian view is adequate, its requirement of indeterminism is superfluous; some compatibilist account will be equally adequate.

Indeed, it is sometimes objected that such a libertarian view does *worse* than a compatibilist competitor. A decision that meets the requirements of the former, it is claimed, is made with *less* control than is a decision that meets the requirements of the latter. The requirement of indeterminism is worse than superfluous; it is destructive of the control that we want an account of free will to characterize.

I shall offer some reasons to doubt that this second, stronger objection is correct. However, I believe that the first objection is about half right. A decision that meets the requirements of modest libertarianism is made with no greater degree of control than is a causally determined decision that is in every other respect the same. But the objection may be about half wrong as well. What I acknowledge to be correct in it does not imply that what is offered by modest libertarianism is *of no more value* than what is offered by a competing compatibilist view. For it may be that the chance of not making the decision, or of making an alternative decision instead, though not increasing the degree of control, adds to the value of the agent's control. In the final section of this paper, I shall argue that it is reasonable to maintain that this is in fact so.

Before focusing on this issue, however, an important detail of the modest libertarian view needs some attention. A large part of this paper will concern a difference between two kinds of modest libertarian account.

2. Locating Indeterminism

The version of modest libertarianism that I sketched places indeterminism in the direct production of the decision: the event that is required to be nondeterministically rather than deterministically caused is the decision itself. Such an account requires what we might call "action-centered indeterminism" (since making a decision is performing a mental action). Call this type of modest libertarian view an "action-centered" account.[3]

Several writers (Dennett 1978; Fischer 1995; and Mele 1995, 1996, and 1999) have offered versions of an importantly different type of modest libertarianism, one on which indeterminism is located not precisely in making a decision or performing an action but at an earlier point in the process of deliberation. With this type of view, the events that are required not to be directly deterministically caused are not actions of any sort; the required indeterminism is non-action-centered. Call this type of modest libertarian view a "non-action-centered" account. In this section I shall defend an action-centered account against some objections that have been raised against it, and I shall present a reason for preferring it to a non-action-centered libertarian view.

2a. An Argument against an Action-Centered Account

Mele (1995) holds that libertarians should accept a compatibilist account of the relation between a deliberator's evaluative judgment concerning which course of action is best (or better or good enough) and his acquisition of an intention (and between the intention-acquisition and the performance of the action that has been decided upon); that is, they should allow but not require deterministic causal connections here. As do similar views proposed by Dennett and Fischer, the account recommended by Mele requires indeterminism only at an earlier stage of the deliberative process. The account may be satisfied when, for example, it is undetermined which of a certain subset of the agent's non-occurrent beliefs come to mind in the process of deliberation and combine with other events and states to bring about the agent's evaluative judgment (214).[4] The subset in question consists of "beliefs whose coming or not coming to mind is not something that one would control even if determinism were true" (216). Moreover, Mele suggests,

> even when an agent is on the verge of reaching a decisive better judgment, the (undetermined) coming to mind of a belief might prompt reservations that lead to reconsideration. So, in a scenario of the imagined kind, what an agent decisively judges best can be causally open as long as deliberation continues. Further, as long as deliberation is in progress it can be causally open when that deliberation will end, for it can be causally open whether a belief will come to mind and prolong deliberation. (217)

But indeterminism subsequent to the agent's making an evaluative judgment, as is required by an action-centered account, would be undesirable, Mele argues. He first introduces an important distinction between two types of control that an agent might have over an action or other event or state (211). The first, "proximal control," concerns the direct (and perhaps also nearly direct) production of certain agent-involving events, such as the agent's having certain values, desires, and beliefs, his making a certain evaluative judgment, his acquiring a certain intention, and his performing a certain action. We may suppose that the processes by which such events are produced are causal processes. But there is more to proximal control than just the causal nature of this process; I shall discuss what more there might be below. The second, "ultimate control," concerns the causal influence of agent-external events or conditions. In order for an agent to have ultimate control over the making of a certain decision, there must be at no time any minimally causally sufficient condition for the agent's making that decision which includes no event or state internal to the agent. Thus, agents can have ultimate control over their actions only if determinism is false. Proximal control, on the other hand, is to be understood as compatible with determinism.

Mele then argues that when the direct causation of an agent-involving event such as the making of a decision is nondeterministic, the agent has less proximal control over that event than that possessed by a deterministic counterpart, assuming that the agents have some proximal control, and an equal amount, over some cause of the event. "Imagine," he suggests,

> that it is equally up to each of two agents, $S3$ and $S4$, what they will (individually) judge it best to do in the situation in which they find themselves and that the equal proximal control over this that the agents possess is nonzero control. If it is causally determined that, whatever $S3$ decisively judges it best at t to do at t, $S3$ will intend at t in accordance with that judgment, then the limitations on $S3$'s control over what he intends at t (assuming that it is causally determined that he will judge decisively) are exhausted by any limitations on his control over what he decisively

judges best (and by any limitations imposed by its being causally determined that he will judge decisively). However, internal indeterminism at the relevant juncture brings with it limitations of its own. If it is causally open that whatever $S4$ decisively judges it best to do, he does not intend accordingly, then $S4$'s control over what he intends is limited in a way that $S3$'s control in this connection is not. $S3$ has the power to ensure what he will intend by making a better judgment, and $S4$ does not. (212)[5]

According to this ensurance argument, what is undesirable about indeterminism located where an action-centered account places it is that it diminishes the agent's proximal control over which decision he makes (and hence over which intention he acquires).[6] With the recommended non-action-centered account, it is acknowledged, the agent may lack deterministic proximal control over whether a given belief enters into his deliberative process. But, Mele notes, we do not typically have proximal control over this aspect of deliberation anyway, even if determinism is true. And indeterminism at this point need not diminish the agent's proximal control over "how he deliberates in light of the beliefs that *do* enter his deliberation" (215). He may deliberate carefully and in ways guided by his own deliberative principles. His evaluative judgment may be rational, made for reasons, nondeterministically caused by certain of his values, desires, and beliefs that came to mind during deliberation. An account of this sort, Mele suggests, will give us a view that provides for ultimate control without sacrificing any (or any significant degree of) proximal control.

Two main claims are made here concerning why a non-action-centered account should be favored over an action-centered view. The first is that indeterminism with respect to which considerations come to mind prior to the agent's making an evaluative judgment does not diminish the agent's proximal control (or does not significantly diminish it). The second is that indeterminism subsequent to the agent's evaluative judgment does significantly diminish the agent's proximal control. Although I think that anyone who accepts the second of these claims has reason to reject the first,[7] I shall pass over this point and focus on the second claim. For there are reasons to doubt that it is true.

The crucial premise in the ensurance argument for this second claim is that $S4$'s lacking "the power to ensure what he will intend by making a better judgment" constitutes a decrease in his proximal control over what he intends. Note first that this power is not required for the control that constitutes free will. In akratic or weak-willed decision, an agent may decide contrary to his better judgment. Such an agent does not ensure, by making a better judgment, what he will intend; and it seems that in an ordinary case of akratic decision, the agent may lack the power to ensure this just by making the judgment. He may nevertheless act with the control that constitutes free will.

Such an agent may have a different power to ensure that he will decide in accord with, and on the basis of his better judgment. He may be able to perform certain mental actions—acts of attention, for example—that would so alter the relative strengths of his various motivations that it would then be ensured that he would decide to do what he has judged best. But note that even an indeterministic agent such as *S4* (who decides non-akratically) can have this power. As things stand, it is causally open that he decide contrary to his better judgment. But he may be able to close this off. He cannot ensure what he will intend *just* by making his evaluative judgment; but he may be able to ensure what he will intend by performing certain mental actions that he is able to perform.

Neither of these points directly undermines Mele's conclusion concerning *S4*, for it may be that although *S4* retains enough control for free will, the indeterminism in his case diminishes proximal control to a significant and undesirable extent. Or it may be that the indeterminism undermines *S4*'s freedom by significantly diminishing his proximal control, though not by virtue of eliminating the guarantee that Mele identifies. To evaluate these possibilities, we need to consider what sort of control freedom is and what part proximal control plays in it.

2b. Proximal and Actional Control

The freedom that is the focus of libertarian accounts—and indeed, of competing compatibilist accounts—is essentially a freedom of action. It is a type of what I shall call "actional control," a type of control that an agent can have *directly* only over an action. By way of possessing direct control of this type over action(s), an agent can have indirect actional control over events and states that are not actions, but this latter control is derived from the agent's control over the action(s).

What is the relation of proximal control to this type of actional control? There are several possibilities here; I shall suggest a construal that, it seems to me, is most likely to illuminate the issues before us in this paper.

First, proximal control may be taken to constitute, wholly or partly, several different types of direct actional control. Any action at all, whether performed by a non-rational agent, an unfree agent, or a free agent, is an exercise of some type of direct control by the agent, and the proximal causation of that action—its being caused in a non-deviant way by the agent's having certain desires, beliefs, and a certain intention—is at least part of what constitutes the direct actional control in that instance. (If incompatibilists are correct, then something like what Mele calls "ultimate control" may also partly constitute direct, freedom-level actional control.) Proximal control will also be a constituent in indirect actional control, as when an agent exercises control over the occurrence of some non-active event by purposefully bringing about that event, in a relatively direct way.

Proximal control, as Mele (225) notes, may also have a non-actional form. Such control is something that one might have over the making of an evaluative judgment, even when that event is not an action, and even when one's control over the occurrence of that event does not derive from one's control over earlier actions. An agent's proximal control over the making of an evaluative judgment would be a matter of the way in which the agent's deliberative process produces that judgment. This will be a causal process, one that proceeds in a certain way. Its non-actional freedom, Mele suggests, will be its freedom from certain influences that would undermine the freedom of the subsequent action that it produces, freedom from such things as compulsion, manipulation, and insanity.

We might usefully regard the agent's non-actional proximal control here as freedom as well from certain sorts of inefficiency and irrationality that would not be so severe as to undermine the freedom of the agent's subsequent action.[8] For example, if an agent routinely has a number of quite irrelevant considerations come to mind while deliberating or routinely makes evaluative judgments in a way that is mildly irrational, then the agent may be said to have less control over this non-actional process than he would have if he made these judgments more efficiently and rationally, and yet such inefficiency and irrationality need not render his subsequent decisions and actions unfree. Thus, non-actional proximal control may be greater where some non-actional mental process leading to action proceeds in some ideally efficient and rational way, where, for example, only the most relevant values, desires, and beliefs come to mind during the agent's deliberation, and the causal process that constitutes his deliberation proceeds with the utmost efficiency and rationality to produce the most rational judgment concerning which action is best.[9]

2c. Indeterminism and Proximal Control

With these tools in hand, let us return to an evaluation of the ensurance argument. Recall that the agents *S3* and *S4* have equal, nonzero proximal control over what they decisively judge it best to do. How shall we understand this control? Not as even partly constituting direct actional control. Making a judgment concerning which alternative action is best is not typically itself an action; perhaps it never is. (None of Dennett, Fischer, and Mele give any indication that they take it to be an action.) An agent might have indirect actional control over making such a judgment. The proximal part of such control would concern what directly brings about the judgment. That would not typically be a decision to make a judgment that a certain action is best; it might be a decision to make a judgment now. But the crucial aspect of such control would be how the agent's judgment is related, on the one hand, to his reasons and, on the other, to extraneous factors. This aspect of the agent's proximal control over the making of the judgment is non-actional. Hence, in what follows, in considering an agent's proximal control over such deliberative events as the making of an evaluative judgment, I shall focus on non-actional proximal control.

There is a further reason for focusing here on non-actional proximal control rather than indirect actional control. We are concerned ultimately with the question of the agent's actional control over the eventual decision. We cannot in general suppose that freedom-level actional control—control of a variety and degree sufficient to render decision or other action free—derives from earlier freedom-level actional control. If there is any freedom-level actional control at all, there must be some underived or direct freedom-level actional control. (A familiar regress would be generated if for any decision (or other action) by a given agent to be free, the agent must have performed some earlier free action.) Thus, sooner or later we must provide an account of directly free decision (or other action), of free decision (or other action) whose freedom does not derive from the free performance of earlier actions. We may as well face that task here.[10]

Recall that Mele's view allows (though it does not require) that until a judgment is made, it remains causally open that new beliefs come to mind and either prolong deliberation or produce a different judgment. Thus, when an agent makes an evaluative judgment, it may be that the values, desires, and beliefs that caused the judgment did not causally determine it; it was the case that they would cause it unless some new belief came to mind, and none did. This sort of indeterminism in the direct causation of the judgment is said not to detract from the agent's proximal control over the making of the judgment, or not significantly so.

But if the possibility of a new thought's occurring at this stage does not diminish proximal control, it is unclear why the same possibility at later points should diminish proximal control. It might be that even after an agent has decisively judged a certain action best, it remains causally open that a new thought occur to the agent, one that decisively favors a different alternative. Similarly, it might be that even after the agent has acquired an intention to perform the action judged best, it remains causally open that a new thought occur showing the agent that a different alternative is best. When the agent has acted, it may have been the case that the agent's judgment would cause the acquisition of the corresponding intention, unless a new thought occurred, and that the intention-acquisition would cause the intended action, unless a new thought occurred, and no new thought occurred. It may also have been the case that only relevant new thoughts might have occurred, and that if they had, subsequent judgment, intention-acquisition, and action would have been quite rational. On what grounds could indeterminism of this sort here be said to diminish proximal control, while indeterminism of a parallel sort prior to the evaluative judgment is said not to?

It might be said that there are grounds for this claim in our practical need for deliberation effectively to produce action. We cannot drag out deliberation with unending reconsideration of judgments we have already made and intentions we have already formed. With respect to the first of these, an agent needs to be able to make an evaluative judgment that is, as Mele says, "decisive," a judgment that "settles in the agent's mind the question what (from the perspective of his own desires, beliefs, etc.) it is best or better to do given his circumstances" (15). Moreover, the agent needs such judgments to be effective, in some sense, in keeping that question settled in his mind. The causal openness of new considerations' coming to mind after an evaluative judgment has been made may seem to diminish the agent's proximal control because it decreases the effectiveness of the judgment, an effectiveness for which we have a practical need.

But of course we also have a need for the evaluative judgments that we make to be well informed, and when a decisive judgment has been made without the agent's having taken account of some important, relevant consideration (because it did not come to mind), it may be preferable that the consideration come to mind prior to the performance of the chosen action and that the question of what to do be reconsidered. Any view that allows chanciness with respect to which considerations come to mind and when is going to have a hard time defending the claim that such chanciness prior to the evaluative judgment does not diminish proximal control but after the evaluative judgment it does.[11]

A second difference might be appealed to in order to draw this distinction. With regard to the making of an evaluative judgment, the proximal control on which we are focusing is non-actional. However, when at the end of deliberation an agent acquires a certain intention, it is by performing a mental action of deciding that the agent acquires that intention. The proximal control here will be at least partly constitutive of a type of direct actional control.

The indicated difference is certainly there. But I cannot see how it supports the distinction. Hence, if there are grounds for denying that indeterminism prior to the making of an evaluative judgment significantly detracts from proximal control, then a proponent of an action-centered account has grounds for arguing that indeterminism of the sort we have just considered—the chance of new considerations' coming to mind between judgment and decision—need not significantly diminish proximal control either.

The chance that an agent not decide straightaway in accord with an evaluative judgment may be a chance of the agent's deciding to reconsider that judgment, rather than a chance of new considerations' simply occurring to him. We do not always judge well, and in a particular case an agent may have special reason to doubt the judgment he has just made concerning which course of action is best. That reason may leave rationally permissible both his deciding in accord with the judgment and his deciding to reconsider the judgment. Where this is so, again, lacking a power to ensure what he will decide by making a judgment appears not necessarily to constitute any significant decrease in the proximal component of the agent's direct actional control over the making of the decision.

A proponent of an action-centered view may want to make a stronger claim. The sort of indeterminism considered so far involves a chance of new thoughts' coming to mind subsequent to the evaluative judgment or a chance of the agent's deciding to reconsider his judgment. A proponent may claim that independently of there being a chance of either of these things, and even if the chance is just that the agent decide contrary to the evaluative judgment, indeterminism at this juncture need not significantly diminish proximal control.

A moderate libertarian of this stripe accepts that an agent's proximal control in making a decision consists just in the decision's being non-deviantly caused by appropriate agent-involving events. Further, this theorist holds that the degree of proximal control that is exercised depends on which agent-involving events actually cause the decision (and perhaps on what their causal histories are). What he denies is that the degree of proximal control that the agent exercises depends to any significant extent on whether the causation that actually occurs is governed by deterministic or nondeterministic laws. The degree of proximal control actually exercised in direct actional control, on this view, is a matter of what actually causes what, not of what might have caused what. There may have been a chance of the agent's exercising less proximal control in making a decision without the agent's actually having exercised less proximal control.

When an agent decides *contrary to* his evaluative judgment, he does not exercise rational control, but he nevertheless exercises a type of direct actional control. His decision is an intentional action, and he decides for certain of his reasons. He thus exercises proximal control in making his decision, even if, given the irrationality of his action-production process, he exercises less of such control than he would have had he decided rationally. Further, an agent may act with enough proximal control for direct freedom when he decides irrationally, for he may have been able to exercise rational control. Any incompatibilist will hold that such an agent will have been able to decide rationally only if there was some indeterminism in the process leading to his actual decision. And any modest libertarian, it seems, will allow the indeterminism to be located in the direct causation of the decision, for in this type of case there is no prior non-active event that we could reasonably want to ensure that the agent make the actual (irrational) decision.

If an agent deciding contrary to his evaluative judgment may exercise enough proximal control for direct freedom even when there is some indeterminism in the direct causation of his decision, then it appears that an agent deciding *in accord with* his evaluative judgment may exercise more than enough proximal control for direct freedom even when indeterminism is so located. He actually exercises more than enough proximal control, even though there was a chance of his exercising less (though still enough). If indeterminism located here diminishes control, then, the decrease does not appear to be of great significance.

2d. An Argument from Luck

Let us consider a second argument that has been offered to show that indeterminism in the direct causation of a decision would diminish control, an argument from luck. Suppose that Isabelle has been deliberating about whether

to *A* or to *B*, and she has judged that it would be better to *A*. She then straightaway decides to *A* (and then she *A*'s). Her decision is nondeterministically caused
by her judgment and contemporaneous events and states; even after she had
judged that it would be better to *A*, there remained a chance that she decide to
B. Then, the objection goes, it is a matter of luck that Isabelle decides as she
does. And to the extent that something is a matter of luck for an agent, it is out
of that agent's control. Since Isabelle's proximal control over her decision involves luck, that control is less than it would have been had her evaluative
judgment (together with other states and events) causally determined the corresponding decision.[12]

An argument of this sort is, I think, widely accepted. But it is not decisive. First, it is clearly not *just* a matter of luck that Isabelle decides to *A*. For
her decision is caused (we may suppose in a non-deviant way) by her reasons,   .
including her judgment that it would be better to *A*. Still, some sort of luck
seems to be involved; there was a chance that these reasons would not cause
this decision. However, it needs to be established that this is a type of control-
diminishing luck.

It may be thought to be self-evident that the sort of luck involved here
diminishes control. However, I suggest that any appearance of self-evidence
that this claim has is due to a conflation of some importantly different kinds of
luck.

Suppose that an agent performs an action—a relatively basic action—
aimed at bringing about a certain result, and there is some indeterminism in the
process leading from that action to the result. For example, Paula hits her putt,
and due to certain properties of the ball, the air, and the grass on the green, the
process leading from that event to the ball's falling into the hole is a chancy
one. Here we have what we may call action-subsequent luck; it concerns what
happens after Paula's relatively basic action of hitting her putt. If we take Paula's
sinking the putt to be a process that includes the ball's falling into the hole,
then the luck here may also be called action-internal; it concerns as well what
happens within Paula's less basic action of sinking the putt.[13] It is evident, I
think, that this action-subsequent luck and action-internal luck diminish proximal control. Paula would have greater proximal control over the ball's falling
into the hole and over her sinking the putt if her hitting the putt were part of a
deterministic cause of the ball's going into the hole.[14]

But the indeterminism in Isabelle's case is located differently; it is located
in the direct causation of a basic action, in the direct causation of the decision.
Suppose that Isabelle has no actional control, whether direct or indirect, over
the making of her evaluative judgment; her proximal control over this event is
non-actional. (This matches what is often the case; and I have defended this supposition above.) Then, if we want to call the indeterminism here a kind of luck,
we can call it action-centered luck. While it is evident that action-subsequent
luck and action-internal luck diminish proximal control, it is not at all clear that
action-centered luck detracts from proximal control.[15]

An analogous point can be made with regard to the ensurance argument. *S4*, that argument points out, lacks a power to ensure what he will intend by making a better judgment, and this lack is supposed to constitute a decrease in the proximal component of the direct actional control that *S4* has in making the decision—in actively forming the intention. Note that what *S4* lacks is a power to ensure what *action* he performs by first undergoing some *non-active* change (over which, we have supposed, he has no actional control). Now, consider an importantly different case: Sam lacks a power to ensure what emotion he will experience by trying to feel a certain way. Sam's lacking this power does diminish any indirect actional control over what he experiences that he might be able to exercise just by trying to feel a certain way. But it would be a confusion to allow this fact to lead us to find plausible the main premise of the ensurance argument. For what Sam lacks is a power to ensure what *non-active* change he will undergo by first *actively* trying to bring about a certain change, and that is very different from lacking a power to ensure what *action* one will perform by first undergoing some *non-active* change. While it is quite clear that lacking the first of these powers would constitute a diminution of a type of actional control, it is certainly not so clear that lacking the second constitutes a decrease in any component of direct actional control.

Finally, as I suggested above, even if indeterminism located where an action-centered libertarian account places it *does* diminish proximal control, the decrease appears not to be so great as to undermine the agent's freedom. It is significant, I think, that contemporary compatibilists do not *require* the deterministic causation of directly free actions,[16] and that, similarly, Mele's libertarian account does not *require* deterministic causation of the intention-acquisition and the action that has been decided upon. Of course, the intent may just be to allow that there be some insignificant indeterminism, some vanishingly small chance of the occurrence of something bizarre that will never in fact happen (as, we are told, there is a tiny chance that a pebble tossed onto a solid table top will pass right through it rather than bouncing off). But there is good reason to allow for more than this. For a decision whose direct causation is indeterministic may be nonetheless intentional and rational, an exercise of the agent's ability to consider the reasons favoring the relevant alternatives and make his decision rationally on the basis of that consideration and free from influences such as compulsion and brainwashing. And these are the sorts of features that compatibilists, with good reason, generally cite as constituting the freedom of a decision or other action. Thus, there is no clear reason to think that the proximal control provided by an action-centered libertarian view is not enough proximal control for freedom.

2e. An Argument for an Action-Centered Account

Let us turn now to a consideration favoring an action-centered account over its rival. The type of view advanced by Dennett, Fischer, and Mele allows that an agent may have freedom-level actional control over a decision even if that decision is causally determined by events over none of which has the agent ever had any freedom-level actional control whatsoever, whether direct or indirect. The account will have to allow that a free decision (or other action) may be so determined; otherwise, it will not be possible for the account to provide for an individual's first free decision (or other action).[17] But a libertarian may reasonably object that this runs contrary to incompatibilism, that a decision (or other action) so determined cannot be free. (Such a libertarian may allow that a determined action may be *indirectly* free, but only if some part of any determining cause of it either is or is a causal result of an earlier free action of that agent.)

A reason for libertarians to so object stems from the Consequence Argument. The most widely accepted arguments for incompatibilism are detailed versions of this basic argument, which may be informally stated as follows:

> If determinism is true, then our acts are the consequences of the laws of nature and events in the remote past. But it is not up to us what went on before we were born, and neither is it up to us what the laws of nature are. Therefore, the consequences of these things (including our present acts) are not up to us.[18]

Here, the notion of something's being up to us is that of our having, through our capacity to act freely, a certain sort of influence over that thing. In the terminology I have been using in this paper, it is the notion of our having some freedom-level actional control, either direct or indirect, over that thing.

Anyone who accepts this argument should reject the claim that the type of view advanced by Dennett, Fischer, and Mele correctly characterizes decisions that are free—up to the agents who make them. This type of view allows that free decisions may be causally determined by events that are not up to us. It thus allows that free decisions may be consequences of the laws of nature and earlier events that are not up to us. But the consequences of these things, according to the Consequence Argument, are not up to us—are not things over which we have any freedom-level actional control, either direct or indirect.

(It does not matter to one who accepts the Consequence Argument that the events that Dennett, Fischer, and Mele allow may determine our free decisions (e.g., the evaluative judgments) do not occur in the remote past, before we were born. The point of appealing in that argument to events that occurred so long ago is simply that it will be generally accepted that such events are not up to us. But, as we have seen, Dennett, Fischer, and Mele, on pain of regress, must accept that the events that they allow may determine our free decisions are events that are not up to us (in the relevant sense).)

The Consequence Argument supports a different conception of ultimate control, or a conception of a different type of ultimate control from that proposed by Mele. Let us call this "action-centered ultimate control." In order for an agent to have action-centered ultimate control over the making of a certain decision, there must be at no time any minimally causally sufficient condition for the agent's making that decision over which the agent has no direct or indirect, freedom-level actional control. Action-centered libertarian views provide for action-centered ultimate control, while non-action-centered views do not.

On an action-centered view, an agent's freedom-level control stems from his performance of directly free actions. It is by acting with direct freedom that he ensures that certain things are the case, including that those actions are performed. This provides proponents of such a view with a further reply to the ensurance argument. *S4*, Mele pointed out, lacks the power to ensure what he will intend by making an evaluative judgment. However, where the intention is acquired actively, in the making of a decision, the reply is that *S4* may nevertheless have the power to ensure what he will intend *by making a decision*. His control, or his power to ensure what he decides is centered on his action of deciding, not on something that occurs prior to that action and over which he altogether lacks freedom-level actional control. And, according to the argument we have just considered, this is as it should be.

3. Judging the Value of Actional Control

An action-centered, modest libertarian account provides for something that no compatibilist account can secure: action-centered ultimate control. It provides for this variety of control in addition to proximal control. I have presented reasons in support of a claim that the indeterminism required by that account does not diminish the agent's proximal control, or at least does not diminish it so much that it is not enough proximal control for free action. But one may still think that the account cannot secure exactly as much proximal control as can a compatibilist account, and one may wonder why we should not prefer the latter. And even if one thinks there is no less proximal control with the action-centered libertarian account, one may wonder why we should want ultimate control of any sort, whether action-centered or not. Why should we not, indeed, find most desirable an ideally felicitous deterministic action-producing process? Why should we not prefer that always when we deliberate, the most relevant considerations efficiently come to mind, we rationally make evaluative judgments on the basis of them, these judgments effectively cut off further consideration, we rationally decide and act in accord with these judgments, and all this is causally determined to occur, so that there is no chance of anything's going in a less-than-ideal way?

Any version of modest libertarianism faces this challenge. But it is one that I think can be met. There are reasons to prefer that a modest libertarian view—and in particular, an action-centered one—is true, and it can be rational to judge the actional control we have if such a view is correct to be better, of greater value, than what we would have even in an ideal deterministic world.

One of those reasons is *not*, I think, that the ultimate control—whether action-centered or not—plus the proximal control secured by a modest libertarian view is a *greater degree* of control than is the proximal control secured by any compatibilist account. A modest libertarian view adds an additional variety of control to proximal control, but the combination doesn't leave us with greater or more control. That is because the ultimate control secured by such a view is wholly negative: it is a matter of the absence of any determining cause of a certain sort (on an action-centered view, a determining cause over which the agent has no freedom-level actional control). The satisfaction of this wholly negative condition does not leave the agent with any additional positive powers to determine which decision he makes. The positive determinative powers secured by a modest libertarian view are just those stemming from the causal powers of the agent's mental attitudes, some of which are exerted in his exercise of proximal control, and these are no greater than what is secured by a compatibilist competitor. The account, then, does not increase the degree or amount of actional control, even if it secures a new' variety of actional control.

Nevertheless, though negative in this respect, the ultimate control provided by a modest libertarian account suffices to render the future genuinely open on at least some occasions when an agent deliberates. On an action-centered view, sometimes when an agent deliberates and makes a decision, there remains until the making of the decision a genuine chance that the decision not be made. The decision is a genuine branch point in a probabilistic unfolding of history. This sort of openness is absent from any deterministic world. And one may reasonably judge that it is partly constitutive of some things that are intrinsically valuable, some things that are absent from any world without it.

There are a number of candidates for intrinsically valuable things that are partly constituted by the kind of openness just described. I shall discuss a few, but I shall not try to be exhaustive.

Consider first the way things seem to us in deliberation. When an agent is deliberating about whether to *A* or to *B*, it generally seems to that agent as though, in some sense, it is open that he *A* and open that he *B*. It has been argued that an agent *cannot* deliberate without believing of each alternative that he is considering that he *can* pursue that alternative. I think that this claim is too strong.[19] But we do generally take it for granted that each of the alternatives we are considering is in some sense open. Even if, strictly speaking, we are capable of deliberating without believing this, the presumption is practically inescapable. It is deeply a part of our nature, or our second nature, to presume this when we deliberate. Whatever we may think during our philosophical reflections about the openness of the future, when we become engaged in deliberation about what to do, this openness is something we presume.

It is no straightforward matter to say what sort of openness is presumed by us when we deliberate. But an individual may reasonably believe that it is the sort of openness secured by a modest libertarian view—a sort that cannot be present in any deterministic world—that *he* commonly presumes, or that such an account, unlike a compatibilist view, provides a faithful articulation of the rather vague view that he commonly presumes.[20] Such an individual, then, may reasonably hold that if determinism is true, then whenever he deliberates, he is subject to an illusion. He may grant that the illusion is strictly avoidable; it may be possible for him, at least on occasion, to deliberate without making the presumption. But he may find it, as I think we do find it, practically impossible to do this on a consistent basis. And since it is practically impossible for us not ever to deliberate, he may reasonably hold that if determinism is true, then he is routinely subject to a practically unavoidable illusion.

The sort of openness provided by a modest libertarian view, then, may be reasonably valued as partly constitutive of the non-illusoriness of deliberation, which is a property making for goodness. This is one consideration that can provide a reason for preferring the truth of a modest libertarian account even to the sort of ideal deterministic production of decision and action described earlier.[21]

The openness secured by a modest libertarian account, together with the proximal control provided by that account, may be reasonably thought to be partly constitutive of other goods that would not be available in any deterministic world. If which decisions we make is sometimes open in the indicated way, and if in making them we exercise the sort of proximal control secured by a modest libertarian account, then some of our decisions may make a significant difference to how things go (including what kinds of persons we become). Of course, even if determinism is true, there is a way in which our decisions generally make a difference: had we not made them, things would have gone differently. With the truth of an action-centered modest libertarian view, our decisions may still make a difference in this way. But they may make a difference in a second way as well: they may be branch points in a probabilistic unfolding of history, branch points over which we exercise direct, freedom-level actional control. There may have been a real chance of things not going a certain way, and these decisions may be the events that set things going that way. In making the decisions, then, *we* will be making a significant difference in how things go, in this second as well as in the first way. And one may reasonably think that it is intrinsically good to be making a difference in this way with some of one's decisions, that this sort of making a difference is an intrinsically good thing.[22] Since it could not be present in a deterministic world, this consideration provides a reason to prefer a modest libertarian to a compatibilist account.

This same openness combined with proximal control may be what is represented in a kind of life-hope ("our outlooks on our own futures"—Honderich (1988, 380)) that will be realizable only if a libertarian account is true. Our hopes concerning our own futures are not just hopes that certain states of affairs will come about. "My hopes," Honderich (383-84) notes, "are typically hopes that I will make something happen, bring something into existence, keep it, or change it—that I will succeed through my own actions in securing certain states of affairs." Even if determinism is true, my decisions and actions may secure certain states of affairs, in that my decisions and actions bring about these states of affairs. With the truth of a modest libertarian view, my decisions and actions may still secure certain states of affairs in that way. But they may also secure the states of affairs in a second way, by bringing about (by an exercise of freedom-level actional control) things for which, until the occurrence of certain decisions and actions of mine, there had always been some real chance of their not obtaining. One may reasonably judge that it is better if one may have realizable life-hopes representing one's decisions' and actions' securing things in both of these ways.[23]

The issue most frequently discussed in connection with free decision and action is moral responsibility. Here I think it is not reasonable to think that a modest libertarian account improves on a good compatibilist view. This is a significant limitation on the claims that can be made for the former account.

If determinism is true, it is still the case that there are certain kinds of justifications for praise and blame, reward and punishment. These sorts of reactions express our feelings and our judgments about past behavior; they may contribute to moral education and may encourage good behavior and deter bad; and they may help to protect us from miscreants. Incompatibilists typically hold, however, that a very important type of justification would always be lacking: none of these reactions could ever be deserved. Less categorically, some incompatibilists allow that, in a deterministic world, there might be a type of desert of these kinds of reactions or of some version of these reactions, or that they may be deserved to a degree. But it is then said that there would be an important type of desert missing, or that an important version of these reactions would not be deserved, or these reactions would not be fully deserved.[24]

Whatever the implications of determinism for desert really are, the implications of modest libertarianism for desert are, it seems, the same. The truth of a modest libertarian view provides for a type of ultimate control that is absent from any deterministic world, and that ultimacy secures a type of openness. But the ultimacy and the openness provided by such a view are wholly negative: they are entirely a matter of the absence of a determining cause of a certain sort. The positive agential powers secured by such a view are just those provided by a good compatibilist account. And if compatibilist accounts fail to provide an adequate grounding for desert, this shortcoming is to be remedied not just by subtracting something from these views but by (also) adding something, some additional positive agential powers to determine what one decides and does. Hence, only a libertarian account that secures greater positive agential powers can provide more of a grounding for desert than can a good compatibilist view.[25] Since a modest libertarian view secures no greater positive agential powers, it provides no more of a grounding for desert.

(Similar remarks apply regarding the appropriateness of reactive attitudes such as guilt, indignation, resentment, pride, and gratitude. Whatever the right view is regarding the compatibility of determinism with the appropriateness of these attitudes, it seems clear that the same holds for the compatibility of their appropriateness with the truth of a modest libertarian account, for a reason exactly analogous to that just given with respect to desert.)[26]

What about the summational judgment that, overall, the non-illusoriness, difference making, and life-hopes secured by the truth of a modest libertarian account render the truth of such a view better than the truth of any compatibilist view, even under ideal circumstances? The latter would guarantee for us a certain efficiency and rationality in deliberation, decision, and action. Of course, in ideal cases, the truth of a modest libertarian view would deliver the same efficiency and rationality; but it could not provide the guarantee. This guarantee would have to be weighed against what the libertarian view would provide.

Where there is often a chance that an agent will decide contrary to his evaluative judgment, it is likely that some of his decisions and subsequent actions will be irrational. Although even rational judgments about which alternative is better or best can be mistaken, in many cases acting contrary to rational evaluative judgments will constitute and produce less of what is good than would acting in accord with them. There will be a loss of good, then, if rather than our having ideally deterministic action-production systems, our decisions are produced as characterized by an action-centered modest libertarian account.

Can one reasonably judge that such a loss is more than compensated for by the good things secured by a modest libertarian account but not by any compatibilist view? That depends on what the libertarian account says about the probabilities of irrational decisions. What is an acceptable trade-off may vary from case to case, but in general it would seem better that where the costs of deciding and acting irrationally were great, the chance of so deciding was small. One might, then, prefer a modest libertarian view on which, in many cases at least, judging an alternative better or best rendered it highly probable that one would decide in accord with that judgment.

A proponent of such a view must face the question whether libertarian freedom must be diminished as the chance of doing otherwise decreases. If there had to be some inverse relation between the difficulty of doing something or the amount of effort required to do it, on the one hand, and the probability of one's doing it, on the other, that might support an affirmative answer to this question. But clearly there need be no such relation. (After all, there is none in deterministic worlds, where it may be extremely difficult for an agent to do something despite the fact that there has never been any chance that he would fail.) And other than such a relation, it is hard to see what would support an affirmative answer.

It seems to me that one can reasonably judge that the truth of a modest libertarian account that incorporates the suggested view about probabilities would be better than the truth of a compatibilist competitor. But the judgment is certainly not rationally required; it seems that reasonable individuals may rationally come down on either side of this question.[27]

There is, then, a third respect in which the libertarianism discussed here is modest. An adherent of it may well think that his compatibilist opponents are mistaken. But he should not think that they need be less rationally justified in holding their view than he is in holding his, nor that their justification need depend on their ignorance of anything he can bring to their attention. Of course, it may be that he can persuade some of them to change their minds, but if he can't, it may be neither his fault nor theirs. His claim for his view, it seems, should acknowledge that it is less than compelling. But we should all be so modest when it comes to this issue.[28]

Notes

1. I take decision to be a type of mental action, an action of forming an intention to perform a certain type of action. It may be that not all intention-acquisition is action, and of course there is action that is not the formation of an intention. Though I shall focus here on decision, similar things can be said concerning other types of action.

   Note also that here I am concerned with requirements for *direct* freedom. The distinction between direct and indirect freedom will be discussed in section 2b.

2. For some examples, see Lewis (1973, postscript B); Eells (1991); and Tooley (1987, 289–96).

3. It is important to be clear about the type of indeterminism that is required by an action-centered account. Such a view does *not* add an event to those that figure in a compatibilist account of the production of a free decision; what is required is *not* that some additional, undetermined event occur between the agent's having certain reasons and his making a certain decision, or between his making a certain evaluative judgment and his making the decision, where that undetermined event then contributes to causing the decision. Nor are there required to be any gaps or breaks in the causal chain leading to the decision. What is required is just that the direct causation of the decision by the agent's having certain reasons, or by his having those reasons and his making a certain evaluative judgment, be governed by a nondeterministic law rather than a deterministic one.

4. This "doxastic" indeterminism is presented as just one illustration of a type of process that Mele finds conducive to libertarian control. He notes:

   > Other indeterministic scenarios may also be considered. For example, one may explore the benefits and costs of its being causally undetermined which of a shifting subset of *desires* come to mind at a time, or which of a changing segment of beliefs an agent actively *attends* to at a given time, or exactly *how* an agent attends to various beliefs or desires of his at certain times. (221)

5. An incompatibilist might object to the claim that "the limitations on *S3*'s control over what he intends at *t*...are exhausted by any limitations on his control over what

he decisively judges best... ." For it might be held that the very fact that *S3*'s intention-acquisition is causally determined constitutes a limitation on his control over what he intends at *t*. However, it must be noted that Mele's claim about the limitations on control concerns limitations on *S3*'s *proximal* control, and it is *proximal* control that is said to be greater in the case of *S3*. Mele does not believe there is a different, valuable, freedom-relevant type of control that might be possessed by *S4* but not by *S3* because the latter's intention-acquisition is causally determined. Even if Mele is mistaken about this point, he might be right in what he says regarding proximal control. (I shall return in section 2e to the issue of whether there might be this additional type of control.)

6. A somewhat different objection might be raised against an action-centered view. It might be said that were the agent to judge that it is best to *A* and then decide to *B*, then the agent would be deciding irrationally; and it may be claimed that it is irrational (or "insane") to want to be able to decide irrationally. As will become clear in section 2c, the first claim here is mistaken; it may happen that an agent judges a certain course of action best and then, before making a decision, realizes that he was mistaken. The second claim as well is quite dubious; for an illuminating discussion of it, see Fischer and Ravizza (1992).

   Even if one can rationally want to have an ability to decide contrary to one's evaluative judgment, it may be thought that an action-centered modest libertarian account provides merely for the *chance* of one's so deciding and not for the *ability* to so decide. The issue here is the agent's control over which decision he makes. That is the issue on which I focus in the text.

7. Recall that Mele restricts indeterminism to those beliefs whose coming or not coming to mind we do not control even if determinism is true. Indeterminism here will not detract from any proximal control that we *actually* have over those beliefs. However, in addition to considering a scenario in which the uncontrolled coming or not coming to mind of these beliefs is not determined, we should consider scenarios, both deterministic and indeterministic, in which we *do* have some proximal control over which beliefs come to mind. For example, it might be that, whenever an agent deliberates, all and only the most relevant beliefs, or all and only those that he has time to consider, come to mind, and that those beliefs then figure in a highly efficient and rational way in the production of an evaluative judgment. If this process were deterministic, then just by setting himself to deliberate, an agent could ensure a high degree of efficiency and rationality in his deliberations. This would seem to constitute a desirable type of proximal control in deliberation. Then, if indeterminism subsequent to an evaluative judgment significantly diminishes proximal control at that stage, it appears that indeterminism that affected which beliefs come to mind in deliberation would likewise leave us with significantly less proximal control than we *might* have at this stage. If we believe that indeterminism subsequent to an evaluative judgment significantly diminishes control, then, it seems, we should prefer a deterministic world in which we have the described proximal control over which beliefs come to mind in deliberation to a world in which a view like that proposed by Dennett, Fischer, and Mele is true. Indeterminism of the sort posited by that view might not diminish what we *do* have, but if we are concerned with which varieties of control are best, we should not take our (contingent) imperfections as fixed. (A similar point is raised in Clarke (forthcoming).)

Note, however, that this criticism assumes that indeterminism subsequent to an evaluative judgment significantly diminishes proximal control. I shall question that assumption.

8. The rationale for this expansion of the notion of non-actional proximal control is that such control concerns features of an action-production process that contribute to the control the agent has in acting. This actional control or practical freedom requires an ability to exercise *rational* control in acting. Features of an action-production process that decrease rationality may detract from that actional control without undermining freedom altogether.

9. It is in terms of such a notion of non-actional control that we might understand such Kantian slogans as "the realm of reason is the realm of freedom." Certainly reasoning need not involve any actional control or practical freedom. But it may always involve some degree of non-actional control.

10. A libertarian account might require that, in order for a decision (or other action) to be directly free, the agent must have had some actional control—though not necessarily freedom-level—over earlier events. This sort of requirement would not produce the vicious regress described in the text. I shall ignore this possibility for the time being, but I return to it in section 2e, note 17.

11. Here it may be said against all types of modest libertarianism that what we should find most desirable is an ideally felicitous deterministic action-producing process. We should prefer that the most relevant considerations efficiently come to mind, that we rationally make evaluative judgments on the basis of them, that these judgments effectively cut off further consideration, that we rationally decide and act in accord with them, and that all of this be determined to happen whenever we deliberate. We should prefer that we have a power to ensure all of this just by beginning to deliberate concerning which of certain alternative actions to perform. We should value this sort of felicitous determinism over a deliberative process that has indeterminism located at any juncture whatsoever.

There are, I think, three types of reply that can be made to this objection. One is that we are not in fact so ideally efficient and rational, and that for creatures with our practical limitations it is better to have, somewhere in the deliberative process, genuine chance. But this is a strikingly poor reply for a libertarian to make. Libertarians should hold that *no* sort of actional control that even an idealized deterministic agent could have is as valuable as is direct libertarian control. Indeterminism is not supposed to be needed to give us something second-best.

Two claims that would make better replies are considered in the text below. They are that indeterministic proximal control need not be *less* proximal control than deterministic proximal control, and that even if it is less proximal control, its combination with action-centered ultimate control may be more valuable than anything we could have given determinism.

12. Mele (1999) raises this sort of problem of luck for libertarian views.

13. If one prefers to think that Paula's sinking the putt is (identical with) her hitting the putt (or some even more basic action—e.g., her moving her arms in a certain way), then one may say that the luck here is just action-subsequent.

14. A similar point is made by Kane (1996, 144). He describes what he calls "antecedent determining control," a power to determine ahead of time how things will turn

out. Indeterminism located between one's doing something and an outcome will, he acknowledges, undermine antecedent determining control. But this is not the only location that indeterminism might have, and this sort of control is not the only desirable sort.

15. The point can be put differently. Compare Isabelle with Diane, who is exactly the same except that Diane's judging that A is better, together with contemporaneous events and states, causally determines her deciding to A. I have been putting the action-centered theorist's claim as stating that the indeterminism does not diminish Isabelle's proximal control over her decision. But the claim could be made differently: the determinism does not increase Diane's proximal control. The issue here is what degree of the proximal component of direct actional control *Diane* might have over the making of her decision. The fact that some agent-involving event over which she has no actional control is part of a deterministic (rather than part of an indeterministic) cause of her decision does not clearly increase any component of *her* actional control over that decision.

16. For a compatibilist's argument that such deterministic causation should not be seen as necessary for the control that is required for moral responsibility, see the final section of Fischer (forthcoming).

17. As I noted earlier, a non-action-centered account could require that this proximal control be indirect actional control. However, on pain of regress, the account could not require that it be *freedom-level* actional control. And according to the objection about to be considered, it is precisely what the non-action-centered account cannot require—viz., that if there is any determining cause of a free decision or other action, it must have as a part something over which the agent has (direct or indirect) *freedom-level* actional control—it is precisely this that must be required by an adequate libertarian view.

　　The argument in this section tells as well against the view advanced in Ekstrom (1999, ch. 4). She requires that, in order for a decision to be directly free, some action—viz., the active formation of a preference—that precedes the decision must be nondeterministically caused. It is allowed that the preference-formation causally determine the decision, and it is not required that the active formation of the preference be a *free* action. Then, as with the kind of view advanced by Dennett, Fischer, and Mele, it is allowed that there may be a determining cause of the decision over no part of which has the agent ever had any *freedom-level* actional control.

18. Van Inwagen (1983, 16).

19. For discussion of this point, see Clarke (1992).

20. Some individuals believe that the sort of openness that seems to them to lie ahead in deliberation is a sort that could be there even if determinism were true. See, for example, Mele (1995, 135–37). I do not claim that such individuals are mistaken in so believing, nor that they are not rationally justified in holding that belief. My claim is that some other individuals may be rationally justified in holding the contrary belief.

21. Nathan (1992, 30–31 and 38) suggests that we may desire free will for the sake of not being subject to a certain illusion, one closely related to the illusion I discuss.

22. Swinburne (1996, 37) writes that "It is a good for any agent to have a free choice, for that makes him an ultimate source of the way things happen in the universe... .

And if he exercises that choice in forwarding the good, that is a further good for him. But the good of forwarding the good is a lot better if the agent has a free choice between good and evil, not just between alternative goods, for then his choice is deeply significant for the way the world goes." By a free choice, he means one that is not causally determined. I would suggest that the "deep significance" of an undetermined free choice is better seen as not restricted to cases where the open alternatives are good and evil.

23. Honderich holds that it is part of the content of our life-hopes that we will "initiate" at least some of our actions (1988, 384 and following). The idea of initiating, he says, implies "that our futures are in part *open, alterable,* or *unfixed*" (385). But it implies more: "Talk of initiating, making, giving rise to, bringing about, producing, and so on implies...an activity that is not itself a product." (387) A modest libertarian view cannot do justice to this latter notion, even if it can secure something more than can any compatibilist account.

   Similarly, Honderich (389) maintains that "True chance, at any rate on a large scale, would be about as damaging to hope as fixity. To take it that I, in or as my self, give rise to my actions, is not to make them a matter of randomness." It is clear that given the truth of a modest libertarian view, which decisions an agent makes is not a matter of *mere* chance. The agent exercises proximal control—and not a greatly lesser degree than would a deterministic counterpart—in making directly free decisions. This may not suffice for the hope Honderich has in mind, but it may suffice for a kind of libertarian life-hope.

24. For a subtle treatment of these issues, see Honderich (1988, ch. 10).

25. If there is a libertarian view that provides for greater positive agential powers it is, I believe, an agent-causal view. In Clarke (1996) I discuss different versions of such an account and identify reasons favoring one particular version. A major drawback of such views is, of course, that there is more reason to doubt their truth than there is to doubt the truth of a modest libertarian account.

26. I have said that one might *reasonably* judge that certain things partly constituted by the openness secured by a modest libertarian account are good or better than their compatibilist versions. I intend that one may be rationally justified in making and holding these judgments. Such judgments may, of course, be consistent with others made by an individual, and what is judged regarding libertarian control may stand in some explanatory relations to what is judged regarding some related matters.Whether there can be more to the justification of these value judgments depends on the broader issue of how value judgments may be rationally justified. It seems to me that justification can turn on a value judgment's relations not just to other value judgments but also to the individual's beliefs about other matters, his desires, his preferences, his caring about certain things, and his reflection on the objects of value judgments. When, for example, an individual carefully considers a variety of actional control, thinks clearly about how it compares with competing varieties and how it relates to other things he values, and finds that he prefers that variety, that he cares more about having it, and that it seems to him to be better, the judgment that it is better may well have some degree of rational grounding in the reflections from which it arises.

27. There may also be summational judgments that are different but not inconsistent. For example, an individual may judge that in the context of a certain kind of life,

the control secured by a modest libertarian view is better. That judgment might be consistent with one made by a second individual that in the context of a different kind of life, the control secured by a compatibilist view is better. (And it might be reasonable to judge that neither of these kinds of life is, on the whole, better than the other.)

Alternatively, an individual might judge that, given certain fairly fixed features of his personality, it is better for him to have one of these types of control. A second individual might, again, make a different but not inconsistent judgment about which it would be better for him to have. Lack of agreement here need not be disagreement.

28. I wish to thank Ish Haji, Al Mele, and Michael Zimmerman for helpful comments on earlier versions of this paper. I am grateful also to audiences at Davidson College, University of North Carolina, Greensboro, and University of Vermont.

References

Armstrong, D. M. (1983). *What is a Law of Nature?* Cambridge: Cambridge University Press.

Chisholm, Roderick M. (1966). "Freedom and Action." In Keith Lehrer, ed., *Freedom and Determinism*. New York: Random House.

Clarke, Randolph (forthcoming). Review of Alfred R. Mele, *Autonomous Agents. Mind.*

———— (1996). "Agent Causation and Event Causation in the Production of Free Action." *Philosophical Topics* 24, No. 2, 19–48.

———— (1995). "Indeterminism and Control." *American Philosophical Quarterly* 32, 125–38.

———— (1992). "Deliberation and Beliefs about One's Abilities." *Pacific Philosophical Quarterly* 73, 101–13.

Dennett, Daniel C. (1978). "On Giving Libertarians What They Say They Want." In *Brainstorms*. Montgomery, Vermont: Bradford Books.

Earman, John (1986). *A Primer on Determinism*. Dordrecht: D. Reidel.

Eells, Ellery (1991). *Probabilistic Causality*. Cambridge: Cambridge University Press.

Ekstrom, Laura Waddell (1999). *Free Will*. Boulder: Westview.

Fischer, John Martin (forthcoming). "Recent Work on Moral Responsibility." *Ethics*.

———— (1995). "Libertarianism and Avoidability: A Reply to Widerker." *Faith and Philosophy* 12, 119–25.

Fischer, John Martin and Mark Ravizza (1992). "When the Will is Free." *Philosophical Perspectives* 6, 423–51.

Honderich, Ted (1988). *A Theory of Determinism*. Oxford: Clarendon Press.

Kane, Robert (1996). *The Significance of Free Will*. New York: Oxford University Press.

Lewis, David (1973) [1986]. "Causation." *The Journal of Philosophy* 70, 556–67. Reprinted (with postscripts) in *Philosophical Papers*, Volume II. Oxford: Oxford University Press.

McKay, Thomas J. and David Johnson (1996). "A Reconsideration of an Argument against Compatibilism." *Philosophical Topics* 24, No. 2, 113–22.

Mele, Alfred R. (1999). "Ultimate Responsibility and Dumb Luck." *Social Philosophy and Policy* 16, 274–93.

———— (1996). "Soft Libertarianism and Frankfurt-Style Scenarios." *Philosophical Topics* 24, No. 2, 123–41.

———— (1995). *Autonomous Agents*. New York: Oxford University Press.

Nathan, N. M. L. (1992). *Will and World*. Oxford: Clarendon Press.

O'Connor, Timothy (1993). "On the Transfer of Necessity." *Nous* 27, 204–18.

Pereboom, Derk (1995). "Determinism *al Dente.*" *Nous* 29, 21–45.

Strawson, Peter (1962). "Freedom and Resentment." *Proceedings of the British Academy* 48, 1–25.

Swinburne, Richard (1996). "Some Major Strands of Theodicy." In Daniel Howard-Snyder, ed., *The Evidential Argument from Evil.* Bloomington: Indiana University Press.

Tooley, Michael (1987). *Causation.* Oxford: Clarendon Press.

Van Inwagen, Peter (1983). *An Essay on Free Will.* Oxford: Clarendon Press.

Widerker, David (1987). "On an Argument for Incompatibilism." *Analysis* 47, 37–41.

46

Philosophical Perspectives, 14, Action and Freedom, 2000

TRANSFER PRINCIPLES AND MORAL RESPONSIBILITY

Eleonore Stump
Saint Louis University

John Martin Fischer
University of California, Riverside

It is useful to divide contemporary arguments for the incompatibility of causal determinism and moral responsibility into two types: indirect and direct. The indirect arguments present reasons why causal determinism is incompatible with the possession of the relevant kind of alternative possibilities and conclude from this that causal determinism is incompatible with moral responsibility. It is, of course, a presupposition of the indirect arguments that moral responsibility requires alternative possibilities. The direct arguments contain no such presupposition, although some of their proponents may believe that moral responsibility does indeed require alternative possibilities.

The direct arguments employ what might be called "transfer" principles. These are principles that transfer a certain property; the relevant property here *is lack of moral responsibility*.[1] Let "Np" abbreviate "p and no one is even partly morally responsible for the fact that p." Then this is a transfer principle introduced by Peter van Inwagen:

Rule B: Np and N(p $>$ q) implies Nq.[2]

Van Inwagen's Rule B is a transfer principle insofar as it transfers the property of lack of moral responsibility from one fact to another by the medium of lack of responsibility for the pertinent conditional.

Van Inwagen's direct argument for the incompatibility of causal determinism and moral responsibility can be presented simply as follows. For present purposes, we can understand causal determinism as the doctrine that a complete description of the (temporally nonrelational) state of the universe at a time, and a description of the laws of nature, entail every truth about subsequent times. Let P be a proposition describing the state of the universe before there were any human beings, let L be a proposition describing the laws of nature, and let F be a truth about the way the world is today. Then, if causal determinism is true,

(1) (P and L > F).

Clearly, no one is even partly morally responsible for this fact, and so this is also true:

(2) N[(P and L) > F].

Since [(P and L) > F] is equivalent to [P > (L > F)], this is true as well:

(3) N[P > (L > F)].

Now

(4) NP,

and so by Rule B, from (3) and (4) we can conclude

(5) N(L > F).

Since

(6) NL,

by another application of Rule B, from (5) and (6) we reach the conclusion,

(7) NF.

Since F is an arbitrary truth, this conclusion can be generalized. Consequently, the argument appears to show in a direct fashion that if causal determinism is true, no one is even in part morally responsible for any fact.

But Rule B can be called into question. Mark Ravizza offers the following kind of case to impugn Rule B.[3] At T1, Betty freely detonates explosives as part of a plan to start an avalanche that will destroy an enemy camp; and, in fact, her explosion does succeed in causing an avalanche that is sufficient to destroy the camp at T3. Unbeknown to Betty, however, there is another cause of the camp's destruction by avalanche. At T1, a goat kicks loose a boulder, and it causes an avalanche which is also sufficient to destroy the camp at T3 and which contributes to the actual destruction of the camp at T3. In the story, no one is even partly morally responsible for the goat's kicking the boulder. And no one is even partly morally responsible for the fact that if the goat kicks that boulder at T1, then the camp is destroyed by avalanche at T3. Nonetheless,

Betty is at least partly responsible for the camp's being destroyed by avalanche at T3. Thus, Ravizza's case apparently shows that Rule B is invalid. In cases of simultaneous causation, the rule fails.[4]

In a recent paper, Ted Warfield has suggested a reply on behalf of the incompatibilist.[5] He concedes that Ravizza's case presents a challenge to Rule B. Warfield claims, however, that there is a related but non-equivalent rule—he calls it 'Rule Beta □'—which can play a similar role in an argument for the incompatibility of causal determinism and moral responsibility. According to Warfield, Rule Beta □ is not subject to Ravizza-style counterexamples.

This is Rule Beta □:

[Np and □($p > q$)] implies Nq.

The key difference between Rule B and Rule Beta □ is in the connection between p and q. For Rule B, it must be the case that if p, then q, and no one is responsible for this fact. For Rule Beta □, the connection between p and q is one of logical necessity. Because the connection between p and q in Warfield's Rule Beta □ is so much stronger than the connection between p and q in Rule B, Warfield supposes that it will be much harder to construct scenarios which present a challenge to his rule. For Ravizza's scenario to serve as a counterexample to an inference licensed by Rule Beta □, the connection between the goat's kicking the boulder at T1 and the camp's being destroyed by avalanche at T3 would have to be a logical one; and, of course, it is not. As Warfield says, "The conditional premise (if the goat kicks the boulder at T1, then the avalanche destroys the camp at T3), though not a proposition anyone is even partly morally responsible for, does not express a relation of logical consequence, and so Ravizza's example fails to apply to my argument [for incompatibilism]." (p.222–223)

Contrary to what Warfield claims, his Rule Beta □ *is* subject to Ravizza-style counterexamples, in our view. In what follows, we present two such counterexamples, each of which is sufficient to show that Rule Beta □ is invalid.

Counterexample A. Let it be the case that, necessarily, if the actual laws of nature obtain and the conditions of the world at T2 (some time just before T3) are C, then there will be an avalanche that destroys the enemy camp at T3. Let it also be the case that at T1 Betty *freely* starts an avalanche which is sufficient to destroy the camp at T3 and which contributes to its destruction at T3. Finally, let it be the case that Betty's freely starting an avalanche is the result of some suitable indeterministic process.

Then let r be the conjunction of

(r1) the actual laws of nature obtain

and

(r2) the condition of the world at T2 is C.

And let *q* be

(*q*) there is an avalanche which destroys the enemy camp at T3.

In this example, *r* is true. N*r* is also true: nobody is even partly morally responsible for the obtaining of the actual laws of nature and the condition of the world's being C at T2. By hypothesis, it is also true that □(*r* > *q*). Any world in which (*r*1) and (*r*2) are true is a world in which *q* is true. And yet it seems clear that N*q* is false. Insofar as Betty at T1 freely starts an avalanche, she is at least in part morally responsible for the camp's being destroyed by an avalanche at T3.

Warfield anticipates such a case. He says,

> Can a Frankfurt-type case (or a Ravizza overdetermination case) be constructed that is a counterexample to Rule Beta □? I don't see how. To illustrate notice that making...the avalanche a logical consequence of the goat's kicking the boulder requires that we assume that [the avalanche] is a *deterministic* consequence of the arrangement of natural forces. This change would provide a case that is at least of the right form to serve as a counterexample to Rule Beta □. But to be a counterexample to Rule Beta □ the example must be an example in which the Frankfurtian judgment of moral responsibility [Betty's moral responsibility for the camp's being destroyed by an avalanche] holds up. With the additional assumption of determinism that is needed to make the case applicable to Rule Beta □, however, this Frankfurtian judgment is equivalent to the claim that determinism and moral responsibility are compatible. It is hardly of interest to point out that the assumption of the compatibility of determinism and moral responsibility implies that Rule Beta □ is invalid. (p.223)

But note that we have not assumed causal determinism in our example. Contrary to Warfield's claim, such an assumption is *not* "needed to make the case applicable to [Rule] Beta □." This is because, even in an indeterministic world, *some* events and states of affairs can be causally determined. One can suppose that the enemy camp's being destroyed by an avalanche at T3 is causally determined by the goat's kicking a boulder at T1 *without* thereby supposing that Betty's deliberations or actions are causally determined. Even in an indeterministic world, there can be "pockets of local determination".[6] To deny this is to suppose that, for any state of affairs *p* whatever, the laws of nature and the condition C of the world at T2 is compatible with *p* at T3 and also compatible with *not-p* at T3. But this is to suppose that absolutely everything in the world is indeterministic, and presumably even libertarians don't want to make so strong a claim.

Counterexample B. For those still inclined to worry about the issue of causal determinism, however, we can construct a counterexample which doesn't depend on there being even local determinism. This time let *r* be a conjunction of these propositions

(r1) the actual laws of nature obtain

and

(r3) there is an avalanche which destroys the enemy camp at T3.

Now, without doubt, there is a logically necessary connection between r and q (since q is identical to [r3]), but the question of whether causal determinism of any sort obtains is irrelevant. Here we have

(8) Nr

and

(9) $\Box \, (r > q)$,

but it isn't the case that

(10) Nq,

for the sort of reasons given in connection with Ravizza's story.

Warfield has an objection to this sort of counterexample, too. He maintains that

(W1) if no one is even partly morally responsible for a conjunction, then no one is even partly morally responsible for either conjunct of the conjunction. (p.218)[7]

This claim calls into question Nr in our counterexample B. It is not the case that no one is even partly responsible for (r3). On (W1), then, it isn't the case that no one is even partly morally responsible for r. Consequently, Nr is false.

But is Warfield's claim (W1) right? We think it isn't, because of the connection between conjunctions and conditionals.

To see this, consider again Ravizza's story. It is not the case that if the actual laws of nature obtain, there will not be an avalanche that destroys the enemy camp at T3. So this is true:

(11) not (L $>$ not-q).

Furthermore, it seems odd to think that anyone is even partly responsible for (11). It is peculiar to suppose that a human being is to blame for (11), is the source of the state of affairs described by (11), could have brought it about that that state of affairs didn't obtain, and so on. So this also seems true:

(12) N[not (L > not-q)].

Of course, (11) is equivalent to this:

(13) (L and q).

So it seems as if this also has to be true:

(14) N(L and q).[8]

But now we have a problem, if (W1) is correct. In Ravizza's story, Betty is partly responsible for q. Therefore, it isn't true that no one is even partly responsible for the conjuncts of (13); Betty is at least partly responsible for q. On (W1), however, for it to be the case that no one is even partly responsible for the conjunction, it would also have to be the case that no one was even partly responsible for either of the conjuncts. Consequently, if Warfield's claim (W1) is true, (14) is *false*.

In that case, however, Warfield must also hold that (12) is false. But the claim that (12) is false strikes us as counter-intuitive.

Furthermore, as the preceding discussion shows, if (W1) is true, so is this:

(W2) Given a true antecedent of a conditional,[9] a person is partly responsible for the conditional's being false if he is partly responsible for the falsity of the consequent of the conditional. [10]

That's why commitment to (W1) turns out to require rejecting

(12) N[not (L > not-q)].

But if (W2) is true, it seems that this ought also to be true:

(W3) Given a true antecedent of a conditional, a person is partly responsible for the conditional's being true if he is partly responsible for the truth of the consequent of the conditional.

Why should we accept that a person is partly responsible for the falsity of a conditional with a true antecedent because of his responsibility for the falsity of the consequent, and yet deny that a person is partly responsible for the truth of a conditional with a true antecedent because of his responsibility for the truth of the consequent?

Another way to see the connection between (W1) and (W3) is to consider the reason Warfield gives for accepting (W1). To make (W1) seem plausible, Warfield says, "being at least partly morally responsible for a conjunct is a way of being partly morally responsible for a conjunction" (p.218). But if that is right, then it seems that a similar point ought to apply to conditionals: being partly responsible for the truth of the consequent of a conditional with a true antecedent is a way of being partly responsible for the truth of the conditional.

And yet (W3) is clearly mistaken. To see this, consider (9) again:

(9) $\Box\, (r > q)$,

where r is

($r1$) the actual laws of nature obtain,

and

($r3$) there is an avalanche which destroys the enemy camp at T3,

and q is identical to ($r3$). Warfield also accepts this rule of inference, taken from Peter van Inwagen:

Rule A: $\Box\, p$ implies Np.

Rule A seems entirely uncontroversial. In fact, Warfield says,

> van Inwagen's Rule A is (nearly) as trivial and inconsequential as a rule of inference could be. No one has, to my knowledge, challenged this principle nor has anyone challenged any principle closely related to Rule A.[11]

Now, from (9), by Rule A, we get

(15) N $(r > q)$.

On (W3), however, a person is partly responsible for the truth of a conditional with a true antecedent if she is partly responsible for the truth of the consequent of the conditional. So, on (W3), we will have to say that (15) is *false*, just as (12) is, because Betty is partly responsible for q. By Rule A, however, it then follows that (9) is false, since by Rule A (9) implies (15). Without doubt, this is absurd. So either Rule A is after all invalid, or (W3) is false. And if (W3) is false, then by parity of reasoning it seems that (W1) is false also.

For these reasons, we think Warfield's claim (W1) should be rejected. The logic of responsibility is more complicated than (W1) implies. Given the relation between conjunctions and conditionals, it is right to hold that someone can be partly responsible for a conjunct of a conjunction without being partly responsible for the conjunction. Consequently, our counterexample B is also effective against Rule Beta □.

Finally, we think it is worth pointing out that one of us believes that causal determinism is incompatible with moral responsibility and the other does not. But we unite in thinking that causal determinism cannot be proved incompatible with moral responsibility by Warfield's Rule Beta □.[12]

Notes

1. In the context of the indirect arguments for the incompatibility of causal determinism and moral responsibility, one can have "Transfer of Powerlessness" principles. For a discussion of such principles, see John Martin Fischer, *The Metaphysics of Free Will: An Essay on Control*, (Oxford: Blackwell Publishers, 1994), pp.23–66.
2. Peter van Inwagen, *An Essay on Free Will*, (Oxford: Clarendon Press, 1983), p.184.
3. Mark Ravizza, "Semi-Compatibilism and the Transfer of Nonresponsibility," *Philosophical Studies* 75 (1994), pp.61–93, esp. p.78. For similar examples, see also John Martin Fischer and Mark Ravizza, *Responsibility and Control: A Theory of Moral Responsibility*, (Cambridge: Cambridge University Press, 1998), pp.151–169.
4. One of us (Stump), but not the other, thinks it isn't clear that the invalidity of Rule B shown by Ravizza's example renders Van Inwagen's argument irremediably invalid. That is because Rule B fails only in certain cases, and it isn't clear to one of us that cases of moral responsibility can be assimilated to those cases of simultaneous causation in which Rule B fails.
5. Ted A. Warfield, "Determinism and Moral Responsibility Are Incompatible," *Philosophical Topics* 24 (1996), pp.215–226. In addition to the suggestion explored in the text, Warfield also presents other strategies for replying to the compatibilistic strategy of Ravizza; see, especially, pp.221–222. Subsequent references to Warfield's paper will be given by page number in parentheses in the text.
6. Daniel Dennett introduces the term 'local fatalism' to refer to a related but different notion: Daniel C. Dennett, *Elbow Room: The Varieties of Free Will Worth Wanting*, (Cambridge, Mass. and London: MIT Press, 1984), pp.104–106.
7. One possible reason for thinking that (W1) is true is the supposition that one is at least partly morally responsible for a conjunction if one is morally responsible for a part of a conjunction. But being morally responsible for a part of a conjunction and being partly morally responsible for a conjunction are not the same thing, as our argument in what follows helps to make clear.
8. This inference is licensed by the fact that if p and q are logically equivalent, then Np if and only if Nq.
9. It's possible to interpret (W1) as applying only to true conjunctions; in that case, this qualification in (W2) is needed.
10. Obviously, we can switch the conjuncts in the conjunction from (L and q) to (q and L), which is equivalent to

$$(12^*)\ \text{not}\ (q > \text{not-L}).$$

Since Betty is partly responsible for (q and L), she will also be partly responsible for (12*). Consequently, accepting (W1) requires accepting not only (W2) but also

> (W2*) Given a false consequent, a person is partly responsible for a conditional's being false if he is partly responsible for the truth of the antecedent of the conditional.

11. Pp.218–219. Similarly, Van Inwagen says, "The validity of Rule (A) seems to me to be beyond dispute. No one is responsible for the fact that $49 \times 18 = 882$, for the fact that arithmetic is essentially incomplete, or, if Kripke is right about necessary truth, for the fact that the atomic number of gold is 79." (Van Inwagen 1983, p.184).
12. We are grateful to David Widerker, Al Mele, Chris Pliatska, and Ted Warfield for helpful comments on an earlier version of this paper.

Philosophical Perspectives, 14, Action and Freedom, 2000

THE DUAL REGRESS OF FREE WILL AND THE ROLE
OF ALTERNATIVE POSSIBILITIES

Robert Kane
The University of Texas at Austin

I

Modern debates about the incompatibility of free will and determinism have focused almost exclusively on the condition of alternative possibilities, the requirement that the free agent "could have done otherwise." I have argued in the past that this focus on alternative possibilities has obscured important features of traditional debates about free will and moral responsibility and that focusing on alternative possibilities alone is too thin a basis on which to rest the case for incompatibility of free will and determinism.[1] In this paper, I want to explain my reasons for believing this and then apply the results to important controversies in the recent philosophical literature on free will and moral responsibility.

Section II considers initial grounds for thinking that alternative possibilities cannot be the whole story about why one might think free will is incompatible with determinism. There are possible actions in which the agents have alternative possibilities, or could have done otherwise, and the actions are undetermined—and yet the agents lack free *will*. Such actions show that the power to do otherwise and indeterminism together are not sufficient for free will (even if these two conditions should be necessary). Section III considers a different set of arguments, more familiar in recent philosophy, purporting to show that alternative possibilities are not even necessary for free will or moral responsibility. These arguments (of Daniel Dennett, Harry Frankfurt and others) only partially succeed, for reasons to be explained in section III. But if we look at them in unfamiliar ways, they provide further support for the belief that traditional issues about free will and determinism cannot be resolved by focusing on alternative possibilities alone.

What else is required to adequately address traditional issues about free will and determinism? In section IV and V, I argue that the discussion of earlier sections leads to another condition in the history of debates about free will, whose importance to those debates has often been obscured by the exclusive focus on alternative possibilities. I call this additional condition "the condition of ultimate responsibility" and explain its significance and its relations to determinism and alternative possibilities in sections IV and V. These discussions lead in section VI to the "dual regress of free will" referred to in the title of this paper. While regresses often enter into debates about free action and free will, the existence of this dual regress has gone largely unnoticed by philosophers; and its importance to free will debates has not been generally appreciated. One of my purposes in this paper is to bring this neglected topic to the attention of philosophers, for I think it provides a key to understanding the tangled connections between free will, moral responsibility, alternative possibilities and indeterminism.

Finally, section VII applies the results of sections II-VI to recent controversies about free will and moral responsibility, including debates (1) about "when the will is free," (2) about so-called "Frankfurt-style examples" and (3) about new positions, such as "hyperincompatibilism," that have come on the scene in recent years in the attempt to rethink the role of alternative possibilities in disputes about freedom and responsibility.

II

I suggested that there are possible actions for which agents have alternative possibilities and the actions are undetermined—and yet the agents lack free *will*. This is the first clue that free will requires more than the power to do otherwise even if the alternative possibilities should be undetermined as well. To identify the actions which show this, one has to go back to examples put forward thirty or more years ago in debates about "could have done otherwise" by J. L. Austin (1966) , Philippa Foot (1966), Michael Ayers (1968), Elizabeth Anscombe (1971) and others. These "Austin-style examples," as I shall call them, were originally conceived for a different purpose, but I shall argue that they have a significance beyond that envisaged when they were first introduced.

Here are three examples of this kind, each with usefully different features. The first is J. L. Austin's example from his celebrated essay, "Ifs and Cans." Austin imagined that he must hole a three-foot putt to win a golf match, but owing to a nervous twitch in his arm, he misses. The other two examples are ones I have used on other occasions. An assassin is trying to kill the prime minister with a high-powered rifle when, owing to a nervous twitch, he misses and kills the minister's aide instead. I am standing in front of a coffee machine intending to press the button for coffee without cream when, owing to a brain cross, I accidentally press the button for coffee with cream. In each of these cases, we can further suppose, as Austin suggests, that an element of genuine chance or indeterminism is involved (perhaps the nervous twitches or brain crosses are brought about by actual undetermined [amplified] quantum events in the nervous systems of the agents). We can thus imagine that Austin's holing the putt is a genuinely undetermined event. He might miss it by chance and, in the example, does miss it by chance.

Now Austin's inspired question about his example was this: can we say in such circumstances that "he could have done otherwise" than miss the putt? His answer is that we can indeed say this. For he had made many similar putts of this short length in the past (he had the capacity and opportunity); and since the outcome of this one was undetermined, he might well have succeeded in holing it, as he was trying to do. But this means we have an action (missing the putt) that is (i) undetermined and (ii) such that the agent could have done otherwise; and yet missing the putt is not something that we regard as *freely* done in any normal sense of the term because it is not under the agent's voluntary control. The same is true of the assassin's missing his intended target and my accidentally pressing the wrong button on the coffee machine.

One might initially be tempted to think that these three occurrences are not *actions* at all in such circumstances because they are undetermined and happen by accident. But Austin rightly warns against drawing such a conclusion. Missing the putt, he says, was clearly something he *did*, even though it was not what he wanted or intended to do; similarly, killing the aide was something the assassin did, though unintentionally; and pressing the wrong button was something I did, even if only by accident or inadvertently. The point is that many of the things we do *by accident* or *mistake*, *unintentionally* or *inadvertently*, are nonetheless things we *do*. We may sometimes be absolved of responsibility for doing them (though not always, as in the case of the assassin), but it is for *doing* them that we are absolved of responsibility; and this can be true even if the accidents or mistakes are genuinely undetermined.

To see this, imagine the assassin's lawyer standing before a jury insisting that his client's killing the aide was an accident, and insisting moreover that, since it was a genuinely undetermined accident, killing the aide was not really something his client *did* at all. Rather it happened by chance ("chance" did it, not his client); and his client was therefore not responsible. Such an "indeterminism defense," as I have elsewhere called it, is absurd on the face of it; and the jury would rightly reject it. They would realize what Austin clearly saw— that even if some indeterminism and chance should be involved in the explanatory chains that lead from our motives and intentions to actions, that would not of itself undermine the claim that the actions were ours and that we could sometimes be held responsible for them. We can be responsible for what we probabilistically cause as well as for what we deterministically cause.

The following example of my own brings this out in a striking way. A disgruntled nuclear plant employee hides radioactive material in his boss's office with the intent of giving the boss cancer. The physics of radiation together with circumstances of the case may well imply that the boss has only, let us say, a thirty percent chance of contracting the disease usually produced by exposure to this material; but he does contract it and dies. No sensible jury would refuse to convict the employee of murdering his boss on the grounds that the boss's death was the result of undetermined quantum mechanical events (as, by hypothesis, it may have been). This example, like the others, shows that our ordinary language of action and responsibility is flexible enough to accommodate indeterminism and probabilistic causation in circumstances like these. We can be responsible for raising or lowering the probabilities that certain good or bad things will happen by our intentions and efforts; and this is what the nuclear employee did by planting the material in the office. There was a chance he would fail to do what he was trying to do, kill his boss, but he succeeded and was guilty.

Austin's intent when introducing his original example of the missed putt in "Ifs and Cans" was more narrowly focused than my intentions here. Austin wanted to criticize certain "hypothetical" analyses of "could have done otherwise" favored by compatibilists (according to which it means that an agent "*would* have done otherwise, *if* the agent had desired or intended or tried to do otherwise"). Most philosophers now believe Austin was successful in the limited task he set himself of showing that such analyses are flawed. But there is much more to be learned from the style of example Austin introduced; and my goal here is to focus on what such examples tell us specifically about the relation of alternative possibilities to free *will*. Recall the thought that what we have in examples such as missing the putt, killing the aide, and pressing the wrong button are actions that are (i) undetermined and (ii) such that the agents could have done otherwise, and yet they are not freely performed in the sense of being under the agents' voluntary control. To see what this implies about free will, let us now add the following scenario.

Suppose God creates a world in which there is a considerable amount of genuine indeterminism. Chance plays a significant role in this world in human affairs as well as in nature. People set out to do things and often succeed, but sometimes they fail in an Austinian manner. They set out to kill prime ministers or bosses, hole putts, press buttons on coffee machines, thread needles, punch computer keys, scale walls, and so on—usually succeeding, but sometimes failing by mistake or accident in a manner that is undetermined. But now we further imagine in this world that all actions of all agents, whether they succeed in their purposes or not, are such that their reasons, motives and purposes for trying to act as they do are always predetermined or pre-set by God. Whether the assassin misses the prime minister or not, his intent to kill the prime minister in the first place is predetermined by God. Whether or not Austin misses his putt, his wanting and trying to make it rather than miss are preordained by God. Whether I press the button for coffee without cream, my wanting to do so because of my dislike of cream is predetermined by God; and so it is for all persons and all of their actions in this imagined world.

I would argue that persons in such a world lack free *will*, even though it is often the case that they have alternative possibilities and their actions are undetermined. They can do otherwise, but only in the limited Austinian manner—by mistake or accident, unwillingly or inadvertently. What they cannot do in any sense is *will* otherwise; for all of their reasons, motives and purposes have been pre-set by God. We may say that their wills in every situation are already "set one way" before and when they act, so that if they do otherwise, it will not be "in accordance with their wills."

What this scenario brings out is that when we wonder about whether the wills of agents are free (rather than wondering only about whether they have freedom of action), it is not merely whether they could have done otherwise that concerns us, even if the doing otherwise is undetermined. What interests us is whether they could have done otherwise *voluntarily* (or *willingly*), *intentionally* or *rationally*. Or to put it more generally, we are interested in whether they could have acted in *more than one way* voluntarily, intentionally and rationally, rather than only in one way voluntarily, intentionally and rationally and in other ways merely by accident or mistake, unintentionally, inadvertently, or irrationally. ("Voluntarily" [and "willingly"] mean here acting "in accordance with one's will [character plus motives]"; "intentionally" means "knowingly" [as opposed to "inadvertently"] and "on purpose" [as opposed to "accidentally"] and "rationally," means "having reasons for acting and acting for those reasons." I shall have more to say about these terms later.)

I have elsewhere referred to such conditions—of *more-than-one-way*, or *plural*, voluntariness, intentionality and rationality—as "plurality conditions" for free will.[2] Such plurality conditions seem to be deeply embedded in our intuitions about free choice and action. Most of us naturally assume that freedom and responsibility would be deficient if it were always the case that we could only do otherwise by accident or mistake, unintentionally, involuntarily or irrationally, in the manner of Austin-style examples. But *why* do we assume this so readily; and why are these plurality conditions so deeply embedded in our intuitions about free will? These are questions that have not received the attention from philosophers they deserve. For if the arguments to this point are correct, free will involves more than alternative possibilities and indeterminism; and the "plurality conditions" appear to be among the additional requirements. Philosophers would do well to focus more attention on these conditions rather than on alternative possibilities alone.

III

The preceding arguments show that alternative possibilities are not sufficient for free will and moral responsibility, even if indeterminism is added. We now turn to a different set of arguments whose intent by their originators was to show that alternative possibilities (and consequently indeterminism as well) are not even necessary for free will and moral responsibility. Two distinct kinds of arguments of this sort have surfaced in the recent literature on freedom and responsibility. The first kind appeals to what David Shatz (1997) has called "character examples"[3]; the second kind appeals to what have come to be known as "Frankfurt-style examples."

One of the best-known arguments of the first kind—appealing to character examples—comes from Daniel Dennett's *Elbow Room* (1984). Dennett says "I have not yet declared a position on the 'could have done otherwise' principle: the principle that holds that one has acted freely (and responsibly) only if one could have done otherwise" (p. 131). Dennett thinks this principle is false, citing as a counterexample the case of Martin Luther. According to Dennett, when Luther said "Here I stand. I can do no other" upon finally breaking with the church in Rome, he meant "that his conscience made it *impossible* for him to recant" (p. 133). Suppose, says Dennett, Luther was literally right about this: he could not then and there have done otherwise because his act was determined by his character and motives at the time. This would not matter to Luther's free will or responsibility, says Dennett, for "we simply do not exempt someone from blame or praise for an act because we think he could do no other" or because we think his act was determined by his character (p. 133). In saying "I can do no other," Luther was not renouncing free will or moral responsibility, but rather taking full responsibility for acting of his own free will. Dennett concludes that neither free will nor moral responsibility require "could have done otherwise" *or* the absence of determinism.

Though I do not think this argument fully succeeds, I do think Dennett is on to something important that even incompatibilists about free will, like myself, should concede. I think we should concede that Luther's "Here I stand" *could* have been a morally responsible act done "of his own free will," even if Luther could not have done otherwise at the time he performed it and even if his act was determined by his then-existing character and motives. But I think this should be conceded only to the extent that one can assume other things about the background of Luther's action that made him responsible or accountable for it—that made it an act of "his own" free will. If Luther's affirmation did issue inevitably from his character and motives at the time it was made, then his moral accountability for it would depend on whether he was responsible for having made himself into the kind of person he then was, whose character and motives would issue in such an act. Compare Aristotle's claim that if a man is to be responsible for wicked acts that flow from his character, he must at some time in the past have been responsible for the wicked character from which these acts flow[4], or Kant's claim (1960: 40) that a "man... must make or have made himself into whatever in the moral sense, whether good or evil, he is or is to become."

Those who know Luther's biography know the inner struggle he endured leading up to his fateful affirmation. By numerous choices and actions in this period, he was gradually shaping the character and motives from which his affirmation would flow. If we do not hesitate to judge Luther responsible for the final affirmation, I think it is because we believe he is responsible by these past choices and acts for making himself into the person he was at the time. But then, the question of whether he could have done otherwise shifts backwards to earlier choices and acts through which his present character and motives were formed. If some of these earlier choices or actions were not such that he could have done otherwise, there would have been nothing he could have *ever* done to make himself different than he was—a consequence, I believe, that is incompatible with his being ultimately accountable for what he was. To put the point graphically: if God had made us so that we *never* could have done anything to make ourselves different than we are, could a just God turn around and blame or punish us for *failing* to be other than we are?

Dennett's point should therefore be qualified. Character examples, like Luther's, do show that alternative possibilities are not required for *every* morally responsible act done "of our own free wills." This is a significant result for our purposes, for it lends further support to the idea that alternative possibilities are not the whole story about free will. Yet if we take a broader perspective, rather than focusing on individual acts isolated from "a whole lifetime," it does not necessarily follow from this result that free will and moral responsibility do not require alternative possibilities *at all*, i.e., at any times in the course of an agent's life. A stronger argument than Dennett's would be needed to show this; character examples alone will not suffice.

But I said there were two kinds of arguments in contemporary philosophy purporting to show that alternative possibilities are not necessary for free will or moral responsibility. Some philosophers feel that the second kind of argument, which appeals to so-called "Frankfurt-style examples," does provide the stronger argument needed to show that alternative possibilities are not needed at all for free will or moral responsibility. "Frankfurt-style examples" are particularly relevant to our concerns because they were originally introduced by Harry Frankfurt (1969) with the intent of undermining what he called the "principle of alternative possibilities" (PAP): "a person is morally responsible for what he has done only if he could have done otherwise" (p. 829). Such examples have since played a major role in contemporary discussions of freedom and moral responsibility.

Frankfurt-style examples usually involve a controller (called "Black" in Frankfurt's original example) who wants an agent (Jones) to perform an action A (p. 835). If the agent, Jones, decides to do A on his own, the controller, Black, will not intervene, but if it becomes clear that Jones is going to do something else, Black has the power to "take effective steps" to ensure that Jones does A. We are to imagine that the controller has great power—perhaps he has direct control over Jones's brain or a drug that will allow him to control Jones whenever he chooses. Frankfurt argues that if Jones does A on his own in such circumstances (and the controller does not in fact intervene), Jones can be morally responsible even though he literally could not have done otherwise (because the controller would not have let him). If this is so, it follows that being morally responsible does not imply being able to do otherwise; and the principle of alternative possibilities, PAP, would be false.

Such examples of "pre-emptive" (or "counterfactual") control have proliferated since Frankfurt introduced them. The literature on them is now enormous,[5] but we can fortunately restrict ourselves to those aspects of Frankfurt-style examples that are directly related to our purposes. The first thing to notice is that, in the above discussion of character examples, such as the Luther example, we have already conceded that the principle Frankfurt is attacking, namely PAP, is false. Jones could in principle be responsible for his action (just as Luther was) even *if* he could not have done otherwise and even if his action was determined by his character and motives, so long as he was to some degree responsible for making himself into the sort of person he then was by virtue of other actions or choices in the past with respect to which he could have done otherwise. Black's non-interference is required, of course, but it is not enough to ensure Jones's responsibility. We have to know more about the background of Jones's action in its own right, including how he got to be the way he is. As a consequence, Frankfurt-style examples of this kind (like character examples) do not necessarily show that moral responsibility does not require having alternative possibilities at all in the course of a lifetime.

But it is just here that Frankfurt-style examples provide some extra leverage that character examples do not provide. For one might go on to imagine a "global Frankfurt controller" hovering over Jones throughout his entire lifetime, so that Jones *never* could have done otherwise; and yet the controller never in fact intervenes because Jones always does on his own what the controller wants. Since such a global controller would be a mere observer of events, never actually intervening in Jones's affairs, Jones would be left to his own devices and might therefore be responsible for many of his actions even though he never could have done otherwise because the controller (ever-present, though non-intervening) would never have let him. This seems to imply that moral responsibility (and the free will that moral responsibility requires) could be consistent with never having any alternative possibilities.

Some philosophers believe that global Frankfurt-style examples of this sort provide powerful support for the claim that alternative possibilities are not required *at all* for free will or moral responsibility.[6] Yet Frankfurt-style examples in general (and global ones, in particular) are unusual and esoteric, as even their proponents admit[7]; and standing in opposition to them are persistent ordinary intuitions that alternative possibilities have *something* to do with our ability to act freely and responsibly. How do we sort out these conflicting intuitions? I believe they can be sorted out, but doing so turns out to be another instance in which the answers cannot be found by focusing on alternative possibilities alone (even though the issues in this case are about alternative possibilities). One has to dig more deeply into the underlying reasons why persons have thought alternative possibilities are required for free will and moral responsibility in the first place. This is a a task toward which all of our reasoning thus far has been pointing; and it requires wading into deeper waters than we have yet encountered.

IV

I believe the clues one needs to resolve these contemporary disputes about alternative possibilities lie deep within the history of debates about free will and determinism. When one looks into this history, one finds that the requirement of alternative possibilities, or "could have done otherwise" (AP, as I shall hereafter call it), is only one consideration leading people to believe that free will must be incompatible with determinism. There is a second requirement, less frequently discussed, which turns up in the history of debates about free will and is to my mind even more important. I call it the "condition of ultimate responsibility" (or UR, to distinguish it from AP).[8] I do not think one can resolve issues about free will, responsibility and determinism without also bringing in this second condition along with AP, any more than one can explain what a carrot is by describing only that part of it which grows above the ground. When it comes to free will, ultimate responsibility is the root and alternative possibilities the leaves.

I have discussed the history behind these claims in more detail elsewhere.[9] Here I will go directly to the UR condition and explain its motivation and meaning. To do so, I will focus on only one historical figure, namely Aristotle, to illustrate the difference between UR and AP. Aristotle talks about free and responsible actions being "up to us" and he notes that "when acting is up to us, so is not acting" (1915:1113b6)—thus affirming the condition of alternative possibilities or AP for actions that are "up to us." Yet, as Richard Sorabji (1980) has noted, Aristotle usually cites two conditions, not one, for an action's being "up to us" in a sense required for responsibility or blameworthiness (pp. 233–4). AP is one of these conditions, but Aristotle also asserts in other passages, in Sorabji's words, that "the concept of an action being up to us is connected... with the concept of our being or having within us, the 'origin' (*arche*) of the action" (p. 234). This second condition puts the emphasis for responsible action not on the power to do otherwise, but on the *source* or *ground* (*arche*) of the action that is actually performed. This source must be "in us."

Moreover, some of those passages in which Aristotle talks about the source of our actions being within us make clear that he is particularly worried about whether agents are responsible for the characters and motives that are the sources (*archai* and *aitiai*) of their actions. He acknowledges that it may no longer be possible for a man of ingrained character not to be wicked, but he also insists (as indicated earlier) that if the man is responsible for his wicked acts, he must at some time in the past have been responsible for forming the character and motives that issued in such an act. Aristotle himself says little more about this. But many philosophers have held that if we were to take this idea seriously, it would lead to a potentially vicious regress in which agents would have to be responsible by still earlier acts for the characters and motives that led to the acts by which they formed their present characters and motives, and so on *ad infinitum.*[10] Or, even more absurdly, one would have to assume that at some time agents were "prime movers unmoved," with respect to some of their acts, as Roderick Chisholm (1982) has put it—somehow causes of themselves (*causae suorum*), or creators *ex nihilo*

In sum, one encounters deep puzzles with the idea of an ultimate source or ground of character and action wherever one turns—which is perhaps why many philosophers (including many with incompatibilist instincts) have given up on the idea of ultimate responsibility, preferring to talk instead about alternative possibilities. But rather than give up on the idea of ultimate responsibility altogether, my thought has been to try to tame it and rid it of the absurdities with which it is often associated (such as prime movers unmoved, creation *ex nihilo*, and the like). The first step would be to acknowledge that our actions are always limited by circumstances and that they cause only as parts of complex webs of background causes and circumstances, including nature and upbringing. What we should therefore say is that to be responsible for our characters and motives being the way they are, some of our past actions must have "made a difference" in the sense that they were essential parts of the actual web of causes and conditions that resulted in our characters and motives being the way they are; and if these actions of ours had not been involved, our characters and motives would not have been such that our present actions would have issued from them as they did.[11]

This is to recognize that we are never prime movers "unmoved." What ultimate responsibility requires is not that, but something different. The further clues lie in character examples, like Luther's, and in the references to Aristotle. What the condition requires is that there not be any sufficient ground or reason (condition, cause, or motive) of our actions for which we are not ourselves to some degree responsible. Or, putting it positively, we must be responsible to some degree by virtue of our own voluntary actions for anything that is a *sufficient ground* (*arche*) or *reason* (condition, cause, or motive) for our acting as we do. (Call this the condition of ultimate responsibility, or UR.[12]) (The term "voluntary" in it signifies that we acted for reasons or motives we wanted to act upon when we acted—and in that sense acted "in accordance with our wills.")

If, for example, our characters and motives together with background circumstances are sufficient to move us to do A, then we must be responsible for our characters and motives being such that they so move us, given those circumstances; and being so responsible in turn implies (in a manner spelled out two paragraphs earlier) that some of our past voluntary actions must have been essential parts of the complex web of causes and conditions that resulted in our characters and motives being the way they are. This captures the idea that if persons are responsible for the wicked (or noble, shameful, heroic, generous, cruel, kind, treacherous, just...) acts that flow from their characters and motives (their *wills*), they must at some time in the past have been responsible for forming the characters and motives (the wills) from which these acts flow. Such a conception makes explicit something that is often obscured in contemporary free will debates—namely, that free *will*, as opposed to mere freedom of action—is about the forming or shaping of character and motives which are the *sources* of praiseworthy or blameworthy, virtuous or vicious, actions.

But it takes no great insight to see that by defining the condition of ultimate responsibility this way, we have eliminated only some of the difficulties attending it. In particular, we have not eliminated the possibility that it will generate a vicious regress. If I must have formed my present will (character and motives) by voluntary actions, A1... An, in my past, UR requires that if any of these earlier voluntary actions by which I formed my present will also had sufficient grounds or reasons, R1... Rn, in my character and motives (plus background circumstances) when I performed *them*, then I must have been responsible for those earlier sufficient grounds by still earlier voluntary actions, B1... Bn, and so on indefinitely. There is indeed a *potential* regress lurking here, but it becomes actual only if every one of the voluntary actions in this backwards chain *do* have sufficient grounds or reasons in the agent's character and motives (plus background conditions), or in some other set of circumstances. So what the potential regress tells us is that free will is only possible if some voluntary actions in an agent's life history do *not* have sufficient conditions, causes or motives that would have required the agent to have formed them by still earlier voluntary actions.

Therein lies the connection to determinism. For, if determinism is true, every act would have sufficient conditions or causes in the conjunction of prior circumstances and laws of nature. So the potential regress tells us that *if free will requires ultimate responsibility in the sense of UR, free will is incompatible with determinism*. Some voluntary acts in our life histories through which we formed our present wills must have been undetermined if we are to be to any extent the ultimate sources or grounds (*archai*) of our own wills. Note that this does not establish that a free will requiring ultimate responsibility exists or even that it is intelligible. One might question whether actions lacking sufficient conditions, causes or motives could in fact be free and responsible actions at all, since they would be undetermined and therefore might happen merely by chance. This is a legitimate concern about incompatibilist freedom, as anyone knows who has followed free will debates—a concern I have addressed at length in other places (for I believe one can make sense of undetermined actions without assuming they happen merely by chance).[13] But that is not the main concern here. The concern here is about what free will would require if it did require ultimate responsibility; and the argument is that it would require the absence of determinism for at least some actions in one's life history by which one's present character and motives were formed. (If that should mean free will could not exist, so be it.)

But there is something even more important in this reasoning for our present purposes. You will notice that the above argument for incompatibility of free will and determinism does not at any point invoke *alternative possibilities*, or the requirement of alternative possibilities (AP). It focuses rather on the sources or grounds of what we actually do rather than on the power to do otherwise. When we argue about the incompatibility of free will and determinism from alternative possibilities, or AP, we tend to focus on notions of "necessity," "possibility," "power," "ability," "can" and "could have done otherwise." The argument from UR focuses on a different set of concerns about the "sources," "grounds," (*archai*)," "reasons" or "explanations" (*aitiai*) of our actions, characters, motives and purposes. Where did they come from, who produced them, and who is responsible for them? Was it *we* ourselves who are responsible for forming our characters and motives, or someone or something else—God or fate, heredity and environment, nature or upbringing, society or culture, behavioral engineers or hidden controllers? Therein lies the core of the traditional "problem of free will."

Does this mean then that alternative possibilities have nothing to do with the free will problem or the incompatibility question? One might be tempted at this point to think so (though I am going to argue that it would be a mistake to think so). If one could get directly to incompatibilism from UR, AP might appear to to be unnecessary. To incompatibilists, this may look like a way of reconciling their incompatibilist beliefs with the arguments from Frankfurt-style examples considered at the end of section III, which seemed to show that moral responsibility (and any free will that moral responsibility entails) does not require alternative possibilities.[14] Whether Frankfurt-style examples actually do show this is something I left undecided at the end of section III. (Later I will argue that they do not.) But incompatibilists who are convinced by Frankfurt-style arguments, and yet do not want to give up their incompatibilism, might be tempted to take the following line: while free will and moral responsibility do not entail alternative possibilities, free will and moral responsibility nonetheless entail indeterminism for other reasons (namely, UR).

V

But I now want to argue that this line of reasoning—tempting as it may be—would be wrong. For it turns out that UR not only entails indeterminism, it also entails alternative possibilities (hence AP) for at least some acts in an agent's life history. Yet the surprising thing is that UR entails alternative possibilities for different reasons and by a different argumentative route than the one that leads to indeterminism. This is part of the reason, I believe, why issues about alternative possibilities are so tangled and complex and why their connections to ultimate responsibility are easily missed. To see how alternative possibilities are related to UR we have to focus attention elsewhere—not on the ultimate sources of grounds of *actions* alone, but on the ultimate sources of the *wills* (characters, motives and purposes) of agents to perform those actions.

To see this, let us return to the imagined world of section II in which all of the reasons, motives and purposes of agents were predetermined or pre-set by God. Whether the assassin misses the prime minister, whether Austin misses his putt, whether I press the button for coffee without cream, our intentions or purposes, wants and other motives for trying to do the things we are trying to do have been pre-set by God; and so it is for all agents and all of their actions in this world. I argued that persons in such a world would lack free will, even though they might sometimes be able to do otherwise in the Austinian manner—by mistake, accident, or chance. What they could not do in any situation is will otherwise. For their wills in the form of their reasons, motives and purposes are already "set one way" before they act and they are never the ultimate sources of their own wills.

This shows in a striking way why, to have free will, it is not only necessary to be the ultimate source of one's actions, but to be the ultimate source of one's will to perform the actions as well. It would not be enough to be unhindered in the pursuit of one's motives and purposes, if all of one's motives and purposes were created by someone or something else (God or fate or whatever) as in the above imagined world. Even one's motives or purposes for wanting to change one's motives or purposes would be created by someone or something else in such a world. UR in fact captures this additional requirement. For it says that we must be responsible by virtue of our voluntary actions for anything that is a sufficient condition, cause, *or motive* for our acting as we do. One has a *sufficient motive* for doing something, when one's will is "set one way" on doing it before and when one acts—as the assassin's will is set on killing the prime minister. Among the available things he might do, only one of them will be done voluntarily and intentionally. Anything else he might do would be done only by accident or mistake, inadvertently or unintentionally.[15]

UR says that if you have a sufficient motive for doing something in this sense—if your will is "set one way" on doing it rather than anything else available to you—then to be ultimately responsible for your will, you must be to some degree responsible by virtue of past voluntary acts for your will's being set the way it is. This is significant because when we look to the responsibility of the assassin for what he did, we look to his evil motives and intentions. They are the source of his guilt, whether he succeeds in killing the prime minister *or* fails and kills the aide instead. Luther too, we assumed, had a sufficient motive for his final affirmation, "Here I stand." But if his will was set one way by the time he made it, this would not count against his ultimate responsibility, so long as he was responsible for his will's being set that way. Such is what UR requires.

But now it looks like we have another regress on our hands. If your will was already set one way when you performed those earlier voluntary actions by which you set your present will, then you must have been responsible by virtue of still earlier voluntary actions for its being set that way, and so on backwards. Once again, however, this is only a *potential* regress. Just as the earlier regress discussed in section IV could be stopped by assuming that some actions in one's history lacked sufficient grounds or reasons in the sense of sufficient *causes or conditions*, so this regress can be stopped by supposing some actions in one's past lacked sufficient grounds or reasons in the sense of sufficient *motives*. These would be actions in which the agents' wills were not already set one way before they performed them; rather the agents would set their wills one way or another in the performance of them.

I have elsewhere called such actions "will-setting" actions (Kane, 1997). When, for example, agents make choices or decisions between two or more motivationally viable options and do not settle on which they want more, all things considered, until the moment of choice or decision itself, then their choices or decisions are "will-setting" in this way: the agents set their wills one way or another in the act of choosing itself. (Choices or decisions are not the only such actions that can be will-setting in this way, but they are the most familiar.[16]) The potential regress of sufficient motives can only be stopped by supposing that some voluntary actions in the agent's past are will-setting in this way and not already "will-settled." If all actions were like the assassin's killing of the prime minister, where the agent's will is already set one way, we would have to ask how the agent's will got to be set that way and the regress would continue backwards.

But then it follows that will-setting actions will satisfy the requirement of being *more than one way*, or *plural*, voluntary and intentional (i.e., the "plurality conditions" mentioned at the end of section II). To see why, consider a variation on the assassin example that would make his choice to kill the prime minister a will-setting one. Suppose that just before pulling the trigger, the assassin has doubts about his mission. Pangs of conscience arise in him and a genuine inner struggle ensues about whether or not to go through with the killing. There is now more than one motivationally viable option in his mind—his will is no longer set one way—and he will resolve the issue one way or the other by consciously deciding and thereby setting his will in one direction or the other. Unlike the original assassin example, neither outcome in this case will be a mere accident or mistake; either will be a voluntary and intentional decision to go through with the killing or to stop.

We have thus returned to the plurality conditions of section II. At the end of that section, I asked why these conditions, such as plural voluntariness and intentionality, are so deeply embedded in our intuitions about free will—why so many people readily assume that their free will would be deficient if they were always able to do otherwise only by accident or mistake, unintentionally or involuntarily, as in the Austin-style examples. We now have a clue. If (i) free will requires (ii) ultimate responsibility for our wills as well as our actions, then it requires (iii) will-setting actions at some points in our life histories; and (iv) will-setting actions satisfy the plurality conditions. But now, taking this argument one obvious step further, if free will implies the power to do otherwise voluntarily and intentionally, it implies *a fortiori* (v) the power to do otherwise *simpliciter*, i.e., alternative possibilities, for some actions in one's life history.

Note, however, that this argument from (i) free will to (v) alternative possibilities (AP) is not direct. It goes through (ii) ultimate responsibility (UR), (iii) will-setting and (iv) plurality. Some of our actions must be such that we could have done otherwise, *because* some of them must have been such that we could have done otherwise *voluntarily* and *intentionally*; and the latter condition is required at some points in our lifetimes in order to be ultimate sources of our own wills.

VI

We are now finally in a position to understand what is meant by "the dual regress of free will" of this paper's title. Two potential regresses have been considered—one in section IV, the other in section V. The first regress begins with the requirement (of ultimate responsibility, UR) that agents be responsible by virtue of past voluntary actions for anything that is a sufficient ground (*arche*) or sufficient reason for their actions in the sense of a set of sufficient *conditions or causes*. (Call it the SC-regress). It leads to the conclusion that if agents are to have free will, some actions in their life histories must be undetermined (must lack sufficient conditions or causes). The second regress begins with the requirement (of ultimate responsibility, UR) that agents be responsible by virtue of past voluntary actions for anything that is a sufficient ground or reason for their actions in the sense of a sufficient *motive*. (Call it the SM-regress.) It leads (by way of will-setting and plurality) to the conclusion that if agents are to have free will, some actions in their life histories must be such that they could have done otherwise, or had alternative possibilities, with respect to those actions.

The first of these regresses results from the requirement that we be ultimate sources of our actions, the second from the requirement that we be ultimate sources of our wills (to perform those actions). If the second requirement were not added, we might have a world in which all the will-setting was done by someone or something other than the agents themselves. Agents in such a world might be unhindered in the pursuit of their purposes, but it would never be "up to them" what purposes they pursued. They would not be the ultimate creators or originators of their own ends (i.e., purposes).

In such manner, the requirements of indeterminism and alternative possibilities are arrived at by different routes—though they have a common origin in the idea that we must be the ultimate sources or grounds of our willed actions. But do the two requirements converge? Are the actions in our life histories that must be undetermined if the SC-regress is to be stopped the same actions as the will-setting actions required to stop the SM-regress? It is natural to think that they would be, but an argument is needed to show it. Suppose the undetermined occurrences required to stop the SC-regress were not will-setting and plural, or *more than one way*, voluntary and intentional. Then these undetermined occurrences would either be *one-way* voluntary and intentional (as in the Austin-style examples). Or, they would be *no-ways* voluntary or intentional. In the latter case, all possible alternatives would happen without voluntary or intentional control; and since they are also by hypothesis undetermined, they would be mere chance occurrences. Thus, there would be no reason to think they were *actions* at all, much less responsible actions. In the former case—if the undetermined occurrences were one-way willed (as in Austin-style examples)—the agents wills would have been set one way in making them and we would have to ask whether the agents were responsible by virtue of earlier actions for their wills' being set that way. The SM-regress would continue backwards. So the undetermined actions that stop the SC-regress must also be will-setting and plural voluntary, if the SM-regress is to be stopped as well.

Conversely the will-setting actions that stop the SM-regress must also be undetermined. For if those actions by which agents set their own wills one way or the other were determined, the agents would have to be responsible (via UR) for the conditions or causes determining them, and the SC-regress would continue. Thus we arrive at the conclusion that if both regresses of free will are to be stopped—if we are to be ultimately responsible for our actions and our wills to perform the actions—then the will-setting actions that stop one regress (and satisfy the requirement of alternative possibilities (AP)), and the undetermined actions that stop the other regress must converge on the same actions.

VII

In this final section, I apply the results of these reflections to several controversies in the recent literature of free will and moral responsibility.

When is the Will Free? It follows from the preceding arguments that even if one holds that free will—and the (ultimate) moral responsibility associated with free will—are incompatible with determinism, one is not thereby required to hold that every morally responsible act done "of one's own free will" must be undetermined. Undetermined actions for which we could have done otherwise are only a subset of all of the actions for which we are ultimately responsible and which are done of our own free wills. I called actions in this subset "will-setting" actions. They might also be called "self-forming actions" (SFAs), since they are character and motive-forming acts through which we make ourselves into the sorts of persons we are.

The view that undetermined actions need only be a subset of all of the morally responsible actions performed of our own free wills has been called "restricted incompatibilism" by John Martin Fischer and Mark Ravizza (1992).

(Others have called it "restricted libertarianism" (Shatz, 1997)). Such a view is "incompatibilist" or "libertarian" because it insists that free will and responsibility are incompatible with determinism. It is "restricted" incompatibilism by virtue of the fact that it does not require that all responsible actions done of our own free wills must be undetermined. Peter van Inwagen has defended a restricted incompatibilist view in a well-known essay "When is the Will Free" (1989), which appeared in an earlier volume of this series. His view was subsequently criticized by Fischer and Ravizza (1992), among others (e.g., McCann, 1996), giving rise to a controversy about when the will is free.

I side with van Inwagen in this controversy and have also defended a restricted incompatibilist view since the publication of my first book on free will (Kane, 1985). (Van Inwagen cites this work in his 1989 paper.) But our versions of restricted incompatibilism differ in details that have emerged in this paper and are relevant to the dispute with Fischer and Ravizza. First, van Inwagen arrives at restricted incompatibilism by focusing on alternative possibilities and utilizing his Rule Beta (which I will not discuss here). By contrast, I arrive at restricted incompatibilism by way of reflection on UR. Many of the criticisms Fischer and Ravizza make against van Inwagen's restricted incompatibilism apply to his use of Rule Beta; and those criticisms do not apply if the matter is approached through UR. Second, van Inwagen claims that undetermined actions would be very rare if his arguments for restricted incompatibilism are correct. With respect to many of our everyday actions, we have no good reasons for doing otherwise. For example, when the telephone rings in my office I answer it—deliberately to be sure—but the fact is that I had no good reason not to answer it, given my character and motives at the time. Many of our everyday actions are like that, van Inwagen argues; and there is no good reason to think they must be undetermined.

I agree with van Inwagen about this, but I think he restricts the range of undetermined self-forming actions more than is necessary. He includes cases where agents are torn between moral obligation and self-interested desires, or prudential conflicts between present inclinations and long-term goals. He also cites cases where we are torn between incommensurable goals—such as trying to decide whether or not to become a lawyer or doctor, to stay with one's ailing mother or to join the resistance—where there are strong, and not easily comparable, reasons for choosing different options. I also include these three possibilities as examples of undetermined free choices in Kane, 1985. But I also emphasize that if one takes note of the fact that these are all cases where the agent has more than one "motivationally viable" option to choose from, and is torn inside about just what to do, then such cases occur more commonly in everyday life than one might think.[17]

But, in addition, I now hold that undetermined self-forming actions (SFAs) form a much wider class of actions than would be indicated by the three above examples; and this is a major theme of my most recent book (Kane, 1996). Not only do undetermined SFAs include cases where we must choose between more than one motivationally viable option, they also include cases where we must make efforts to sustain our purposes or intentions against countervailing desires, fears, aversions, laziness and other conditions which make it difficult to carry out our plans and purposes once chosen (pp. 152–8). Such efforts against resistance in the will are common occurrences of everyday life and far from rare. (On some days they begin when we have to drag ourselves out of bed in the morning.) This is important because Fischer and Ravizza also argue that restricted incompatibilism would imply (counterintuitively) that genuinely free actions for which we could have done otherwise would be more rare than we normally assume in everyday experience. I respond in two ways. First, undetermined self-forming actions turn out to be more common in everyday life, when viewed more broadly in the manner just described. Second, even in those cases where agents could not have done otherwise because of their existing characters and motives (such as Luther's affirmation or my picking up the telephone when it rings), the actions of such agents can still be responsible (even ultimately responsible) and done "of their own free wills," if the agents are responsible for the wills from which they act.

But would the actions (Luther's and mine, for example) have been "free" actions in ordinary senses of the term, if they were determined and the agents could not have done otherwise? Well, that depends on what you mean by "free"; for it must be emphasized that this word has different meanings in ordinary usage. If "free" means done "of one's own free wills" the answer (already given) is Yes; Luther's action and mine could be such. Also, if "free" means uncoerced or uncompelled as it often does in ordinary language, the answer is again Yes; Luther's affirmation and my picking up the telephone could well have been uncoerced and uncompelled actions, even if determined. Unlike many incompatibilists, I believe these "compatibilist" senses of "free" (uncoerced, uncompelled, unconstrained) are legitimate senses of "free" and they are the senses we often have in mind when in ordinary contexts we say of actions such as Luther's or my picking up the phone that we acted "freely" even though there were no motivationally viable options at the time.

What incompatibilists should insist upon, I claim, is that these compatibilist senses of "free" (uncoerced, uncompelled, etc.) are not the only ones that matter. Acting "of one's own free will" in a sense that requires ultimate responsibility also matters. But this sense of "free" (acting "of one's own free will") can also be ascribed to actions like Luther's and my picking up the phone if they are determined. So there are a number of senses of "free" and "responsible" (including "ultimately responsible") that can be legitimately ascribed to actions by restricted incompatibilists, even if the agents could not motivationally have done otherwise when they acted. Restricted incompatibilism need not be counterintuitive, as Fischer and Ravizza claim.[18]

Hyperincompatibilism. At the end of section III, I suggested that many contemporary philosophers are convinced by Frankfurt-style examples (especially the "global" variety) that free will and moral responsibility do not require alternative possibilities at all. Yet some of those same philosophers continue to have strong incompatibilist intuitions. They may therefore be tempted to argue for the view mentioned at the end of section V that, while free will and moral responsibility do not require alternative possibilities, free will and moral responsibility are none the less incompatible with determinism for other reasons.[19] Such a view has sometimes been called "hyperincompatibilism." One contemporary philosopher who has defended such a view is Eleonore Stump (1996). She in fact ascribes it also to Thomas Aquinas. Aquinas is certainly an incompatibilist about free will. He believes that the will is not causally determined ("efficiently caused," in his terms) when it makes free choices. Stump claims further that, for Aquinas, what is required for free will in addition to causal indeterminism is that free and responsible actions be internally caused by the wills of the agents themselves and not by causes external to the agent; and for this, she claims, having alternative possibilities is not required.

I do not know if Stump is right about Aquinas on alternative possibilities. Her accounts of his view are generally astute and insightful; and, for my part, I believe that Aquinas is one of the most perceptive and original thinkers to have ever written on the topic of free will. But I think there is something wrong with *hyperincompatibilism*; so I hope Stump is wrong in thinking that Aquinas holds it. The problem confronting hyperincompatibilists is to say *why* we should think free will is incompatible with determinism if it does *not* imply alternative possibilities. Stump is aware of this problem and has addressed it in a number of places. In one of her papers (n.d.), she suggests that what may lie behind incompatibilist intuitions, if alternative possibilities are not required, is the idea of ultimate responsibility; and she cites my writings in support of this suggestion. Needless to say, I think Stump is right to focus on ultimate responsibility in this connection, since focusing on the ultimate sources of free will and action will get one to incompatibilism directly without bringing in alternative possibilities, as we saw in section IV. Moreover, focusing on ultimate responsibility fits nicely with Stump's view (and Aquinas's) that free will requires that actions have their sources or origins "in us" and not in causes wholly external to us.

So far so good. But what must be added, as we saw in section V, is that free will not only requires ultimate responsibility for our actions but ultimate responsibility for our wills; and this requires that some of our actions be will-setting actions in which agents set their own wills in one way or another rather than having them set by someone or something else; and will-setting actions in turn require alternative possibilities. So if hyperincompatibilists look to the idea of being the ultimate source of one's own will as the reason for incompatibilism (as I think they should) they are going to get a requirement for alternative possibilities anyway for at least some of the actions in the life histories of agents.

Frankfurt-style cases. But what then are we to make of Frankfurt-style examples (including the global variety) which lead hyperincompatibilists to their unusual view and which have led so many other contemporary philosophers to believe that alternative possibilities are not required at all for moral responsibility or free will? Does it not seem reasonable to say that if a global controller never actually intervened in the lives of agents (because they always did what the controller wanted), then the agents could still be responsible for their actions, and even *ultimately responsible* in my sense, though they never could have done otherwise (because the controller would not have let them)? Stump herself poses this question (n.d.); and it is a good one. For in the last analysis, it is the Frankfurt-style cases that provide hyperincompatibilism with its chief support.

My answer is this: if agents really are ultimately responsible for their actions in the sense of UR, and they sometimes genuinely exercise their free wills through will-setting actions or SFAs, a global Frankfurt controller cannot always exercise counterfactual control over them and they will sometimes have the power to do otherwise. Why is this so? Because UR not only implies alternative possibilities for will-setting or self-forming actions (SFAs), it implies indeterminism as well for such actions (by the other part of the dual regress). And a Frankfurt controller faces a dilemma in trying to control undetermined choices or actions. I first stated the reasons why this is so in Kane, 1985 (p. 51) and have developed them further in Kane, 1996 (pp. 142–4). (Similar arguments have been made independently by David Widerker (1995 and 1995a).[20])

The argument, briefly stated, is this. If a choice is undetermined up to the moment when it occurs (as SFAs would be), the controller cannot tell before the choice itself is made which option the agent is going to choose; and then it will be too late to intervene. Thus, the controller faces a dilemma. On the one hand, if he stays out of it, waiting until one or another choice is actually made, the agent could have chosen otherwise, since the choice was undetermined and could have gone the other way. On the other hand, if the controller intervenes to ensure that the choice he wants is made, he must do so *in advance*, no longer leaving it undetermined until the last moment which choice will be made. But in that case, while the agent cannot do otherwise, the controller has actually intervened to determine the outcome in advance and the agent is not ultimately responsible for the outcome, the controller is. (This is no longer "counterfactual" intervention, but "actual" intervention.) So with regard to undetermined will-setting actions or SFAs: if the global controller never actually intervenes in them, the agents will be ultimately responsible (UR), but the agents will also have alternative possibilities (AP); and if the controller does actually intervene in advance to determine the outcomes, the agents will lack alternative possibilities (not-AP), but the controller and not the agents will be ultimately responsible for the outcomes (not-UR).

There have been numerous attempts by defenders of Frankfurt-style examples to respond to this objection (and to similar objections by Widerker and others) over the past five years, but no response, to my mind, has been satisfactory.[21] To answer all such responses, however, would be a task that goes well beyond the scope of this paper.[22] Let me conclude by saying that if this argument does withstand criticism, as I think it does, it provides further support for the claim that ultimate responsibility, and hence free will, require alternative possibilities as well as indeterminism. This is what most of us incompatibilists have traditionally believed.

Notes

1. Kane, 1985, 1989, 1994, 1996 (chapters 3–5), 1997.
2. Kane, 1996, chapter 7.
3. Shatz,1998, is one of the best and most thorough discussions of character examples in the recent literature. His conclusions about what they do and do not show are similar to my own.
4. Aristotle, 1915, 1114a13–22; also 255a8, 110a17,1113b21, 1114a18–19.
5. For a thorough discussion of the topic and further examples, see Fischer, 1994, chapter 7; Fischer and Ravizza, 1998, passim; Haji, 1996, chapter 2; Mele and Robb, 1998, and Hunt, n.d. For dissenting views on Frankfurt-style examples, see Davidson, 1973, van Inwagen, 1983, Naylor, 1984, Heinaman, 1986, Rowe, 1991, Lamb, 1993, Widerker 1995 and 1995a, Ginet, 1996, Copp, 1997, Wyma, 1997, and McKenna, 1997. Some incompatibilists such as Stump, 1990, 1996 and n.d., and Zagzebski, 1991, reject PAP on Frankfurtian grounds, but resist the conclusion that free will and moral responsibility are therefore compatible with determinism. I consider this "hyperincompatibilist" view later in the paper (section VII).
6. See, e.g., Fischer, n.d.
7. See, e.g., Fischer and Ravizza, 1998, p. 30.
8. Kane, 1996, chapter 3. Several other recent philosophers who have recognized the importance of this condition for free will debates (though they give it different names and/or view it differently than I do) are Gomberg, 1975, Strawson, 1986, Nagel , 1986 and Klein, 1990.
9. Kane, 1996, chapters 1 and 3.
10. The best known and most sophisticated version of this regress argument in recent philosophy is by Galen Strawson, 1986.
11. This means that ultimate responsibility would always be a matter of degree. Moreover, given the complexity of most persons' pasts, it is formidably difficult to determine how much ultimate responsibility persons bear for their actions. Only an all-knowing God would know for sure. Finite knowers like ourselves must make our best guesses in the ordinary affairs of life, personal and legal. I do not regard the difficulties of doing this as an objection against the idea of ultimate responsibility so much as a reflection on the human condition.
12. A formal statement of this condition appears in Kane, 1996, p. 35. I would now modify the statement given there by deleting the clause "and for which the the agent could have voluntarily done otherwise." It turns out for reasons given later in this paper (section V and VI) and in Kane, 1996 (chapter 7), that this clause is not necessary since it is implied by other aspects of the definition. I am indebted to criticisms of John Fischer (n. d.) for helping me to see this.
13. See especially Kane, 1996, chapters 8 to 10, and Kane, 1999 and 1999a.
14. For incompatibilists who are tempted in this direction, see the references in note 4.
15. Note that actions can have a sufficient motive in this sense without having a sufficient cause, as the Austin-style examples show.
16. I discuss a variety of other examples in chapter 9 of Kane, 1996.

17. I made this point as the commentator on van Inwagen's 1989 paper when it was presented at the APA Central Division meeting in Chicago, 1987. This commentary was never published, but its themes found their way into some of my later writings (e.g., Kane, 1996, pp. 77–8).
18. For other compelling arguments to this effect, see Shatz, 1998.
19. See note 4 for references.
20. Also by Wyma (1997); another set of arguments with affinities to this one appears in Ginet, 1996.
21. See e.g., Fischer, 1995, Stump, 1996 and n.d., Mele and Robb, 1998, Speak, 1999, Hunt, n.d. Widerker and Katzoff (1996) is a response to Fischer, 1995. Goetz, 1999, is a response to Stump, 1996.
22. I have made an attempt to answer responses to this argument in Kane, 1999a, and in an as-yet-unpublished paper entitled "Responsibility, Incompatibilism and Frankfurt-style Cases."

References

Anscombe, G. E. M. 1971. *Causality and Determinism*. Cambridge: Cambridge University Press.
Aristotle. 1915. *Nichomachean Ethics*. Vol. 9 of *The Works of Aristotle*. Ed. by W. D. Ross. London: Oxford University Press.
Austin, J. L. 1966. "Ifs and Cans." In B. Berofsky, ed., *Free Will and Determinism*, New York: Harper and Row, 295–321.
Ayers, M. R. 1968. *The Refutation of Determinism*. London: Methuen.
Chisholm, Roderick. 1982. "Human Freedom and the Self." In G. Watson (ed.) *Free Will*, Oxford: Oxford University Press, 24–35.
Copp, David. 1997. "Defending the Principle of Alternative Possibilities: Blameworthiness and Moral Responsibility." *Nous* 31: 441–56.
Davidson, Donald. 1973. "Freedom to Act." In *Essays on Freedom and Action*, Ted Honderich (ed.). London: Routledge and Kegan Paul.
Dennett, Daniel. 1984. *Elbow Room*. Cambridge, MA: MIT Press
Fischer, John Martin. 1994. *The Metaphysics of Free Will*. Oxford: Blackwell.
———. 1995. "Libertarianism and Avoidability: A Reply to Widerker." *Faith and Philosophy* 12: 119–25.
———. n.d. "Freedom and Moral Responsibility." *Philosophy and Phenomenological Research*, forthcoming.
Fischer, John Martin and Mark Ravizza. 1992. *Philosophical Perspectives* 6: 423–51.
———. 1998. *Responsibility and Control*. Cambridge: Cambridge University Press.
Foot, Philippa. 1966. "Free Will as Involving Determinism." In B. Berofsky (ed.) *Free Will and Determinism*, New York: Harper and Row, 95–108.
Frankfurt, Harry. 1969. "Alternative Possibilities and Moral Responsibility." *Journal of Philosophy* 66:829–39.
Gomberg, Paul. 1975. "Free Will as Ultimate Responsibility." *American Philosophical Quarterly* 15: 205–12.
Haji, Ishtiyaque. 1996. "Moral Responsibility and the Problem of Induced Pro-Attitudes." *Dialogue* 35:703–20.
———. 1998. *Moral Appraisability*. New York: Oxford University Press.
Heinamen, Robert. 1986. "Incompatibilism Without the Principle of Alternative Possibilities." *Australasian Journal of Philosophy* 64:266–76.
Hunt, David. n.d. "Moral Responsibility and Unavoidable Action." *Philosophical Studies*, forthcoming.
Ginet, Carl. 1996. "In Defense of the Principle of Alternative Possibilities: Why I Don't Find Frankfurt's Argument Convincing." *Philosophical Perspectives* 10:403–17.

Goetz, Stewart. 1999. "Stumping for Widerker." *Faith and Philosophy* 16: 83–9.

Kane, Robert. 1985. *Free Will and Values*. Albany, N.Y.: State University of New York.

———. 1989. "Two Kinds of Incompatibilism." *Philosophy and Phenomenological Research* 50: 219–54.

———. 1994. "Free Will: The Elusive Ideal." *Philosophical Studies* 75: 25–60.

———. 1996. *The Significance of Free Will*. Oxford and New York: Oxford University Press.

———. 1996a. "Freedom, Responsibility and Will-Setting." *Philosophical Topics* 24: 67–90.

———. 1999. "Responsibility, Luck and Chance: Reflections on Free Will and Indeterminism." *The Journal of Philosophy* xcvi: 217–40.

———. 1999a. "On Free Will, Responsibility and Indeterminism: Responses to Clarke, Haji and Mele." *Philosophical Explorations* 2: 105–21.

Kant, Immanuel. 1960. *Religion Within the Bounds of Reason Alone*. Trans. by T. Greene and H. Hudson. New York: Harper & Row.

Klein, Martha. 1990. *Determinism, Blameworthiness and Deprivation*. Oxford: Oxford University Press.

Lamb, James. 1993. "Evaluative Compatibilism and the Principle of Alternative Possibilities." *Journal of Philosophy* 90:517–27.

McCann, Hugh. 1997. "On When the Will is Free." In G. Holmstrom-Hintikka and R. Tuomela (eds.) *Contemporary Action Theory* I (Dordrecht: Kluwer): 219–32.

Mele, Alfred and David Robb. 1998. "Rescuing Frankfurt-style Cases" *Philosophical Review* 107:97–112.

Nagel, Thomas. 1986. *The View From Nowhere*. New York: Oxford University Press.

Naylor, Margery. 1984. "Frankfurt on the Principle of Alternative Possibilities." *Philosophical Studies* 46:249–58.

Rowe, William. 1991. *Thomas Reid on Freedom and Morality*. Ithaca: Cornell University Press.

Shatz, David. 1998. "Irresistible Goodness and Alternative Possibilities." In C. Monpkin and M. Kellner, eds. *Free Will and Moral Responsibility: General and Jewish Perspectives*. College Park: University of Maryland Press

Speak, Daniel James. 1999. "Fischer and Avoidability: A Reply to Widerker and Katzoff." *Faith and Philosophy* 16: 239–47.

Sorabji, Richard. 1980. *Necessity, Cause and Blame: Perspectives on Aristotle's Philosophy*. Ithaca, N.Y.: Cornell University Press

Strawson, Galen. 1986. *Freedom and Belief*. Oxford: Oxford University Press.

Stump, Eleonore. 1990. "Intellect, Will and the Principle of Alternative Possibilities." In *Christian Theism and the Problems of Philosophy*, ed. Michael Beaty, Notre Dame: University of Notre Dame Press, 254–85.

———. 1996. Libertarian Freedom and the Principle of Alternative Possibilities." In *Faith, Freedom and Rationality*. London: Rowman and Littlefield, 73–88.

———. n.d. "Alternative Possibilities and Responsibility: The Flicker of Freedom." In L. Overton and S. Buss (eds.) *Essays in Honor of Harry Frankfurt* (forthcoming).

van Inwagen, Peter. 1989. "When is the Will Free?" *Philosophical Perspectives* 3:399–422.

Widerker, David. 1995. "Libertarianism and Frankfurt's Attack on the Principle of Alternative Possibilities." *Philosophical Review* 104:247–61.

———. 1995a. "Libertarian Freedom and the Avoidability of Decisions." *Faith and Philosophy* 12:113–18.

Widerker, David and Charlotte Katzoff. 1996. "Avoidability and Libertarianism: A Response to Fischer." *Faith and Philosophy* 13: 415–21.

Wyma, Keith. 1997. "Moral Responsibility and Leeway for Action." *American Philosophical Quarterly* 34:57–70.

Zagzebski, Linda. 1991. *The Dilemma of Freedom and Foreknowledge*. Oxford: Oxford University Press.

Philosophical Perspectives, 14, Action and Freedom, 2000

AUTONOMY AND MANIPULATED FREEDOM

Tomis Kapitan
Northern Illinois University

1. Introduction

In recent years, compatibilism has been the target of two powerful challenges. According to the so-called *consequence argument*, if everything we do and think is a consequence of factors beyond our control (past events and the laws of nature), and the consequences of what is beyond our control are themselves beyond our control, then no one has control over what they do or think and no one is responsible for anything. Hence, determinism rules out responsibility. A somewhat different argument—here called the *manipulation argument*—is that by allowing agents to be fully determined, compatibilist accounts of practical freedom and responsibility are unable to preclude those who are subject to global manipulation from being free and responsible.[1]

Both unwelcome conclusions have prompted a variety of compatibilist responses. To the consequence argument, some favor dropping the principle of alternate possibilities inasmuch as that principle is thought relevant to the notion of control (Fischer 1994). Others have denied that the past or the laws of nature are beyond our control (Lewis 1979), and still others have questioned the validity of the argument, specifically, the closure principles upon which it relies (Slote 1981). I have argued that the appropriate combination of such responses yields an adequate rebuttal to the consequence argument (Kapitan 1996). The manipulation argument has been challenged by those who find that responsibility is not ruled out by external controllers (e.g., Frankfurt 1988, Blumenfeld 1988), and by those who think a historical conception of autonomy provides a way of disqualifying the manipulated agent from being either free or responsible (Mele 1995, Fischer and Ravizza 1998, Haji 1998). Not satisfied with these replies, I will show how they fall short and offer an alternative account of why the manipulation argument fails to refute compatibilism.

2. Conditions of Responsibility

Some philosophers argue that no one is ever truly responsible for what they have done since no one is truly self-determining (Strawson 1986, chp. 16, and see Double 1991, chps. 6–7, and Waller 1998, chp. 4). As a stipulation on a technical use of 'responsible' there is no need for dispute, but there are sound reasons for thinking that in some sense the existence of responsible agents is beyond doubt. For one thing, societies are fully justified in setting standards of behavior and in applying mechanisms for maintaining those standards, specifically, educational requirements and practices of praising/rewarding and blaming/punishing people for what they do. For another, these sanctioning practices are justifiably applied only to those for whom there is evidence of being *worthy* of praise or blame. When the evidence is at hand, agents can legitimately be *held responsible* and, to that extent, *are* responsible, even if they are not "truly responsible" in some philosophers' technical sense.

Let us speak unapologetically of agents being responsible for performances or omissions of actions, and construe responsibility for any other type of situation in terms of bringing about, sustaining, or preventing that situation. Retrospectively, an agent S is worthy of praise or blame for having performed action A at time t only if there is reason to suppose that the following conditions are met at some suitably prior time:

Intention/Foresight: Doing A at t was an intentional action of S's or a foreseeable result of some intentional action of S's.
Control: Doing A at t was under S's control.
Obligation: S was subject to a moral demand concerning doing A at t.

Analogous requirements apply for omissions. While necessary, the joint satisfaction of these conditions does not settle whether S is deserving of praise or deserving of blame. For example, even if a student is obligated not to shout in class, yet exercises control in shouting intentionally, he might not be blameworthy if he believed that overriding factors were present. Again, Sam and Sal might separately steal $100, an act they are similarly obligated to avoid and over which they have the same control. But if Sam steals from a motive of helping a poor person in an emergency whereas Sal steals in order to buy himself expensive cognac for impressing his friends, then, other things being equal, Sam is less blameworthy than Sal. Accordingly, to determine whether S is responsible and to what degree, one must know what additional psychological states accompanied S's action, specifically, S's beliefs about prevailing circumstances and pertinent obligations together with pro-attitudes he possessed (desires, values, preferences, etc.) that were relevant to—that is, about or causally influential upon—the action or its results. Schematically:

Relevant States: S's motivational and doxastic states M1, M2,... , Mn were the relevant states with which S did A at t.

For a given agent, action, and time, a fourth responsibility condition will be an instance of this schema. Joint satisfaction of these four conditions is sufficient for responsibility.

Some qualifications are in order. First, it is adequate *evidence* that the conditions are satisfied that justifies one in *holding* S responsible for A-ing. A mere joint satisfaction of the conditions is not sufficient for anyone's holding S responsible. Nor is it necessary given that evidence is defeasible. Second, inasmuch as the conditions provide non-question-begging criteria for judging whether S is responsible, then they must be decidable independently of assessments of S's worthiness of being praised or blamed. Third, each condition can be refined to suit the specifics of particular theories of free action and responsibility. In particular, the obligation condition may or may not be construed as implying that S actually is morally obliged with respect to A (see Zimmerman 1988, pp. 40–46 and Haji 1998, chps. 9–10). On the other hand, either this condition or the relevant states condition should guarantee that S was in a position to have understood he was subject to that demand.

The control condition is central to, if not definitive of, practical freedom, and at least two factors are involved. The first is that of *efficacy*: performance of the action would result in an anticipated manner from relevant pro-attitudes (intentions, desires, values, goals, etc.), so that the agent lacks control if compelled to do the action or prevented from doing it against these attitudes. The notion of efficacy can be extended to include omissions, and to the certain consequences of performances and omissions. Some hold that efficacy must be *dual* by including abilities both to do and to refrain from an action according to "the determination or thought of the mind" (Locke's *Essay* Book II, Chapter XX, section 8). Regardless whether a demand of duality can be sustained, a second ingredient of S's control over his A-ing at t is that S *presumes* that both doing A at t and omitting A at t are open alternatives for him. This embodies a pair of presumptions on S's part, namely, (i) that he would perform A (or refrain from A) at t were he to undertake (intend, choose) so doing, and (ii) his undertaking A at t is, as yet, contingent—where the presumed efficacy and contingency are indexed to what he takes himself to believe (Kapitan 1991, pp. 31–33, and 1996, pp. 435–439). If S is minimally rational, then by presuming his A-ing as open relative to what he takes himself to believe, it follows that his A-ing—represented by S to himself by the first-person "my A-ing"—actually is open *relative to* what he takes himself to then believe. This *doxastic* openness of A-ing implies that S's undertaking (choice) to do A is, at the same time, doxastically contingent and, hence, provides a sense in which S takes his undertaking to do A at t to be "up to himself" or "his own" (Kapitan 1989, pp. 31–34). Satisfaction of the control condition, then, implies the agent's presumption of duality even when not matched by an ability to do otherwise given the actual circumstances. In Kantian terms, responsible agency occurs "under the idea of freedom" even if the agent is not free in a "theoretical" respect.[2]

It is unreasonable to require that S's control over A-ing implies S's control over all the pro-attitudes and character traits that led to his A-ing. He may be unable to think *about* some of these attitudes and traits, and some of them may be deeply entrenched and unshakeable features of his personality. At the same, time, higher degrees of responsibility for A-ing might accrue if S has control over some relevant attitudes, and if S is responsible for *having* an attitude or a trait P during interval t then S must have control over P at t or during a time suitably prior to t.

3. Autonomy and the Manipulation Argument

A man who is coerced at knifepoint to relinquish his wallet may very well be in control of his behavior, and his control may be dual if he is able to refrain from complying with the thief's demand. Yet he is not acting in a way that he prefers; he is not fully self-governing and the consequent actions are not wholly "his own." Again, an addict might act from irresistible desires for a drug while, at the same time, not want to so act or to be so motivated. His autonomy is also offset by the influences that frustrate his will or prevent him from acting in a manner he would otherwise prefer. Perhaps S's practical freedom requires satisfaction of yet a further responsibility condition, namely, that S was *autonomous* in doing A.

One might suspect that these cases are readily handled by the previous conditions. A coerced agent is exempted from blame because the circumstance of the threat produces an obligation that overrides the usual demand to do or omit an action, namely, to spare oneself (or someone else) the threatened harm. One subjected to irresistible desires, or akratic agents in general, lack self-control with respect to certain actions. Alternatively, perhaps what is lacking in both cases is the agent's identification with the proximal psychological causes of the action, in which case a specification of the relevant states condition is what fails to be satisfied. This is not to say that autonomy is not a component of practical freedom, but rather, that is captured in the conditions already identified.

But suppose S were controlled by another agent who causes S to behave, think, in accord with its own desires, not by causing S to act in a manner contrary to S's own intentions or preferences, but by manipulating S's choices, preferences, and beliefs through non-coercive means such as indoctrination, information control, hypnosis, drugs, or brain implants. Oblivious to these causes, S is subject to *covert, non-constraining* control (CNC control) exercised by external agents (Kane 1985, p. 35). If the control is so comprehensive that *all* S's desires, values, deliberations, choices, intentions, etc. within a certain interval are what they are because of the manipulation, then it is *global* during that interval (Schoeman, 1978, p. 295). If introduced at a point after the beginning of S's history then it is *interruptive*, while if S's whole mental life from birth is so determined then it is *total*. S's psychological life might be disconnected and episodic if the manipulators are constantly inducing the states, but it might be coherent and well-integrated if manipulation occurs through successful programming (Frankfurt 1988, p. 53). Maybe Skinnerian behavioral engineers are capable of imposing this sort of global control over an individual, or perhaps total control could be achieved through devices implanted in S's brain, beginning, say, with the insertion of microchips into S's fetus, permitting the external controllers to both monitor and direct the course of S's psychological development within given genetic constraints. The implants might even be preprogrammed, allowing the manipulators to retire from the scene, confident their aims will be carried out. The picture is extreme, but advances in micro-processing and robotics that would make it possible cannot be ruled out. What seems clear to a good many observers is this: a covertly manipulated agent is much like a robot, perhaps a living, breathing, conscious organic being capable of informed rational deliberation, but not an autonomous agent, and, by that very fact, neither free nor responsible.

Manipulation undermines responsibility if it moves an agent against his will or better judgment, or if breaks psychological continuity by introducing a hiatus between an agent's current preferences and previously entrenched dispositions (Haji 1998, pp. 116–119). But suppose continuity is not broken and the manipulated agent has a coherent, well-integrated character complete with a sufficiently well-informed sense of responsibility and a high degree of *self-control* (in the sense contrasted with akrasia). Perhaps there are thoroughly brainwashed yet well-disciplined individuals who fit this description. We might think that he cannot be responsible since he is not autonomous. But how does he lack autonomy *if* he is self-controlled? Moreover, how is he any different from a "naturally determined" self-controlled agent?

The question spawns an intriguing analogical argument against compatibilism. Robert Kane asks us to consider a person, Ishmael, in a world W0 where his entire inner life and behavior is the consequence of CNC control by external agents. Kane assumes that by being so controlled, Ishmael lacks what is required to be a responsible agent in W0. Imagine that in a similar world W1, Ishmael, or a counterpart of Ishmael, acts and thinks exactly as Ishmael in W0 does, with exactly the same capacities, abilities, and opportunities that Ishmael in W0 has, but as a result of natural forces rather than manipulation. Suppose, moreover, that Ishmael in W1 satisfies the conditions of responsibility that compatibilists have set forward, in particular, he possesses all the control over his actions and mental states that a compatibilist could conceivably propose. Since Ishmael in W0 also satisfies those conditions then he has no less control or autonomy and, hence, is no less practically free. Consequently, he too is responsible. Since this is absurd, then compatibilist theories about practical freedom and responsibility are mistaken. In sum:

1. A manipulated agent is not practically free in, and not responsible for, any of its behavior or states that result from the actions of external manipulators.
2. There can be a totally manipulated agent who is practically free in any sense a compatibilist can offer, in particular, who can satisfy the conditions of control and autonomy to the degree that any naturally determined agent can.

Therefore,

> 3. The naturally determined agent is neither practically free nor responsible with respect to any of its behavior or states.

Kane concludes that since "no existing compatibilist account of freedom" can block the CNC control of a compatibilistically construed "free" agent by another agent, then all such accounts of responsibility fail (1985, pp. 37–42).

Kane classifies a compatibilist response to this manipulation argument as *hard* if it denies premise 1, and *soft* if it draws the line at premise 2 (Kane 1985, 38). The hard compatibilist takes the totally manipulated agent to be free and responsible for whatever behavior, mental states, and character are the products of its control. The obvious problem with this position is that we would exculpate someone from responsibility were we to discover that he was subject to total CNC control in behaving as he did, just as we would were we to discover that he was a victim of malicious indoctrination since youth or of an injury to his prefrontal cortex that radically changed all his decision processes.[3]

The soft compatibilist denies premise 2 and faces the task of explaining why covert manipulation diminishes responsibility and practical freedom while the natural influences to which a person is subject, viz., genetic inheritance, parental guidance, socialization, education, an so forth, do not (Kane 1996, 68, 225, n.15). One approach insists that the totally manipulated agent is not autonomous because its inner states are produced by something alien to the "self." It repudiates the notion that autonomy can be captured by purely internalist descriptions, e.g., efficacy of pro-attitudes with respect to proximal states or conformity of these states with higher-order identifications, values, or a deeper self. Instead, autonomy is a matter of the historical genesis of an agent's psychology and can only be described through an *externalist* account of the acquisition and retention of pro-attitudes. Obviously this approach cannot preclude these attitudes from being the product of some external influences, nor *merely* preclude manipulation from being among the permissible external causes. What it must offer is a non-circular explanation of why manipulation erodes autonomy whereas causation by "natural" means does not (see Dworkin 1976, p. 24; Christman 1989, pp. 10-22; Kane 1996, pp. 68–69).

In what follows, two externalist accounts of autonomy are examined and rejected. It is then argued that while manipulation does not automatically rule out responsibility, cases where it does are explainable in terms of the four conditions of responsibility without invoking an independent requirement of autonomy.

4. Autonomy and Historicity: Alfred Mele

Alfred Mele acknowledges that agents who possess ideal *self-control* over their own motivations and decisions fail to be autonomous if they are controlled by external manipulators (Mele 1995, p. 122). He clearly sees the threat of the manipulation ("mind-control") argument to a compatibilist theory of responsibility. In examining cases of brainwashing, he asks,

> How is the control that manipulators exert over an agent in the brainwashing scenarios examined here, for example, relevantly different from the effect of the distant past on an agent at a deterministic world? (Mele 1995, p. 173)

He considers two agents, Ann and Beth, who are similarly motivated by an entrenched or "unsheddable" value of being an industrious philosopher, but whereas Ann has arrived at her motivation "on the basis of careful critical reflection over many years," Beth's motivation is due to the intervention of brainwashers who have successfully altered her values and priorities. Were Beth motivated to perform wicked Charles Manson type deeds then she "is not responsible for her Mansonian character—values principles, and the like" (p. 161), and "we would not hold her *responsible* for her Mansonian character" (p. 159). Ann, by contrast, is responsible for what she has become. Why the difference? Ann, unlike Beth, is an *autonomous* agent because she has autonomously developed her values (p. 155). Lacking autonomy, a manipulated agent like Beth fails to be practically free.[4]

Etiology is at the core of Mele's concept of psychological autonomy. Internalist conceptions of autonomy are vulnerable to the manipulation objection even when control is dual (pp. 147–152). What a manipulated agent lacks is *authenticity*, the ability to subject its own drives to rational scrutiny (see also Feinberg 1989, p. 32 and Dworkin 1989, p. 61). According to Mele, an agent S does not authentically possess a pro-attitude P during interval t if S was *compelled* to have P in a way not arranged by S, that is, if in acquiring P, S's own capacities for control over his mental life were bypassed by external causes (pp. 166–167)—where capacities are *bypassed* insofar as they play no role in the acquisition (Blumenfeld 1988, 222). More fully, if (i) S comes to have P in a way that bypassed capacities for control over his mental life in a way he did not himself arrange, (ii) P is "practically unsheddable," (p. 153), and (iii) S does not have other pro-attitudes that would support his identifying with P (excepting those unsheddable ones that have themselves been induced in a bypassing manner) then S is *compelled* to possess P and is not autonomous (p. 172).[5]

Unlike Ann, Beth is compelled to have her values because they were induced by external agents in a manner not endorsed by her. Even if her change of character resulted from passing through a randomly occurring electromagnetic field in the Bermuda Triangle, she would still be compelled to have a pro-attitude because her capacities for control were bypassed. Similarly, a person can have compelled pro-attitudes as a result of indoctrination, for example, a child whose religious convictions resulted from brainwashing by a religious fanatic who taught that critical reflections about these doctrines will earn eternal damnation in hell. The child's capacities are bypassed either because its modest capacity to believe and desire on the basis of an assessment of evidence was circumvented, or, if this capacity had not yet emerged, because its capacity to develop into an ideally self-controlled agent was bypassed, "and, indeed, destroyed" (p. 168). Besides psychological compulsion, autonomy can also be undermined by controlling the information to which agents have access, or by preventing agents' deliberative processes from reliably resulting in intentions and actions (pp. 179–185). In the latter event, a capacity to develop into agents who have "a significantly greater role in shaping their own deliberative habits" is bypassed by the fact that unreliable or inefficient deliberative habits are engineered.

Corresponding to the three ways in which agents may fail to be autonomous, then, Mele offers (p. 187) the following trio of conditions as *sufficient* for an agent S to be psychologically autonomous:

1. S has no motivational states that are compelled or coercively produced.
2. S's beliefs are conducive to informed deliberation about matters of concern to him.
3. S is a reliable deliberator (i.e., can effectively act upon deliberations and intentions).

While not claiming satisfaction of these conditions to be necessary for psychological autonomy, Mele argues that an agent satisfying them will not be subject to CNC control despite being determined. The same holds for one who meets the necessary and sufficient conditions that a compatibilist could offer for *strong* psychologically autonomy, namely, regularly exercises ideal self-control, is mentally healthy, and satisfies conditions 1–3. Since manipulation entails compulsion and compulsion blocks autonomy, then the manipulated agent cannot be autonomous in a way that the naturally determined agent can. Their difference is a matter of how their respective pro-attitudes were generated. Mele concludes that compatibilism is saved by exploiting the standard compatibilist distinction between mere causation and psychological compulsion, employed not only at the level of choice and action, but at the level of "character" (p. 173).

Despite its impressive detail, Mele's account is not an adequate response to the manipulation argument. Either it makes autonomy too rare to be of much use in a theory of responsibility or it cannot block a CNC controlled agent from being autonomous. Let us see why this is so.

Mele holds that if an unsheddable pro-attitude is acquired in a way that bypasses capacities for self-control, say, by being manipulated, exposed to a randomly occurring electro-magnetic disturbances, or involuntarily ingesting a mind-altering drug, then the agent is compelled to possess it and is not autonomous. Suppose Beth acquired a new value in a less spectacular fashion, say, as a result of moving to a new locale, taking a new job, and being subjected to a different life style and set of environmental stimuli. Imagine that the new value is singular—say, an aversion for people with high-pitched voices—in that does not cohere with the rest of her standing values though it does not necessarily contradict them either. Suppose further that she did not consciously adopt this new attitude as a result of "rationally assessing and revising" her values and principles, or "identifying" with it "on the basis of informed, critical reflection, and of intentionally fostering new values and pro-attitudes" in accordance with her considered evaluative judgments (pp. 166–167). According to Mele's theory, her standing capacities for self-control were bypassed and her new attitude was not acquired authentically. If the aversion becomes practically unsheddable, perhaps because of deep physiological causes, then Beth is compelled to have the new value and does not possess it autonomously. Conceivably, it might play a role in a well-informed deliberate decision of Beth's, for instance, a negative vote on a personnel matter. If responsibility requires autonomy then Beth is not responsible for her vote. This result is odd because this manner of attitude-acquisition does not seem unusual. Perhaps many of us have picked up such singular aversions or desires by being exposed to a novel confluence of environmental stimuli. Yet, unless we take the drastic expedient of ruling out "moral luck" altogether, they do not seem to be automatic barriers to responsibility for actions ensuing from them.

Recall that a victim of brainwashing is said to lack autonomy because its pro-attitudes were acquired in a way that bypassed or "destroyed" a capacity to *develop* into an individual capable of exercising control over the compelled attitudes (p. 168). Now suppose that Beth acquired her aversion to people with high-pitched voices by a process of critical evaluation, yet had she been given the right sort of education in primary school then she would have developed in such a way so as to control her newly acquired aversion. So, she *had* the capacity to develop into a person with such control, but because of the education and upbringing she actually received, the capacity was bypassed or destroyed. Consequently, she is compelled to have that aversion and is not autonomous. This result seems far too sweeping: perhaps at the time of our births, most of us *could* have developed a capacity to exert control over a wide variety of pro-attitudes even though we did not. In our early development each of us is subjected to physical and social forces of which we are largely ignorant, over which we have no control, yet from which we acquire values, beliefs, motivations, and capacities for rational evaluation that subsequently guide our choices and actions. These forces "destroyed" any capacity to become a different sort of person with self-control regarding *any* unsheddable pro-attitude that we happen to have. Consequently, every unsheddable pro-attitude is compelled, and anyone with firm unshakeable principles of action ends up being inauthentic and non-autonomous, e.g., Ann, whose unsheddable values for industriousness "were acquired under her own steam" (p. 155).[6]

To avoid this unhappy result, suppose we amend the account so that the destruction of a capacity that never develops is neither an instance of psychological compulsion nor a barrier to autonomy. A different problem then arises. Mele states that any agent who has ideal self-control, exercises that control, is mentally healthy, and satisfies the compatibilist trio with respect to a given pro-attitude, is strongly psychologically autonomous but not CNC-controlled (p. 189). Why not? Mele allows that a CNC controlled agent—call him "Ned"— can exercise ideal self-control and be mentally healthy (pp. 122–126). Presumably he can also satisfy conditions 2 and 3 of the "compatibilist trio." Apparently Ned can satisfy condition 1 as well, for on the amended account the manipulators might endow him from childhood or early fetal stages with capacities for critical reflection that he regularly exercises in regards to his values and priorities. That his reflections are themselves the product of manipulation does not imply that they lack causal efficacy within Ned's psychology. Indeed, the manipulators might utilize these causal patterns in controlling Ned. But then Ned meets all the conditions for strong psychological autonomy.

Curiously, Mele seems warm to this possibility when he allows that an adult, Fred, might be created with a certain set of sheddable desires and values that his creator knows will eventuate in certain sorts of behavior. Since Fred can reflect intelligently on these sheddable attitudes then he satisfies the three conditions for psychological autonomy, and by exercising ideal self-control and being mentally healthy, is strongly autonomous. Mele contends that compatibilists should accept this result and not conclude that Fred is *controlled* by his creator:

> In one respect, Fred is like any autonomous agent at a deterministic world: his path is causally determined. He is special in having been endowed at the time of his creation with a collection of motivational attitudes for his creators' own purposes. But since these are sheddable attitudes, this detail of his creation does not render him non-autonomous, on the assumption that compatiblism is true (pp. 190–191).

To the contrary, granting that Fred has the capacity to examine and revise his values, it remains that the creator has instilled Fred with the values constitutive of this capacity. Moreover, the creator understands that Fred's pro-attitudes will produce the desired actions as outputs given certain environmental inputs, inputs which the creator knows Fred will be subject to. So, Fred is caused, indeed, deliberately caused, to behave in a certain way in much the same way that designers of robots program the responses of their machines to various stimuli. In the absence of a precise definition of "X controls Y," this is reason to think that, despite his autonomy, Fred is CNC controlled by his creator.[7]

If this assessment is correct, then a manipulated agent like Fred can autonomously possess pro-attitudes. Is Fred also responsible for what he does? If so, then Mele's account of practical freedom is acceptable only by hard compatibilists. If not, we are back at the initial question of how a manipulated agent differs from a naturally determined agent. Without more being said about psychological compulsion, sheddability, or autonomous action (p. 193) I see no clear answer to this question within Mele's theory. Consequently, it does not provide a decisive rebuttal of the manipulation argument.

5. Control and Historicity: Fischer and Ravizza

Incorporating historically-based notion of autonomy into practical freedom is also a feature of John Fischer's and Mark Ravizza's response to the manipulation argument (Fischer and Ravizza 1998). Unlike Mele, they make autonomy a part of control and their treatment is more closely driven by a concern with responsibility. A responsible agent is one who is an "appropriate candidate for the reactive attitudes," a status achieved on the basis of either behavior or character (p. 6). Persuaded that the Frankfurt examples show that one can be responsible for behavior so long as no "responsibility-undermining" factors are operative in the actual sequence leading up to the action, they advocate a *semicompatibilism* according to which causal determinism is compatible with moral responsibility but not with a freedom to do otherwise. The control required by responsibility is *guidance control*, understood in terms of properties of the *mechanism* that leads to the relevant behavior, specifically:

(1) The mechanism must be *reasons-responsive*: given roughly the same conditions of behavior and with the same mechanism operating, the presentation of various reasons to the agent would have resulted in different behavior. Thus, an agent possesses guidance control over the behavior if there exist scenarios in which the agent would have done otherwise, even though the agent is not able to bring about such scenarios (p. 52).
(2) The mechanism must be the agent's *own* in that the agent *takes responsibility* for it, that is, he views himself as an agent subject to reactive attitudes by virtue of the way he has behaved as a result of that mechanism (pp. 210–213).

Failure to satisfy (1) can be caused by forms of subliminal advertising, hypnosis, brainwashing, or direct brain manipulation that create physical mechanisms that are not reasons-responsive (pp. 48–49). An agent subject to covert manipulation might satisfy (1), but being unaware of the relevant behavior-producing mechanism it is unable to take responsibility for that mechanism and, therefore, would fail to meet condition (2). If the agent were made aware of it, he would likely not regard it as the causal source of his behaving as he does and, therefore, would not think himself responsible for what emerges from it.

It is unclear what qualifies as a *mechanism* of behavior on Fischer's and Ravizza's account, much less *the* mechanism of behavior. Presumably not every set of factors that results in behavior B is a mechanism of B, otherwise, causal determinism would rule out (2) from ever being satisfied. Fischer and Ravizza write that "there is no plausibility to the suggestion that all conditions in the past—no matter how remote or irrelevant—must be included as part of the 'mechanism that issues in action'" (p. 52). What justifies this claim? Taking 'mechanism' to be synonymous with 'process leading to action' or 'way action comes about' (p. 38), they acknowledge that different mechanisms can operate in a case of any given action, but go on to say that as a "presupposition of the theory" there is "an intuitively natural mechanism that is appropriately selected as the mechanism that issues in action for the purposes of assessing guidance control and moral responsibility" (p. 47). They offer very little by way of saying how this mechanism is "selected" beyond the following. First, the relevant mechanism must not be described in such a way that it entails the action, otherwise it could not satisfy condition (1) of guidance control, that is, the mechanism must be described in a "temporally intrinsic" fashion rather than an "extrinsic" manner inclusive of the action in question (p. 47). Second, since the fact that there are a number of "actions" a person performs at a time does not preclude singling out one of them as relevant in ascribing responsibility, so too, we can pick out which mechanism is the relevant mechanism that "issues in action."[8]

The manipulation argument is supposedly defused by appealing to clause (2) in the characterization of guidance control: a manipulated agent cannot take responsibility for the mechanism that led to action. Here, however, Fischer and Ravizza promise more than they deliver. Observe how they characterize the concept of S's "taking responsibility" for the mechanism that results in his A-ing:

(1) S sees himself as an agent, viz., "that his choices and actions are efficacious in the world" and, thus, that his own motivational states are the causal source of his A-ing;

(2) S accepts that his is a fair target of the reactive attitudes as a result of how he exercises agency in A-ing; and

(3) S's view of himself as satisfying (1) and (2) is based, in an appropriate way, on evidence (pp 210–213).

Now suppose that the behavior of both the CNC controlled agent and the naturally determined agent result from the same sorts of *proximal* mechanisms, that is, from "ordinary practical reasoning" (p. 233) guided, in turn, by their desires, beliefs, reasonings, intentions, and so on. Suppose, further, that each had a hand in forming a good number of these states, even though this formation process in the manipulated agent was engineered by the external manipulators. Since the covertly manipulated agent might take responsibility for the proximal states that led to his action (p. 234), why don't these qualify as *the* mechanisms of action?

Fischer's and Ravizza's response is that responsible agency requires the satisfaction of certain historical conditions:

In certain cases involving direct manipulation of the brain (and similar influences), it is natural to say that the mechanism leading to the action is not, in an important sense, the agent's own. (p. 230)

We can readily agree that this is so for *a* mechanism leading to action, namely, the manipulation itself. But why is manipulation *the* relevant mechanism if *another* reason-responsive mechanism is operative for which the covertly controlled agent does take responsibility, namely, his own deliberations? What is relevant, they insist, is *"how* that mechanism has been put in place" (p. 231), and they motivate this by discussing three cases of covert manipulation (pp. 230–236). The first can be dismissed because irresistible desires are implanted that undermine reasons-responsiveness. In the second, while the implanted desires are strong, the mechanism leading to action, namely, the manipulation that induces the desire, is not one for which the agent takes responsibility. Why not? Because the agent does not know about the manipulation and, hence, "has not taken responsibility for the kind of mechanism that actually issues in the action" (p. 233). This response assumes that the relevant mechanism must be the manipulator's machinations but, unfortunately, does not explain *why* the proximal psychological states are not equally relevant.

The treatment of a third case is more puzzling. Here, the dispositions that constitute "taking responsibility" are themselves implanted. Fischer and Ravizza conclude that condition (3) above might not be satisfied, yet they decline to specify what an "appropriate way" of basing one's beliefs upon evidence is, saying only,

> This condition is intended (in part) to imply that an individual who has been electronically induced to have the relevant view of himself (and thus satisfy the first two conditions on taking responsibility) has not formed his view of himself in the appropriate way. (p. 236).

This is no answer at all. Since an appropriately formed view of oneself can be causally determined (p. 236), then unless the appropriate basing relation is characterized in a rigid externalist fashion so as to rule out the presence of total manipulation, it is unclear that there need be any difference between the totally manipulated agent and the naturally determined agent with respect to how they obtained that evidence. The authors are aware of the externalist expedient (pp. 236–237 n.31) but do not develop it. I am skeptical that a difference with respect to evidence gathering and assessment can be secured given that total manipulation can duplicate much of the ordinary causal processes involved in conscious experience, belief acquisition, retention, and evaluation.[9]

If covert manipulation is *the* mechanism that generated the action then, to be sure, it is not something for which the agent can take responsibility. But it is equally true that agents generally do not take responsibility for the processes of character formation—e.g., parental guidance, public education, peer influence, emotionally-charged delights and traumas of youthful experience, or the family-building projects of grandparents. Why aren't these antecedents *the* relevant mechanisms that issue in action? How do such processes differ in any way that is relevant to moral responsibility? These are the questions with which we began. The answer in terms of "taking-responsibility" won't do since agents rarely, if ever, take responsibility for remote processes that caused them to be the sorts of agents they are, yet might take responsibility for their practical reasoning so produced. And it will not do to locate the relevant mechanism within an internal state if external manipulation undermines responsibility. Hence, without specifying what determines the uniqueness of the mechanism that is relevant to responsible action and what an appropriate way of basing one's view of one's own agency upon evidence consists in, I conclude that the Fischer-Ravizza attempt to preclude the covertly manipulated agent from being morally responsible fails. Since it does not obviously preclude the manipulated agent from taking responsibility, then they are absolutely right to admit that "we cannot pretend to have a *decisive* defense of compatibilism." (p. 236).[10]

6. When Historical Considerations Matter

Let us look more closely at how manipulation affects responsibility. Some writers shift easily between talk about an agent's "being responsible" to it being justifiable to "hold" the agent responsible in the same breath (for instance, Mele 1995, pp. 159–161). On the face of it, whether a person can be justifiably *held* responsible is different from that person's actually *being* responsible, since those justified in holding S responsible for A-ing might be mistaken about whether S satisfied the responsibility conditions. One might insist that there is no difference here and take responsibility to be constituted by the justification for holding people responsible, but it is more commonly thought that an agent's responsibility is a matter of being *worthy of* (deserving of, being an appropriate candidate for) praise or blame (Wallace 1994, Copp 1997, Haji 1998, Fischer and Ravizza 1998).

Yet the formula "S is worthy of praise or blame" is itself ambiguous. A good deal has recently been written about the actions of "praising" and "blaming" as responses to behavior that include reactive attitudes or emotions (e.g., gratitude, indignation, resentment, etc.) and, perhaps, sanctioning actions (punishment, reward, verbal praise or criticism, etc.) directed towards agents. These *reactive responses*, as we may call them, are constitutive of holding an agent accountable (Strawson 1962; Wallace 1994, chp. 3). Accordingly, "S is worthy of praise or blame" can mean that some agent X would be justified by certain standards for either blaming or praising S for what he did or omitted. X must occupy a position of proper authority and possess evidence that S satisfied the responsibility conditions with respect to A, including that his A-ing is subject to those standards, for this to be so (Watson 1996, 235–236). So construed, being worthy or praise or blame is a property that S possesses in relation to agents within a specified normative framework, hence, partly constituted by factors external to S. If the normative framework is one of morality, then we are speaking of moral responsibility from an *external* perspective or, alternatively, of *moral accountability*.

Judgments from the external perspective must be distinguished from what Gary Watson has called "aretaic judgments," assessments of an agent's "excellences and faults" that might be true independently of anyone's being justified in any reactive responses towards the agent (Watson 1996, 231). Such judgments consider moral blameworthiness and praiseworthiness as monadic properties determined by the agent's motivational, cognitive, and intentional states, and character traits, so that "S is worthy of praise or blame" means that S is either morally virtuous or vicious in acting as he does. Here it is essential that the agent actually satisfy the responsibility conditions. The dependence upon inner states—so prominent in Kant's treatment of moral agency and the good will—allows us to speak of moral responsibility from an internal, aretaic perspective, that is, from a concern with *moral character*.[11]

It should not be concluded that there are separate kinds of moral responsibility here; there might be just one phenomenon with different aspects. Indeed, the requirement of *mens rea* in the legal setting suggests more than an occasional overlap.[12] Yet, justification for responsive reactions requires more than evidence in support of certain aretaic judgments. The practice of holding people responsible also depends upon what can be called the *responsive value* of particular responsive reactions, that is, their value as mechanisms of correcting, reinforcing, or deterring various types of behavior, attitudes, or character traits. Of particular importance is the responsive value accruing to reactive attitudes and emotions themselves. In plain fact, people want to be the objects of favorable reactive attitudes and not the targets of the negative ones, and will often act accordingly quite apart from the prospect of overt sanctions. Moreover, the reactive attitudes gain value through their ability to move their possessors to act in ways that they might not otherwise do.[13]

To achieve a workable conception of justification, let us speak of a reactive response of type R as being *standardly correlated* with a responsive value V, that is, with the customarily expected benefits of R-type responses regarding the deterrence, reinforcement, or correction of certain sorts of behavior. This can be relativized further by correlating R-type responses of a population P with V in circumstances of sort C. Accordingly, a *general practice* of responding in an R-manner to A-type behavior in circumstances or sort C is morally justified within a population P just in case an R-response by members of P to someone's A-ing is standardly correlated with effects having a sufficiently high degree of positive responsive value V. Then, a *particular* R-type response by X to S's A-ing is morally justifiable when X possesses adequate evidence that (i) the general practice of R-responding to A-type behavior in circumstances of sort C is morally justified; (ii) circumstances or sort C obtain; and (iii) S satisfies the responsibility conditions with respect to A. An additional qualification is possible if we want to make explicit X's office or position of authority with respect to S's A-ing in those circumstances. Also, since our assessments of the responsive values associated with given practices are constantly being updated and refined, then what practices are justifiable responses to which behaviors is subject to variation over time inasmuch as customarily expected benefits change.

Historical factors have an undeniable bearing upon both moral character and moral accountability. Facts about how a person's mental states or character traits were formed and developed are relevant to his or her moral virtue and vice. For instance, one might be responsible for a murder committed today but planned five months ago, and this is important to explaining the differences in the degree of vice involved in that premeditated murder and a case of manslaughter brought about by a sudden provocation and unanticipated homicidal urge. Again, one who spent years overcoming deeply inculcated prejudices in an effort to become a more tolerant person might exhibit greater moral virtue in permitting certain behaviors in his presence than one who was the beneficiary of tolerance-training since youth, even though their intentions and obligations concerning those behaviors might be the same on given occasions. Personal history partly determines the precise degree to which an agent is reprehensible or laudable.

Because these historical factors concern the change, formation, and integration of attitudes and character traits, they are internal to the agent's character and development. By contrast, moral accountability is also attuned to external situations. For example, the mere fact that I intentionally refrained from showing up at a party to which I was invited, but not obligated to attend, is not enough to make me culpable, nor for others to be justified in negative reactive attitudes towards me. But I may be blamed for failing to attend if five months ago I had promised the host to attend. The extent to which I merit a responsive reaction depends not only upon my earlier promise but also that I have not done anything to cancel my agreement in the meantime. Again, suppose an instructor gives a passing grade to a negligent student upon the student's payment of $500. If this comes to be known by those with the proper authority then standard punitive responses are in order. However, if the teacher were threatened at gunpoint to record a passing grade then the historical circumstance of coercion is reason to override the standard responses. A similar conclusion holds if it was learned that the teacher's recording of the passing grade resulted from involuntarily ingesting a drug which produced irresistible sympathetic desires to accommodate all student requests.

The four responsibility conditions are sensitive to historicity. By failing to attend a party I neglect a present obligation fixed by my past promise, and he who would blame me must be apprised of this promise. If I forgot the promise, a different reaction might be called for, but only because forgetting is a relevant state accompanying an omission. The moral demands upon a coerced teacher can different from those of the uncoerced teacher given that it is more important to avoid the threatened penalty than to comply with the demand. Coercion is relevant in determining what obligation is binding, thus, in deciding whether the obligation condition is satisfied. In the case of the drug-induced irresistible urge, it is control over one's behavior that is diminished because one is unable to either resist the urge or shed it. Again, knowledge of the agent's history is central in determining the amount of control possessed and what reactive responses are justified. Different responses would be called for were it learned that the teacher was careless in ingesting what he or she did, or deliberately took the drug without knowing what it might produce, or deliberately took the drug knowing what effect it would have.

How does manipulation of psychological states affect responsibility? Everything depends upon what the effects of the manipulation are. Consider moral character first. It is assumed by the manipulation argument that a totally CNC controlled agent can have a coherent psychological profile. He might be endowed with a relatively consistent set of pro-attitudes, possess a considerable amount of self-control, regularly review and reorganize his priorities and commitments in accord with his accumulating experience and reflection, and act in response to well-informed practical reasoning. If so, does he possess a moral character? Suppose a globally manipulated agent, Dan, believes that torture is morally wrong yet takes on a job as an eye-gouger because he enjoys the spectacle of human torment, even though the desire to witness suffering is not irresistible. Does Dan act wickedly? Imagine that he acts with a firm sense of open alternatives, viz., that he can refrain from eye-gouging for all he knows. Is his choice morally depraved? I see no reason to think otherwise. Yes, Dan is the unfortunate victim of his manipulators, his wicked character is engineered, but it is a character, and it is wicked nonetheless. One can be manipulated to wish wickedly just as one can be manipulated to believe falsely. Were Dan manipulated into believing that eye-gouging is a great service to mankind, his character might be less reprehensible, but no less engineered. His situation would be little different from that of an Aztec priest whose commitment to the virtues of human sacrifice was instilled through early indoctrination and reinforced by a steady barrage of praise, honors, and rewards. We shudder equally at the spectacle of either.

One might object that Dan is devoid of any moral character because he is not sufficiently autonomous, his choices are not his own. It was pointed out in section 2, however, that if Dan takes eye-gouging to be "open" for him then he presumes the choice of that profession to be "his own." If it is added that Dan "identifies" with his choice, "takes responsibility" for it, and even possesses "ideal self-control," as it was argued that a totally manipulated agent might, then I claim that he has the autonomy needed to underscore his moral depravity. To paraphrase Kant: one who acts with a sense of openness—implied by the control condition—and with an acceptance of a moral demand—implied by the obligation condition—acts "under the idea of responsibility." And one who acts under the idea of responsibility is, thereby, really responsible in the sense of having a moral character.

Things are more complicated when we shift our focus from moral character to moral accountability. Initially, it might seem that one could be no more justified in blaming Dan for his actions than in chastising a hungry lion for snaring an unwary tourist. However, should Dan's actions and the salient circumstances yield no obvious signs of being subject to covert control, and there is evidence that Dan satisfies the responsibility conditions, then one can have sufficient reason to blame Dan for his actions, indeed, to apply the strongest sanctions standardly allowable to the perpetrators of such incredibly horrendous deeds. Thus, the mere *fact* of being CNC controlled does not necessarily defeat the claim that Dan is morally accountable, that is, worthy of blame from the external standpoint.

The situation changes if it becomes known that Dan is manipulated, for then it is apparent that there are additional determinants of Dan's actions beyond his practical reasoning, namely, the goals, intentions, beliefs, and powers of his manipulators. This information alone casts doubt upon whether Dan satisfies any of the responsibility conditions. Perhaps his behavior appears intentional but isn't, or perhaps his induced moral beliefs are vividly opposed to the demands people would normally take him to be subject to, or maybe the manipulators might trump the control Dan would otherwise exercise. For example, they might induce irresistible desires that do not cohere with his values, or diminish the number of apparent options, or induce beliefs that impair his efficacy with respect to actions that otherwise appear open. Again, if the requirement is for dual control, the manipulators might be counterfactual interveners that would prevent Dan from doing otherwise if he chose or even to be able to choose otherwise. As long as there is evidence of that manipulation interferes with satisfaction of the responsibility conditions, then it is appropriate to judge that Dan is neither autonomous nor responsible in each of these cases.

Typically, if there is evidence of manipulation then an agent may be exempted from blame (or praise) despite satisfaction of the responsibility conditions, and it is here that a requirement of alternate possibilities is important even if the agent's actual control is not dual. Thus, to be justified in blaming or praising an agent for an action, one must be able to discern that an opportunity existed for the agent to have refrained if he or she had chosen. Because it is so difficult to determine what a person's motives, perceived options, and intentions actually are, external indicators are vital in appraising whether the agent satisfied the responsibility conditions, particularly the condition of control. If I surmise that S had no opportunity to refrain from A-ing, for example, if I have evidence that S is subject to counterfactual interveners, then, for all I know, perhaps S *did* chose to refrain but was prevented from so doing. I would then have evidence that S did not satisfy the control condition or the relevant states condition so to justify my blaming him. To increase my confidence that this was not so and that he did satisfy the responsibility conditions, then the following conditional supplies a *criterion* to be followed in order to establish justification for holding S responsible:

> If S is morally accountable for A-ing at t, then at some suitably prior time, S was able to have refrained from A-ing at t.

Analogous criteria are appropriate for omissions and for consequences of actions. So, if one has evidence that an agent is CNC controlled but does not know if the manipulators would not intervene, then this criterion is not satisfied, one lacks evidence that the agent satisfies the control condition and, therefore, one is not justified in holding the agent responsible.[14]

Moreover, by preventing agents from having a suitable degree of control over their inner states or what ensues from them, manipulation threatens to disrupt the standard correlations between specific reactive responses and the expected responsive values. We know this from experience. Just as disciplinary techniques that usually correct unwanted behavior in children, e.g., verbal disapproval, will not work for those whose neurological conditions leave them mentally impaired, so too, they can fail for individuals who have been brainwashed. In severe cases, negative reactive responses are out of order. Consequently, information that an agent is subject to covert manipulation typically defeats the evidence one has that standard correlations between types of reactive responses and the expected responsive value will hold, and justification for praise or blame is not forthcoming. I say "typically" for the following reason. If there is evidence that the manipulated agent is manipulated so as *not* to destroy the standard correlations, perhaps because the agent is pre-programmed to respond in an appropriate fashion or because the manipulators would cause the agent to so respond, then there is reason to think that the usual reactive responses will retain their expected responsive value. In such an event, the responses may be justified.

7. Conclusion

I have argued that the mere presence of manipulation does not automatically defeat the claim that the agent is morally responsible—worthy of praise or blame—from either an internal or an external perspective. Manipulation does matter when (i) it prevents an agent from satisfying the responsibility conditions, or (ii) evidence of its presence undermines the justification of standard reactive responses. Here, then, we have an explanation of those instances where a manipulated agent differs from the naturally determined agent with respect to responsibility, underwriting a soft compatibilist denial of the second premise of the manipulation argument. In all other cases, the hard compatibilist rejection of the argument's initial premise is in order.

Notes

1. Versions of the consequence argument are advanced in van Inwagen 1975, 1983, Lamb 1977, and Ginet 1983, 1990. Van Inwagen 1983, pp. 183–188 presents a version tailored to responsibility alone. The manipulation argument is set forth in Taylor 1974, pp. 49–51 and, more fully, in Kane 1985, chp. 3 and Kane 1996, chp. 5.
2. See Section 3 of Kant's *Grundlegung zur Metaphysik der Sitten*. The presumption of openness is central to the account of ability I offer in Kapitan 1996. Similar conditions are supported in Dennett 1984, pp. 116–118; Strawson 1986, p. 196; Zimmerman 1988, pp. 21–22; Vihvelin 1988, p. 238; Glannon 1995, pp. 267–9; and Bok 1998, chp. 3.
3. Recent research by Antonio Damasio *et al* (forthcoming in *Neuroscience*, November 1999) reports that injuries to the prefrontal cortex can alter a person's the capacity to distinguish right from wrong.

4. Mele notes that one can be morally responsible for an action one did not *perform* autonomously, but not unless one was at some point or other autonomous agent (1995, p. 140).

5. When subject to psychological compulsion of this sort, the agent not only fails to autonomously develop a pro-attitude, but fails to autonomously possess (retain) it since it is unsheddable. Of course, an agent might autonomously *develop* a pro-attitude without possessing it autonomously, e.g. a drug addict who autonomously develops a desire for heroin but is subsequently unable to shed that desire (Mele 1995, p. 138).

6. On page 168 Mele claims that if an agent is "magically produced" by some devil to have certain pro-attitudes innately then these states are compelled and not possessed authentically. In such a case, no capacity to develop into an agent capable of controlling those pro-attitudes is bypassed, but then any innate unsheddable value is compelled.

7. In correspondence of October 25, 1999, Mele wrote to me that on page 179 he took Kane's description of the CNC-controlled agent as one whose choice "necessarily comes out as the controller plans or intends" (Kane 1985, p. 36), to imply that "some attitude that gave rise to the choice was one that the agent was compelled to have." I assume that Kane is talking about causal necessity here, and a compatibilist need not take causal necessitation of a choice to imply either its compulsion or that of any attitude giving rise to it.

8. See Fischer and Ravizza 1998, p. 47, n.19. One way of specifying which of an agent's many actions are the ones relevant for responsibility are those that satisfy the obligation and intention/foresight conditions, determined in part, by the agent's intentional and doxastic states, including the agent's previous commitments. If this were how "the relevant mechanism" that issues in action is selected then the agent's psychological states are the determining factors, but these provide no means of distinguishing between a normal agent and a manipulated agent.

9. Fischer and Ravizza suggest in note 28 on pp. 234–235, that no coherent self emerges or develops in a totally manipulated agent. Again, they are short on explanation. Why can't the totally manipulated agent be a "coherent self" if he or she possesses enough self-reflection and self-control? What about indoctrinated-from-youth agent? Why should the child who emerges from a controlled environment, beginning in the womb if we like, lack the ability to develop into a self anymore than a child who developed has been determined under other, more normal, influences? On these points, I find excessive hand-waving.

10. Ishtiyaque Haji (1998) attempts to block the manipulation argument in a way that combines elements of both Mele's and Fischer's and Ravizza's account. Haji speaks of *moral appraisability*, viz., being morally blameworthy or morally praiseworthy for the action (1998, p. 8), arguing that it is historically based (p. 123). S is morally appraisable for doing A iff (1) S exercised volition control over A (did A intentionally and holding constant S's motivation for A-ing and S's evaluative scheme, there is a scenario in which S both intends and performs an alternative to A); (2) S believed that doing A had moral value; and (3) S's doing A issues from actional springs that are authentic or are truly S's own. (1998, p. 237). Haji uses condition (3) to block the manipulation argument, where the "actional springs" are constituted by the "evaluative scheme" in terms of which S assesses reasons for action. The scheme

is "truly the agent's own," if it is (i) not normative-wise unauthentic, and (ii) appraisability-wise authentic. These two notions are characterized as follows: An evaluative scheme is *not normative-wise authentic* if it involves destruction or repression of an agent's initial normative agency (i.e., it destroys or replaces an "original evaluative scheme" of the agent) (p. 126). An agent's evaluative scheme is *appraisability-wise authentic* if its pro-attitudinal and doxastic elements (i) include all those, if any, that are authenticity demanding; (ii) do not include any that authenticity destructive; and (iii) have been acquired by modes that are not authenticity subversive (p. 136) In turn, an attitude is *authenticity-destructive* if having it precludes satisfaction of other conditions (epistemic and control ones) for appraisability; *authenticity-demanding* if having it is required for appraisability; and *authenticity subversive* if its instillment is incompatible with appraisability for later behavior (p. 131). The totally manipulated agent is not appraisability-wise authentic since its initial evaluative scheme is induced and, hence, not normative-wise authentic.

There are two problems with Haji's response. First, it seems that the totally manipulated agent's evaluative scheme can be normative-wise authentic inasmuch as it is the agent's *initial* evaluative scheme. Second, the heavy reliance upon the notion of "appraisability" in Haji's definitions threatens to violate a desideratum for a responsibility condition, namely, that it be decidable independently of assessments of responsibility (or, in this case, of appraisability). Unless we know what the conditions for appraisability are, we cannot say whether the totally manipulated agent is appraisability-wise authentic. A manipulated agent might satisfy the intent/foresight, obligation, control, and relevant states conditions, and have an attitude of seeing himself in control of his actions and as a suitable subject for moral responsibility— attitudes Haji thinks are required to ensure appraisability for subsequent behavior (p. 130). We might think it obvious that the manipulated agent is not "appraisable," but the criteria Haji provides are not sufficiently *independent* to justify this claim. For these reasons, I find that Haji is unable to preclude the totally manipulated agent from satisfying the authenticity conditions and, given satisfaction of the other conditions, from being morally appraisable.

11. See Watson 1996, p.231. A similar distinction between moral accountability and moral character can be found in Zimmerman 1988, p. 38, and in Fischer and Ravizza 1998, pp. 8–10, n.12. I have made it in Kapitan 1986, p. 248; 1989, p. 36; and 1996, p. 439. The following example highlights the difference. Suppose Hardy intentionally trips Lefty in order to amuse himself by seeing Lefty sprawl in the dust, an act that Hardy himself believes is of dubious propriety. Anders and his young son Dieter know—and believe it to be generally known—that Lefty is a notorious fugitive from justice who has repeatedly robbed elderly people in their homes. Lefty is at this moment fleeing his pursuers (who include Anders and Dieter) after having just deprived Granny Seelittle of her most prized and valuable heirlooms. Upon seeing rounding a corner, Hardy trips Lefty. Observing this, thinking that Hardy is among those anxious to stop Lefty's escape, and desiring to set an example for his son Dieter, Anders would be morally justified in praising Hardy for his action. From the standpoint of moral accountability, Hardy is praiseworthy for having tripped Lefty relative to Anders. Yet, motivated as he was, Hardy is also *not* worthy of being praised for tripping Lefty; from the standpoint of moral character, he is blameworthy because he exhibited wickedness in tripping Lefty. So, there are at least two

different ways in which someone can be morally praiseworthy or blameworthy for having performed a certain act.

12. Fischer and Ravizza note that the two views may be combined into one "mixed" view of MR if one is an appropriate candidate for reactive attitudes just in case one has a "credit" or a "debit" in one's "ledger of life" (pp 9–10), that is, if one possesses the appropriate excellence or fault. Watson also doubts whether the two perspectives on responsibility can be held apart, though he thinks it important to see "that they have distinct sources." (p. 243). See also, Davis 1979, pp. 137–138), and the discussion of *mens rea* in Perkins 1972, chp. 7, and in LaFave and Scott 1986, chp. 3.

13. In *Republic* 440c–441e, Plato emphasized that the Spirited element (θυμός) serves as an ally of Reason when activated through attitudes like anger (also, indignation, gratitude, pride), thereby moving the person to act justly.

14. I have discussed principles of alternate possibilities at greater length in Kapitan 1996, pp. 435–441, where versions are stated in terms of a compatibilist notion of ability.

References

Bok, Hilary. 1998. *Freedom and Responsibility*. Princeton: Princeton University Press.

Blumenfeld, David. 1988. "Freedom and Mind Control." *American Philosophical Quarterly* 25/3: 215–228.

Christman, John, ed. 1989. *The Inner Citadel*. (Oxford: Oxford University Press).

Davis, Lawrence. 1979. *Theory of Action*. Englewood Cliffs, NJ: Prentice-Hall.

Double, Richard. 1989. "Puppeteers, Hypnotists, and Neurosurgeons." *Philosophical Studies* 56: 163–173.

Dworkin, Gerald. 1976. "Autonomy and Behavior Control." *Hastings Center Report* 6: 23–28.

Dworkin, Gerald. 1989. "The Concept of Autonomy." In Christman 1989: 54–62.

Feinberg, Joel. 1989. "Autonomy." In Christman 1989: 27–53.

Fischer, John and Mark Ravizza. 1998. *Responsibility and Control*. Cambridge: Cambridge University Press.

Frankfurt, Harry. 1988. *The Importance of What we Care About*.

Ginet, Carl. 1983. "In Defense of Incompatibilism." *Philosophical Studies* 44: 391–400.

Ginet, Carl. 1990. *On Action*. Cambridge: Cambridge University Press.

Glannon, Walter. 1995. "Responsibility and the Principle of Possible Action." *The Journal of Philosophy* 92, 261–274.

Haji, Ishtiyaque. 1998. *Moral Appraisability*. Oxford: Oxford University Press.

Kapitan, Tomis. 1986. "Freedom and Moral Choice." *Nous* XX, 241–60.

Kapitan, Tomis. 1989. "Doxastic Freedom: A Compatibilist Alternative." *American Philosophical Quarterly* 26, 31–42.

Kapitan, Tomis. 1991. "Ability and Cognition: A Defense of Compatibilism." *Philosophical Studies* 63, 231–243.

Kapitan, Tomis. 1996. "Modal Principles in the Metaphysics of Free Will." In J. Tomberlin, ed., *Philosophical Perspectives 10, Metaphysics*. Oxford: Blackwell, 419–445.

LaFave, Wayne and Austin Scott. 1986. *Criminal Law*, 2nd edition. St. Paul: West Publishing Co.

Lamb, James. 1977. "On a Proof of Incompatibilism." *Philosophical Review* 86: 20–35.

Mele, Alfred. 1995. *Autonomous Agents*. Oxford: Oxford University Press.

Perkins, Rollin. 1972. *Criminal Law and Procedure*. Mineola NY: The Foundation Press Inc.

Schoeman, Ferdinand. 1978. "Responsibility and the Problem of Induced Desires." *Philosophical Studies* 34: 293–301.

Strawson, Galen. 1986. *Freedom and Belief*. Oxford: Oxford University Press.

Strawson, Peter. 1962. "Freedom and Resentment." *Proceedings of the British Academy* 48: 187–211.

Taylor, Richard. 1974. *Metaphysics*. Engelwood Cliffs NJ: Prentice-Hall.

Van Inwagen, Peter. 1983. *An Essay On Free Will*. Oxford: Oxford University Press..

Vihvelin, Kadri. 1988. "The Modal Argument for Incompatibilism," *Philosophical Studies* 53, 227–244.

Wallace, R. Jay. 1994. Responsibility and the Moral Sentiments. (Cambridge MA: Harvard University Press).

Waller, Bruce. 1998. *The Natural Selection of Autonomy*. Albany: SUNY Press.

Watson, Gary. 1996. "Two Faces of Responsibility." *Philosophical Topics* 24, 2:227–248

Philosophical Perspectives, 14, Action and Freedom, 2000

CAUSALITY, MIND, AND FREE WILL

Timothy O'Connor
Indiana University

Whatever the totality of our nature might be, we human beings have bodies that situate us in a physical space. Many of our actions are at least partially constituted by causally connected sequences of events within such bodies. Do these evident facts constrain, on purely conceptual grounds, the account we advance concerning the metaphysical nature of our minds, from which our actions spring?

One familiar affirmative answer to this question holds that these facts suffice to entail that Descartes' picture of the human mind must be mistaken. On Descartes' view, our mind or soul (the only essential part of ourselves) has no spatial location. Yet it directly interacts with but one physical object, the brain of that body with which it is, 'as it were, intermingled,' so as to 'form one unit.' The radical disparity posited between a nonspatial mind, whose intentional and conscious properties are had by no physical object, and a spatial body, all of whose properties are had by no mind, has prompted some to conclude that, pace Descartes, causal interaction between the two is impossible. Jaegwon Kim has recently given a new twist to this old line of thought.[1] In the present essay, I will use Kim's argument as a springboard for motivating my own favored picture of the metaphysics of mind and body and then discussing how an often vilified account of freedom of the will may be realized within it.

I Kim's Argument

Kim contends that the existence of a spatial framework, or something strongly analogous to such a framework, is a necessary condition on causal interaction among objects. He supports this thesis by an analysis of the 'pairing problem,' which invites us to give a principled way of identifying individual causal relationships in a scenario in which parallel sequences occur. Suppose rifles A and B are fired simultaneously and result in the simultaneous deaths of Andy and Buddy. Kim asks two questions (which he does not clearly distinguish): (1) What makes it true that A's firing killed Andy, and not the other way around? (2) What principles or criteria would lead us to correctly pair individual causes with their effects? Kim answers both these questions in terms of the spatial relations among the rifles and the two individuals. Rifle A's distance from, and orientation in relation to, Andy, is an important general feature of the situation that both made it possible for A to result in Andy's death and gives us a principled reason for supposing these two items to be causally paired, rather than A with Buddy and B with Andy.

I think Kim's treating these two questions as inextricably linked is unwise. He gives no reason to suppose that there could not be a situation in which objects are so distributed that their patterns of causal interactions exhibit a deep symmetry, making it impossible to decide the true causal pairings on empirical grounds. It is instead the first of Kim's questions, concerning the truthmaker for individual causal pairings, that interests me. Kim is implicitly supposing that causality necessarily exhibits a kind of *generality*. If an object or system A acts on B at time t, this will be due to general characteristics of B: its being the right sort of thing for A to act upon and its being in the right relationship to A at the time. Had it been a different object C that had those characteristics at t (both intrinsic and in relation to A), then A would have acted on it instead. Causality, we might say, is *non-haecceitistic*: objects do not have a primitive disposition to act on certain other individual objects; they are instead disposed to act on any objects having the right characteristics. At different times, the same object will achieve much the same effect on different tokens of some general type.

I accept this thesis about causal generality.[2] Kim wields it against Cartesian dualism as follows: we can imagine two nonphysical minds with identical intrinsic states at time *t0*. Yet one acts on body *B1* and the other acts on body *B2*. Why? Given that the minds bear no spatial relationships with these bodies, we must find some other kind of external relationship that explains the causal selectivity. Kim can think of none and concludes that there probably couldn't be one. So if causation cannot be haecceitistic, selective dualistic interaction (one mind with one body, and vice versa) appears to be impossible. Note that an appeal to God as the one who ordains certain permanent mind-body pairings will not help. For just as God cannot make a round square, likewise God cannot create a haecceitistic model of an essentially non-haecceitistic make.

Kim goes further. He suggests that the same consideration should lead us to suppose that causal interaction even *among* nonphysical minds is probably incoherent. For what kind of relationship could play the role of a structuring environment that is played by space for physical objects? If none is proffered, and we embrace the Eleatic linkage of existence with causal powers, we should suspect the coherence of the very idea of a nonphysical mind altogether.

II A Souler System?

It will be profitable to begin our assessment of the options for dualistic causality with a quick look at this last, fanciful scenario of a monistic system of interacting souls. Kim rather quickly places it outside the bounds of intelligibility, due to the lack of spatial relations that could structure the conditions of selective interaction. But there are other forms of order. One can readily imagine a scenario in which such an alternative to spatial relationships serves to structure the interactions of nonphysical minds, provided they have a suitably rich psychology. Suppose that God, in generating a series of souls, ordains that in their initial state they conform to a mathematically describable array, with each soul carrying the information of its present 'location' in the array as a primitive intentional state. Souls 'move' through the array over time by forming intentions to occupy a specified location. Among the basic laws of this souler system is a dynamical one that governs the actual re-arrangements as a function of all such intentions. (Perhaps, analogous to a time-sharing condominium arrangement, souls continually form ordered preferences as to their subsequent location. The dynamical law might factor in previous success in obtaining highly-ranked preferences, give a certain weight to preferences to remain in one's present 'neighborhood', and so forth. The reader is invited to fill in the details as he wishes.) Causal capacities come in two basic types: the ability to form specific intentions concerning oneself or another and the ability to modify the intentional state of another via one's intentions. I shall say more about the ability to generate intentions later. Let us concentrate now on the effect of such intentions on one's fellows. An example might be this: by intending to communicate to Jaegwon the thought that it would be nice to have a body as humans do, I cause him to register this thought, along with a belief that it is *my* thought that he is now entertaining. Again, there will be some sort of dynamical law that governs the degree of 'success' in bringing about such states in others: perhaps it will be directly proportional to the recipient's attentiveness and inversely proportional to his present informational load and 'distance' in the array. Perhaps instead of a function dictating continuously diminishing clarity and accuracy in the reception of the thought, these features of the effect will be measurable in discrete quanta of only a few magnitudes.

It will be noticed that I have used spatial metaphors to characterize the ordering that structures the interaction of souls in a space-less world. This should not in itself be objectionable, however. It is analogous to the nonliteral talk of phase space in quantum mechanics. We find it natural and easy to encode information in spatial terms. Propositional logic can be given a spatially encoded formalization, but we can do so without supposing that the logical relationships so represented are actually spatial. One might, though, shape the worry about reliance on spatial metaphor into the following objection:

> You have not actually described a framework of objective external relations. Instead, you have merely gestured at an abstract formalism and asserted without argument that there could be a kind of external relation so characterizable that is distinct from spatial relations and holds among nonphysical minds. Your reference to divine decree in instituting the array seems

ineliminable, and in consequence the changing sequence over time that you described smacks of occasionalism, rather than real interaction.

In reply, I grant that a mathematical characterization of an objective ordering does not disclose the qualitative character of the ordering it is meant to describe, in the way that we ordinarily suppose ourselves to directly apprehend suitable instances of spatial relations. The only such external relations among concrete objects that we do seem to apprehend in this way are spatial and temporal. Nonetheless, sketching the picture as I did above encourages the thought that there might be other possible instances of such mathematical structures. (Indeed, if one accepts relativity theory, one is committed to denying, contrary to appearances, that space and time are objective relations and accepting instead an underlying reality—the spacetime interval—that is *not* directly apprehended in experience.)

If necessary, we might mount a further defense of the possibility of soul-soul interactions that exploits the fact that it is easier for us to accept the existence of intrinsic properties that are alien to our world. (Why? Probably because we are committed to the existence of a wider range of such properties together with the fact that we can functionally specify properties in terms of their causal role within a system, whereas external relations merely provide a background, or structured framework, within which properties manifest their dispositional character.) So suppose one remains skeptical of the very possibility of external relations within a system of nonphysical souls. One could recast my description of such a system by eschewing external relations within an array in favor of a primitive sort of intrinsic informational state had by each soul, such that it knows 'where' it is 'in relation to' all the others. Whether a given soul may act upon another will depend in part on these informational states, along with their other intrinsic properties. In such a scenario, all causal interactions would be a function entirely of intrinsic properties, without reference to any structuring external relations. But I do not see that it can be dismissed on that account. For the necessary *role* that external relations play in our world's physical transactions— providing an objective structuring of objects that allows for completely general dispositional tendencies to work selectively from context to context—*is* carried out in the envisioned scenario.

III The Trouble with Cartesian Interactionism

Can the strategy just employed on behalf the coherence of a parliament of souls be adapted to the picture of the Cartesian dualist? It seems not. We should require not just the system of ordered relations among the nonphysical souls, along with the system of spatial relations among the physical objects, but also a cross-grid mapping of the two, identifying in general terms which body will impact which mind, and vice versa, in terms of their locations within their respective systems. And the trouble here is that on the Cartesian picture, we continually have the same pairings of individual souls and bodies, despite constant relational changes on at least the physical space side of the duality. The Cartesian picture of causal interaction seems unrepentantly haecceitistic.

(Is there the barest of possibilities in the following scenario? Suppose a two-dimensional mind-body array, involving external relations on both sides— *not* including spatiality—in which individual minds and bodies never in fact *change* locations. In consequence, they always act on the same object cross gridwise. Meanwhile, the bodies are acting and acted upon by constantly changing physical objects as their spatial relations change. We may suppose the souls lack potentiality for soul-soul interaction. In principle—at least by the power of God—souls and bodies could be reconfigured within the two-dimensional array, coming to act on different objects of the other category. If this scenario were coherent, it would involve the most exquisitely small distance from the objectionable idea of haecceitistic causality. Whether truly possible or not, for it to be true of our world, we must assume a system of physical relations entirely hidden from ordinary observation and indeed irrelevant to body-body interaction. I judge this sufficiently high a price to motivate the alternative presented in the sequel.)

What the dualist needs, as even Descartes saw but failed to provide, is a metaphysics on which the mind and body constitute a unified natural *system*. We want a plausible picture on which a particular mind and body are not independent objects that somehow continually find one another in the crowd of similar such objects, but instead constitute a unified single system whose union is grounded independently of particular mental-physical interactions. For note that Kim's argument does not anywhere address *self*-causality—a single object or natural system's acting upon itself. The problem of generality does not sensibly arise in this context, apart from the easily satisfied requirement that if a given system has the propensity to act upon itself in a certain manner, a similar propensity should be had by a qualitatively identical system.[3]

IV Mind and Emergence

Here is a way individual souls and bodies might constitute a single natural system. At some specific juncture in the development of the human organism, the body generates the soul, a nonphysical substance. Provided the requisite degree of structural complexity and life-conserving functions are preserved, the soul will likewise persist. Thus, it is completely dependent on the body not just for its coming to be but also for its continuing to be. Given such a baseline, asymmetrical dependency-of-existence relation, it is not arbitrary that these two entities should also interact continuously in more specific ways over time. On this picture, the soul is not entirely an entity in its own right, but is more properly seen as an aspect of the overall, fundamentally biological system that is the human person.

While I do think this emergentist variety of substance dualism is able to overcome Kim's objection to the traditional variety, the kind of causal capacity it attributes to the requisite biological systems is extraordinary. Differentiating details aside, causal agents in the universe of every sort are taken to act by introducing a qualitative change (or sustaining a persisting qualitative state) within themselves or other entities. The present sort of emergence, by contrast, would involve the generation of fundamentally new substance in the world— amounting to creation ex nihilo. That's a lot to swallow. Note that it's not sufficient, for addressing Kim's problem, that one retreat to supposing a pre-established harmony. For then the apparent dependence of the soul on the body is not real, they do not constitute a single natural system, and the pairing problem is not solved.

I suggest instead that those of us with dualist predilections try to live with a weaker form of dualism, on which token mental events are ontologically sui generis, distinct from any complex token physical state, without there being any substance distinct from the body which is the direct bearer of those events. This is a substance monism on which human persons are fundamental biological entities that also have emergent mental states. In the present section, I will sketch in formal terms the notion of emergence I have in mind.[4] In the remainder of the paper, I will address one reason some traditional dualists are dissatisfied with the weaker form of emergence: its implications for freedom of the will.

The informed reader is admonished that what we're after from an account of emergence in the present context is quite different from other, epistemologically-rooted conceptions of emergence employed in some contemporary theories of mind in philosophy and cognitive science. Our notion is ontological. We shall say that a state of an object is emergent if it instantiates one or more simple, or nonstructural, properties and is a causal consequence of the object's exhibiting some general type of complex configuration (whose complexity will probably be a feature of both its intrinsic and functional structure). By calling a property 'nonstructural', I mean that its instantiation does not even partly consist in the instantiation of a plurality of more basic properties. By calling the emergent state a 'causal consequence' of the object's complex configuration, I mean this: in addition to having a locally determinative influence in the manner characterized by physical science, fundamental particles and systems also naturally tend (in any context) toward the generation of such an emergent state. But their doing so is not discernible in contexts not exhibiting the requisite macro-complexity, because each such tending on its own is 'incomplete.' It takes the right threshold degree of complexity for those tendings, present in each micro-particle, to jointly achieve their characteristic effect, which is the generation of a specific type of holistic state.

So far I have given only a sufficient condition for a state's being emergent. The reason is that the picture becomes more complicated once we consider not just the generation of an emergent state, but the kinematics of an object's having one or more emergent features for a period of time. Think of the above as a baseline case, involving just such an initial generation of an emergent state. Consider that, as a fundamentally new kind of feature, it will confer certain causal capacities on the object that go beyond even the summation of capacities directly conferred by the object's microstructure. Its effects might include directly determining aspects of the microphysical structure of the object as well as generating other emergent states. In setting forth a general account of how this might go, I am guided not by abstract intuition about how it must go in any possible emergent scenario, but about how it is plausible to suppose it goes with respect to our own mental life, on the supposition that qualitative and intentional mental features of our states are emergent.

On that supposition, it seems plausible that there are enduring baseline mental states that partially underwrite more specific and often momentary mental states. Suppose, then, that when a neurophysiological system H comes to have a certain kind of complex configuration $P*$ at time $t0$, the baseline emergent state E is the direct result at $t1$. ($P*$, of course, will have to be of a sufficiently general type as to persist through constant and over time dramatic change.) $P*$ will also partly determine the underlying physical state of H at time $t1$. Let $P0$ be the remaining aspect of H's intrinsic state at $t0$, and $P@$ be the summation of those factors in H's immediate environment that will bear upon the physical state of H at $t1$. Letting "$\rightarrow$" represent the causal relation, we have

$P*$ at $t0 \rightarrow E$ at $t1$

and

$P*+P0+P@$ at $t0 \rightarrow P*+P1$ at $t1$

(the latter conjunction being the total intrinsic physical state of H at time $t1$, with $P1$ being the remainder beyond $P*$). Now E at $t1$ will help to determine in part the physical state of H at the subsequent moment, $t2$, but not its continuing to exhibit $P*$, of course, as that would involve causal circularity. E, we may suppose, will also help to determine the occurrence at $t2$ of another emergent state, $E2$. Diagramatically, the overall picture is this:

(For simplicity of representation, I'm treating '$P@$' schematically; at each moment it represents the sum total of those immediate environmental factors bearing on the intrinsic state of H at the subsequent moment.)

We are now in position to answer two standardly asked questions about any doctrine of mental causation. First, do the emergent properties of H supervene on its physical properties? By 'supervenience,' I here mean a synchronic relation between families of properties. The family of emergent properties would supervene on the family of physical properties just in case having an emergent property implies, of causal necessity, (1) that an object has some physical properties and (2) that its having any specific set of physical properties suffices to determine which, if any, emergent properties one has.

The first condition is evidently satisfied. The slogan used to capture the second condition is: 'No mental difference without a physical difference.' Consider first the status of our baseline emergent feature E, with reference to times $t0$ and $t1$ in the diagram. E is absent at $t0$ and present immediately thereafter. The underlying physical properties are different, too, but that is not the reason for the difference in emergent properties. For the differentiating factors ($P0$, $P1$, and the variable $P@$) are, by hypothesis, not directly relevant to the occurrence of E. $P*$ alone is so relevant. Yet E is absent at the first time, since $P*$'s obtaining at $t0$ causally determines not what will occur at that very time, but immediately thereafter. So at the first instant of its instantiation in H, H will not bear E. This indicates that there might be two objects having identical intrinsic physical properties (including $P*$) and existing in the same external circumstance, yet one has E and the other lacks it.

But this is only a slight departure, restricted to the first instant at which the 'base' property $P*$ occurs. More interesting divergence between emergent properties in the face of physical similarity can be seen when we turn from the baseline emergent property E to the more specific features $E2$, $E3$, and $E4$. Consider $E2$ at time $t2$. You might have the underlying physical properties $P*$ and $P2$ without having had $E2$. For $E2$ is a product of the immediately prior state of H (comprised of $P*$, $P1$, and E). This prior state presumably could have been different (such that $E2$ would not then occur at $t2$), consistent with the same subsequent physical state at $t2$, given a suitably fortuitous change in the environmental circumstance $P@$. The possibility of a difference with respect to $E2$ without an underlying physical difference is clearer when we suppose that the causal connections are probabilistic only. For then we can hold fixed the immediately prior state of H, and suppose a scenario in which it causes the same underlying physical state at $t2$, but, owing to a different chancy outcome, causes the occurrence not of $E2$, but of some distinct property, $E*2$.

So emergent states do not in general supervene on physical states. A second question we might have is whether they are epiphenomenal, at least with respect to the purely physical states of H and its immediate environment. Is the system in its purely physical aspect—is physics more generally—causally closed? Here, too, the answer is No. $P3$'s obtaining at $t3$ is in part a product of E and $E2$'s obtaining at $t2$. Had one or both of these failed to obtain at that previous time, something other than $P3$ would have occurred subsequently. Consistent with this, it is true in an emergentist scenario that everything that occurs rests on the *total* potentialities of the physical properties. For the occurrence of any emergent properties are among those potentialities, and so the effects of the emergent features are indirectly a consequence of the physical properties, too. The difference that emergence makes is that what happens transcends the immediate, or local, interactions of the microphysics.

In summation, we have seen that property emergentism allows for a form of dualism that escapes Kim's problem, since the mental-physical interactions it posits occur within the context of a natural unitary system, and hence is a form of self causality, rather than multiple-object transaction. I now turn to one test of its being sufficiently robust: whether it is consistent with the kind of freedom of will to which many dualists subscribe.

V Causal Generality and Free Will

Freedom of the will, in my judgment, involves the exercise of a distinctively personal form of causality, one which differs in certain respects from the mechanistic form of causation operative in impersonal causal forces.[5] In the mechanistic case, objects have specific causal powers, or dispositional tendencies, associated with their fundamental intrinsic properties. The powers might concern a unique outcome or a range of possible effects that is structured by a specific probability measure. Either way, they exercise certain of these causal powers as a matter of course when they are placed in the appropriate circumstances. Such circumstances either stimulate a latent mechanism or remove inhibitors to the activity of a mechanism already in a state of readiness. Strictly speaking, the cause here is the *event* of the object's having these power-conferring properties in those circumstances.

According to some of us, there is another species of the causal genus, involving the characteristic activity of purposive free agents. Such agents can represent possible courses of action to themselves and have desires and beliefs concerning those alternatives. Against that background motivational framework, they themselves directly bring about immediately *executive* states of intention to act in various ways. This direct causing by agents of states of intention goes like this: As with mechanistic causes, the distinctive capacities of agent causes ('active powers') are grounded in a property or set of properties. So any agent having the relevant internal properties will *have it directly within his power to* cause any of a range of states of intention delimited by internal and external circumstances. However, these properties function differently in the associated causal process. Instead of being associated with direct causal functions from circumstances to effects, they (in conjunction with appropriate circumstances) *make possible* the agent's producing an effect. These choice-enabling properties ground a different type of causal power or capacity—one that in suitable circumstances is freely exercised by the agent himself.

Now given his concern with causal generality, Kim might wonder whether I am trying to have things both ways by embracing the causal powers account of mechanistic causation while also defending agent causation. The causal powers account is resolutely 'anti-singularist,' in the sense discussed above. Yet I have purported to identify as one of its species something (involving agent causation) that seems to imply singularism. But there is not really a problem here, except perhaps with the way some draw the singularist/ anti-singularist distinction. Mechanistic and agent causation both require generality with respect to the grounding of causal powers. A given particular has a given type of causal power because of its intrinsic properties, and properties are universals. Where agent and mechanistic causal capacities diverge is in their *exercise*. The exercise of mechanistic capacities conforms to tendencies of some measure (the limiting case being deterministic). In the agent causal case this is not necessarily so, at least as a conceptual matter.[6] Agents may choose any of the options within the range of their power at a given time without having some fixed probabilistic tendency to do so. In any case, the important point here is that this does not fall afoul of Kim's stricture on non-haecceitistic causal tendencies, since agent causation is grounded in generalized capacities and is a form of self causality within a unitary system.

Can we make sense of agent causation as an *emergent* capacity of a fundamentally biological system? Note that such a theorist is committed to the emergence of a very different *sort* of property altogether. Instead of producing certain effects in the appropriate circumstances itself, of necessity, this property enables the individual that has it in a certain range of circumstances to freely and directly bring about (or not bring about) any of a range of effects. It might be thought that because of this distinctive character, it isn't possible that it could naturally emerge from other properties. Such a property could be instantiated only in a very different kind of *substance* from material substances, as on the problematic Cartesian view.

This thought does not bear well under scrutiny, however. Given that there is nothing inconsistent about the emergence of an "ordinary" causal property, able to causally influence the environments in which it is instantiated, it is hard to see just why there could not be a variety of emergent property whose novelty consists in enabling its possessor directly to effect changes at will (within a narrowly limited range, and in appropriate circumstances). If properties are able, as a matter of nomological necessity, to produce an entirely novel type of property, what reason do we have to assert that, when it comes to the property-kind distinction just noted, properties can spawn others of their own kind alone? At least, this would seem to be an empirical, not philosophical or conceptual, matter.

Still, taking the agency theory seriously within an emergentist framework raises a whole host of more detailed theoretical problems and issues. The most fundamental of these is determining the precise underlying properties on which an agent-causal capacity depends. Put differently, what types of features— either functionally or intrinsically characterized—constitute a physical system's being a free agent in the technical sense? Conversely, what structural transformations in the human nervous system would result in long-standing (or permanent) loss of the agent-causal capacity generally? This is an empirical matter (one answerable only by neurobiological science), and not in the province of philosophical action theory. Yet even a casual acquaintance with how neurobiologists approach their craft is enough to give an appreciation of the enormous difficulty this most basic issue poses. A plausible general conjecture is that such a capacity is bound up with the capacities for action representation and for conscious awareness, in their specifically human (and probably certain other mammalian) manifestations. It is highly plausible that this self-determining capacity strictly requires each of these other abilities, as they appear to follow from the very characterization of active power as structured by motivating reasons and as allowing the free formation of executive states of intention in accordance with an action representation.

If there are agent-causal events, there is no neat and simple way of dividing those events from mechanistic-causal ones. It surely must be allowed that some human behavior, even conscious behavior, is directly brought about by mechanistic-causal factors. (Not all action is *free* action.) This is likely to be true of behavior governed by unconscious factors and highly routinized actions. Precisely to what extent, then, is an ordinary human's behavior directly regulated by the agent himself, and to what extent is it controlled by subpersonal processes? Even when I act freely, I am usually not trying to control directly the precise degree of muscle contraction, limb trajectory, and so forth. This makes it plausible to hold that our memory system stores action sequences that we simply activate through conscious choice. (It also explains the facility of an experienced performer in carrying out complex movements, such as a sequence of dance steps.[7]) It may be that these choices are at times even brought about event-causally, while we simply monitor the result and retain the capacity to agent-causally redirect things as need be.

One might also worry that free will requires the emergence of a degree of indeterminism far beyond what we have any reason to believe is operative (as a function of quantum indeterminacy) at the complex level of neural structures. My reply is that since an emergent property has, relative to its underlying properties, a unique, nonstructural nature, we have no *a priori* reason to think it must result in processes exhibiting precisely the same degree of indeterminism as is present in its sustaining lower-level processes. Still, we are not supposing 'something's coming from nothing,' as many have thought: the presence of any emergent, on the view I have sketched, will be determined by more fundamental features of its possessor. What it does allow is a stable set of processes giving rise, at certain critical junctures, to a somewhat different order of affairs via 'top-down' controlling features. It is just this possibility that allows the right sort of emergentist view to overcome the opposite complaint from Cartesian sympathizers that agents with such emergent capacities are 'ontologically superficial'—not among the truly basic entities whose activities determine the way the world is.[8] While it is true, on my picture, that the presence of agent-causal capacities in select complex entities has always been among the potentialities of the world's primordial building blocks, the way those potentialities are exercised is not so prefigured. The agents themselves determine these outcomes. In consequence, any way of completely characterizing what happens in the world must make reference to these agents and their distinctive capacities. This is as ontologically 'deep' as any entity that is not necessary being could aspire to.

Notes

1. "Dualism, Causality and Being a Person," in a proposed volume of essays entitled *Persons, Bodies, and the Prospects of Survival*, edited by Kevin Corcoran.
2. It is denied by 'singularists' who hold that causation is first and foremost a relation between particular events, and the holding of that relation in a given instance has no implications (strict or probabilistic) for what happens elsewhere or elsewhen. C might cause E even though no other C-type event causes or has a tendency to cause an E-type event. It may *happen* to be true of our world that all causal transactions fall into patterns of certain types, but this, for the singularist, is at best owing to some contingent feature of the way causation is manifested in our world. There might have been ubiquitous causation in a chaotic, anomic world—including causal patterns between pairs of objects that are not amenable to general analysis of the sort Kim requires.

   The implausibility of this view is apparent when one considers the ultimate positions on the nature of causation in the actual world held by the two contemporary philosophers who have most emphatically argued that causation is a singular relation—positions which look decidedly *anti*-singularist to the causal observer. David Armstrong has responded to a serious problem for earlier versions of his position by holding that causation is manifested in our world as a relation among *types* of states of affairs. (See *A World of States of Affairs* Cambridge: Cambridge University Press, 1997.) And Michael Tooley's 'speculative proposal' in response to that same problem is to posit unusual features in the mereology of transcendent universals. If it is a law of nature that all things having property P have property Q, then, he says, we might suppose that P "exists only as part of the conjunctive universal, P and Q." (*Causation: A Realist Approach* Oxford: Clarendon Press, 1987, p.124). It would then follow that *any* time P is instantiated, Q is as well. Although these moves are critical to salvaging their respective theories of the general nature of causal processes in our world, they insist that these are merely contingent facts about causation, so as to preserve the singularist 'intuition' that there might have been instances of causation in an anomic world—in a world where events having the effects they do has nothing to do with the kind of events they are. This contingency is mysterious and unmotivated.
3. I note in passing that one might suppose that the problem presently under consideration applies equally to the classical conception of God as a nonphysical mind who causally acts upon the physical universe. But this would be a mistake. The physical universe is not a pre-given object which, as it happens, God encounters, as on the Cartesian picture the soul is an originally independent substance in its own right and is then 'fitted' to a specific body. Instead, God's acting on the universe in particular ways at particular times is of a piece with His giving being to the universe at that time: the universe is entirely dependent on Him at all times for its very existence and character, and there is no neutral environment akin to space in which He and it and

possibly other entities co-exist, which might prompt the question of the general conditions which govern selective interaction among them.

4. I explain this less formally and address objections not considered here in chapter 6 of my *Persons and Causes: The Metaphysics of Free Will* (New York: Oxford University Press, 2000).

5. I have argued this in several places, most recently in the book cited in the previous note. (Much of the present section of this paper excerpts material from that work.) When I say that agent causation is "purposive," and thereby contrasts with "mechanistic" causation, I don't mean to imply that it is not law-governed in any way. (See the following note.) Nor do I mean to imply that were reasons directly to cause choices, the activity would be nonpurposive in the ordinary sense. Rather, I intend to highlight the fact that agent causation is essentially purposive, whereas mechanistic causality is not. Agent causality is triadic—it involves an agent's causing an intention for a reason. The dyadic form of mechanistic causality is indifferent to whether the causes be reasons or impersonal states.

6. There are some contingent features of human agents that indicate that the exercise of active power has further causal structure in the way reasons govern it. Reasons move us to act, and some do so much more strongly than others. In ch.5 of my book, I propose that we think of the agent's states of having reasons to act in various ways as structuring the agent causal capacity, such that the agent's freely choosing an action type will have some objective tendency to occur, one which fluctuates over time. Even if this is accepted, it remains true that, in contrast to mechanistic causation, it remains up to the agent to decide how to act. The tendency-conferring state of having a reason does not itself generate the action; it disposes the agent himself to initiate an action sequence.

7. This is discussed by the philosopher A. Farrer in *The Freedom of the Will* (London: Adam & Charles Black, 1958) and cognitive scientists S. Kosslyn and O. Koenig in *Wet Mind* (New York: Free Press, 1992).

8. This phrase is taken from some recent unpublished work by Peter Unger.

References

Armstrong, D. (1997) *A World of States of Affairs*. Cambridge: Cambridge University Press.

Farrer, A. (1958) *The Freedom of the Will*. London: Adam & Charles Black.

Kim, J. (forthcoming) "Dualism, Causality and Being a Person," in Corcoran, K., ed. *Persons, Bodies, and the Prospects of Survival*.

Kosslyn, S. and Koenig, O. (1992) *Wet Mind*. New York: Free Press.

O'Connor, T. (2000). *Persons and Causes: The Metaphysics of Free Will*. New York: Oxford University Press.

Tooley, M. (1987) *Causation: A Realist Approach*. Oxford: Clarendon Press.

Philosophical Perspectives, 14, Action and Freedom, 2000

ALTERNATIVE POSSIBILITIES AND CAUSAL HISTORIES

Derk Pereboom
University of Vermont

1. Two libertarian attempts to revitalize a principle of alternative possibilities.

Two kinds of objections against Frankfurt-style arguments have recently received significant attention. A first sort, advocated by Robert Kane and systematically formulated by David Widerker, has the following structure. For any Frankfurt-style case, if causal determinism is assumed, the libertarian will not have and cannot be expected to have the intuition that the agent is morally responsible.[1] If, the other hand, libertarian indeterminism is presupposed, an effective Frankfurt-style scenario cannot be devised, for any such case will fall to a dilemma. In Frankfurt-style cases, in the actual situation there is always a prior sign by which the intervener can know that the agent will perform the action she does, and which signals the fact that intervention is not necessary. If in the proposed case the sign causally determines the action, or if it is associated with something that does so, then the intervener's predictive ability can be explained, but then the libertarian would not have the intuition that the agent is morally responsible. If the relationship between the sign and the action is not causally deterministic in such ways, then the libertarian can claim that the agent could have done otherwise despite the occurrence of the prior sign. Either way, some principle of alternative possibilities emerges unscathed.

The second type of objection to Frankfurt-style arguments has been developed by Michael Otsuka, Keith Wyma, and Michael McKenna.[2] The main idea behind this approach is to propose an alternative-possibilities requirement distinct from the more common sort, one which can withstand arguments of the sort that Frankfurt developed.[3] Abstracting away from the details of specific proposals, this strategy claims that for an agent to be morally responsible for an action what is required is that she could have avoided the moral responsibility she actually has for her action, and that, further, no Frankfurt-style case can falsify this requirement. For Frankfurt-style cases all involve some alternative possibility that would serve as the trigger for intervention, and if the intervention had occurred the agent would have avoided the moral responsibility that in the actual situation she has for her action.

I will present a case that defends Frankfurt against the sort of objection that Kane and Widerker raise. This example differs in important respects from others recently devised to answer this objection, and I shall contend that it avoids difficulties that threaten these other cases. Moreover, against the second objection I will argue that any alternative-possibilities condition of the sort that Otsuka, Wyma, and McKenna have proposed that plausibly might explain why an agent is morally responsible falls to this new sort of case as well. (This claim leaves open the prospect, which I acknowledge, that there is an alternative-possibilities condition not relevant to explaining why an agent is morally responsible that is necessary for moral responsibility.)

2. The first objection against Frankfurt-style arguments.

The current discussion of each of the two objections prominently features the notion of a *robust* alternative possibility. I agree with Fischer's claim that for a principle of alternative possibilities to be plausible, the kinds of alternative possibilities that it specifies must be robust, and indeed the notion of robustness plays a prominent part in my own account.[4] The intuition underlying the alternative-possibilities requirement is that if, for example, an agent is to be blameworthy for an action, it is crucial that she could have done something to avoid being blameworthy—that she could have done something to get herself off the hook. If having an alternative possibility does in fact play a role in explaining an agent's moral responsibility for an action, it would have to be robust in the sense that as a result of securing that alternative possibility, the agent would *thereby* have avoided the responsibility she has for the action she performed—it would be her securing of that alternative possibility *per se* that would explain why the agent would have avoided the responsibility. Following Fischer, here is an example of the non-robust sort of alternative possibility. Imagine a Frankfurt scenario in which Jones very much wants to kill Smith, but it turns out that he will kill Smith only if he in fact blushes beforehand. Then Jones's failure to blush might be the sign that would trigger the intervention of Black, who wants to ensure that Jones kills Smith. Suppose that Jones acts without intervention. Then we might well have the intuition that he is morally responsible, despite the fact that (as it appears) he could not have done otherwise. A libertarian might respond that there was an alternative possibility available to Jones after all: he could have failed to blush. However, failing to blush does not meet our criterion of robustness. For if Jones had failed to blush, he would not *thereby* have avoided responsibility for evading killing Smith—it would not be the failure to blush *per se* that would explain why Jones would not be blameworthy. By typical libertarian intuitions, a robust sort of alternative possibility would involve *willing* to do otherwise than to perform the action the agent in fact wills to perform.[5]

Widerker's version of the first objection has the following structure.[6] The case at issue is the one we have just encountered, in which Jones wants to kill Smith, but Black is afraid that Jones might become fainthearted, and so he is prepared to intervene if Jones fails to show a sign that he will kill Smith. The sign that he will kill Smith is his blushing at t1. The important features of the scenario are these:

(1) If Jones is blushing at t1, then, provided no one intervenes, Jones will decide at t2 to kill Smith.

(2) If Jones is not blushing at t1, then, provided no one intervenes, he will not decide at t2 to kill Smith.

(3) If Black sees that Jones shows signs that he will not decide at t2 to kill Smith, that is, sees that Jones is *not* blushing at t1, then Black forces Jones to decide at t2 to kill Smith; but if he sees that he is blushing at t1, then he does nothing.

Finally, suppose that Black does not have to show his hand, because

(4) Jones is blushing at t1, and decides at t2 to kill Smith for reasons of his own.[7]

Although the case is meant to show that Jones is morally responsible despite the fact that he could not have done otherwise, Widerker claims that this conclusion is not forced on the libertarian:

Note that the truth of (1) cannot be grounded in the fact that Jones's blushing at t1 is, in the circumstances, causally sufficient for his decision to kill Smith, or in the fact that it is indicative of a state that is causally sufficient for that decision, since such an assumption would... [not be] accepted by the libertarian. On the other hand, if (1) is not thus grounded, then the following two options are available to the libertarian to resist the contention that Jones's decision to kill Smith is unavoidable. He may either reject (1), claiming that the most that he would be prepared to allow is

(1a) If Jones is blushing at t1, then Jones will *probably* decide at t2 to kill Smith...

But (1a) is compatible with Jones's having the power to decide not to kill Smith, since there is the possibility of Jones's acting out of character. Or the libertarian may construe (1) as a conditional of freedom in Plantinga's sense...that is, as

(1b) If Jones is blushing at t1, then Jones will *freely* decide at t2 to kill Smith, [in a sense that allows that the agent could have decided otherwise][8]

in which case the libertarian may again claim that in the actual situation when Jones is blushing at t1, it is within his power to refrain from deciding to kill Smith at t2.[9]

Widerker's is a very important objection, and it serves as a test for the effectiveness of any Frankfurt-style argument. One point of clarification: If the libertarian that Widerker supposes Frankfurt must convince is simply presupposing a principle of alternative possibilities, then one could not expect that a Frankfurt-style argument would dislodge his view. But Widerker, I think, does not intend that his libertarian simply presuppose this principle, but rather only the claim that moral responsibility is incompatible with an action's having a deterministic causal history. I will proceed with this understanding of Widerker's objection.

3. Problems for recent attempts to answer Widerker.

Several critics have attempted to construct Frankfurt-style arguments that escape this objection. The kinds of cases that have been used in these arguments can be divided into two categories:

(a) those in which the relationship between the prior sign and the action is causally deterministic, and the indeterminism that makes for the agent's libertarian freedom is present in the causal history of the action before the prior sign

and

(b) those in which the prior sign is eliminated altogether.

Eleonore Stump and Ishtiyaque Haji have constructed examples in category (a),[10] while David Hunt, and Alfred Mele together with David Robb have devised scenarios in category (b).[11]

In my view, the cases that have been devised in each of these categories face significant problems. First, (a)-type situations are difficult to construct so that they are effective against Widerker's objection. Stump's and Haji's examples have serious drawbacks. In Stump's case, Grey, the neurosurgeon, wants to ensure that Jones will vote for Reagan. Grey finds that every time Jones decides to vote for Republicans, the decision regularly correlates with *the completion* of a sequence of neural firings in Jones's brain that always includes, near the beginning, the firing of neurons a, b, and c. Jones's deciding to vote for Democratic candidates is correlated with the completion of a neural sequence that always includes, near the beginning, the firing of neurons x, y, and z. Whenever Grey's neuroscope detects the firing of x, y, and z, it disrupts that sequence, with the result that this sequence is not brought to completion. Instead, the device activates a coercive mechanism that makes Jones vote Republican. Crucially, Stump specifies that the firing of x, y, and z does not constitute a decision, and in her view the occurrence of this sequence would not count as a robust alternative possibility. If, on the other hand, the neuroscope detects the firing of a, b, and c, it allows the sequence to proceed to completion and the decision to vote Republican to occur.[12] Stump specifies that the decision is indeed a causal outcome of the neural sequence.[13] What makes the agent libertarian is that the neural sequence is not the outcome of a causal chain that originates in a cause outside him. Rather, it is the outcome of a causal chain that originates, at least to a significant extent, *in an act of the agent which is not the outcome of a causal chain that originates in a cause outside the agent*. Here Stump suggests the Aquinas-inspired view that the neural sequence is the outcome of a causal chain that originates in the agent's intellect and will.[14]

But as Stewart Goetz points out, to assess this case, one needs to know more about the psychological features of the act performed by the agent to cause the neural process. If this act is causally determined, then Stump's agent would appear not to be free in the libertarian sense. But if it is not causally determined, then he might well have robust alternative possibilities for action. If it is the act of intending to make a decision, for example, and if the indeterminism of that act allows for the agent also to have avoided intending to make the decision, then the case might well include a robust alternative possibility after all.[15] Note that in Stump's setup, the agent's performance of that act— which constitutes the agent's crucial libertarian causal role—precedes the possible intervention.[16]

More generally, the challenge for Stump is to characterize the agent's causal role so that (i) her action is not causally determined (by factors beyond her control) and (ii) her action does not involve robust alternative possibilities. A case of the sort that Stump devises is subject to the following dilemma: If the indeterminism (whether or not it is a characteristic of the sort of agent's act she has in mind) that occurs prior to the neural sequence is significant enough to make the action a libertarian freely-willed action, then it has not been ruled out that the indeterministic juncture features a robust alternative possibility. If Stump were to reject the claim that there is a robust alternative possibility at this point, then it would remain open to a libertarian (like Widerker) to deny that the agent has genuine libertarian free will. Perhaps it is possible to embellish Stump's example to answer this objection. But to me it is not clear that there could be a plausible Frankfurt-style case in which the action is not causally determined by factors beyond the agent's control (in a way that would satisfy the libertarian) and she lacks robust alternative possibilities if the intervention would occur after the crucial indeterministic juncture.

In Haji's example, the sort of libertarian agency attributed to the agent consists in its being undetermined which of various considerations will enter the mind of the agent in deliberation. So, at the outset of Jones's deliberation it is causally open whether he will kill Smith, because it is causally undetermined whether various considerations will enter his mind at the onset of his musings. The infallible predictor, Black,

> intervenes if and only if he believes that Jones will not make the decisive best judgment that favors the decision to kill Smith which he, Black, wants Jones to

make. Specifically, should Jones make the judgment that he ought not to kill Smith, *then* (and only then) will Black intervene and cause Jones to alter the judgment.[17]

There is no need for Black to intervene "as Jones decides appropriately on his own," and one's intuition is that Jones could be morally responsible for his decision. However, one problem for Haji's case is that it was open to Jones to have made the decisive best judgment that he ought not to kill Smith, and this alternative possibility seems robust. For it appears plausible that if Jones had made the decisive best judgment that he ought not to kill Smith he would thereby have avoided the responsibility he has for the action he actually performed—it would be his securing of this alternative possibility *per se* that would explain why he would have avoided this responsibility. Another difficulty for Haji's example is that many libertarians would not allow that the sort of indeterminacy he specifies could be significant for moral responsibility because it fails to provide the agent with enhanced control. A case in which the relevant considerations indeterministically enter the mind of the agent, whereupon his judgment and decision are determined, would seem to exhibit no more control by him than a situation in which such considerations deterministically enter the mind of the agent, whereupon the agent's judgment and decision are causally determined.[18]

4. Frankfurt-style scenarios without prior signs.

Cases in category (b) exemplify a different of strategy for opposing alternative-possibility conditions. In these cases there are no prior signs to guide intervention, not even non-robust flickers of freedom. One ingenious scenario in this category is presented by Mele and Robb.[19] The example features Bob, who inhabits a world in which determinism is false:

> At t1, Black initiates a certain deterministic process P in Bob's brain with the intention of thereby causing Bob to decide at t2 (an hour later, say) to steal Ann's car. The process, which is screened off from Bob's consciousness, will deterministically culminate in Bob's deciding at t2 to steal Ann's car unless he decides on his own to steal it or is incapable at t2 of making a decision (because, e.g., he is dead at t2)... . The process is in no way sensitive to any "sign" of what Bob will decide. As it happens, at t2 Bob decides on his own to steal the car, on the basis of his own indeterministic deliberation about whether to steal it, and his decision has no deterministic cause. But if he had not just then decided on his own to steal it, P would have deterministically issued, at t2, in his deciding to steal it. Rest assured that P in no way influences the indeterministic decision-making process that actually issues in Bob's decision.

Mele and Robb claim that Bob is plausibly morally responsible for his decision. I think that their argument may in fact be successful, but that their development of the case raises one problem that could undermine it. Mele and Robb discuss several potential problems for their scenario, one of which is whether we can make sense of what would happen at t2 if P and Bob's indeterministic deliberative process were to diverge at t2. Here is how they handle the difficulty:

> The issue may be pictured, fancifully, as follows.[20] Two different "decision nodes" in Bob's brain are directly relevant. The "lighting up" of node N1 represents his deciding to steal the car, and the "lighting up" of node N2 represents his deciding *not* to steal the car. Under normal circumstances and in the absence of preemption, a process's "hitting" a decision node in Bob "lights up" that node. If it were to be the case both that P hits N1 at t2 and that x does not hit N1 at t2, then P would light up N1. If both processes were to hit N1 at t2, Bob's indeterministic deliberative process, x, would light up N1 and P would not. The present question is this. What would happen if, at t2, P were to hit N1 and x were to hit N2? That is, what would happen if the two processes were to "diverge" in this way? And *why*?
>
> We extend Bob's story as follows. Although if both processes were to hit N1 at t2, Bob's indeterministic deliberative process, x, would preempt P and light up N1, it is also the case that if, at t2, P were to hit N1 and x were to hit N2, P would prevail. In the latter case, P would light up N1 and the indeterministic process would not light up N2. Of course, readers would like a story about why it is that although x would preempt P in the former situation, P would prevail over x in the latter. Here is one story. By t2, P has "neutralized" N2 (but without affecting what goes on in x). That is why, if x were to hit N2 at t2, N2 would not light up.[21] More fully, by t2 P has neutralized all of the nodes in Bob for decisions that are contrary to a decision at t2 to steal Ann's car (e.g., a decision at t2 not to steal anyone's car and a decision at t2 never to steal anything).[22] In convenient shorthand, by t2 P has neutralized N2 and all its "cognate decision nodes." Bear in mind that all we need is a conceptually possible scenario, and this certainly looks like one.[23]

The aspect of this story that might raise the libertarian's eyebrows is P's neutralization of *N2* and all its cognate decision nodes. For he might be tempted to claim that P's neutralizing procedure is equivalent to P's causal determination of Bob's decision to steal the car. On the other hand, Mele and Robb do specify that P's neutralizing activity does not affect what goes on in Bob's indeterministic decision making process, and so it would seem that P would not causally determine the decision. How can we shed light on this difficulty?

Let us examine an approach in category (b) that more vigorously exploits the neutralization idea. A strategy of this type has become known as "blockage," and has been developed by David Hunt.[24] Here is a way of presenting this sort of approach that I think is especially powerful. Consider two situations.

> Situation A: Ms. Scarlet deliberately chooses to kill Colonel Mustard at t1, and there are no factors beyond her control that deterministically produce her choice. When she chooses to kill the Colonel, she could have chosen not to kill him. There are no causal factors that would prevent her from not making the choice to kill Colonel Mustard.

In these circumstances, Ms. Scarlet could be morally responsible for her choice. But then, against an alternative-possibilities principle one might employ a counterfactual version of this situation:

> Situation B: Ms. Scarlet's choice to kill Colonel Mustard has precisely the same actual causal history as in A. But before she even started to think about killing Colonel Mustard, a neurophysiologist had blocked all the neural pathways not used in Situation A, so that no neural pathway other than the one employed in that situation could be used. Let us suppose that it is causally determined that she remain a living agent, and if she remains a living agent, some neural pathway has to be used. Thus every alternative for Ms. Scarlet is blocked except the one that realizes her choice to kill the Colonel. But the blockage does not affect the actual causal history of Ms. Scarlet's choice, because the blocked pathways would have remained dormant.

One might, at least initially, have the intuition that Ms. Scarlet could be morally responsible for her choice in B as well. Yet for an incompatibilist this intuition might well be undermined upon more careful reflection on whether in B Ms. Scarlet retains libertarian freedom. One important question about such blockage cases is one Fischer asks: *Could* neural events bump up against, so to speak, the blockage?[25] If so, there still may be alternative possibilities for the agent. But if not, why aren't the neural events causally determined partly by virtue of the blockage? Kane's response to blockage cases reflects this worry:

> In [a case in which every other alternative is blocked except the agent's making A at t], of course, there *are* no alternative possibilities left to the agent; every one is blocked except the agent's choosing A at t. But now we seem to have determinism pure and simple. By implanting the mechanism in this fashion, a controller would have predetermined exactly what the agent would do (and when); and, as a consequence, the controller, not the agent, would be ultimately responsible for the outcome. Blockage by a controller that rules out all relevant alternative possibilities is simply predestination; and on my view at least, predestination runs afoul of ultimate responsibility.[26]

In response, one might claim that in the standard Frankfurt-style cases the relevant action is inevitable, but the intuition that the agent is morally responsible for it depends on the fact that it does not have an actual causal history by means of which it is made inevitable. What makes the action inevitable is rather some fact about the situation that is not a feature of its actual causal history, and hence, the action's being inevitable need not make it the case that it is causally determined. But how is the blockage case different from the standard Frankfurt-style cases? After all, the blockage does not seem to affect the actual causal history of the action.

Nevertheless, perhaps Kane's response can be defended. Two-situation cases of the above sort might be misleading just because it is natural to assume that the actual causal history of an event is essentially the same in each, given that the only difference between them is a restriction that would seem to have no actual effect on the event. But consider a simple two-situation case modelled on a reflection of Hunt's.[27] Imagine a universe correctly described by Epicurean physics: what exists at the most fundamental level is atoms and the frictionless void, and there is a determinate downwards direction in which all atoms naturally fall—except if they undergo uncaused swerves.

> Situation C: A spherical atom is falling downward through space, with a certain velocity and acceleration. Its actual causal history is indeterministic because at any time the atom can be subject to an uncaused swerve. Suppose that the atom can swerve in any direction other than upwards. In actual fact, from t1 to t2 it does not swerve.

A counterfactual situation diverges from C only by virtue of a device that eliminates alternative possibilities and all differences thereby entailed:

> Situation D: The case is the identical to C, except that the atom is falling downward through a straight and vertically oriented tube whose interior surface is made of frictionless material, and whose interior is precisely wide enough to accommodate the atom. The atom would not have swerved during this time interval, and the trajectory, velocity, and acceleration of the atom from t1 to t2 are precisely what they are in C.

One might initially have the intuition that the causal history of the atom from t1 to t2 in these two situations is in essence the same. However, this intuition could be challenged by the fact that the restrictions present in D but not in C may change this causal history from one that is essentially indeterministic to one that is essentially deterministic. For since the tube prevents any alternative motion, it would seem that it precludes any indeterminism in the atom's causal history from t1 to t2. And if the tube precludes indeterminism in this causal history, it would appear to make the causal history deterministic. Whether this line of argument is plausible is difficult to ascertain, but neither is it obviously implausible.

This problem could make it hard to assess moral responsibility in blockage cases. Sympathy for Frankfurt-style arguments is generated by the sense that moral responsibility is very much a function of the features of the actual causal history of an action, to which restrictions that exist but would seem to play no actual causal role are irrelevant. However, in a scenario in which such restrictions, despite initial appearances, could be relevant to the nature of the actual causal history of an action after all, one's intuitions about whether the agent is morally responsible might become unstable. My own view is not that actual causal histories in blockage cases are clearly deterministic, but only that these considerations show that they may be. This type of problem should make one less confident when evaluating these difficult kinds of Frankfurt-style cases. Since Mele and Robb's development of their case involves something very much like a blockage scenario, one might as a result also be less confident about the ultimate success of their argument.

5. A new Frankfurt-style scenario.

Here is my case:

Tax evasion, Part 1: Joe is considering whether to claim a tax deduction for the substantial local registration fee that he paid when he bought a house. He knows that claiming the deduction is illegal, that he probably won't be caught, and that if he is, he can convincingly plead ignorance. Suppose he has a very powerful but not always overriding desire to advance his self-interest no matter what the cost to others, and no matter whether advancing his self-interest involves illegal activity. Furthermore, he is a libertarian free agent. But his psychology is such that the only way that in this situation he could fail to choose to evade taxes is for moral reasons. His psychology is not, for example, such that he could fail to choose to evade taxes for no reason or simply on a whim. In fact, it is causally necessary for his failing to choose to evade taxes in this situation that a moral reason occur to him with a certain force. A moral reason can occur to him with that force either involuntarily or as a result of his voluntary activity (e.g. by his willing to consider it, or by his seeking out a vivid presentation of such a reason). But a moral reason occurring to him with such force is not causally sufficient for his failing to choose to evade taxes. If a moral reason were to occur to him with that force, Joe could, with the his libertarian free will, either choose to act on it or act against it (without the intervener's device in place). But to ensure that he decide to evade taxes, a neuroscientist now implants a device which, were it to sense a moral reason occurring with the specified force, would electronically stimulate his brain so that he would decide to evade taxes. In actual fact, no moral reason occurs to him with such force, and he chooses to evade taxes while the device remains idle.

In this situation, Joe could be morally responsible for deciding to evade taxes despite the fact that he could not have chosen otherwise. The prior sign does not causally determine his decision. There is indeed an alternative possibility, that a moral reason occur to him with a certain force. But such a possibility is insufficiently robust to ground his moral responsibility for tax evasion. For, again, the deeper intuition underlying alternative-possibilities requirement is that if, for example, an agent is to be blameworthy for an action, it is crucial that she could have done something to avoid this blameworthiness. If alternative possibilities were to play a role in explaining an agent's moral responsibility for an action (in a way independent of an intuition about its actual causal history), it would be because as a result of securing an alternative possibility instead, he would thereby have avoided the responsibility he has for the action he performed. However, if Joe had made a reason for an alternative action occur to him with a certain force, he would not *thereby* have avoided responsibility for evading taxes. For his making the reason for an alternative action occur to him is compatible with his never deciding to perform the alternative action, or even ever being inclined to perform that action, and choosing to evade taxes instead.

This example fits neither description (a) or (b). Rather, it is a case that has the following features:

(i) The agent clearly has free will according to most libertarian views.
(ii) What would trigger the intervention is a "flicker" that is insufficiently robust to explain the agent's moral responsibility for the decision in question.
(iii) It does not ground the truth of the analogue of Widerker's

(1) If Jones is blushing at t1, then, provided no one intervenes, Jones will decide at t2 to kill Smith,

which is

(1′) If a moral reason does not occur to Joe with a certain force, then, provided no one intervenes, Joe will decide to evade taxes,

in causal determinism, while at the same time not endorsing the analogues of Widerker's

(1a) If Jones is blushing at t1, then Jones will [only] *probably* decide at t2 to kill Smith,

and

(1b) If Jones is blushing at t1, then Jones will *freely* decide at t2 to kill Smith, [in a sense that allows that the agent could have decided otherwise],

which are

(1a′) If a moral reason does not occur to Joe with a certain force, then he will [only] probably decide to evade taxes,

and

(1b′) If a moral reason does not occur to Joe with a certain force, then he will freely decide to evade taxes (in a sense that allows that the agent could have decided otherwise).

The absence of what would trigger the intervention at some particular time (the role of this absence is played by Jones's blushing at t1 in Widerker's case, and by the non-occurrence of a moral reason with the requisite force at some particular time in Tax Evasion), or a state indicated by this absence, will not together with all the other actual facts about the situation, causally determine the decision. Joe's decision is not causally determined by the non-occurrence at any particular time of a moral reason with sufficient force. For at any point in the causal history of the action prior to the choice a moral reason could have occurred to him with sufficient force, even as a result of his own (undetermined) voluntary activity. But (*contra* 1a) the decision *will* occur (and not just probably occur) in the absence of what would trigger the intervention, even though it is not causally determined, because what would trigger the intervention is causally necessary (but not causally sufficient—thus not causally determining) for the decision's not occurring. Hence, (*contra* 1b) there is a libertarian sense in which the agent can *freely* decide to perform the action, but *without* its being the case that she could have decided otherwise.

Seeing how this example responds to Kane's version of the objection highlights the value of having the cue for intervention be causally necessary but not sufficient for the action, while ensuring that up to the time of the decision itself, the agent is not causally determined to make it. Kane argues, first of all, that supposing the case is to convince the libertarian, then if the agent in the example decides on his own, then this decision must be causally undetermined. Now if the intervention does occur, then the agent is not morally responsible. But if the neuroscientist "does not intervene to predetermine the outcome and the indeterminacy remains in place until the choice is made—so that the outcome is [a "self-forming willing"]—then the agent...is ultimately responsible for it. However, then it is also the case that the agent *could have done otherwise*."[28] However, let the cue for intervention be a causally necessary condition of the alternative, such as, in our example, the occurrence to the agent of a moral reason with a certain force. Then if the neuroscientist does not intervene, even though the indeterminacy remains in place until the choice is made, *it is not the case*, contrary to Kane's supposition, that the agent could have decided or could have done otherwise. For in order to decide otherwise, a moral reason would have had to occur with the requisite force, and then the device would have been activated.

One might reply that in order for Joe to be responsible for his action, his moral psychology must have been set up by crucial choices of his for which there were robust alternative possibilities.[29] But to see that this sort of answer is mistaken, consider:

> Tax Evasion, Part 2: Joe was raised in a context in which people are typically self-interested in the sort of way he is now. His parents, for example, had this sort of psychological profile. But he was also raised to reflect critically on his values as soon as he was able. Like most of us, he initially

accepted his family's values, and he held them very strongly. Joe then learned about competing positions, but upon serious reflection, he rejected them. Suppose that for him to abandon his initial moral view it was causally necessary that a reason for accepting a competing position occur to him with a certain force, and this could occur either involuntarily or as a result of his voluntary activity. Were such a reason to occur to him with that force, he could still choose to retain or reject his values (in the absence of the neuroscientist's device). But the neuroscientist, knowing all of this about his psychology, sets up his device before Joe begins critical reflection on his moral views, so that if a reason to accept a competing view were to occur to him with the specified force, it would electronically stimulate his brain to retain his initial moral position. But in actual fact, the device remains inert, for although he considers reasons to accept competing views, these reasons never occur to him with sufficient force to trigger the device.

Thus, although Joe's moral psychology was not set up by crucial choices of his for which there were robust alternative possibilities, he could still be morally responsible for evading taxes.

Consequently, this type of objection can be answered. Even presupposing libertarianism, we have not yet encountered a principle of alternative possibilities that plausibly has a significant role in grounding moral responsibility.

6. Answering the second objection.

As we have seen, the second type of attack on Frankfurt-style strategies has been advanced by Michael Otsuka, Keith Wyma, Michael McKenna.[30] Otsuka claims that a necessary condition on blameworthiness for an act of a given type is that the agent, as a result of his voluntary endeavor, could have instead behaved in a manner for which he would have been entirely blameless.[31] Wyma, in a similar vein, claims that a person is morally responsible for something she has done, A, only if she has failed to do something she could have done, B, such that doing B would have rendered her not morally responsible for A. McKenna argues that in all of the successful Frankfurt-style cases, the agent has the power either to be the author of his action or not, and that it is precisely this sort of alternative possibility that is significant for moral responsibility.

These philosophers assume that their conditions could not be falsified by Frankfurt cases because the successful versions involve the possibility that the agent could have voluntarily done, or been the author of, something that would have triggered the intervention, whereupon she would not have been morally responsible for the act in question. Fischer argues that these conditions could be undermined by cases in which intervention would be triggered by an involuntary flicker, in which the agent does not have a voluntary alternative possibility.[32] However, in setting up an involuntary flicker case, one must be careful to avoid the problem that Kane and Widerker raise by ensuring that Joe remains a libertarian free agent. We might try to do so by changing Joe's psychology in Part 1 so that in his situation a vivid presentation by an external source would now be required for a moral reason to occur to him with the requisite force. Given the strength of his self-interest and the level of his commitment to morality, since the benefit to himself at stake is significant and the damage to others that would result is not especially great, he could not make a moral reason occur to him with the right force voluntarily, and he could not voluntarily seek the sort of external presentation of moral reasons that would make them occur to him with this force. The relevant facts about the history of his psychology are given by Tax Evasion, Part 2, with the addition that he could not make a moral reason occur to him with sufficient force because of the strength of his self-interest and the weakness of his moral commitment, and the extent to which these features of his psychology have become ingrained. This specification is psychologically plausible—there is much that typical agents could not bring themselves to do because of their commitments. But again (without the intervener's device in place), if a moral reason were to occur to him with the specified force, Joe could, with the power of his libertarian free will, either decide to act on it or act against it. The neuroscientist's device is set up so that it senses when a moral reason occurs to him with such force, and he decides without the device intervening. If Joe could be morally responsible for deciding to evade taxes in this case, then it would directly undermine Otsuka's condition, since Joe could not, *as a result of his voluntary endeavor*, have behaved in such a manner for which he would not have been entirely blameless. It would show McKenna's to be mistaken, for Joe lacks the power *not to be the author of* the tax evasion, and similarly for Wyma's, since it is not the case that he failed to do something he *could have done*, such that doing it would have rendered him not morally responsible for evading taxes.

But the advocate of an alternative-possibilities requirement might argue that if Joe were morally responsible despite his not meeting these conditions it would be because his not doing so is explained by his moral psychology, which, in turn, results from certain crucial choices that he made that do fulfil conditions of the general sort we are now examining. Joe's inability to make a moral reason occur to him with sufficient force is explained by the fact that he chose to retain the self-interested moral conception that he was raised to hold, and although he could not have chosen otherwise, he failed to do something he could have done (i.e., have a reason for accepting a competing moral position occur to him with a certain force), such that doing so would have rendered him not morally responsible for making this choice (because then the device would have been activated). This claim suggests the following alternative possibility principle:

(Z) An agent is morally responsible for something she has done, A, only if she has failed to do something she could have done, B, such that doing B would have rendered her not morally responsible for A, or if she could not have done something that would have rendered her not morally responsible for A, this fact is explained by choices this agent made, $C_{1\ldots n}$, which are such that at the time she made them she could have done something, $D_{1\ldots n}$, such that doing $D_{1\ldots n}$ would have rendered her not morally responsible for $C_{1\ldots n}$.

It is not obvious to me that this principle has a counterexample, and that therefore (Z) could be an alternative-possibilities condition that is necessary for moral responsibility. We might revise Part 2 of Tax Evasion so that for Joe to have abandoned his initial moral view it was causally necessary that a reason for accepting a competing position occur to him with sufficient force, but that such a reason could occur to him only involuntarily, and never as a result of his voluntary activity. However, then we would want to know why his psychology has this feature, and the sort of explanation that suggests itself is that he has been so thoroughly indoctrinated by his upbringing that his ability to evaluate his moral view rationally has been impaired by factors beyond his control. As a result, there is a strong pull to the claim that Joe is not morally responsible in this situation. There many be another way to construct a counterexample to this principle, but it is not obvious to me how this might be done.

I favor a different kind of objection to the sort of condition that McKenna, Wyma, and Otsuka advocate. First of all, it may be that a condition is necessary for some phenomenon A but sometimes holds by virtue of features that are irrelevant to explaining the nature of A, that do not illuminate the nature of A. I believe that even if it turns out that conditions of the sort at issue are necessary for moral responsibility, they can hold by virtue of features of a situation that are explanatorily irrelevant to what would make an agent morally responsible, and that as a result the condition at issue fails to illuminate the nature of the phenomenon.

Consider Wyma's view, according to which an agent is morally responsible for something she has done, A, only if she has failed to do something she could have done, B, such that doing B would have rendered her morally nonresponsible for A. Suppose that Joe could have voluntarily taken a sip from his coffee cup prior to his deciding to take the illegal deduction, not understanding that this action would preclude his evading taxes, because unbeknownst to him, taking the sip would have triggered a bomb that would have killed him. In this situation, he could have behaved voluntarily in such a manner that would have precluded the action for which he was in fact blameworthy, as a result of which he would have been morally non-responsible for this action. But whether he could have voluntarily taken the sip from the coffee cup, not understanding that it would render him blameless in this way, is intuitively irrelevant to whether he is morally responsible for tax evasion. We might say that despite the fact that Joe could have voluntarily taken a sip from his coffee cup, and doing so would have rendered him morally non-responsible for evading taxes, this alternative possibility is nevertheless insufficiently robust to have an important role in grounding moral responsibility. Because this sort of alternative possibility would render Wyma's proviso satisfied, conditions of this sort, even if they are necessary for moral responsibility, would appear not to have a significant role in explaining its nature. (In fairness to Otsuka, the problem fails to undermine the sort of position he actually holds, since he resists the claim that an alternative possibilities condition would explain why an agent is morally responsible for an action.)

A condition more plausibly relevant to explaining moral responsibility for an action A is that the agent could have willed otherwise in the following more robust sense: she could have willed to refrain from doing A, or she could have willed to perform an action that she understands would preclude her doing A (or that she understands would preclude her performing an action of A's general sort). However, Tax Evasion does have the right characteristics to undermine this condition, for it shows that Joe could be morally responsible despite the fact that this condition is not satisfied. True, Joe could have willed that a moral reason not to evade taxes occur to him with a particular force. But if Joe were voluntarily to make such a moral reason occur to him with this force, the intervention would take place. He could not then have willed to refrain from evading taxes, or willed to perform an action that he understood would preclude his evading taxes. Nevertheless, Joe is morally responsible for his action. Consequently, if Wyma's condition is refined in this way, so as to eliminate the factors that make it hold for a situation due to features irrelevant to explaining moral responsibility, then it can be shown false. The same type of point can be made about Otsuka's and McKenna's provisos. Conditions of this sort seem to purchase technical indefeasibility at the cost of explanatory relevance to moral responsibility.

7. Causal history incompatibilism.

For the record, I do not intend my arguments to support a compatibilist position. Rather, I endorse incompatibilism, but I believe that the most plausible and fundamentally explanatory incompatibilist principles concern the causal history of an action, and not alternative possibilities. For a powerful and common incompatibilist intuition is that if all of our behavior was "in the cards" before we were born, in the sense that things happened before we came to exist that, by way of a deterministic causal process, inevitably result in our behavior, then we cannot legitimately be blamed for our wrongdoing. By this intuition, if causal factors existed before a criminal was born that, by way of a deterministic process, inevitably issue in his act of murder, then he cannot legitimately be blamed for his action. If all of our actions had this type of causal history, then it would seem that we lack the kind of control over our actions that moral responsibility requires. This intuition does not involve a claim about alternative possibilities. Accordingly, I favor *causal history incompatibilism* over *leeway incompatibilism*. However, I will not develop my positive proposal here.[33]

One might place incompatibilists on a continuum ranging from those who hold that moral responsibility requires that an agent could have done or chosen otherwise, to the most radical causal history incompatibilists, who maintain that even in a blockage case an agent can be morally responsible so long as the actual causal history of the action has the right features. Advocates of an alternative-possibilities requirement would tend to advocate an indeterminist condition on the actual causal history of an action only because it would make the existence of alternative possibilities a prerequisite for moral responsibility, for it is a condition about alternative possibilities that is most significant for explaining why agents would be morally responsible. My own incompatibilist view is that moral responsibility requires that the action's actual causal history have certain indeterministic features, but that it might well be that alternative possibilities—not necessarily of the robust sort—are entailed by the actual causal history having these features. Nevertheless, the aspect of the action that has the important role in explaining why agents would be morally responsible is the nature of the actual causal history, and not the alternative possibilities.[34]

Notes

1. Robert Kane, *Free Will and Values*, (Albany: SUNY Press, 1985), p. 51 n. 25, and *The Significance of Free Will* (New York: Oxford University Press, 1996), pp. 142–4, 191–2; David Widerker, "Libertarianism and Frankfurt's Attack on the Principle of Alternative Possibilities," *The Philosophical Review* 104 (1995), pp. 247–61; see also Keith D. Wyma, "Moral Responsibility and Leeway for Action," *American Philosophical Quarterly* 34 (1997), pp. 57–70. Fischer provides a clear and helpful account of these views in "Recent Work on Moral Responsibility," forthcoming in *Ethics*.
2. Michael Otsuka, "Incompatibilism and the Avoidability of Blame," *Ethics* 108 (1998), pp. 685–701; Keith D. Wyma, "Moral Responsibility and Leeway for Action;" Michael McKenna, "Alternative Possibilities and the Failure of the Counterexample Strategy," *Journal of Social Philosophy* 28 (1997), pp. 71–85. Fischer provides a valuable account of these positions in "Recent Work on Moral Responsibility."
3. Examples of more common principles of alternative possibilities are:

> An action is free in the sense required for moral responsibility only if the agent could have done otherwise than she actually did.

and

> An action is free in the sense required for moral responsibility only if the agent could have chosen otherwise than she actually did.

4. Fischer, *The Metaphysics of Free Will*, (Oxford: Blackwell, 1994), pp. 131–159.
5. See also Mele's characterization of robustness, which I endorse, in "Soft Libertarianism and Frankfurt-Style Scenarios," *Philosophical Topics* 24 (1996), pp. 123–141, at pp. 126–7.
6. cf. Ishtiyaque Haji, *Moral Appraisability* (New York: Oxford University Press, 1998), pp. 34–5.

7. Widerker, "Libertarianism and Frankfurt's Attack on the Principle of Alternative Possibilities," pp. 249–50.
8. The bracketed phrase does not occur in Widerker's text, but it clearly expresses his meaning.
9. Widerker, "Libertarianism and Frankfurt's Attack on the Principle of Alternative Possibilities," p. 250.
10. Stump, "Libertarian Freedom and the Principle of Alternative Possibilities," in *Faith, Freedom, and Rationality*, Jeff Jordan and Daniel Howard Snyder, ed. (Lanham, MD, Rowman and Littlefield, 1996), pp. 73–88;" Haji, *Moral Appraisability*, p. 36.
11. Alfred Mele and David Robb, "Rescuing Frankfurt-Style Cases," *The Philosophical Review* 107 (January 1998), pp. 97-112; David Hunt, "Moral Responsibility and Unavoidable Action," forthcoming in *Philosophical Studies*, cited by Mele and Robb and by Fischer in "Recent Work on Moral Responsibility".
12. Stump, "Libertarian Freedom and the Principle of Alternative Possibilities," pp. 77–8.
13. Stump, "Libertarian Freedom and the Principle of Alternative Possibilities," pp. 79.
14. Stump, "Libertarian Freedom and the Principle of Alternative Possibilities," pp. 80–5.
15. Stewart Goetz, "Stumping for Widerker," *Faith and Philosophy* 16 (1999), pp. 83–9. In this article he develops this and other criticisms in further detail.
16. Stump replies to Goetz's objection in "Dust, Determinism and Frankfurt: A Reply to Goetz," in *Faith and Philosophy* 16 (1999), pp. 413–22, but in my view, she does not lay to rest the worry I just described.
17. Haji, *Moral Appraisability*, p. 36. Haji attributes the inspiration for this sort of libertarianism to Mele, in *Autonomous Agents*, (New York: Oxford University Press, 1995), p. 216. This kind of libertarianism is also suggested by Daniel Dennett, in "Giving Libertarians What They Say They Want," in his *Brainstorms* (Montgomery, VT: Bradford Books, 1978), at p. 295.
18. See, for example, Randolph Clarke, "Agent Causation and Event Causation in the Production of Free Action," *Free Will*, Derk Pereboom, ed. (Indianapolis: Hackett Publishing Company, 1997), p. 286, (a longer version of this article appears in *Philosophical Topics* 24, 1996, pp. 19–48).
19. Mele and Robb, "Rescuing Frankfurt-Style Cases."
20. (Mele and Robb's note.) The picture obviously is neuro-fictional, but it is useful nonetheless.
21. (Mele and Robb's note.) What would happen if Bob's indeterministic deliberative process were to hit N2 at some time tn *prior* to t2? In one version of the story, N2 would light up at tn—Bob would decide at tn not to steal the car—but then at t2, when P hits N1, Bob would change his mind and decide to steal it. In another version—the one we prefer, owing to its relative simplicity—P neutralizes N2 as soon as Black initiates P.
22. (Mele and Robb's note.) David Hunt independently makes a similar suggestion in a forthcoming article (Hunt, ["Moral Responsibility and Unavoidable Action"]).
23. Mele and Robb, "Rescuing Frankfurt-Style Cases," pp. 104–5.
24. Fischer, contribution to a symposium on *The Significance of Free Will*, in *Philosophy and Phenomenological Research*, forthcoming, 1999.
25. Fischer, "Recent Work on Moral Responsibility."
26. Kane, in his reply to Fischer in a symposium on *The Significance of Free Will*, forthcoming in *Philosophy and Phenomenological Research*.
27. From Hunt's personal correspondence with Fischer, cited in Fischer's "Recent Work on Moral Responsibility."

28. Kane, *The Significance of Free Will*, p. 142.
29. Kane suggests a reply of this sort to a similar case, in correspondence.
30. Michael Otsuka, "Incompatibilism and the Avoidability of Blame;" Keith D. Wyma, "Moral Responsibility and Leeway for Action;" Michael McKenna, "Alternative Possibilities and the Failure of the Counterexample Strategy," *Journal of Social Philosophy*, pp. 71–85. Fischer provides a helpful account of these positions in "Recent Work on Moral Responsibility."
31. By way of clarification, Otsuka states:

> When I say that one could instead have behaved in a manner for which one would have been entirely blameless, I mean that it was within one's voluntary control whether or not one ended up behaving that way. But I need not claim that the behavior itself must have been voluntary ("Incompatibilism and the Avoidability of Blame," pp. 688–9)

32. Fischer, "Recent Work on Moral Responsibility."
33. I argue for this view in "Determinism *Al Dente*," *Noûs* 29, March 1995, pp. 21–45. For similar positions see Robert Heinaman, "Incompatibilism without the Principle of Alternative Possibilities, *Australasian Journal of Philosophy* 64 (1986), pp. 266–76, and Eleonore Stump, "Libertarian Freedom and the Principle of Alternative Possibilities."
34. I wish to thank David Christensen, John Fischer, Hilary Kornblith, Alfred Mele, and Linda Zagzebski for helpful comments and conversations.

Philosophical Perspectives, 14, Action and Freedom, 2000

LIBERTARIAN COMPATIBILISM

Kadri Vihvelin
University of Southern California

Jack was pushed by Jill, and is now tumbling down the hill. The push didn't break Jack's legs; a few minutes from now, he will get up and walk. But right now, thanks to Jill's push, Jack cannot help tumbling down the hill and thus cannot walk.

The incompatibilist thinks that there is an important sense in which there is no relevant difference between Jack's fall and the actions of any deterministic agent at any time. For example, consider deterministic Dana, who has been giving a speech to a mostly English-speaking audience and who is, at this moment, uttering an English sentence in response to a question. Dana knows how to speak Spanish, and a few minutes from now, she will say something in Spanish (when asked a question by a Spanish speaker). But right now, thanks to the deterministic causes of her English utterance, Dana *cannot* help speaking English and thus cannot say something in Spanish.

The compatibilist disagrees, and points to the differences between Jack and Dana to explain why. Jack's falling is not a voluntary action; even if he chose to walk, he would still fall. But Dana's speaking English is a voluntary action, under her volitional control; if she chose to speak Spanish instead, she would do so.

True enough, replies the incompatibilist, but the relevant question is whether Dana *can*, in the circumstances that in fact obtain, *choose* to speak Spanish. To the incompatibilist, it seems obvious that the deterministic causes of Dana's choosing to speak English are in all relevant respects like the deterministic causes of Jack's falling down the hill; they render Dana powerless to choose to speak in Spanish, or, for that matter, to make any choice other than the choice she actually makes.

Here, where argument should start, is where it usually ends. Instead of defending the assumptions about causation and laws of nature which underlie the claim that deterministic causes are, in all relevant respects, like pushes and shoves, libertarians and other incompatibilists appeal to "intuitions" about the "fixity" of the past and the laws of nature.[1] And instead of addressing seriously these modal and metaphysical concerns, the standard compatibilist response is still some variation on the "we're the only game in town" strategy, which consists chiefly of arguing that the libertarian conception of freedom is metaphysically dubious, perhaps downright incoherent, and, at any rate, not the kind of freedom worth wanting.[2]

The only way to get past this impasse is to take seriously the legitimate incompatibilist worry that Dana is as unable to do otherwise as Jack is unable to avoid falling downhill. And the only way to do this is to understand how our ordinary ways of thinking about what we can and cannot do make libertarianism such a natural and appealing view. I think that once we've done this, we'll see that what has gone wrong in the traditional debate is that compatibilists and incompatibilists have been talking past each other. Compatibilists should be understood as arguing that determinism doesn't rule out the possession of abilities, including the abilities that have traditionally been thought necessary for free will and moral responsibility. But incompatibilists are right to insist that free will also requires the genuine opportunity of doing something other than what one in fact does. There is no incoherence or mystery in an account of free will that combines both elements. It may look as though this account is committed to incompatibilism, but I will argue that this is not the case. Just as we may have the freedom compatibilists want regardless of whether determinism is true or false, so too we may have the freedom libertarians want regardless of whether determinism is true or false.

All this will take some arguing. Before I begin, let's take a quick look at the current state of the art in the debate between incompatibilists and compatibilists.

The Incredible Ability Argument for Incompatibilism

There is really just one *argument* in the current literature in support of incompatibilism.[3] It's a reductio that goes like this:

Suppose that determinism is true. Then for every action X that I perform, there is a true historical proposition H about the intrinsic state of the world at some time prior to my birth and a true proposition L specifying the laws of nature, such that H and L jointly imply that I do X. Now let's suppose that I nevertheless have the ability to do otherwise. If so, then I have the ability to do something such that if I did it, then either H or L, or both, would be false. And if that's so, then I have either the ability to change the past or the ability to change the laws or, perhaps, the ability to do both. But to suppose that I have either of these abilities is incredible. Therefore, it cannot be the case both that determinism is true and that I have the ability to do otherwise.

This argument—let's call it the 'Incredible Ability' argument—doesn't work. The standard compatibilist reply[4] is to distinguish between two counterfactuals:

(C1) If S had done otherwise, the past would have been different.

(C2) If S had done otherwise, this would *have caused* the past to have been different.

Having distinguished **C1** from **C2**, the compatibilist points out that there is a corresponding ambiguity between two ability claims:

(A1) S has the ability to do something such that if she did it, the past would have been different.

(A2) S has the ability to do something such that if she did it, this would *have caused* the past to have been different.

The problem with the Incredible Ability argument is that it equivocates between these two ability claims. To count as a reductio against the compatibilist, the argument must establish that the compatibilist is committed to **A2**. But the compatibilist is committed only to **C1** and hence only to **A1**. The compatibilist is committed only to saying that deterministic agents have abilities which they would exercise *only if* the past had been different in the appropriate ways and there is nothing incredible about this. Consider the ability to shoot and wound a human being. Joe's got the ability, but he would exercise it only in a narrow range of circumstances—self-defense or defense of his family. As a matter of fact, these circumstances never arise and Joe never shoots anyone. But he's still got the ability.

The incompatibilist needs a new argument. But when we look to the literature, there is not much argument to be found, as opposed to appeal to "intuitions" about our powerlessness with respect to the past and the laws of nature.

Ability, Opportunity, and the Beginnings of a New Argument for Incompatibilism

Compatibilists argue that in our everyday sense of 'free', 'can', or 'is able', we do not take the claim that someone is able to walk, talk, or play the piano as entailing that the person can do these things, given the circumstances that in fact obtain. Incompatibilists insist that if we are asking what someone is able to do, then we must be asking what that person can do *in the circumstances that in fact obtain*; that is, in asking what that person can do, *given the actual past and the laws*. In the literature on free will and determinism, this debate often seems to come down to an irresoluble dispute about what we *ought* to mean by words like 'free', 'can', 'power', and 'ability'.

I think we can make progress by recasting the free will/determinism debate in terms of two concepts that are part of our ordinary thinking about what we can and cannot do.

Commonsense recognizes a distinction between abilities (understood as skills, capacities, or knowing how) and opportunities. Someone may have the ability to do something (e.g., play the piano) but be unable to do it because she lacks the opportunity (there is no piano handy). Someone else may have the opportunity (the piano's right in front of her) but be unable to play because she lacks the ability (she never took lessons). And another person may be unable to play because she lacks both ability and opportunity.

Facts about ability and opportunity are relevant to questions of freedom and responsibility in at least two different ways.

First, we ordinarily think that someone is morally responsible for failing to do something (as opposed to merely failing to *try* to do something) only if she had the opportunity as well as the ability to do it. We don't hold someone responsible for failing to play the piano if she doesn't know how to play. But we also don't hold her responsible if any of the following are true: there is no piano handy; there's a piano but it's not working; there's a piano but the person is in chains or otherwise prevented from reaching the piano.[5]

Second, we think that the range of alternatives among which we have reason to deliberate is limited to those acts that we in some sense *can* do, and we think that the relevant sense of 'can' entails both ability and opportunity. If there's no way for you to rescue a drowning child, then there's no point in deliberating about how to do so. But there are two different ways in which you may be unable to save the child. You may be unable because you lack a relevant ability—the only way to reach the child is by swimming and you cannot swim. Or you may be unable because you lack opportunity, e.g. if any of the following are true: the only way to reach the child is by boat and there is no boat; by the time you notice the child, it's already too late to save her; there are sharks in the water which will eat you before you get to the child.

We may use this distinction between ability and opportunity to help us get more clear about why determinism is supposed to be incompatible with free will and moral responsibility. Is it because determinism robs us of opportunities or is it because determinism deprives us of abilities?

To answer this, we have to say a bit more about what it is to have an ability. We make judgments about ability on the basis of evidence of a reliable causal correlation between someone's attempts to do a certain kind of act and the success of her attempts. There is a continuum of cases, ranging from the person with no ability to do X who keeps trying and sometimes gets lucky, to the person just learning to do X who succeeds more often, to the person highly skilled at X-ing, who typically succeeds most often. But since success depends partly on circumstances outside the person's control, this correlation is evidence of ability, not constitutive of ability. What, then, is it to have the ability to do X?

Here's a sketch of an account: Someone has the ability to do X just in case it's true that there are some reasonably specifiable circumstances C (e.g., working piano nearby, the person is not bound or otherwise physically prevented from reaching the piano) such that if she tried, in circumstances C, to do X, she would probably succeed.[6] We evaluate this counterfactual by considering possible worlds where our laws obtain, where the person is as similar to the way she actually is as is compatible with her trying to do X, and where circumstances C obtain. If all or some reasonably high percentage of these worlds are worlds at which the person's attempt succeeds, then she has the ability to do X.

There are cases where it's not clear whether someone is unable to do something because she lacks the ability or because something prevents her from exercising the ability she continues to possess. Consider, for instance, the pianist who suffers from stage-fright so extreme that her hands begin to shake when she tries to play in front of an audience. Should we say that her stage-fright prevents her from exercising her ability to play? Or should we say that her stage-fright temporarily deprives her of the ability to play? Or should we say that she has one ability (the ability to play while no one's watching) while lacking another ability (the ability to play while someone's watching)? How we answer these questions depends on two variables: what we think the relevant ability is, and what we choose to include in the circumstances C in terms of which the ability is defined. There is room to argue about these kinds of cases. But I think that everyone should agree that the having of abilities, understood as skills or knowhow, is compatible with the truth of determinism. After all, abilities are defined in terms of conditionals about what would probably be the case, given our laws and the relevant enabling circumstances C, *if* someone tried to do an act of the relevant kind. Such conditionals may be true even if it's also true (as the incompatibilist thinks) that no person can ever *try* to do anything that she doesn't in fact try to do. Given this, we should not think that determinism deprives us of freedom by depriving us of abilities.

Note that everything I've just said applies to "inner"or mental abilities as well as abilities to perform bodily actions like piano-playing and swimming. A deterministic agent may have the kinds of mental abilities that have traditionally been thought necessary for free will—the ability to reason and deliberate concerning possible actions, the ability to make decisions about what to do on the basis of prudential and moral considerations, and so on. Indeed, for any *ability* you might think relevant to the question of free will and moral responsibility, there is no reason to think that deterministic causal laws would deprive us of this ability.[7]

I think that the disagreement between compatibilists and incompatibilists is best understood as a disagreement about whether the deterministic causes of an action prevent a person from doing anything else, including those things she has the ability to do. That is, the incompatibilist thesis should be understood as the claim that determinism deprives persons of the *opportunity* to do anything other than what they in fact do.

Remember Jack, who was pushed by Jill, and who is now tumbling down the hill. Jack still has the ability to walk because in the relevant circumstances C (standing on solid ground, not chained or otherwise prevented from moving his limbs) if he tried to walk, he would probably succeed. But Jill's push has rendered him temporarily unable to exercise his ability. He still has the ability, but lacks the opportunity.

And remember deterministic Dana, who is at this moment answering a question in English. No one denies that Dana has the ability to speak Spanish or the ability to deliberate concerning the pro's and con's of speaking in English versus speaking in Spanish. The only sensible question is whether the deterministic causes of Dana's English utterance temporarily prevent her from exercising her ability to speak Spanish. That is, the question at issue is (or should be) whether deterministic causes deprive Dana of the *opportunity* to speak Spanish.

If this is right, then we should understand the free will debate as a debate about whether deterministic causes are like pushes and shoves, temporarily depriving us of the opportunity to exercise our unexercised abilities. And once we understand this, incompatibilist intuitions start to make a lot more sense.

Although Jack has the ability to walk, he can't walk right now. Why not? Well, if he had walked, it *would have to have been the case that the past was different*—that Jill didn't push him. Given that she did push him, he cannot walk—he lacks the opportunity. Suppose that Dana is a deterministic robot, designed to respond in English to English questions and in Spanish to Spanish questions. Dana has the ability to speak in Spanish because there are relevant circumstances C (e.g.. she's asked a question in Spanish, she is not gagged or otherwise physically prevented from speaking) in which it's true that if she tried to speak in Spanish, she would probably succeed. But if Dana had spoken in Spanish right now, *it would have to have been the case that the past was different*—that the question to which she is responding was a Spanish question. Given that the question was in fact an English question, she cannot reply in Spanish—she lacks the opportunity.

Compare Dana to indeterministic Ingrid, who has also been giving a speech in English and who is also uttering an English sentence in response to a question. Like Dana, Ingrid has the ability to speak Spanish. But it's *false* that if she had spoken in Spanish right now, *the past would have to have been different*. If she had spoken in Spanish, the past would still have been exactly the same. Well, perhaps that's going too far. She's got no reason to speak in Spanish, so perhaps it's true that if she had spoken in Spanish, this might have been because something about the past was different (e.g.. she was asked a question in Spanish). But the past would not *have to have been different*. It might have been exactly the same—Ingrid might simply have decided to utter a Spanish sentence, perhaps as a philosophical example, perhaps as a private joke.

This apparent counterfactual difference between indeterministic Ingrid and deterministic Dana, is, I think, what fuels the incompatibilist intuition that there is a real and interesting difference between deterministic and indeterministic agents. And the counterfactual true of Ingrid—that if she did otherwise, the past would or at least *might* still have been exactly the same—is, I think, what lies behind the otherwise obscure thought that what's necessary for free will is the "categorical" or "unconditional" power to do otherwise—the power to do otherwise given *all the facts*, or, at least, the power to do otherwise *given all the facts about the past*. Let's give a name to this somewhat obscure thought and understand it as follows:

> **Fixed Past Assumption (FPA):** A person has free will only if it is at least sometimes true[8] that she has the *opportunity* as well as the ability to do otherwise; that is, only if it's at least sometimes true both that she has the ability to do something else X and also true that *if she had tried and suc-*

ceeded in doing X, the past prior to her choice would or at least might still have been exactly the same.[9]

If **FPA** is true, then it looks as though there is a fairly straightforward argument for the thesis that free will is possible, if possible at all, only at indeterministic worlds, that is, only at those worlds where more than one future course of events is nomologically possible, given the same past. But should we accept **FPA**?

FPA has this much going for it. It is part of a deeply engrained picture we have of ourselves as agents, a picture which represents our relation to the past as fundamentally different from our relation to the future. The past is "fixed", over and done with; when we make decisions we must assume that the past is the way it is. The future, on the other hand, is not yet fixed, it is in some sense "open", up to us, under our control. By making a choice (or reaching a decision or forming an intention) and then acting on it, we actualize the future; it is *we* who are responsible for the future being the way it is.

But the fact that a picture is intuitively appealing doesn't mean that it's correct, or even that it can survive closer scrutiny.

Here's a first attempt at an argument in defense of **FPA**: We are trying to give an account of the facts that make it true that *nothing* prevents someone from exercising her ability to do X. If it's really true that nothing prevents S from exercising her ability to do X, it must be true that S can do X, *given all the circumstances which in fact obtain*. But that's just shorthand for "S can, given *all the facts*, do X". If we ask whether the imprisoned lifeguard can save the drowning child, we understand this as a question about what she can do, given all the facts, including the fact that the door was locked a few minutes ago. We aren't asking the *different* question of what she might have been able to do if the past had been different.

But this is not a good argument. *All* the facts include facts about the *future*. For any action X that anyone fails to do, the totality of facts includes the fact that she will *not* do X. If we insist on saying that someone can do X only if she can do X, given *all* the facts, then no one can ever do otherwise, regardless of whether determinism is true or false.

We can give a better argument in defense of **FPA**. It goes like this: The difference between past and future is not ontological; it is relational. The difference is that *we* can *cause* future events, but not past events. Of course the future would be different—would have to be different—if Jill had not pushed Jack. But that's because Jill would have *caused* it to be different, and so doesn't count against Jill's opportunity to do otherwise. If Jill had done otherwise—if she had not pushed Jack—everything might still have been just the same except for Jill's choice and its causal consequences. But if Jack had done otherwise—if he had walked—the world would have to have been different in ways that he would not have caused. If he had walked, it would have to have been the case that he isn't tumbling down the hill and for this to be true, it would have to have been the case that Jill didn't push him.

We may now formulate the claim that underlies **FPA**:

Agent Causation Assumption (ACA): A person has free will only if it's at least sometimes true that she has the *opportunity* as well as the ability to do otherwise; that is, only if it's at least sometimes true both that she has the ability to do something else X and also true *that if she had tried and succeeded in doing X, everything except her choice, action, and the causal consequences of her choice and action would or at least might have been just the same.*[10]

The assumption being made here is the following: Someone has the opportunity to exercise her ability to do X just in case there is no impediment to her doing X. If there is no impediment to her doing X, then *nothing would have to be different* in order for it to be true that her attempt to do X succeeds—except, of course, her choice, action, and the causal consequences of her choice and action.

This assumption seems reasonable. Consider another kind of case, a case that has traditionally been regarded as a counterexample to compatibilist attempts to provide a conditional analysis of 'could have done X'. Mary, a native English speaker, is under general anesthetic while she undergoes surgery. According to a standard conditional analysis of 'can do X', it's true that Mary can speak English just in case it's true that if Mary chose (or tried, decided, intended, etc.) to speak English, she would succeed in speaking English. Since Mary's choosing (trying, etc.) to speak English requires her to be conscious, the conditional 'if Mary chose (tried, etc) to speak English, she would succeed' is true, so according to the conditional analysis of 'can', Mary can speak English. But since Mary is *in fact* unconscious, she cannot speak English.

Incompatibilists use cases like that of Mary to argue that 'can' is "categorical" rather than "conditional". I would draw a somewhat different moral. I think that this kind of case[11] illustrates how compatibilists and incompatibilists so often talk past each other. There is a sense in which Mary can speak English, but there is also an important and relevant sense in which she cannot. In one sense, the ability sense, Mary *can* speak English. It continues to be true of Mary, at all times while she remains unconscious, that *if* she tried, in the appropriate enabling circumstances C, to speak English, she would probably succeed. Her state of unconsciousness no more deprives her of the *ability* to speak English than Jack's state of tumbling downhill deprives him of the ability to walk. On the other hand, there is a significant sense in which Mary *cannot* speak English. Her state of unconsciousness prevents her from choosing, deciding, intending or in any way trying to bring it about that she speaks English and thus prevents her from exercising her ability. So long as she remains unconscious, Mary retains the ability to speak English, but lacks the opportunity.

Mary's case isn't a counterexample to the compatibilist thesis that *abilities* are correctly analysed in terms of conditionals. But the fact that she can't, *in the relevant sense*, speak English during the time that she's under general anesthetic shows that there is more to our ordinary sense of 'can' (or 'free', or 'is able') than simply having the ability to do something. And it shows that we can meaningfully speak of someone being unable to exercise an ability despite the fact that there are no external impediments to her doing so. It thus supports the incompatibilist's thesis that a person may be deprived, by conditions "beneath the skin", of the opportunity to exercise any of her unexercised abilities. And it also supports **ACA**, which explains Mary's lack of opportunity in terms of a different kind of conditional: If Mary had succeeded in speaking English, there would have to have been a difference not caused by her choice or action; she would have to have been conscious.

With these distinctions in hand, we are now ready to formulate a new argument for incompatibilism.

The No Opportunity Argument for Incompatibilism

1. Someone S has free will only if it's at least sometimes true that she is able to do otherwise.
2. S is able to do otherwise iff she has the ability to do something else X and the opportunity to do X (that is, iff she has the ability to do X and nothing prevents her from exercising the ability).
3. For any X such that S has the ability to do X, S also has the opportunity to do X only if it's true that if S had tried and succeeded in doing X, everything except her choice, action, and the causal consequences of her choice and action would or at least might have been just the same.
4. If determinism is true, then for any X such that S does not do X, if S had done X, neither her choice nor her action would have *caused* the past (prior to her choice) to be different.
5. If determinism is true, then for any X such that S does not do X, if S had done X, the past prior to S's choice would have been different.
6. Therefore, if determinism is true, for any X such that S has the ability to do X but S does not do X, S lacks the opportunity to do X.
7. Therefore, if determinism is true, S is never able to do otherwise.
8. Therefore if determinism is true, S lacks free will.

The first two premises are (or should be) common ground between the compatibilist and the incompatibilist. The third premise is entailed by **ACA**. The fourth premise relies on the uncontroversial assumption that there is no backwards causation, neither at the actual world nor at the closest worlds where determinism is true. The fifth premise is an assumption about counterfactuals at deterministic worlds which seems plausible.[12] Premise 6 follows from 3, 4, and 5. Premise 7 follows from 2 and 6. The conclusion follows from premises 1 and 7.

The compatibilist can't object to this argument on the grounds that it's based on a conception of free will which is incoherent, unsatisfiable, or requires a mysterious, nonnaturalistic conception of our abilities. The argument does not claim that indeterministic agents have *abilities* lacked by deterministic agents and is therefore compatible with a naturalistic understanding of abilities as complex dispositional properties. The argument is neutral between different accounts of what abilities constitute free will; it insists only that a *necessary* condition of free will is that it is at least sometimes true that the person has the opportunity as well as the ability to do otherwise. Finally, the opportunity component of free will, understood in terms of **ACA**, is neither mysterious nor logically unsatisfiable—indeterministic Ingrid satisfies it.

The problem for the compatibilist *seems* to be that she has to reject premise 3 and therefore **ACA**. But it isn't clear that there are good reasons for rejecting **ACA**. **ACA** says that a necessary condition for having free will is the truth of a counterfactual that is, I have argued, intuitively relevant to our beliefs about what we have the opportunity to do. The compatibilist cannot insist that facts about opportunity are facts "outside the skin" (e.g.. facts about the absence of locked doors and chains). For nothing turns on our use of the word 'opportunity'. The incompatibilist's worry about deterministic causes is that they are the internal equivalent of pushes and shoves, temporarily preventing the agent from exercising most of the abilities she continues to possess. I have argued that **ACA** is the best way of making precise this worry.

Given this way of understanding the incompatibilist's argument, it is hard to resist the conclusion that the freedom to do otherwise is incompatible with determinism.[13] And some compatibilists have not resisted. An increasing number of compatibilists have embraced the view that John Fischer has christened "Semi-Compatibilism"; they grant that free will (understood as entailing the freedom to do otherwise) is incompatible with determinism, but insist, following Harry Frankfurt, that moral responsibility is nevertheless compatible with determinism.[14]

Agency and Counterfactuals

But it's not clear that the compatibilist *has* to reject **ACA** and premise 3. The No Opportunity argument relies on a thesis about counterfactuals—premise 5. For premise 5 to be true, it must be the case that, for every deterministic agent S, and every relevant context of utterance, the sentence below expresses a true proposition:

Deterministic Backtracker (DB): If S had done otherwise, the past prior to her choice would have been different.

If, on the other hand, there is a relevant context at which **DB** fails to express a true proposition, then premise 5 is false and the No Opportunity argument fails.

I will argue that we should reject the claim that **DB** is always true. I will argue for this in two stages. First, I will make some observations about how we in fact evaluate counterfactuals in certain contexts. Then I will argue that we are justified in evaluating the relevant counterfactuals this way and that our justification is independent of the truth or falsity of determinism.

Consider the kinds of counterfactuals we take seriously in contexts of deliberation or decision-making *before* action and in contexts where someone is called upon to defend her action *after* the time of action. Let's call these "agency counterfactuals". Here's an example: Sara is deliberating at noon about whether or not to step on the ice after a warm winter morning during which the ice has mostly melted. Sara is a sensible and cautious person who would never step on ice unless she were sure that it's strong enough to support her weight. Knowing this fact about Sara's character, we might try to lure her onto the ice with this argument: "If you stepped on the ice, it would not have melted and it would be strong enough to support your weight." Sara would not take this argument seriously. She would agree that her character is such that we have good reason for believing that if she steps on ice, it's safe, and thus good reasons for believing that if she steps on ice, it didn't melt shortly before she stepped on it. She might even agree that there is a way of understanding the "backtracking" counterfactual "if Sara stepped on the ice, it would not have melted" which makes it true. But she believes that the counterfactual *relevant to her decision* is this one: "If I step on the ice, it would still have melted this morning, and it would not be strong enough to support my weight." And when we later asked her why she didn't walk on the ice, she replies: " Because if I had stepped on it, I would have fallen through." [15]

In considering whether or not to step on the ice, Sara assumes that, regardless of what she chooses, the past prior to her choice would still have been the way it in fact is—the ice would still have melted, she would still weigh what she actually weighs, she would still not have been supported by a helium-filled balloon, and so on. When thinking this way, Sara rejects **DB** and assumes that the following counterfactual is both true and relevant to her decision-making:

Fixed Past Counterfactual (prospective): If I stepped on the ice now, at noon, the past prior to my choice would still have been just the same.

Sara's rejection of **DB** isn't restricted to the context of deliberation prior to action. When we ask her the next day why she declined to take advantage of the opportunity to walk across the ice, her reply suggests that she believes that the following counterfactual is both true and relevant to the justification of her action:

Fixed Past Counterfactual (retrospective): If I had stepped on the ice just then, at noon, the past prior to my choice would still have been just the same.

Here's another fact about Sara: She believes that agency counterfactuals have truth-conditions that are objective in the following sense; she believes that they are true or false in virtue of facts that are independent of her reasons for believing them. These facts include facts about the past. She believes that if she relies on a mistaken belief about the past in believing a counterfactual, then her counterfactual belief may turn out to be mistaken, even though it was rational for her to believe it, given everything she knew at the time. For instance, suppose that she is standing, on a different day, with her friend Stan at the edge of the ice having an argument about whether the ice would support their weight. She says: " It's safe; I went skating yesterday." He answers: "Yes, but there was a thaw this morning." They don't go on the ice, but a few minutes later they watch Jill performing the experiment and falling through. Sara says: "You were right and I was wrong; I thought the thaw could not have melted all that ice, but I see now that it did. If I had stepped on it, I would have fallen through."

I claim that Sara is representative; this is how we in fact evaluate agency counterfactuals. This is an empirical claim. My evidence consists in the following. Despite the fact that the sentences used to assert or entertain counterfactuals are highly context-sensitive and often ambiguous between different readings[16], there are some counterfactuals which we so uncontroversially accept as true that the philosophical problem (as Goodman first pointed out[17]) is to give a theory of counterfactuals which explains how this knowledge is possible. Goodman was primarily interested in the singular causal counterfactuals associated with laws[18], but everything he said applies also to that species of singular causal counterfactual I've been calling 'agency counterfactuals'. Somehow we know how to go about determining whether these counterfactuals are true or false. How do we do it? My claim, in a nutshell, is that our knowledge of the truth-conditions for agency counterfactuals is best explained by our implicit acceptance of a theory which tells us to evaluate these counterfactuals by using everything we know about the past until just before the agent's choice[19], and then reasoning from the choice onwards in accordance with what we know about the laws and causal generalizations. And our knowledge of the truth-conditions of other singular causal counterfactuals suggests that we do so by using a theory which is an extension of our theory of agency counterfactuals; we hold the past constant until either the time of the antecedent or as near to it as is compatible with the occurrence of a local "divergence miracle"[20] and then reason from there in accordance with what we know about the laws and causal generalizations. In other words, we evaluate singular causal counterfactuals in the way that David Lewis tells us we should.[21] And if determinism is true, then, whether we realize this or not, we evaluate agency counterfactuals by considering worlds where the *agent's choice* is the divergence miracle.[22]

I think, moreover, that we are justified in evaluating agency counterfactuals this way. We are justified because the theory which tells us to evaluate them this way is the theory that best accounts for the data—our knowledge of the counterfactuals we uncontroversially accept as true.

A brief historical digression will help to defend my claim. In his seminal article, Goodman drew our attention to something he called 'the problem of cotenability'. Consider a dry well-made match which in fact is not struck. In the absence of specific reasons for believing otherwise (eg. someone lurking by, ready to pour water on the match at the first sign of an attempt to light it), we believe that if the match had been struck, it would have lit. But if, as Goodman assumed, the truth-conditions of a counterfactual are given by the fact that there is a valid argument from the antecedent and some true premises to the consequent, then why do we believe *this* counterfactual about the match rather than any of the other counterfactuals whose consequents may also be deduced from the antecedent, the laws and other true premises—eg. if the match had been struck, it would have been wet; if the match had been struck, there would have been no oxygen? In other words, why do we regard the dryness of the match and the fact that there is oxygen as "cotenable" premises while rejecting its unlit state as a cotenable premise? More generally, on what grounds do we choose, from among *all the truths* about the world, which ones are eligible to be counted as the premises for the purpose of constructing a valid argument to evaluate a counterfactual? Goodman named this "the problem of cotenability" and he thought it fatal to the prospects of giving a noncircular account of the truth-conditions of counterfactuals. For it seems that our grounds for accepting the dryness of the match and the presence of oxygen as cotenable premises are our beliefs in other *counterfactuals*: eg. our belief that if the match had been struck, it would still be dry and our belief that if the match had been struck, there would still be oxygen.

Goodman wrote in 1947, and what philosophers think about counterfactuals has changed considerably since then. Some philosophers have argued that what Goodman showed us is that *no* counterfactuals have objective truth-conditions; whether a counterfactual is true or false (or, on some views, "assertible" or not) is *always* determined by the facts the speaker chooses to hold fixed. On this view, there are no empirical grounds for choosing between "if the match had been struck, it would have lit" and "if the match had been struck, it would have been wet". (Or between "if Sara had stepped on the ice, she would have fallen through" and "if Sara had stepped on the ice, it would have been safe".) Other philosophers have drawn the opposite conclusion; they have taken the moral to be that our knowledge of causal truths—both actual and counterfactual—outruns our knowledge of laws. Somehow we know that striking that match *would cause* it to light, whereas striking the match would *not cause* it to get wet and wouldn't cause it not to be in the presence of oxygen even though, so far as the *laws* are concerned, all that's ruled out is that all of the following facts obtain: the match is dry; it's wellmade; it's in the presence of oxygen; it's struck; it doesn't light.

I think the first view—the rejection of objective truth-conditions for counterfactuals—is the counsel of despair, not justified at this relatively early stage of the game in our understanding of counterfactuals. After all, the first big advance in understanding counterfactuals did not come until the advent of possible worlds semantics in the early 1970's.[23] This isn't a solution to Goodman's problem but it does provides a helpful neutral framework for discussing the problem. On the possible worlds approach, the counterfactual "if P, it would be the case that Q" is true just in case the closest worlds where P is true are all worlds where Q is also true.[24] The problem of cotenability then becomes the problem of providing an account of the factors that determine which worlds count as the closest for the purpose of evaluating the counterfactual. The philosophers who reject objective truth-conditions for all counterfactuals are in effect saying that there is *never* a standard way of resolving the vagueness and ambiguity of counterfactual sentences; 'closest' *always* means 'most like the actual world in the ways that matter to the speaker'. Note that if this view is right, then the No Opportunity argument fails. For the No Opportunity argument relies on the claim that **DB** is always true. If counterfactuals lack objective truth-conditions, then we may reject **DB** by simply choosing to evaluate agency counterfactuals by holding the past fixed.

The second approach is, I think, the correct one, but we need to say more to turn it into a theory. It's not enough to gesture in the direction of "a causal theory of counterfactuals"; we need an account that tells us *which* causal facts are the ones that determine which worlds count as closest for the purpose of evaluating the counterfactual "if E had happened, then F would have happened".[25] For as a matter of fact, E *didn't* happen, so the causal facts include facts about the causes of the non-occurrence of E, facts about the effects of the non-occurrence of E, as well as facts about causal regularities. Any world where E happens will differ from the actual world with respect to some of these causal facts. So until we have an account which tells us which causal facts are the relevant ones, we don't have a solution to Goodman's problem.

Here's a first thought. (For reasons that will become obvious in a moment, let's call it 'the Naive theory'.) The relevant causal facts are facts that *we lack the power to causally affect*. We lack the power to causally affect either the *laws* or the *past*, so we hold these facts constant when we evaluate a counterfactual. So, for instance, we evaluate 'if the match had been struck, it would have lit' by considering worlds where the laws are exactly the same and the past is exactly the same until just before the time of the antecedent, when some person picks up the (dry, wellmade, unlit, in the presence of oxygen) match and strikes it. This *seems* to solve Goodman's problem in a way that accounts for our knowledge of the relevant counterfactual. For our knowledge includes, not just knowledge of regularities and laws, but also knowledge of our past interactions with the world, including our attempts, both successful and unsuccessful, to manipulate objects to bring about results we want. And our experience tells us that by striking a dry wellmade, etc. match we often succeed in lighting it, but don't (barring unusual circumstances) succeed in bringing it about that the match is wet or deprived of oxygen or not well-made.

There is something to this idea. Our beliefs about counterfactuals, causation, and our causal powers as agents are closely linked. Some philosophers have argued that we would not have the concept of causation if we didn't believe that we are agents with the power to manipulate objects and to originate causal chains.[26] Other philosophers have argued that our beliefs about agency and fixed past counterfactuals are so deeply rooted in our way of thinking of ourselves and the world that, even though "backwards" causation is not a logical impossibility, we would not accept any evidence as showing us that an *agent* has the power to causally affect the past.[27] Nevertheless, the Naive theory cannot be right, for at least two reasons. First, not all causal counterfactuals are about causes that may, even in principle, be brought about by the intervention of an agent. Second, the truth of determinism doesn't rule out either the truth of singular causal counterfactuals or our knowledge of them. But if determinism is true, there are *no worlds* with our laws and the same past where anyone chooses otherwise, thereby making something different happen. A theory of singular causal counterfactuals should apply to causes that are not manipulable by agents as well as those which are, and it should apply to deterministic as well as indeterministic worlds. So our theory of these counterfactuals should not *insist* that both the laws and the past be kept constant.

Since the counterfactuals about which we seem to be most confident are agency counterfactuals, let's begin by trying to give an account of these counterfactuals that will apply to deterministic as well as indeterministic worlds. (Perhaps we can later find a way of applying or extending the account to other singular causal counterfactuals, but we won't start by assuming we can do this.) If determinism is true, there are *no* worlds with exactly the same laws and exactly the same past where anyone chooses and does otherwise, so we must decide which respect of similarity matters more. Let's begin historically and assume it's the laws. This, of course, doesn't solve Goodman's problem, since what gave rise to that problem is the fact that the truth about the laws underdetermines the true counterfactuals. But perhaps we can use our general causal knowledge to help us out. We know that causes are temporally prior to their effects and we know that there is no direct causation at a temporal distance; the past causes the future only by way of the present. These two facts about causation suggest the following theory, which we will call "the Fixed Law" theory.[28]

The Fixed Law theory says that the closest worlds where an agent S does something X at time t are worlds with the *same laws* as the actual world and which are otherwise as *similar to the actual world at time t* as is compatible with S doing X. If determinism is true, then these worlds have the same deterministic laws as ours and thus a different causal history leading up to S's doing X. But since the past causes the future only by way of the present, we can ignore these differences, focusing on the relevant facts at time t. So, for instance, we evaluate "if S had struck the match at t... ." by considering worlds which *at time t* are very much like the actual world in all the intuitively relevant respects (the match is dry, wellmade, in oxygen, unlit) except for the fact that the match is in S's hand, being struck. Since these worlds have our laws, they are all worlds at which the match lights a moment later.

This theory *seems* able to accommodate the agency counterfactual about Sara and the ice. Granted, there are worlds with our laws where Sara steps on the ice without falling through. But, as Jonathan Bennett points out[29], these are worlds which are more like ours so far as *Sara* is concerned (same weight, character, desires, reliable sense detectors) at the cost of a greater dissimilarity with respect to other facts obtaining at the time of the antecedent—facts about the state of the ice and the beliefs that Sara and others have about the state of the ice, etc. It seems plausible to suppose that the worlds which are *overall most similar* to our world at the time of the antecedent are worlds where the ice is in the same melted state it's actually in, and Sara is the same as she actually is except for the fact that she has somehow acquired the false belief that the ice is safe. If that's right, then the Fixed Law theory agrees (albeit for different reasons) with the counterfactual endorsed both by commonsense and the Naive theory: that if Sara had stepped on the ice, she would have fallen through.

But while the Fixed Law theory may give the correct truth-conditions for some agency counterfactuals, it's not clear that it works for all agency counter-factuals, either in terms of accounting for our knowledge of them or account-ing for what we believe are the counterfactual facts. Here are two problems.

First, this theory allows us to consider particular facts obtaining at times earlier and later than the time of the antecedent only insofar as those facts may be deduced from the laws together with particular facts obtaining *at the time of the antecedent*. But it's not clear that this provides a sufficiently rich factual base to account for all the counterfactuals we think are true. For instance, in contemplating whether to climb a particular mountain, Sara might wonder whether she would be the first woman to do so. On the Fixed Law theory, there is an answer to this counterfactual question only if the present contains traces *either* of the fact that some woman previously climbed the mountain or of the fact that no woman has ever climbed the mountain. But it seems intelligible to suppose that the present provides us with no evidence either way. If so, then according to the Fixed Law theory the counterfactual "if Sara had climbed that mountain, she would have been the first woman to do so" is neither true nor false. But this is wrong for the same reasons that verificationist accounts of the past are wrong. Whether or not we can ever know it, it's either true or false that some woman has already climbed that mountain. And this historical fact suf-fices for the truth or falsity of "if Sara had climbed that mountain, she would have been the first woman to do so."

Second, if the laws must be held constant and determinism is true, then if anyone had done other than what she actually did, the causes of her choices would have been different, and the causes of those causes would have been different, and so on, all the way back to the Big Bang. And these would not be the only differences. For any world where our laws hold are worlds where these different causes will have different effects, and these effects will in turn have different effects, and so on, all the way from the Big Bang back to the time of the antecedent of the counterfactual we are considering. Given this, the Fixed Law theory seems incapable of explaining our knowledge of even the most uncontroversial counterfactuals about the undone acts of deterministic agents. For instance, in knowing that if Dana had pushed the button, the light would have come on, we rely on our knowledge of many other counterfactuals, including counterfactuals about what would still be the case *at the time of the antecedent*. (The light bulb would still be working, the fuse would still not have blown, the cord would still not have come unplugged, and so on.) These counterfactuals *might* often be true, for every potentially causally relevant fact F. But there seems no guarantee, given the Fixed Law theory, that these counterfactuals will always be true. And if there is no guarantee, then the Fixed Law theory has not solved Goodman's problem; it has not given us a theory that makes it plausible that we have the counterfactual knowledge we seem to have.

These problems suggest a different kind of theory, one which is closer in some ways to the Naive theory. This theory—we'll call it the "Fixed Past" theory—tells us to evaluate agency counterfactuals by considering worlds where the past (prior to the person's choice) *is exactly the same* and the laws are, if need be, just different enough to allow the agent to choose differently. In other words, the laws are just different enough to allow the agent's choice to be an event that counterfactual theorists call "a divergence miracle".

The Fixed Past theory provides the right truth-conditions for the match counterfactual and for the various ice-stepping counterfactuals. But it also provides the right truth-conditions for counterfactuals, like the "first woman" counterfactual, that are true in virtue of historical facts. And since it holds the past constant, it's not subject to the "backtracking" worry that the Fixed Law theory is subject to. Finally, it provides a more plausible account of our knowledge of agency counterfactuals than does the Fixed Law theory. According to the Fixed Law theory, we are allowed to use our knowledge of the past (relative to the time of the antecedent) only insofar as this knowledge provides evidence about the state of the world at the time of the antecedent; according to the Fixed Past theory, we are allowed to rely on our knowledge of the past for the more straightforward reason that the past would be the same no matter what the agent does.

The Fixed Past theory looks pretty good. Is anything wrong with it? Well, if you were brought up on Goodman and the metalinguistic pre-possible worlds approach to counterfactuals, you may be suspicious of an account that seems to be playing "fast and loose" with the laws. Doesn't this lead to modal anarchy, you might wonder? If the laws at the closest antecedent-worlds are different from our own, who's to say what would happen at such worlds?

But this objection misunderstands how Lewis has taught us to think about the laws at the closest worlds.[30] Don't think of the closest worlds as worlds where one of our deterministic laws have been replaced by a different law, with far-reaching consequences for different agents at different times. Think rather of worlds which share our past history until the occurrence of an event (eg. Sara's choosing to step on the ice) which, by the standards of *our laws*, is a "local miracle" and think of the laws at these "divergence miracle" worlds as being as much like our laws as is possible, given the occurrence of this event. At these worlds, one of our laws has been replaced by something that is, I think, best described as an "almost-law"; a generalization "weakened and complicated by a clause to permit the one exception".[31] To put it another way, the closest worlds, on this view, are worlds where events happen according to our laws at all places and times *except* in the small spatiotemporal region where the divergence miracle occurs.

Does this way of thinking about the laws at the closest worlds make any unacceptable assumptions either about the nature of laws or about possible worlds? I don't think so. No matter what your view of laws—whether you view them as true in virtue of the regularities that in fact obtain or whether you view them as true in virtue of relations of contingent necessitation—there are possible worlds where things happen in the way described above. And no matter what your view of possible worlds—whether you accept Lewis's robust realism about worlds or whether you think of worlds as abstract entities or useful fictions—what I described above is logically possible. It is possible that everything happens just as it actually does until the moment of Sara's choice, and that everything after her choice happens in accordance with our laws.

Given this, I see no reason for rejecting the Fixed Past theory of agency counterfactuals, and every reason for adopting it.

Let's review where we are. The success of the No Opportunity argument requires the truth of **DB**, and the truth of **DB** requires the truth of a theory of counterfactuals that tells us to always evaluate counterfactuals by holding the *laws* fixed. But while this is a natural assumption, it's equally natural to evaluate some counterfactuals—the ones I called "agency counterfactuals"—by holding the *past* fixed. If we combine these two natural assumptions, we end up with the Naive theory of agency counterfactuals. The Naive theory is a natural starting point, but it's naive insofar as it provides nontrivial truth-conditions for agency counterfactuals only if determinism is false (since if determinism is true, every world where someone does otherwise has either a different past or different laws). So we must reject the Naive theory and choose *either* a Fixed Law theory[32] or a theory that permits small divergence miracles as a trade-off for a greater match with respect to past and present particular fact. David Lewis has convinced many of us that the latter kind of theory is the right theory for the counterfactuals we entertain and assert in contexts where our primary concern is with answering questions about the causal upshots of the occurrence or non-occurrence of a particular event. I've been arguing that, so far as agency counterfactuals are concerned, the closest worlds are those where the *entire past* (prior to the agent's choice) is the same as it actually is. If I'm right about this, then **DB** is false and the No Opportunity argument fails.[33]

Ability, Opportunity, and Laws

We are now in a position to explain why our commonsense view of free will is, despite appearances, compatible with determinism. I have argued that our commonsense view embodies two elements; we assume that we have various mental skills or *abilities* (eg. to reason, deliberate, make choices, and so on) and we assume that when we act we ordinarily have the *opportunity* of choosing and doing otherwise, where this is understood so that it satisfies **FPA**. (If we had tried and succeeded in doing otherwise, the past prior to our choice would or at least might still have been just the same.) Finally, we assume that it's ordinarily true, at least on occasions when an agent deliberates, chooses, and acts, that she *could have done otherwise* in the following sense: she had both the ability to do something else and also the opportunity to do so.[34]

Given this view of free will, it's natural to suppose that if determinism is true, then we are *less* free than we would be if determinism were false (in the right kind of way). Determinism doesn't rule out the possession of any abilities, for we may have the ability to do something even when we are in circumstances where we lack the necessary conditions for exercising the ability (cf. the pianoless pianist). But if determinism is true, then it seems that we *can never do otherwise*; even if we have the relevant ability, we always lack the opportunity. For suppose that I have the ability to do some basic action X (eg. raise my hand) and suppose that on a particular occasion there is nothing that we would ordinarily count as an impediment to the exercise of my ability (I'm not in chains, unconscious, hypnotized, etc.). I consider doing X, but decide not to do it, and don't. Commonsense says that, barring unusual circumstances[35], I could have done X; in addition to the ability, I also had the opportunity. But if determinism is true, it seems that this belief must always be mistaken. For surely if I exercise (or try to exercise) any of my abilities, the laws of nature would still hold. So if I had done X, our deterministic laws would still have obtained and *the past would have been different*, indeed, *would have to have been different*. But if that's so, then appearances were misleading and I could not have done X; I had the ability, but lacked the opportunity.

This reasoning is natural and seductive, but I have argued that it rests on a mistake about counterfactuals. The mistake comes in supposing that we always evaluate counterfactuals about what we do (or try to do) by holding the laws fixed. Depending on the context and our interests, it *may* be appropriate to keep the laws fixed. For instance, when we try to answer the question: "Does S have the ability to do X?", it seems reasonable to suppose that we do so by considering the closest worlds where the laws are the same, where S is as similar to the way she actually is as is consistent with her lawfully trying to do X, and where the past is as different as it needs to be in order for it to be true that circumstances C obtain and S tries to do x. And when we seek to answer the question: "How might it come about that S would do X?", then it seems reasonable to suppose that we consider worlds where the laws are the same and S is the same with respect to character, abilities, dispositions, and so on, and where the past is as different as it needs to be in order for it to be true that S lawfully, and in character, does X.[36] But in a situation where someone is trying to decide what to do by asking, of each considered act X, "What would be the causal consequences if I did X?", then, I argued, we consider worlds where the *past* prior to S's choosing to do X is exactly the same and the laws, if need be, are just different enough to accommodate S's choice. And in these contexts— agency contexts, as I called them—it's true that if S had done otherwise, the past prior to her choice would have been exactly the way it actually was. But then it's true, *even if determinism is true*, that we have, not just the ability to do something other than what we in fact do, but also the opportunity to do so. That is, we have free will in a sense that satisfies **FPA** *even if determinism is true*.

Is this enough to show that our commonsense view of free will is compatible with determinism? I think so. But my incompatibilist opponents are not convinced. They object for different reasons. Some are unconvinced by my claim about Fixed Past agency counterfactuals; they think that it's always true, in *every* relevant context of counterfactual utterance, that if a deterministic agent had done otherwise, the past would have been different. To these incompatibilists, I have nothing more to say except: "Show me a better theory of agency counterfactuals." Other incompatibilists are willing to accept the Fixed Past theory of agency counterfactuals, but they regard Commonsense Compatibilism (the claim that we have free will that satisfies **FPA** even if determinism is true) as an incredible thesis, even less plausible than standard varieties of compatibilism. It is to these incompatibilists that I address the remainder of my arguments in this section.

First, let's get clear about the source of the incredulity. In defending Commonsense Compatibilism, I am committed to the claim that if determinism is true, then there are occasions when it's true, of some agent S, and some action X, that:

> **Law-breaking Choice (LC):** S can do X and if she did X, her choice would be a law-breaking event; that is, the laws would be different and her choice would be the event in virtue of which this is true.

I grant that **LC**, considered in isolation, looks incredible, but I will argue that appearances are deceptive. I will argue that if you have agreed with me so far—that is, if you accept my claim about the abilities of deterministic agents, and you accept **FPA**, and you accept the Fixed Past theory of agency counterfactuals—then you should accept **LC**. **LC** is surprising, but it is neither incredible nor philosophically objectionable.

To see why, let's take a closer look at why it's natural to think that **LC** says something incredible.

We think that the laws constrain us, by setting limits on what we can do, but **LC** seems to deny this. **LC** seems to say that we can (if determinism is true) choose in ways forbidden by the laws and act on these miraculous (law-breaking) choices. **LC** doesn't actually say that we can *do whatever* we like, despite the laws, but it seems arbitrary and ad hoc to say that we are able to make miraculous choices while denying that we are able to perform miraculous actions. But if we are able to *act* miraculously it seems that there are no limits at all to what we can do. This is not just incredible but clearly false. There are all sorts of things we cannot do—walk on water, run faster than the speed of light, defy gravity, etc. Since Commonsense Compatibilism has no grounds for denying that we can do these things, we must reject Commonsense Compatibilism.

There are two parts to this objection. The first part says that it's arbitrary to say that we are able to make law-breaking choices, while being unable to perform law-breaking actions. The second part says that Commonsense Compatibilism is committed to both claims and therefore denies that the laws place *any* restrictions on what we can do.

Let's look at the second part first. Commonsense Compatibilism says that we can do something only if we have the *ability* as well as the opportunity to do it, and Commonsense Compatibilism accepts the account of ability I proposed as common ground between compatibilists and incompatibilists. Someone has the ability to do X only if some worlds *with the same laws* where the person is in circumstances C and tries to do X are worlds where she succeeds in doing X. Given this account of what it is to have an ability, it follows that no one has the ability to do any act contrary to the laws. For there are no worlds with our laws at which anyone tries and succeeds in walking on water, running faster than the speed of light, or doing any other act which (either in itself, or together with circumstances C) entails the falsity of the laws. So the second part of the objection is answered. Commonsense Compatibilism does not deny that the laws place substantive constraints on what we can do; laws constrain us by setting limits on our abilities.

What about the first part of the objection, which says that it's arbitrary and ad hoc to say that agents have the ability to *choose* contracausally, while denying that they have the ability to *act* contracausally?

But Commonsense Compatibilism doesn't say that anyone has the *ability* to choose contracausally. Our doings include mental or psychological doings as well as doings of what are sometimes called basic actions (arm-raisings, foot-movings, etc.) and doings of nonbasic actions (riding a bicycle, playing the piano, etc.) Commonsense Compatibilism does not draw any arbitrary distinctions between our mental or psychological abilities and other abilities; the laws of nature constrain our mental abilities in exactly the same way they constrain our other abilities. We've got the ability to do a mental action just in case it's true that given the relevant circumstances C and given our laws, if we tried to do an act of the relevant mental type, we would probably succeed.

So both parts of this objection have been answered. Since we can do only what we have the ability to do, and since our abilities are constrained by the laws, it's false that Commonsense Compatibilism endorses the incredible claim that the laws are irrelevant to questions of what we can do, including mental doings, including the doings which result in choices.

LC is misleading insofar as it seems to be attributing to S a certain kind of *ability*—the ability to make law-breaking choices. But **LC** must be read in the context of Commonsense Compatibilism, and, given this, what **LC** in fact asserts is a conjunction of two claims:

(A) S can, in the ability sense, do X

and

(O) If S now tried and succeeded in doing X, the past prior to her choice would be the same and so her choice would be the divergence miracle, that is, a law-breaking event.

The two conjuncts are logically independent of each other.

A is not sufficient for **O**. S may have the ability to do X without it also being true that if she now tried and succeeded in doing X, the past would be the same and her choice would be the divergence miracle. Unconscious Mary, tumbling Jack, and the pianoless pianist are examples.

And **O** is not sufficient for **A**. It may be true that if S now tried and succeeded in doing X, her choice would be the divergence miracle without it also being true that S has the ability to do X. For instance, suppose that S lacks the ability to pick the winning ticket out of the box, but that on a particular occasion nothing stands in the way of S getting lucky and picking out the winning ticket. If so, then it's true that *if* S had tried and succeeded in picking out the winning ticket, the past would have been the same until the occurrence of her choice which (if determinism is true) would have been a divergence miracle.

It shouldn't be surprising that **A** and **O** are independent of each other. **A** says that S has the ability to do X. **O** says, in part, that if S tried and succeeded in doing X, *the past prior to her choice would be exactly the same*; that is, **O** says that S has the opportunity to do X in the sense partly defined by **FPA**. Since we may have the opportunity to do something without having the ability to do it, we cannot draw any inference from the law-breaking counterfactual *also* asserted by **O** to the conclusion that S has any incredible abilities.

Libertarian Compatibilism

I've been calling my view "Commonsense Compatibilism", but I think it deserves a somewhat more provocative name. I hereby name it "Libertarian Compatibilism" because it is a compatibilist view which captures the intuitions behind our commonsense view, a view which is usually thought to be libertarian in the standard philosophical sense (that is, as entailing incompatibilism). We believe that we are agents, importantly different from the rest of nature. We believe that we have the ability to transcend the forces that have made us what we are, that we are able somehow to "rise above" our desires and the chains of causation that bind the lower creatures. We believe that we enjoy, not unlimited freedom of the will, but a freedom that is absolute in this sense: barring very unusual circumstances, when we intentionally do something, we *could have chosen and done otherwise, given the actual past.* This commonsense view has traditionally been understood in the literature as the thesis that the laws which govern us are, at best, indeterministic, or more radically, that we aren't governed by laws at all but that we govern ourselves by a special brand of causation—agent-causation, where this is understood so that it reduces neither to event nor to fact causation.

What I have been arguing is that we can do justice to much in these intuitions without departing either from naturalism or from determinism. (I take no stand on whether determinism is in fact true or false, but follow the time-honored compatibilist tradition of saying it doesn't matter.) I've done this by arguing that what lies behind these intuitions is best understood counterfactually, in terms of **FPA**, and, more fundamentally, in terms of **ACA**. **FPA** says that we have free will only if it's true that if we did otherwise, *the past prior to our choice would or might still be the same.* **ACA** says that we have free will only if it's true that if we did otherwise, *the only differences would be our choice, action, and the causal consequences of our choice and action.* At first glance, it may seem that both **FPA** and **ACA** entail the incompatibility of free will and determinism; but I have argued that this is not the case. We have reasons independent of the free will/determinism debate for believing that the relevant counterfactuals are true.

Libertarian Compatibilism is an unorthodox form of compatibilism, but I think it's not only defensible but plausible. I think it captures what's intuitively right about compatibilism, on the one hand, and orthodox (that is, incompatibilist) libertarianism, on the other hand.

The following counterfactuals are consistent:

> **(C)** If the past had been suitably different, S would have had different reasons and she would have chosen, tried, and succeeded in doing otherwise.
>
> **(L)** If S had tried and succeeded in doing otherwise, the past prior to her choice would or at least might still have been exactly the same.

C is the claim traditionally stressed by compatibilists, who insist that a free agent is one whose actions casually and counterfactually depend on her reasons and whose reasons depend on facts about the past. **L** is the claim traditionally stressed by libertarians who insist that a person is free to do otherwise only if the past is counterfactually *independent* of her choice and action. But **C** and **L** are consistent, and, if I'm right about how we evaluate counterfactuals, then *both* are in fact sometimes true.[37]

Notes

1. The most sophisticated and rigorous arguments for incompatibilism are versions of the so-called "modal argument" articulated independently by Carl Ginet and Peter van Inwagen in a series of articles and in their books, Ginet's *On Action* (Cambridge, 1990) and van Inwagen's *An Essay on Free Will*, (Clarendon Press, Oxford, 1983). But these defenses of incompatibilism end up relying, at points that seem to me crucial, on undefended "intuitions" about the ways in which the past and laws are "fixed".

2. For a classic instance of this compatibilist strategy, see R.E. Hobart's "Free Will as Involving Determinism and as Inconceivable Without It", *Mind* 43 (1934), 1–27. For more recent examples, see Daniel Dennett's *Elbow Room: The Varieties of Free Will Worth Wanting*, Bradford Books, 1984, and Susan Wolf's *Freedom Within Reason*, Oxford University Press, 1990.

3. Van Inwagen articulates and defends three formal arguments for incompatibilism, but says that all three are versions of one basic argument. The one that's closest to the one I give here is the one he calls "The First Formal Argument". (*An Essay on Free Will*, ibid., pp. 68–78.)

4. Versions of this reply have been made by a number of philosophers, including John Fischer, "Incompatibilism", *Philosophical Studies* 43 (1983), 127–137 and David Lewis, "Are We Free to Break the Laws?", *Theoria* 47 (1981), 113–121.

5. Some people think that Harry Frankfurt has shown that being able to do otherwise is not a necessary condition of moral responsibility. (See his "Alternate Possibilities and Moral Responsibility", *Journal of Philosophy* 66 (1969), 829–839.) In my "Freedom, Foreknowledge, and the Principle of Alternate Possibilities" (*Canadian Journal of Philosophy*, forthcoming), I argue that so-called "Frankfurt stories" fail to establish this; if we have been so persuaded, it's because we have been taken in by a bad *argument*.

6. Although this is rough, it will do for our purposes. A satisfactory analysis of the ability to do X will have to be more carefully formulated. For recent discussion of the related project of trying to give a conditional analysis of dispositions, see C.B. Martin, "Dispositions and Conditionals", *Philosophical Quarterly* 44 (1994), 1–8, and David Lewis, "Finkish Dispositions", *Philosophical Quarterly* 47 (1997), 143–158.

7. On the contrary, a venerable compatibilist strategy has been to argue that the possession of the relevant abilities requires the truth of determinism. This strategy fails because it assumes that there is no causation in the absence of determinism. It's now generally accepted that there may be causation—understood either in terms of subsumption under probabilistic laws or in terms of probabilistic counterfactual dependence—even if determinism is false. Given this, it's false that an undetermined event is for that reason a random event, not in anyone's causal control. And it's false that the falsity of determinism entails that there are no abilities.

8. Why "at least sometimes" instead of 'always'? Because it would be implausible to understand the incompatibilist thesis as the claim that free will requires that we are always free to do otherwise. It seems implausible to suppose that we cease to have free will each time we fall asleep even though our state of unconsciousness prevents us from exercising any of our unexercised abilities. Given this, we have to understand the incompatibilist as *either* saying that we have free will only if we at least sometimes have both ability and opportunity to do otherwise or as saying that

we have free will only if it's ordinarily true, on *each occasion of choice or action*, that we have both ability and opportunity to do otherwise.

9. For "choice", you may substitute "decision", "intention", "volition" or whatever you think the causal antecedent (or first part) of action is. I remain neutral in this paper about different theories of action; my arguments can be reformulated so they apply regardless of your view about what actions are.

10. Note that **ACA** is weak in several ways. It states only a necessary condition for having free will, and it allows for the possibility that someone has free will even if there are relatively few occasions on which she has opportunity as well as ability to do otherwise. I've formulated **ACA** so weakly for two reasons: First, to avoid the unattractive consequence that we cease to have free will whenever we fall asleep. (See note 8.) Second, because I want to capture the common core of a wide range of different views about what it takes for someone to have free will; these differences are, I think, best understood as different views about what *abilities* are necessary for free will.

11. Tell any story where you believe that all of the following are true: Someone cannot do X; if she chose (tried, etc.) to do X, she would succeed; she cannot do X because she suffers from some state (a pathological aversion, phobia, extreme panic, hypnosis, etc.) which renders her unable to choose, decide, intend or in any way try to bring it about that she does X. The moral I draw applies to any story that meets these conditions.

12. Recall our discussion of the Incredible Ability argument, in which we distinguished the innocuous "backtracking" C1 from the incredible causal "backtracking" C2 and argued that the compatibilist is committed only to C1.

13. I don't mean to imply that it cannot be resisted. It can be resisted by providing a compatibilist account of "is able to do x". A promising beginning is the idea that someone is able to do X provided that the following are true: i) she has the ability to do X; ii) she has the relevant mental abilities and capacities—e.g. the ability to deliberate concerning the reasons for and against doing X, the ability to form a judgment based on her consideration of the reasons for and against doing X, and the ability to act according to her judgment; iii) none of the relevant abilities or capacities are impaired or malfunctioning (e.g.. due to drugs, hypnosis, extreme panic, etc.) and iv) there is no external impediment to her doing x.

14. See Fischer's *The Metaphysics of Free Will*, Blackwell, 1994, p. 178. Harry Frankfurt's famous argument for the thesis that we may be morally responsible even if determinism renders us unable to do otherwise was based on a thought experiment involving an agent who does something for his own reasons and who is intuitively responsible for what he does despite the existence of a powerful being, in the background, who would prevent him from acting in any other way. ("Alternate Possibilities and Moral Responsibility", *ibid.*)

15. P.J. Downing first directed our attention to the fallacious "backtracking" argument rejected by Sara in "Subjunctive Conditionals, Time Order, and Causation", *Proceedings of the Aristotelian Society* 59 (1958–59), 125–140. The fallacious argument is: "If Sara stepped on the ice, then it would not have melted this morning; if the ice had not melted this morning and Sara stepped on it, she would not fall through; therefore, if Sara stepped on the ice, she would not fall through."

16. If Bizet and Verdi had been compatriots, would they both have been Italian or would they both have been French? Is there a fact of the matter or does it all depend on what similarity respects matter most to the person considering the counterfactual?

If we focus only on counterfactuals of the Bizet/Verdi kind, we may be tempted to conclude that counterfactuals *never* have objective truth-conditions. But this conclusion would be, I think, premature. There are many different kinds of counterfactuals; it would not be surprising if some have, while others lack, objective truth-conditions.

17. "The Problem of Counterfactual Conditionals", *Journal of Philosophy* 44 (1947), 113–128. Reprinted as Chapter 1 of *Fact, Fiction, and Forecast*, Cambridge, Mass., 1984.

18. This way of putting it is mine, not Goodman's. But from his examples it's clear that he was thinking of counterfactuals which are *causal* (the fact or event referred to by the antecedent would be or would have been a cause of the fact or event referred to by the consequent) and *singular* as opposed to general insofar as they are uttered on some particular occasion with particular background conditions. (Eg. "if this match had been scratched, it would have lit"; "if that radiator had frozen, it would have broken:; "if that piece of butter had been heated to 150 F, it would have melted".)

19. I will use "choice" to refer to whatever mental event is either the cause or the first part of an agent's intentional act. You may substitute "intention", "decision", "volition", or whatever you think the relevant mental event is.

20. A "divergence miracle" is an event that is unlawful by the standards of *our* laws in the following sense: the conjunction of some earlier facts together with the fact that the event occurred entails the falsity of our laws. There are no events that are unlawful by the standards of the world at which they occur, so the worlds where the divergence miracle occurs are worlds where the laws are slightly different from our laws.

21. See, for instance, "Counterfactual Dependence and Time's Arrow", *Nous* 13 (1979), 455–476, reprinted, with Postscripts, in his *Philosophical Papers* Vol II, Oxford, 1986, pp.32–66. Lewis doesn't claim to be giving an account of singular causal counterfactuals; he makes the more ambitious claim that this is how we evaluate counterfactuals given what he calls "the standard resolution" for counterfactual vagueness. (*Philosophical Papers*, pp.33–34) As I read Lewis, the "standard resolution" includes, but is not necessarily limited to, those counterfactuals we entertain in contexts where our primary interest in in figuring out what the *causal upshots* of some particular event or action would be. Before giving his theory, Lewis acknowledges that there are some special contexts where we evaluate counterfactuals differently, and he gives as an example a counterfactual of the "if Sara had stepped on the ice at noon, then (given her cautious character), the ice would not have melted this morning" variety. He offers no theory for these "non-standard" counterfactuals.

I'm not sure whether Lewis is right in drawing the standard/nonstandard distinction in the way that he does, but I think that he is right about that subset of his "standard" counterfactuals in which our main concern is in figuring out the causal consequences of a particular event or action.

22. In saying this, I take myself to be saying something that Lewis would not (or should not) deny. That is, I think that if we apply Lewis's theory of "standard resolution" counterfactuals to the special case of agency counterfactuals, then the closest worlds where the agent intentionally does otherwise will always turn out to be worlds where the agent's choice (or intention, decision, etc.) is the divergence miracle. It should be noted, however, that Lewis does not make this claim in his discussion of the free will/determinism problem in "Are We Free to Break the Laws?", *ibid*. What he says

there is that *if* determinism is true, then if he had done otherwise, for instance, if he had raised his hand, then "the course of events would have diverged from the actual course of events a little while before I raised my hand, and at the point of divergence, there would have been a law-breaking event—a divergence miracle". This is consistent with the divergence miracle being the agent's choice, but it seems to leave it open that the miracle is some other, perhaps slightly earlier event.

23. Possible worlds semantics for counterfactuals was developed independently by Robert Stalnaker ("A Theory of Conditionals", *Studies in Logical Theory, American Philosophical Quarterly*, Monograph 2, Blackwell, 1968, pp. 98–112) and David Lewis (*Counterfactuals*, Harvard University Press, 1973) The use of possible worlds semantics as a tool for evaluating counterfactuals is neutral on different solutions to Goodman's problem, neutral on the question of whether counterfactuals have objective truth-conditions, and neutral on different conceptions of possible worlds.

24. This formula should be understood so that "closest" means "more close than any other" and it should not be assumed that closeness is a matter of degree. It's generally agreed that the closest worlds are similar to the actual world, but not everyone attempts to define closeness in terms of similarity.

25. I put it this way, in terms of events, to highlight that the counterfactuals under considerations are all counterfactuals where the antecedent refers to something that has causes and effects. Most philosophers think that causal relata are events, so that's how I've put it. If you think that causal relata are facts, feel free to substitute "if fact F", keeping in mind that F is the kind of fact that can be a causal relata.

26. See, for instance, G.H. Von Wright, "Causality and Causal Explanation", in *Explanation and Understanding*, Cornell University Press, 1971.

27. See for instance, Michael Dummett, "Bringing about the Past", *The Philosophical Review* 73 (1964), 338–359. See also David Lewis, "The Paradoxes of Time Travel", *American Philosophical Quarterly* 12 (1976), 145–152, and Kadri Vihvelin, "What Time Travelers Cannot Do", *Philosophical Studies* 81 (1996), 315–330.

28. There are different versions of what I'm calling "the Fixed Law" theory. What they have in common is that they try to solve Goodman's problem within the confines of a theory that says that the closest worlds all have the same laws as our world. The version I give below is, more or less, the one articulated by Jonathan Bennett in "Counterfactuals and Temporal Direction", *The Philosophical Review* 93 (1984), 57–91. (Bennett no longer endorses this theory; I describe it because it's the best version of a Fixed Law theory that I know.) See also Paul Horwich, chapter 10 of *Asymmetries in Time*, Bradford Books, MIT Press, 1989.

29. "Counterfactuals and Temporal Direction", p. 73, ibid.

30. See his *Counterfactuals,* ibid, p. 75 and "Counterfactual Dependence and Time's Arrow", in *Philosophical Papers* II, pp. 38–56, ibid.

31. *Counterfactuals,* p.75, ibid.

32. I criticised just one version of a Fixed Law theory—the version defended (but no longer endorsed—see note 28) by Jonathan Bennett. However, I think that similar objections will prove fatal to any attempt to provide a Fixed Law theory for *agency* counterfactuals. In saying this, I don't mean to imply that it's *never* appropriate to hold the laws fixed when we evaluate counterfactuals.

33. In making these arguments, I've appealed only to considerations about the evaluation of counterfactuals. I have not assumed that a deterministic agent has free will in the sense at issue in the free will/determinism debate. An incompatibilist might agree with everything I've said so far about counterfactuals, and still deny that any

deterministic agent can ever do other than what she does. Note, however, that such an incompatibilist needs to defend her position by way of something other than the No Opportunity argument.

34. The qualification "ordinarily" is necessary because there are unusual cases, involving "backup" interveners of the sort described in some Frankfurt stories (see notes 5 and 14) in which someone deliberates, chooses, and acts intentionally but could not have *successfully* acted in any other way.

35. For instance, circumstances of the sort described in some Frankfurt stories. See notes 5, 14, and 34.

36. This is the counterfactual question that we are guided by when we assert or entertain counterfactuals like "if Sara had stepped on the ice, she would have checked first to make sure it's safe" and "we can be sure that if Sara ever stepped on ice, she would not fall through".

37. I am grateful to Mark Balaguer, Jonathan Bennett, Mark Bernstein, Robert Bright, Curtis Brown, Randolph Clarke, John Fischer, Pieranna Garavaso, Carl Ginet, Ishtiyaque Haji, Mark Heller, Hud Hudson, Robert Kane, Tomis Kapitan, Barry Loewer, Michael Otsuka, Howard Sobel, Terrance Tomkow, Gideon Yaffe, and Michael Zimmerman for helpful comments on earlier versions of this paper.

Philosophical Perspectives, 14, Action and Freedom, 2000

CAUSAL DETERMINISM AND HUMAN FREEDOM ARE INCOMPATIBLE: A NEW ARGUMENT FOR INCOMPATIBILISM

Ted A. Warfield
The University of Notre Dame

"If I had to do it all over again, I'd do it all over again." Yogi Berra, 1998.*

I. Introduction

I will use the name "incompatibilism" for the thesis that freedom and causal determinism are incompatible and will call those who accept this thesis "incompatibilists". Most incompatibilists accept some version or other of the well known Consequence argument.[1] In Section II, I will identify and explore what I think is a serious difficulty for the best and most influential presentations of the Consequence argument. I do not, however, come to champion the cause of compatibilism. On the contrary, after my critical discussion of the Consequence argument, I will go on, in Section III, to offer a new argument for incompatibilism.

Consequence style arguments are typically formalistic elaborations upon the following simple line of thought:

> If determinism is true, then our acts are the consequences of the laws of nature and events in the remote past. But it is not up to us what went on before we were born, and neither is it up to us what the laws of nature are. Therefore the consequences of these things (including our present acts) are not up to us. (van Inwagen 1983, p.16)

Consequence arguments are united by their defining feature, the use of some sort of transfer of "powerlessness" (or "power necessity" or "unfreedom") principle. The transfer principle employed in such an argument, to use Timothy O'Connor's (1993) well chosen analogy, (allegedly) "slingshots" our powerlessness with respect to the past and laws of nature to yield powerlessness over the future via the strictly necessary link between the past, (deterministic) laws, and future.[2]

Using "no choice" as the relevant notion of "powerlessness" or "unfreedom", one powerful and influential version of the Consequence argument looks, at least in rough form, like this:

A CONSEQUENCE ARGUMENT

P1. No one has any choice about the past and laws of nature.

P2. Given determinism, the conjunction of the past and laws of nature strictly implies every truth about the future.

P3. No one has any choice about those propositions strictly implied by true propositions that no one has a choice about.

C1. So, given determinism no one has any choice about any future truth (including future truths concerning the allegedly free actions and decisions of human agents).

I am an incompatibilist and I endorse and am willing to defend a suitably developed version of the Consequence argument displayed above.[3] And many of my fellow incompatibilists have, over the past few decades, defended various versions of the Consequence argument with a high level of philosophical sophistication. Strangely enough, however, and though the compatibilist replies to these arguments have been, on the whole, quite weak, these defenses of the Consequence argument have not led to the universal acceptance of incompatibilism among contemporary philosophers. Indeed, the compatibilist position concerning freedom and causal determinism remains without a doubt the dominant position on the topic.[4]

In Section III I will offer a new argument for incompatibilism distinct from, and in my view at least as plausible as, the strongest versions of the Consequence argument. My argument will perhaps resemble some versions of the Consequence Argument in some respects. But my argument does not employ a "transfer of necessity" principle and so is not simply one more version of the Consequence argument.[5]

Before offering my argument in Section III, I will, in Section II, do two things. One thing I will do is attempt to dispel worries about the "proof like" appearance of my argument for incompatibilism. The other thing I will do, taking up the bulk of Section II, is point out and discuss a problematic feature of standard Consequence arguments.

II. "Proof" and a Formal Problem for Consequence Arguments

I will argue for incompatibilism by showing that necessarily, for all propositions X, if determinism is true and X, then no one is free to make it the case that $\sim$X. Some parts of my argument will have a "formalistic" or "proof like" appearance. This appearance, however, should not lead anyone to think that I am trying in any literal sense to provide a *proof* of incompatibilism (or anything else).[6] Rather, what I offer in Section III is merely an argument (a rather strong and convincing one in my view, but still, just an argument). The formalistic character of the presentation should not distract from this fact.

So far as I aware, all versions of the Consequence argument employ a "conditional proof" strategy; many also employ the terminology. Indeed, in most incompatibilist arguments the overall form of the argument is that of conditional proof. The argument typically looks like this: assume determinism and show that, given the assumption, no one has freedom. Most incompatibilists, however, either do not adequately understand or simply fail to adhere to a restriction relevant premises in such an argument must meet if the incompatibilist conclusion is to follow from such an argument. Most incompatibilists, to be precise, seem unaware that in order to get the incompatibilist conclusion that determinism and freedom are strictly incompatible (that no deterministic world is a world with freedom), their conditional proofs must not introduce or in any way appeal to premises that are merely *contingently* true in between the assumption of determinism and the step at which the "no freedom" conclusion is reached.

This is a simple point applying to any alleged conditional proof of a strict conditional. In general, to show by conditional proof that P strictly implies Q, one assumes the truth of P and derives the truth of Q, appealing only to P and necessary truths along the way to Q. In offering such an argument, one is restricted, on pain of modal fallacy, from appealing to merely contingent truths in between the assumption of P (which may be contingent) and the arrival at Q.

My evidence that typical proponents of the Consequence Argument are unaware of this restriction is that they defend only the truth, not the (broad logical) *necessity*, of the relevant steps of their arguments. To use the Consequence Argument displayed above as a model, incompatibilists typically defend the truth, but not the necessity, of (P1) of the argument. Introducing a merely contingently true premise into such an argument, however, weakens the justifiable conclusion of the argument considerably. Arguments weakened in this way show at most that the following conditional is true:

WEAK—If determinism is true then there is no freedom.

But this conclusion is strictly weaker than (it is implied by but does not imply) the proper incompatibilist conclusion:

INC—Necessarily, if determinism is true then there is no freedom.

Notice that (WEAK), if it is a material conditional, is true in every indeterministic world and is true in every world without freedom. While showing that the actual world is indeterministic would establish this reading of (WEAK), doing so would not establish the proper incompatibilist conclusion, (INC). One could defend a stronger contingent reading of (WEAK) as, for example, a counterfactual conditional, by arguing that the contingent premise appealed to in one's conditional proof is of suitable modal strength. Like (WEAK), however, such a conclusion would be strictly weaker than the proper incompatibilist conclusion. Finally, one could, in appealing to a contingent premise in one's conditional proof, defend a strict conditional asserting that the conjunction of determinism with some contingent truth, C, strictly implies the "no freedom" conclusion: necessarily, all deterministic worlds with C contain no freedom. But once again, this conclusion is strictly weaker than the proper incompatibilist conclusion. It is, I conclude, a mistake to appeal to a merely contingently true premise in the body of a "conditional proof" style argument for incompatibilism.[7]

This mistake, however, is apparently made by even the most prominent recent defenders of incompatibilism. Both Peter van Inwagen (1983) and Robert Kane (1996) defend the truth, but not the necessity, of relevant premises of their favorite versions of the Consequence argument. Both van Inwagen and Kane defend the truth, but not the necessity, of premises stating that, for example, "no one has a choice about the laws of nature." Indeed, van Inwagen has made it clear on more than one occasion that he is not even trying to defend the necessity of such premises.[8] The Consequence arguments of van Inwagen and Kane therefore appear to be in danger.

Because this charge of modal fallacy is a serious one and is being made against the flagship argument of contemporary incompatibilists, it is worth pausing to display and explicitly examine the most influential version of the Consequence argument to see that my complaint is justified. The version I have in mind is, of course, the third version of the argument offered by my distinguished colleague Peter van Inwagen.

In an amusing passage beginning Chapter Three of *An Essay on Free Will*, van Inwagen dismisses much of the literature on the incompatibility of free will and determinism. Here's the passage:

> Discussions of this question are usually not on a very high level. In the great majority of cases, they are the work of compatibilists and consist to a large degree in the ascription of some childish fallacy or other to incompatibilists.... . It is not my purpose in this book to defend any previous writer against a charge of fallacious argument. My own arguments will be explicit, and any fallacies they commit should be correspondingly visible. (It is doubtful whether anyone has ever been seduced by the fallacies with which the incompatibilists are customarily charged; if anyone indeed has achieved such a level of philosophical incompetence, I, at least, fall short of it). (1983, p.55)

Though I would never accuse van Inwagen of incompetence, I am making the charge of fallacy. Let's see if I can make the charge stick.

In *An Essay on Free Will*, van Inwagen offers the following argument for incompatibilism. Here are van Inwagen's abbreviations: Let "Np" abbreviate "p is true and no one has or ever had a choice about whether p", "□" abbreviate broad logical necessity, "⊃" material conditional, "P0" abbreviate the complete state of the world at some time in the distant pass, "L" abbreviate the conjunction of the laws of nature, and "P" abbreviate any truth. Here are van Inwagen's rules of inference: ALPHA: From □P, derive NP; BETA: From NP and N(P⊃Q), derive NQ. With this set up in place van Inwagen argues as follows:

Another Consequence Argument (van Inwagen)
1. □ ((P0 & L) ⊃ P)   Consequence of Determinism
2. □ (P0 ⊃ (L ⊃ P))   1
3. N (P0 ⊃ (L ⊃ P))   2, Alpha
4. N P0   Premise—"fixity of the past"
5. N (L ⊃ P)   3,4, Beta
6. N L   Premise—"fixity of the laws"
7. N P   5,6, Beta

Having thus reached the conclusion that no one has or ever had any choice about any truth from his assumption of determinism, van Inwagen concludes that freedom and determinism are incompatible.

Whatever virtues this argument may have (and it has many), and whatever additional vices it may have (and it has some), this argument most certainly exhibits the modal fallacy I have been discussing.[9] For the proper incompatibilist conclusion, (INC), to follow from the soundness of this argument, van Inwagen would need premises formally stronger than premises (4) and (6) above. Among other things, van Inwagen needs to defend not merely the truth, but also the necessity, of his claim that no one has a choice about the laws of nature. Van Inwagen, that is, needs to defend the truth of □ NL, not just NL.[10] Perhaps van Inwagen would be willing to defend this stronger premise (and the similarly strengthened version of premise 4). As the argument is presented in *An Essay on Free Will*, however, the argument, even if sound, does not establish the proper incompatibilist thesis. Instead it establishes only (WEAK) or some similarly weakened thesis. The time is ripe for a new and improved incompatibilist argument. I will provide such an argument in Section III.

As I stressed above, what I will offer in Section III is not a proof of incompatibilism. Rather, I will simply be offering a "semi-formal" argument for incompatibilism. I will, naturally enough, be quite interested to find out what step in the argument compatibilists wish to reject or call into question for I do not think that there is a "defective" step in the argument. But I have no doubt that at least the craftiest philosophers in the compatibilist camp will find something in the arguments that they feel should be rejected. They had better, for if nothing else my argument is valid and, if sound, implies the falsity of compatibilism. It follows that one wishing to confront the argument and hold onto one's compatibilism must reject some step in the argument. This does not imply (at least not by itself) that my argument "begs the question" against the compatibilist.[11] If it did, then, so far as I can tell, any formally valid argument would "beg the question" against those who do not accept its conclusion and all formally invalid arguments would, of course, be unsound: philosophical argumentation would thereby be reduced to absurdity.

III. An Argument for Incompatibilism

I now argue for incompatibilism. So that the argument can move right along once it begins, I introduce the following fairly standard abbreviations up front:

Let "D" abbreviate Determinism.
Let "H" abbreviate the conjunction of the complete state of the world in the distant past with the laws of nature.[12]
Let "Fsa" abbreviate "S is free to make it that case that a".
Use standard symbols for broad logical necessity ("□"), broad logical possibility ("◊"), and negation ("~") and use "⊃" for material conditional.

Compatibilists have traditionally maintained that one being free to, for example, stand at noon, does not require that one so standing be consistent with the actual past and laws of nature. On the contrary, compatibilists have typically maintained that one's being free, in circumstances H, to make it the case that P consists in it being true that one would make it the case that P were circumstances different in some specified respect. I was free to stand at noon just means, according to typical compatibilists, (something like): had I tried to stand at just before noon (or had I wanted to stand at noon) then I would have stood at noon. Such compatibilists therefore deny this key proposition:

1. □ ∀x∀s (Fsx ⊃ ◊ (H & x)).

A compatibilist needn't accept the common conditional analysis approach to freedom to be committed to denying (1).[13] All truths in a deterministic world are strict consequences of the past and laws of nature of the world in question. So any compatibilist committed to there being a deterministic world in which P is the case and in which one is free to make it the case that ~P is committed to denying (1). Furthermore, a simple argument leads from the acceptance of (1) to incompatibilism. Let's see how this argument works. After this argument I will provide a more complicated argument for (1).[14] Putting this simple argument from (1) to incompatibilism together with the later argument for (1) will give me an overall argument for incompatibilism.

I aim to show that the following proposition, expressing the incompatibilist thesis, is true:

CONCLUSION: □ ∀x∀s ((D & x) ⊃ ~Fs~x).

Determinism is the thesis that the conjunction of the past and laws implies all truths; that is

    2. □ ∀x (D ⊃ (x ⊃ □ (H ⊃ x))).

(2) is clearly equivalent to

    3. □ ∀x ((D & x) ⊃ ~ ◊ (H & ~x)).

(1) is trivially equivalent to (1′)

    1′. □ ∀x∀s (Fs~x ⊃ ◊ (H & ~x))

and from (3) and (1′) it follows that

    4. ~ ◊ ∃x∃s (D & x and Fs~x).

(4), plainly enough, is strictly equivalent to the incompatibilist conclusion I'm after, namely

    CONCLUSION: □ ∀x∀s ((D & x) ⊃ ~Fs~x).[15]

This simple argument shows that incompatibilism follows quickly if (1) is true. I will now argue for (1). I argue for (1) by showing that a certain obviously valid inference is in fact valid only if (1) is true.

Consider the following proposition (schema):

    5. P is true and there's nothing anyone is free to do in the circumstances that even might result in ~P.

It seems as obvious as just about anything that (5) strictly implies

    6. P is true and there's nothing anyone is free to do in the circumstances that would definitely result in ~P.[16]

For example, if Kelly is not going to win tonight's lottery and there's nothing anyone is free to do in the circumstances that even might result in Kelly's winning the lottery then it follows that Kelly's not going to win the lottery and there's nothing anyone is free to do in the circumstances that would definitely result in Kelly's winning the lottery. If there's nothing I'm free to do in the circumstances that even might get me out of going to the President's talk, then certainly there's nothing I'm free to do in the circumstances that would ensure that I get out of going to the President's talk. That (5) entails (6) seems obviously correct. (And before anyone complains or worries about possible equiv-

ocation caused by the "context dependence" of the phrase "in the circumstances"
note that (a) we can enforce a univocal reading of "in the circumstances" by
stipulation and (b) the argument would proceed exactly as it does substituting
the clearly univocal phrase "given the actual past and laws" for "in the circumstances" throughout the argument).

Compatibilists, I maintain, must reject the inference from (5) to (6). Compatibilists must do that because, as I will now argue, this inference is valid only
if (1) is true. (5), I maintain, should be understood as

7. P & $\forall s \forall x$ (Fsx $\supset \Box$ ((x & H) $\supset$ P))

and (6) should be understood as

8. P & $\sim \exists s \exists x$ (Fsx & $\Box$ ((x & H) $\supset \sim$P))

or, equivalently, as

8'. P & $\forall s \forall x \sim$ (Fsx & $\Box$ ((x & H) $\supset \sim$P)).[17]

I claim that (7) strictly implies (8') only if (1) is true.[18] I show this as
follows: assume (1) is false and show that given the assumption it follows that
there is a possible world in which (7) is true but (8') is false. The existence of
such a world would conclusively establish that (7) does not strictly imply (8').

Once again recall (1):

1. $\Box \forall s \forall x$ (Fsx $\supset \Diamond$ (H & x)).

Assume (1) is false and we get

9. $\Diamond \exists s \exists x \sim$(Fsx $\supset \Diamond$ (H & x))

equivalently,

9'. $\Diamond \exists s \exists x$ (Fsx & $\sim \Diamond$ (H & x)).

Instantiate and we get

10. $\Diamond$ (Fba & $\sim \Diamond$ (H & a).

Given (10), however, we can see that the truth of (7) does not guarantee the
truth of (8'). Let's see why this is so.

(10) tells us that there is a world, call it w, where agent *b* is free to make it
the case that *a* despite the fact that *a* is incompatible with the past and laws of
w. Because *a* is incompatible with the past and laws of w, it follows that $\sim$a is

a truth of w. Indeed, it follows that ~a is a strict consequence of the past and laws of w.

Recall (7):

7. P & ∀s∀x (Fsx ⊃ □ ((x & H) ⊃ P)).

Since P is just some true proposition, we can, in discussing (7), let P be ~a. Given this, the following proposition is an instance of (7):

11. ~a & ∀s∀x (Fsx ⊃ □ ((x & H) ⊃ ~a)).

We know from (10) that ~a is a truth of w, so the first conjunct of (11) is true. We also know from (10) that ~a is a strict consequence of H. It follows trivially that, for all propositions *x*, ~a is a strict consequence of the conjunction of *x* with H. So it follows that the consequent of the second conjunct of (11) is true and so the second conjunct of (11) is true. So in w, (11), an instance of (7), is true.

Now recall

8'. P & ∀s∀x ~(Fsx & □ ((x & H) ⊃ ~P)).

Having just shown that an instance of (7) is true in w, I now seek to complete this part of my argument by showing that the corresponding instance of (8') is false in w. Again, P is just any truth of the world in question. In discussing (7) we let P be ~a, so let's do that again. It follows that the first conjunct of (8') is true in w. What about the second? Instantiating (8'), and letting P once again be ~a, we can get

12. ~a & ~(Fba & □ ((a & H) ⊃ a)).

As already noted, ~a is a truth of w, so (12) is true just in case the following proposition is true:

13. ~ (Fba & □ ((a & H) ⊃ a)).

But (13) is true only if at least one of the following two propositions is true:

14. ~Fba
15. ~ □ ((a & H) ⊃ a).

But we know from (10) that in w agent *b* is free to make it the case that *a*. So (14) is false in w. And we also know from (10) that H strictly implies ~a and so that the conjunction of H and *a* is a contradiction and therefore strictly implies anything at all including, of course, *a*. (Alternatively, since *a* of course strictly implies a, the conjunction of a with anything, including H, strictly implies a). So (15) is false in w. But since (14) and (15) are both false in w, it follows that (13) is also false in w which implies that the relevant instance of (8') is false in w.

So, given the assumption that (1) is false, we have shown that there is a world, w, in which an instance of (7) is true, but the corresponding instance of (8') is false. This establishes that (7) implies (8') only if (1) is true.

As I showed earlier, however, the truth of (1) leads quickly to incompatibilism. For given the following proposition equivalent to (1),

1′. $\Box \ \forall x \forall s \ (Fs{\sim}x \supset \Diamond \ (H \ \& \ {\sim}x))$

and the following trivial consequence of determinism,

3. $\Box \ \forall x \ ((D \ \& \ x) \supset {\sim} \Diamond \ (H \ \& \ {\sim}x))$

it follows that

4. ${\sim} \Diamond \ \exists x \exists s \ (D \ \& \ x \ \& \ Fs{\sim}x)$.

And (4) is, as we also saw earlier, strictly equivalent to the incompatibilist thesis:

CONCLUSION: $\Box \ \forall x \forall s \ ((D \ \& \ x) \supset {\sim}Fs{\sim}x)$.

So compatibilists must deny the validity of the inference from (7) to (8'). As discussed above, the inference from (7) to (8') is just the formalization of the inference from (5) to (6). That is, this inference is just the inference from

5. P is true and there's nothing anyone is free to do in the circumstances that even might result in $\sim$P

to

6. P is true and there's nothing anyone is free to do in the circumstances that would definitely result in $\sim$P.

Compatibilists are therefore committed to the existence of a world in which P is true and there is nothing I'm free to do (in the circumstances I'm in) that even might make it the case that $\sim$P, but in which there is something I'm free to do (in the circumstances I'm in) that would definitely make it the case that $\sim$P. So, it appears that compatibilists must be open to the possibility, for example, that though there's nothing I'm free to do that even might get me out of attending the President's talk, there may well be something I'm free to do which would definitely get me out of attending the President's talk. To this I say "believe it if you can and if you are a compatibilist you have to believe it". I for one choose incompatibilism.[19]

Notes

* As quoted in *Sports Illustrated*, 9/14/98.

1. A few proponents of the Consequence argument are Carl Ginet (1991, Chapter 5), Robert Kane (1996, Chapter 4), and Peter van Inwagen (1983, Chapter 3).

2. Determinism is the thesis that the complete state of the world in the distant past nomologically necessitates the future. This implies, obviously enough, that the conjunction of the complete state of the world in the distant past with the laws of nature strictly (metaphysically) necessitates the future.

3. Though some additional work is needed (to, among other things, address the concerns of note 10), see Finch and Warfield (1998) and Warfield (1999) for partial defenses of versions of the Consequence argument. Finch and I respond to the common charge that causal indeterminism is incompatible with freedom and so provide assistance to those incompatibilists who also wish to endorse libertarianism (which adds the thesis that freedom exists to incompatibilism). See Crisp and Warfield (forthcoming) for replies to the best recent challenges to the main inference principle employed in most versions of the Consequence argument (van Inwagen's Principle Beta).

4. Peter van Inwagen has recently remarked that "compatibilism is nowadays widely regarded as implausible" (1997, p.373). (As recently as 1983, in *An Essay on Free Will*, van Inwagen called compatibilism the "received opinion (1983, p.v) and said that "incompatibilism can hardly be said to be a popular thesis among present-day philosophers" (1983, p.15)). Van Inwagen is mistaken about the current standing of compatibilism. This mistake is perhaps explained by the fact that most philosophers working professionally on issues concerning freedom and determinism are incompatibilists. Among philosophers generally, compatibilism is the majority position, at least according to my recent informal surveys on the matter.

5. My argument therefore at least seems to support John Martin Fischer in his ongoing dispute with van Inwagen over van Inwagen's claim that plausible incompatibilist arguments must employ (or "presuppose") some version or other of the transfer principle (van Inwagen's Principle Beta). See van Inwagen 1989 and 1994, Fischer and Ravizza 1992 and 1996, Fischer 1994 and 1996 and Warfield 1997. Elsewhere (Warfield 1997) I have severely criticized Fischer's response to van Inwagen on this point and I stand by that criticism. But while Fischer's defense of his thesis was flawed, his thesis may well be true. It is not clear, however, that my argument shows that Fischer's thesis is true. Depending on how van Inwagen and Fischer are understanding "presuppose" (and they do not tell us) my arguments may well presuppose the validity of some Beta like transfer principle. For what it's worth, I think that in the face of my argument the burden is on van Inwagen, should he wish to maintain his position in this debate, to show that my argument does presuppose the validity of a transfer principle.

6. At least if by "proof" one means (in part) a sound argument that no reasonable person could understand but not fully embrace.

7. The argument I provide in Section III will not contain this weakness nor will any part of the argument. My argument will be, without question, an argument for (INC).

My argument is not of the right form (conditional proof) to even possibly exemplify this error.

8. See van Inwagen 1977, p.107 and 1983 Chapter 3. I am not, to be clear, claiming that no argument containing a contingent premise could possibly lend support to the incompatibilist position. Rather, I am claiming that the particular type of incompatibilist argument favored by van Inwagen and Kane (a conditional proof of a broad modal claim) is invalid (and therefore does not support incompatibilism) if a contingent premise is introduced into the argument.

   Jim Stone helpfully discusses what I think is an instance of this general point in Stone 1998. Though I disagree sharply with Stone's overall position (Stone defends compatibilism) I am in broad agreement with his main critical point against the Consequence argument.

9. For a critical discussion of some of the other difficulties facing this particular version of the Consequence argument see Crisp and Warfield (forthcoming).

10. One wishing to defend the strengthened premise, □NL, might, but needn't, defend the thesis that the laws of one world are the laws of every world. "L", as part of such an argument could and probably should be indexed to individual worlds. I hope to elaborate upon this point and explore the possibility of defending such a strengthened Consequence argument on another occasion.

11. Whatever, exactly, that means and I'm sure it means something! See Roy Sorensen's interesting paper "Unbeggable Questions" (1996) for a powerful argument concluding that there is a fallacy of begging the question.

12. By "the complete state of the world" I mean, of course, only the complete *hard* past of the world (excluding, for example, true future tensed propositions). There is, unfortunately, no settled philosophical account of just what features of a time are the "hard" features of a time. Alvin Plantinga has correctly pointed out that typical Consequence arguments depend (and my argument may well depend) on the assumption that the laws of nature of a world are hard facts about times in the distant past. Like most incompatibilists, I accept that the laws are fixed in this way.

13. Compatibilists shouldn't, in my view, accept a conditional analysis of freedom. Such analyses are, so far as I can tell, hopeless for what are by now commonly accepted reasons. For one discussion of these difficulties (and other difficulties for compatibilists) see van Inwagen, 1983, Chapter Four.

14. One might be tempted to assert that no argument for (1) is needed. After all, (1) says only that a necessary condition for one's being free to make it the case that X is that X be broadly logically consistent with the past and laws of nature. This seems to state a quite weak necessary condition for freedom. If this is your reaction, I sympathize. If no argument for (1) is needed, then incompatibilism follows, as shown in the text. Because incompatibilism follows quickly from (1) it is worth trying to see if (1) can be defended in some way beyond the appeal to "obviousness". As argued in the text, I think (1) can be defended in a more productive way: the truth of (1) is required for the validity of certain clearly valid patterns of inference.

15. In an important and neglected paper Thomas Flint (1987, p.438) provided an argument for the conclusion that all compatibilists must deny something very similar to what I have called (1) (Flint's proposition replaces "x" in the consequent of my (1) with "S makes it the case that x"). Though there are important similarities between my argument and Flint's there are also differences. To note two differences: (i) as Flint formulates his argument it appears at most to establish (WEAK) not (INC); (ii) Flint seems to assume that compatibilists are committed to the existence of free-

dom. With suitable clarifications and simple corrections, however, I think that Flint's argument is sound. Flint does not, however, go on to defend the truth of his proposition in an attempt to argue for incompatibilism. Instead he merely points out that it would be dialectically inappropriate to simply assume the relevant proposition in criticizing compatibilism (no doubt he would say the same thing about my (1). Though I'm not sure he's right about this, it is important to note that I do not merely assume the truth of (1). I offer an argument for it.

16. In terminology introduced in Finch and Warfield (1998), the claim that (5) implies (6) is equivalent to the claim that the "might" reading of "no choice" implies the "would" reading of "no choice". In the conventions introduced in that paper, this is the claim that "Mp" implies "Np". Others who have discussed these different understandings of the "no choice" locution have agreed that the "might" reading obviously implies the "would" reading; see for example, McKay and Johnson 1996.

17. One might want to understand (5) and (6) using subjunctives rather than strict conditionals. I think that this would be a mistake. One preferring such a reading however could construct an argument parallel to the one in the text reaching the same conclusion. I leave the task of constructing the argument to those attracted to the subjunctive interpretation of (5) and (6).

18. Because so much turns on the symbolization of (5) and (6) as, respectively, (7) and (8), it is worth saying a bit more about this. In both (5) and (6) I'm understanding the phrase "in the circumstances" as stipulatively equivalent to "given the past and laws of nature". Given this, the translations seem straightforward. (5), translated as (7), says that P is true and every agent/proposition pair is such that if the agent is free to bring about the proposition then P is going to (still) be true even if the proposition is "added" to the past and laws. This is the clearest understanding of a proposition, the "~P" of (5), being such that (given the circumstances) no one is free to make it the case. Similarly, (6), translated as (8), simply says that P is true and there's no agent who is free to make some proposition true (to do something) that would, when "combined with" the circumstances, imply ~P. I take it that's exactly what it means to say that no one could, given the circumstances *ensure* that ~P.

19. My understanding of free will was shaped by an early reading of Peter van Inwagen's influential *An Essay on Free Will* and in discussions with Christopher Hill. I thank Paddy Blanchette, Marian David, Robert Kane, Michael Kremer, Tim O'Connor, Alvin Plantinga, Mike Rea and Dean Zimmerman for helpful discussion of this paper. An earlier version of this paper was presented at the University of Notre Dame where Tom Flint provided insightful commentary. Finally I owe a special thanks to Tom Crisp for his help and comments at several stages in the development of this paper.

References

Crisp, T., and T. Warfield: forthcoming. "The Irrelevance of Indeterministic Counterexamples to Principle Beta," *Philosophy and Phenomenological Research*.

Finch, A., and T. Warfield: 1998. "The *Mind* Argument and Libertarianism," *Mind* 107, 515–528.

Fischer, J.: 1994. *The Metaphysics of Free Will*, Blackwell.

Fischer, J.: 1996. "A New Compatibilism," *Philosophical Topics* 24, 49–66.

Fischer, J., and M. Ravizza: 1992. "When the Will is Free," *Philosophical Perspectives* 6, 423–451.

Fischer, J., and M. Ravizza: 1996. "Free Will and the Modal Principle," *Philosophical Studies* 83, 213–230.

180 / Ted A. Warfield

Flint, T.: 1987. "Compatibilism and the Argument from Unavoidability," *Journal of Philosophy* 84, 423–440.

Ginet, C.: 1991. *On Action*, Cambridge University Press.

Kane, R.: 1996. *The Significance of Free Will*, Oxford University Press.

McKay, T. and D. Johnson: 1996. "A Reconsideration of an Argument against Compatibilism," *Philosophical Topics* 24, 113–122.

O'Connor, T.: 1993. "On the Transfer of Necessity," *Nous* 27, 204–218.

Stone, J.: 1998. "Free Will as a Gift from God: A New Compatibilism," *Philosophical Studies* 92, 257–281.

van Inwagen, P.: 1977. "Reply to Gallois," *Philosophical Studies* 32, 107–111.

van Inwagen, P.: 1983. *An Essay on Free Will*, Oxford University Press.

van Inwagen, P.: 1989. "When is the Will Free," *Philosophical Perspectives* 3, 399–422.

van Inwagen, P.: 1994. "When the Will is not Free," *Philosophical Studies* 75, 95–113.

van Inwagen, P.: 1997. "Fischer on Moral Responsibility," *The Philosophical Quarterly* 47, 373–381.

Sorensen, R.: 1996. "Unbeggable Questions," *Analysis* 56, 51–55.

Warfield, T.: 1997. "Review of John Fischer's *The Metaphysics of Free Will*," *Faith and Philosophy* 14, 261–265.

Warfield, T.: 1999. "Donald Davidson's Freedom," in *Interpretations and Causes: New Perspectives on Donald Davidson's Philosophy* (edited by Mario De Caro), Kluwer.

Philosophical Perspectives, 14, Action and Freedom, 2000

FRANKFURT'S ATTACK ON THE PRINCIPLE OF ALTERNATIVE POSSIBILITIES: A FURTHER LOOK

David Widerker
Bar-Ilan University

I. Introduction

Jones has promised his sick uncle to visit him in the hospital. On his way there, he meets his friend Smith whom he has not seen since their school days. Smith, being eager to talk to Jones, invites him for a cup of coffee in a nearby restaurant. Jones is aware of the fact that if he accepts Smith's offer he will not make it to the hospital during visiting hours. However, after considering the matter briefly, he decides to accept Smith's proposal, succumbing to his curiosity and his desire to spend some time with Smith. So far there is nothing special about our story. It is a simple example of a conflict between duty and self-interest. It goes without saying that Jones is morally blameworthy for not keeping his promise to his uncle. He knew that accepting Smith's offer, in the situation under consideration, would be morally wrong. And although he could have avoided acting in this way, he did not. Now, however, let us modify the above story by adding the following assumption: Let us suppose that, un-beknownst to Jones, there is another person, Black, who for some reason does not want Jones to visit his uncle. Black has the power and the means to force Jones to decide to stay with Smith. But wishing to avoid showing his hand unnecessarily, he has made up his mind to intervene if and only if Jones does *not* show a sign of going to decide to break his promise to his uncle. Call that sign 'S1'. If Jones does show that sign, then Black does nothing, knowing that in this case Jones will decide to accept Smith's invitation. (It is assumed that Black knows Jones very well in this regard). All the other facts are the same as in our initial story. Call this example the 'Promise-Breaking Example'.

Harry Frankfurt is a vigorous opponent of the principle of alternative possibilities (Frankfurt 1969):

(PAP) An agent is morally responsible for performing a given act A only if he could have acted otherwise.[1]

The above story provides an illustration of an important assumption employed by Frankfurt in his attack on PAP:

> (IRR) There may be circumstances in which a person performs some action which, although they make it impossible for him to avoid performing that action, they in no way bring it about that he performs it. (Frankfurt 1969, 830, 837)

Frankfurt insists that in such circumstances (call them IRR-circumstances), the agent is morally blameworthy for what he did, even though he could not have done otherwise. Hence, according to him, PAP is false.

In (Widerker 1995a), I argued, adopting a libertarian position with regard to freedom and moral responsibility, that examples such as the Promise-Breaking Example fail to establish IRR and that, therefore, Frankfurt's argument against PAP does not succeed.[2] Most importantly, I tried to show that his argument fails when applied to simple mental acts such as deciding, choosing, undertaking, forming an intention, i.e., acts which for the libertarian constitute the *loci* of moral responsibility.[3] Essentially, my argument was this: Either the sign S1, which Black employs as a sign for not intervening, is (or is indicative of) something that, in the circumstances, is causally sufficient for Jones's decision at T to break his promise or it is not. If it is, then the example does not describe an IRR-situation, since the latter requires that the decision must not be causally determined. On the other hand, if S1 is not so associated with Jones's decision to break the promise, if S1 is merely a reliable indicator of it, then there is no reason to think that Jones's decision was unavoidable. In either case, the truth of IRR has not been established.[4]

In this article, I wish to advance the debate over the strength of Frankfurt's attack on PAP in two ways. First, I shall consider some new attempts to provide examples of IRR-situations and contend that they do not succeed either. Secondly, and more importantly, granting (for the sake of discussion) Frankfurt's assumption that IRR-situations are possible, I shall provide a comprehensive defense of PAP for one sense of 'morally responsible' that of *moral blameworthiness*.

> An agent is morally blameworthy for performing a given act A only if he could have avoided performing it.[5]

(Henceforth, whenever I refer to PAP, I shall be referring to this construal of it.[6]) I shall develop my defense of PAP (i) by questioning the moral assumptions employed by Frankfurt in his argument against PAP; (ii) by articulating and defending the basic intuition behind PAP; and (iii) by indicating how a defender of PAP might go about explaining away the intuition many share that in an IRR-situation in which the agent performed a morally wrong act, he is morally blameworthy for what he did.[7]

One thing that I hope will become clear as a result of my investigation is that Frankfurt and the PAP-defender are operating with two distinct conceptions of moral blameworthiness. Consequently, the controversy between them can be resolved (if at all) only by determining which of these two conceptions is more plausible. Though on this issue, I side with the proponent of PAP, I shall leave it to the reader to decide which account of blameworthiness she or he prefers.

II. The Examples

The Mele-Robb Example

The first example of an alleged IRR-scenario that I wish to consider is due to Al Mele and David Robb.

> Our scenario features an agent, Bob, who inhabits a world at which determinism is false... At T1, Black initiates a certain deterministic process P in Bob's brain with the intention of thereby causing Bob to decide at T2 (an hour later) to steal Ann's car. The process, which is screened off from Bob's consciousness, will deterministically culminate in Bob's deciding at T2 to steal Ann's car unless he decides on his own at T2 to steal it or is incapable at T2 of making a decision (because, for example, he is dead by T2.) (Black is unaware that it is open to Bob to decide on his own at T2 to steal the car; he is confident that P will cause Bob to decide as he wants Bob to decide.) The process is in no way sensitive to any "sign" of what Bob will decide. As it happens, at T2 Bob decides on his own to steal the car, on the basis of his own indeterministic deliberation about whether to steal it, and his decision has no deterministic cause. But if he had not just then decided on his own to steal it, P would have deterministically issued, at T2, in his deciding to steal it. Rest assured that P in no way influences the indeterministic decision-making process that actually issues in Bob's decision. (Mele and Robb 1998, 101–102)

Does this example establish IRR? I do not think so. There are two problems which seem to cast doubt on its coherence. The first one has to do with the following question: Given the presence of the deterministic process P, how is it that P does *not* cause Bob's decision to steal the car, but rather it is *Bob* who makes that decision on his own? In other words, what happens in that scenario to the causal efficacy of P so that at the time of decision it is absent? Call this problem "the Efficacy Problem". Suppose that this problem can be overcome by stipulating that, when the two processes are *about* to culminate in Bob's decision to steal Ann's car, the deterministic process P is somehow preempted. Then, there arises another problem that would need to be resolved: Given that P is now preempted and Bob decides to steal Ann's car on his own, there is the distinct possibility that at the last moment he might decide not to steal the car. In that case, the following counterfactual

(K) If Bob had not decided on his own to steal the car, P would have deterministically issued, at T2, in his deciding to steal the car,

would be false. The truth of (K), however, is crucial to the success of the Mele-
Robb example. Call this problem "the Divergence Problem".

Mele and Robb are fully aware of both these problems. To dispel them,
they extend their example in the following way:

> [There are] two different "decision nodes" in Bob's brain. The "lighting up" of
> node N1 represents his deciding to steal the car, and the "lighting up of node N2"
> represents his deciding *not* to steal the car. Under normal circumstances and in the
> absence of preemption, a process's hitting a decision node in Bob "lights up" that
> node. If it were to be the case both that P hits N1 at T2 and that [the indeterministic
> process] X does not hit N1 at T2, then P would light up N1. If both processes were
> to hit N1 at T2, Bob's indeterministic deliberative process, X, would light up N1
> and P would not... . [Furthermore], although if both processes were to hit N1 at T2,
> Bob's indeterministic deliberative process, X, would preempt P and light up N1, it
> is also the case that if, at T2, P were to hit N1 and X were to hit N2, P would
> prevail. In the latter case, P would light up N1 and the indeterministic process would
> not light up N2. Of course, readers would like a story about why it is that although
> X would preempt P in the former situation, P would prevail over X in the latter.
> Here is one story. By T2, P has "neutralized" N2 (but without affecting what goes
> on in X). That is why, if X were to hit N2 at T2, N2 would not light up. More fully,
> by T2 P has neutralized all of the nodes in Bob for decisions that are contrary to a
> decision at T2 to steal Ann's car (for example, a decision at T2 never to steal any-
> thing) In convenient short hand, by T2 P has neutralized N2 and all its "cognate
> decision nodes". (ibid., 104–105)

This story still does not vindicate their example. For one thing, it does not solve
the "Efficacy Problem". The reason for this is that, on their account, Bob's
decision to steal the car occurs at the same time (T2) as the hitting of node N1
by processes P and X. This being the case, it is hard to see how X could prevent P from deterministically causing Bob's decision. It would be simply too
late for X to accomplish that.[8]

Suppose now that we modify their story and assume that Bob's decision to
steal the car occurs *after* process P has been preempted by X. In that case,
Mele and Robb are still left with some form of the "Divergence Problem". To
see this, consider the possibility that, given that P has been preempted, Bob
rather than deciding on his own to steal the car, makes *no* decision at all at T2.
Suppose that he simply continues to deliberate what to do, or that he spontaneously stops his deliberation process and turns his attention to something else;
for example, to thinking about his old parents. Each such scenario is a genuine
possibility that is not ruled out by the modified version of the Mele-Robb example. Accordingly, I maintain that Mele and Robb have not given us a convincing example of an IRR-situation, as even on the more plausible construal

of it, Jones has an alternative possibility open to him. He has the power to *avoid* making the decision of stealing Ann's car.

Note that Mele and Robb cannot respond to this objection by arguing that the possibility that Bob makes no decision at all is ruled out by their (modified) example, since they stipulate that (in the absence of preemption) "a process's hitting a decision node in Bob's brain "lights up" that node", implying that Bob's decision to steal the car is caused by X hitting N1. For if they say that, then Bob's decision would be causally determined, in which case, their example again would not satisfy IRR.[9,10]

The Stump Example

Next, consider an example by Eleonore Stump:

> Suppose that a neurosurgeon Grey wants his patient Jones to vote for Republicans in the upcoming election. Grey has a neuroscope which lets him both observe and bring about neural firings which correlate with acts of will on Jones's part. Through his neuroscope, Grey ascertains that every time Jones wills to vote for Republican candidates, that act of his will correlates with the completion of a sequence of neural firings in Jones's brain that always includes near its beginning, the firing of neurons a,b,c (call this sequence 'R'). On the other hand, Jones's willing to vote for a Democratic candidate is correlated with the completion of a different neural sequence that always includes near its beginning, the firings of neurons x,y,z, none of which is the same as those in neural sequence R. (Call this neural sequence 'D'.) For simplicity's sake, suppose that neither neural sequence R nor neural sequence D is also correlated with any further set of mental acts. Again for simplicity's sake, suppose that Jones's only relevant options are an act of will to vote for Republicans or an act of will to vote for Democrats. Then Grey can tune his neuroscope accordingly. Whenever the neuroscope detects the firing of x, y, and z, the initial neurons of sequence D, the neuroscope immediately disrupts the neural sequence so that it is not brought to completion. The neuroscope then activates the coercive neurological mechanism which fires the neurons of neural sequence R, which is correlated with the act of will to vote for Republicans. But if the neuroscope detects the firings of neurons a, b, and c, the initial neurons of sequence R, the neuroscope does not interrupt that neural sequence. It does not activate that coercive neurological mechanism, and neural sequence R continues, culminating in Jones's willing to vote for Republicans, without Jones's being caused to will in this way by Grey.
>
> And suppose that...Grey does not act to bring about the neural sequence R, but that Jones wills to vote for Republicans without Grey's coercing him to do so. (Stump 1996, 76–77 and Stump 1999b, 303–4)

This example also fails to provide a successful illustration of an IRR-situation. It certainly fails to do so as it stands. The reason for this is that in Stump's story Jones's act of will to vote for a Republican candidate (henceforth 'W(R)') turns out to be causally determined by the neural firings a,b,c. This is so, since

186 / David Widerker

these events cause the completion of neural sequence R, which, Stump assumes, is an event (process) that is correlated with W(R). For if a,b,c cause the completion of R, and the latter is correlated with W(R), then they also cause W(R).

Admitting that her example is in need of modification, Stump might explain that the way she was conceiving of the relation between W(R) and the neural sequence R is that W(R), rather than being correlated with the *completion* of the neural sequence R, is correlated with that very sequence itself. On this account, then, a decision or act of will such as W(R) is a temporally extended process which is correlated with a neural sequence whose initial members causally determine the rest of the sequence. Furthermore, W(R) and R are assumed to occur simultaneously.[11] My previous objection does not apply, since now W(R) is not causally determined by a,b,c, whose occurrence, Stump assumes, is also not causally determined.

Although I do not find the above account of a decision plausible, I will not argue against it here. Fortunately, there is a simple and forceful argument that shows that even if one grants Stump's notion of an act of will or a decision, the agent in her story still maintains the power to refrain from his decision to vote for a Republican candidate and also has the power to act otherwise.

To see this, consider a scenario which is like the one described by Stump, except that it does not feature a counterfactual intervener like Grey. In that scenario, there would be no reason to think that Jones could not have decided otherwise. Now recall that, on Stump's view of decisions, once the neural firings a,b,c occur, Jones is bound to make W(R), i.e. he is bound to decide to vote for a Republican candidate. This means that the only way in which Jones could have decided otherwise in the above scenario, is by having the power to bring about the non-occurrence of a,b,c; a power that he would have before the occurrence of a,b,c and not after that. But if he has that power in the said scenario (as he surely does), he must also have it in the scenario featuring Grey. That the latter scenario includes a potentially coercive neuroscope does not change this fact, since its coercive influence would come into play only after the possible occurrence of x,y,z, that is, at a time that is later than the occurrence of a,b,c. Hence, it does not affect Jones's power to bring about the non-occurrence of a,b,c. Now, if Jones has the power to bring about the non-occurrence of a,b,c in the scenario featuring Grey, then, contrary to what is claimed by Stump, he also has it within his power in that scenario to refrain from his actual decision to vote for a Republican candidate.[12] Moreover, he also has the power to act otherwise, namely, by having the power to bring about the neural firings x,y,z whose occurrence in Stump's story is implied by the non-occurrence of a,b,c.[13,14]

The next two examples, which I will treat together, are attempts to construct an IRR-scenario by bringing into the picture an essentially omniscient agent such as God.[15]

The Hunt Example

Consider a possible world which Jones's decision to break the promise (D(B)) is foreknown by God. Hunt argues that this is an IRR-situation, because in these circumstances the decision is both unavoidable and causally undetermined. To establish its unavoidability, Hunt appeals to an influential argument for theological fatalism. According to this argument, if Jones were able to refrain from D(B), there would be a time T1 prior to the occurrence of D(B) and a possible future relative to T1, in which D(B) does not occur. But if divine foreknowledge exists, then the past relative to T1 contains God's infallible belief that D(B) will occur. And this implies that *every* possible future relative to T1 contains D(B). Hence, D(B) is unavoidable.[16]

Another Omniscient Agent Example

In this example, God is said to employ the following strategy to ensure the unavoidability of D(B) without violating the constraints on an IRR-situation specified in IRR: Before Jones makes his decision, God considers the following two conditionals:

(a) If Jones is in circumstances C, then provided no one intervenes, Jones will not decide at T to break his promise.
(b) If Jones is in circumstances C, then provided no one intervenes, Jones will decide at T to break his promise. (C are the circumstances in which Jones deliberates whether or not to break his promise to his uncle.)

Being essentially omniscient, God knows which of these two conditionals is true. Now, if He foreknows that (b) is true, he does nothing. On the other hand, if He foreknows that (a) is true, then shortly after Jones's deliberation process has begun, He intervenes and forces Jones to decide to break his promise. Suppose now that Jones is in C and (b) is true. It is not difficult to see that in these circumstances Jones does not have it within his power *not* to decide to break the promise. For suppose he had that power. Then, there would be a possible world W sharing its past with the real world up until shortly before T in which he exercises that power. Furthermore, this would be a world in which God abandons his policy to intervene iff he knows that (b) is true. But whether or not God abandons this policy is not up to Jones. Hence, though W is a causally possible world, whether or not it is actualized is not up to Jones. Hence, Jones dos not have the power not to decide to break the promise.[17]

Again, I am not convinced that these examples provide non-controversial cases of an IRR-scenario. To see this, let us recall the dialectical situation between Frankfurt and the libertarian. Frankfurt wanted to show that (i) the freedom pertinent to moral responsibility is an agent's acting of his own accord, and that (ii) this freedom cannot be identified with that of an agent's having the power to act otherwise. His attempt to prove IRR was meant to establish precisely these two points. Examining now the above examples from this point of view, it is not at all clear to me that they describe situations in which Jones can be said to be acting on his own. Since in them God is assumed to be infallible, the fact D(B) occurs at T is entailed (in the broadly logical sense) by the prior fact of God's believing at T' that D(B) occurs at T (T' is earlier than T). In this sense, D(B) can be said to be *metaphysically necessitated* or metaphysically determined by that belief of God.[18,19] Now, if a libertarian rejects as an instance of an agent's acting on his own a scenario in which an agent's decision is *nomically* necessitated[20] by a temporally prior fact (or a conjunction of such facts), why wouldn't he reject one in which it is metaphysically necessitated by a prior event? What, in my opinion, is crucial to the libertarian's conception of a free decision is that such a decision is not necessitated or determined in any way by an antecedent event or fact.[21] This condition is not satisfied in the examples under consideration. Now, one might object that metaphysical necessitation is not *nomic* necessitation. But why should this difference be a relevant one? If a decision is rendered unfree by the fact that its occurrence at T is entailed by the conjunction of some temporally prior facts together with the laws of nature, then why wouldn't it be rendered unfree if its occurring at T is entailed by God's prior belief that it will occur at T? If the critic still thinks that there is a difference between the two cases, it is incumbent upon him to explain why this is so.

III. Frankfurt's argument against PAP

My discussion so far suggests that it is far from clear that one can produce an unproblematic example of an IRR-situation. But, for the sake of argument, let us assume that such an example can be provided. How exactly do we get from there to the conclusion that PAP is false? Obviously, to complete his argument against PAP, Frankfurt must show that

(M) An agent who in an IRR-situation performed a morally wrong act is morally blameworthy for it.

How does he do this? The answer to this question is found in the following quotation:

> The fact that a person could not have avoided doing something is a sufficient condition for his having done it. But as some of my examples show, this fact may play no role whatever in the explanation of why he did it. It may not figure at all among the circumstances that actually brought it about that he did what he did... . Now if someone had no alternative to performing a certain action but did not perform it because he was unable to do otherwise, then he would have performed exactly the

same action even if he *could* have done otherwise. The circumstances that made it impossible for him to do otherwise could have been subtracted from the situation without affecting what happened or why it happened in any way.

....When a fact is in this way irrelevant to the problem of accounting for a person's action *it seems gratuitous to assign it any weight in the assessment of his moral responsibility*.(My emphasis) Why should the fact be considered in reaching a moral judgement concerning the person when it does not help in any way to understand either what made him act as he did or what, in other circumstances, he might have done?

This, then, is why the principle of alternate possibilities is mistaken. It asserts that a person bears no moral responsibility—that is, he is to be excused—for having performed an action if there were circumstances that made it impossible form him to avoid performing it. But there may be circumstances that make it impossible for a person to avoid performing some action without those circumstances in any way bringing it about that he performs the action. It would surely be no good for the person to refer to circumstances of this sort in an effort to absolve himself of moral responsibility for performing the action in question. For those circumstances, by hypothesis, actually had nothing to do with his having done what he did. He would have done precisely the same thing, and he would have been led or made in precisely the same way to do it, even if they had not prevailed. (Frankfurt 1969, 836–837)

As we can see, Frankfurt's argument in favor of M reads as follows:

1. The fact that in an IRR-situation an agent could not have avoided performing a certain act plays no role in the explanation of why the agent performed the act.
2. If a fact is irrelevant to the explanation of why the agent performed a certain act, then this fact has no bearing on the agent's moral responsibility for the act.
3. Hence, in the absence of any other excusing factors, M is the case.
4. Therefore, PAP is false.

What are we to say about this argument? Having granted Frankfurt the possibility of IRR-situations, its first assumption is certainly plausible. An IRR-situation is by definition such that though in it an agent could not have avoided performing a certain act, that fact plays no role in the explanation of why the agent performed the act. What about assumption 2. of the argument? Is it incumbent upon the defender of PAP to accept it as well? Here the answer seems negative. To see this, consider the following example by Carl Ginet:

A hurricane is approaching a coastal city. Smith, a resident of the city, mistakenly believes that by chanting an elaborate incantation [he] could cause the hurricane to veer off to sea and never strike the coast. Smith deliberates whether or not to mutter the incantation and (as [he] believes) thereby to prevent the impending disaster. But, [he] decides not to do so.(Unpublished manuscript)

Ginet points out that, on Frankfurt's 2., Smith would be blameworthy for failing to prevent the disaster. For the fact that he could not have prevented it was not among Smith's reasons for not preventing it. He would have decided not to prevent the disaster, even if he could have prevented it. Yet it is quite obvious that, in the situation under consideration, it would be wrong to blame Smith for not preventing the disaster. And part of the reason it would be wrong is that Smith could not have prevented it. To be sure, Smith may be held blameworthy for *not trying* to prevent it, or for *deciding* not to prevent it. But it would be wrong to blame him for failing to prevent it.

Ginet's example shows is that 2. is false, since sometimes the reason why we absolve an agent of the responsibility for performing (failing to perform) a certain act, is not the reason why he performed that act. Here is another example that illustrates this point. Consider a person, Green, who being strongly disinclined to go to work on a certain day because he does not feel like it, incidentally discovers that he is sick. He then decides not to go to work, being however fully aware that this is not the reason for his not going. (He would have missed work, even if he were not sick.) These facts notwithstanding, if Green were challenged later on to justify his not going to work, he could quite legitimately do so by referring to the fact that he was sick on that day.[22]

But there are even stronger counterexamples to 2. than the foregoing. Suppose that Green harms another person for some selfish reason, knowing very well that in doing so he is acting immorally. Surely the fact that Green knew that he was wrong to do what he did has a bearing on our considering him blameworthy for his act. But note that this fact played no role in the explanation of why he performed that act. He harmed the other person not *because* he knew that doing so is morally wrong, but despite his knowing that.

The earlier quotation from Frankfurt also suggests another argument against PAP. Central to it is Frankfurt's claim that

(1) An agent who is in an IRR-situation cannot cite the fact that he could not have avoided doing what he did as an acceptable excuse for his act.

Together with the assumption that IRR-situations are possible and his assumption that

(2) What PAP asserts is that a person bears no responsibility—that is, he is to be excused for having performed an action—if there were circumstances that made it impossible for him to avoid performing it (Frankfurt 1969, 837)

that claim also implies that PAP is false.

Assessing this second argument from the point of view of the PAP-defender, I believe that the latter would agree that *if* PAP is understood in terms of (2), then indeed it would be false for precisely the reason that Frankfurt mentions. For example, Jones would not be able to cite the fact that he could not have done otherwise as a genuine (explanatory) *excuse* for not keeping his promise to his uncle.[23] For he would have acted in the same way even if he could have avoided doing so. Something counts as an (explanatory) excuse for what an agent did, only if its absence would make a difference to the way that agent behaved, i.e. only if were it not to obtain, the agent would have acted differently. This, we know, is not true in the case of Jones. However, the defender of PAP need not accept Frankfurt's reading of PAP. More specifically, he need not and should not accept Frankfurt's identification of 'not being blameworthy' with 'being (explanatorily) excused', which implies that the only way that an agent can escape moral blame is by having an excuse. Both Ginet's earlier example and that of the person who is able to absolve himself of the responsibility for not coming to work by referring to the fact that he was sick, although this was not the reason for his not coming to work, suggest that this assumption is false.

IV. A Defence of PAP (The W-defense)

Can the defender of PAP go further? Can he also show that there are good reasons to accept PAP, reasons that would explain why in an IRR-situation the agent should not be deemed morally blameworthy for the act he performed? This question is important, since although many will agree that Frankfurt's argument against PAP is unconvincing, they may still think that IRR-situations provide intuitive counterexamples to PAP. They may emphasize the fact that in situations of this sort the agent acts freely, doing what he does for reasons of his own without being coerced or causally determined to do so. They may, therefore, rightly wonder why (in the absence of any other excusing factor) the proponent of PAP still thinks that such an agent should be exonerated. Can the PAP-defender allay this worry? I believe he can. To show this, let us focus on a specific example of an IRR-situation, say the Promise-Breaking Example described earlier. Now consider the following reply by the defender of PAP.

> Let me grant, for the sake of discussion, that in the IRR-situation under consideration, Jones acted freely in the sense that what he did he did for reasons of his own without being causally determined or coerced to so act. Still, since you, Frankfurt, wish to hold him blameworthy for his decision to break his promise, tell me *what, in your opinion, should he have done instead*? Now, you cannot claim that he should not have decided to break the promise, since this was something that was not in Jones's power to do. Hence, I do not see how you can hold Jones blameworthy for his decision to break the promise.

Call this defense the 'What-should-he-have-done defense' or for short the 'W-defense'.[24]

The W-defense points to an important reason why it would be unreasonable to judge an agent morally blameworthy in an IRR-situation. When we consider someone morally blameworthy for a certain act, we do so because we believe that morally speaking he should *not* have done what he did. This belief is essential to our moral disapproval of his behavior.[25] Sometimes, however, such a belief may be unreasonable. This happens in a situation in which it is clear to us that the agent could not have avoided acting as he did. To expect in that situation that the agent should not have done what he did is to expect him to have done the impossible. By implication, considering him blameworthy because he has not fulfilled this unreasonable expectation would be unreasonable.

The W-defense thus suggests the following general constraint on ascriptions of moral blame:

(PAE) An agent S is morally blameworthy for doing A only if in the circumstances it would be morally reasonable to expect S not to have done A.[26]

This principle, which may be called "the principle of alternative expectations", enables the PAP-defender to formulate an intuitive argument for PAP.

1. An agent S is morally blameworthy for doing A only if in the circumstances it would be morally reasonable to expect S not to have done A.
2. If S could not have avoided doing A, then on pain of expecting him to have done the impossible, it would be morally unreasonable to expect him not to have done A.
3. Hence, if S could not have avoided doing A, then S is not morally blameworthy for doing A.[27]

Note that PAE is a more general principle than PAP, since it can be used to explain why we sometimes exonerate an agent in situations in which his wrongful behavior was avoidable. These, for example, may be situations in which that behavior resulted from his being unaware of the causal consequences of some act of his, or where it can be traced to insufficient moral knowledge on his part. In each of these cases, there is no reason to assume that the agent could not have avoided acting wrongly. Finally, note that PAE can be further generalized so as to yield a full necessary and sufficient condition for ascriptions of moral blame.

A person is morally blameworthy for doing A iff in doing A he acted in a morally wrong way, and in the circumstances it was morally reasonable to expect him not to have done A.

V. Objections and Replies

In this section, I shall consider some potential objections to the W-defense. Their rebuttal will make my case for it and for PAE more convincing.

Objection 1: It seems implausible to exonerate Jones from blame on the ground that he could not have decided otherwise, or because there is no good answer to the question as to what he should have done in the situation under consideration. After all, Jones *himself* did not know or believe that he could not have decided otherwise.

Reply: The critic misses the point of the W-defense. He claims that one should not absolve Jones of moral responsibility on the ground that he could not have decided otherwise, because this fact cannot be cited by him as an (explanatory) excuse for what he did. He thus assumes that only by having an excuse can an agent escape the charge of moral blame. But this assumption is rejected by the defender of PAP. On his view, an agent can be absolved of moral responsibility even if he lacks an excuse, given that in the situation in question the agent cannot reasonably be expected to have acted differently. And an IRR-situation is precisely a situation of this sort.

But perhaps the critic means to suggest that Jones is blameworthy, because although he did not know that he could not have done otherwise, he nonetheless should have done what *he believed* was the morally correct thing to do, namely, to decide not to break the promise. Again, this is an unreasonable demand. For, in the IRR-situation under consideration, Jones could *not* have done what he believed he should have done.

Objection 2: What Jones's decision reveals about him is the same as what would be revealed by him had he been in a scenario in which he *could* have acted otherwise. Thus, since these two scenarios are morally equivalent and Jones would be deemed blameworthy in the latter scenario, Jones is also morally blameworthy in the actual scenario in which he lacks the ability to decide otherwise.[28]

Reply: The two scenarios are *not* morally equivalent. In the counterfactual scenario Jones is blameworthy for his decision to break the promise, because there he did something he knew was wrong that he could have avoided doing, and hence it was reasonable to expect that he should not have acted in this way. The same is not true of him in the actual scenario. Note, however, that our not considering Jones blameworthy for what he did in the latter scenario does not exhaust all that can be said about his conduct from a moral point of view. For example, Jones's decision in that scenario can still be assessed negatively in the sense that, having been made in disregard of the promise he gave to his uncle, it expressed a preference for his own self-interest over the fulfilling of his moral obligations.

Objection 3: Jones is blameworthy for the decision he made, because he made it freely, for reasons of his own, without being in any way forced or causally determined to make it. What he should have done was to bring it about that he does not make it *freely*.

Reply: The critic's complaint is unreasonable. Notice that not to make a decision freely means either not to make it at all or to be caused to make it. Since, in the situation under consideration, Jones could not have avoided the decision to break the promise, the critic's expectation that Jones should not have made that decision freely reduces to the expectation that Jones should have made it the case that he is caused to make it. But would it be reasonable to subject Jones to such an expectation? Clearly not. A person can be reasonably expected to make it the case that p only if he knows (or should have known) or has good reasons to believe that he should make it the case that p. But in our case the consequent of this principle is false. It is false, because Jones does not know that he is in a situation in which, if he does not decide to break the promise on his own, he will be forced to do so by Black. Consequently, he does not know that the morally correct thing for him to do is to cause Black to force him to decide to break the promise and by implication cannot reasonably be expected to do that.[29]

Objection 4: Contrary to what the W-defense implies, Jones should be held blameworthy for what he did in the IRR-situation under consideration, because he lacked the following characteristic which he should have had.

P: being such that, if placed in the kind of situation described in the example, he would not decide to break his promise.

If he had that characteristic, then Black would know this and would (shortly after Jones's deliberation process has begun) force him to decide to break his promise. And in that case, Jones would not be blameworthy for the decision he made.

Reply: The critic's demand of Jones is again unreasonable. If Jones was supposed to have P, because having it is conducive to his not deciding to break the promise freely, and the critic assumes that Jones had an obligation to that effect (i.e. an obligation not to decide to break his promise freely), then, as was pointed out in the reply to Objection 3, it is doubtful that he indeed had such an obligation.[30] On the other hand, if the critic claims that Jones had an obligation to have P on other grounds, then that may again be questioned. He certainly did not have such an obligation *once* his deliberation process has begun. For at that time, it was not up to him whether or not to have P, since then the only way in which Jones could bring it about that he had P would be by not deciding to break the promise, which in the situation under consideration we know was something that was not in his power to do. And he also did not have such an obligation *before* his deliberation process started, because at that time he did not have any good reason to believe that he lacked the said characteristic. The assumption here is not that Jones is suffering from some kind of character flaw of regularly violating the promises that he gives to his uncle or to other people. Rather, we are assuming that, on the whole, he is a morally conscientious agent who usually keeps the promises he makes.

VI. Explaining Away Frankfurt's Intuition

A complete refutation of Frankfurt's attack on the principle of alternative possibilities requires not only rebutting his argument and providing good reasons for holding that principle. It also requires explaining away his intuition that in IRR-situations the agent is blameworthy or culpable for what he did. Although this latter task requires a paper of its own and hence lies outside the scope of the present essay, I would nonetheless like to say something about the form that such an explanation might take. Basically, it is my view that in holding the agent morally blameworthy in an IRR-situation, Frankfurt (et. alia) are confusing moral blameworthiness with another negative moral evaluation of the agent. To see how this misidentification arises, let us go back to an earlier quotation from Frankfurt.

> What PAP asserts is that a person bears no responsibility—that is, he is to be excused—for having performed an action—if there were circumstances that made it impossible for him to avoid performing it. (Frankfurt 1969, 837)

This, as well as other passages, suggest that Frankfurt is identifying an agent's not being blameworthy for having performed a certain act with his having an excuse for that act. More specifically, it suggests that Frankfurt is operating with the following conception of moral blameworthiness

(F) An agent S is blameworthy for doing A iff in doing A he acted in a morally wrong way, and has no (explanatory) excuse for what he did.[31]

By contrast, the defender of PAP rejects F, replacing it with the principle

(PAE) A person is morally blameworthy for doing A iff in doing A he acted in a morally wrong way, and in the circumstances it was morally reasonable to expect him not to have done A.

Siding with the defender of PAP, let me refer to the negative moral evaluation captured by F as 'F-blameworthiness'[32] and reserve 'blameworthiness' for that captured by PAE. Note that these two evaluations are logically independent. An agent might be F-blameworthy for doing A (omitting A) without being blameworthy for so doing, and *vice versa*. An example of the first type would be an IRR-situation in which the agent acts in a morally wrong way. A less controversial example would be Ginet's example or the "sickness example" mentioned earlier. Still, another example of the same type is Van Inwagen's example in which an agent S witnesses a crime, but not wanting to get involved, decides against calling the police and does nothing. However, unknown to S, the telephone system has collapsed, and every telephone in the city will be out of order for several hours (Van Inwagen 1983, 165–66). Here, S is certainly F-blameworthy for not having called the police, since he does not have an (explanatory) excuse for this omission. But he clearly is not blameworthy for not making the call, since in the circumstances he could not have made it. He may, of course, be blameworthy for not having *tried* to call the police, but this is another matter.

Are there cases in which an agent is not F-blameworthy for doing A but nonetheless can be deemed blameworthy for so acting? I think there are. Consider the following example. S promises his son to pick him up after his soccer game but forgets to do so, thus causing his son to feel distress. Suppose also that, on the whole, S is a morally conscientious agent and that the reason for his forgetting was that he received some bad news about the health of some close friend of his. In this case, S does not seem F-blameworthy for not keeping his promise and for causing his son distress. But one might argue that, provided that S was not overwhelmed by the information he received, he could have been reasonably expected not to forget his duty as a parent and to come to pick up his son on time.

The suggestion that Frankfurt has confused F-blameworthiness with blameworthiness simpliciter nicely explains why he thinks that in an IRR-situation the agent is blameworthy for what he did, despite the fact that he could not have done otherwise. It also accounts for his thought that there is no morally relevant difference between an agent's conduct in an IRR-situation and his conduct in a similar situation in which he can act otherwise, as in each such situation the agent acts in a morally wrong way and has no good (explanatory) excuse for so acting. Finally, let me note that confusing blameworthiness with F-blameworthiness is a mistake one might be tempted to make also for another reason, which is that most often someone who has no good excuse for acting wrongly can reasonably be expected to have acted differently, and *vice versa*.

VII. Conclusion

There is a widely held view among moral philosophers that Frankfurt's attack on PAP constitutes a definitive refutation of the libertarian conception of freedom and moral responsibility. Elsewhere, I have argued against this conclusion by questioning the coherence of the type of scenario on which Frankfurt bases his attack (Widerker 1995a, 1995b). In this paper, I have tried to advance the debate over the plausibility of PAP further (i) by considering and rejecting more sophisticated counterexamples to PAP, and (ii) by casting doubt upon the moral assumptions underlying Frankfurt's attack. Furthermore, I have tried to articulate the basic intuition underlying PAP, and have also indicated how the defender of this principle might go about explaining away the intuition many have that, provided IRR-situations are logically coherent, the agent in such situations is blameworthy for what he did.[33]

Notes

1. I am assuming a fined-grained account of action, according to which an action is a dated particular consisting at least in part in an agent's exemplifying an act-property at a time. I use 'act-property' in Goldman's sense, according to which, an agent's having exemplified such a property does not entail that he performed an action, or that he acted intentionally. See Goldman 1970, 15–17. Although I adopt Goldman's use of 'act-property', I do not endorse his account of action.
2. By a 'libertarian position' I understand the view that an agent's decision (choice) is free in the sense of freedom required for moral responsibility only if (i) it is not

causally determined, and (ii) in the circumstances in which the agent made that decision (choice), he could have avoided making it. By a causally determined decision I shall understand a decision D occurring at time T which is either caused by another event, or is nomically necessitated in the sense that the proposition that D occurs at T is entailed by some conjunction of true propositions describing the laws of nature and state of affairs obtaining prior to T. Some libertarians regard a decision as free even though it was caused, provided it was caused in an appropriate way by an act of the agent that the agent could have avoided. Such decisions would be free at best in a derivative sense, one that I do not intend here.

3. These acts are simple in that they do not contain another act as a part.

4. See Widerker 1995a, 250–252, where I present an elaborate version of this argument. For similar responses to Frankfurt's argument against PAP, see Ginet 1996; Kane 1985, 51; Kane 1996, 142–143, and Lamb 1993. For a libertarian response to Frankfurt of a Reidian type, see Rowe 1991, 82–85.

5. This thesis does not apply to cases of *derivative* responsibility, i.e., cases where the agent is said to be blameworthy for an act by virtue of being blameworthy for the causal conditions that led to it. Obviously, the thesis under consideration would be false if it were meant to cover such cases as well.

6. This construal of PAP is in some sense broader and in another sense narrower than Frankfurt's original formulation. It is broader because, being formulated in terms of avoidability, it also covers the alternative possibility of the agent's not performing any act at all. But it is also narrower, since it concerns itself only with one aspect of moral responsibility. Neither of these differences, however, affects the dialectical situation between Frankfurt and the defender of PAP. If sound, Frankfurt's argument against PAP, would be equally effective against the version of PAP under consideration.

7. For a related, yet different, defense of PAP, see David Copp's illuminating essay in (1997).

8. Note that Mele and Robb cannot overcome this difficulty by appealing to their analogy of a widget-making machine—an analogy introduced by them to explain how it is that, although in their story P and X both hit N1 simultaneously, the decision that Bob ultimately makes is his own (Mele and Robb, 103). In that analogy, they ask us to imagine a widget-making machine which is surrounded by automatic guns shooting ball bearings (bbs) of different color at its receptor. The machine is designed in such a way that when hit by a certain bb, it immediately starts to produce a widget whose color is identical to the color of that bb. Furthermore, when hit simultaneously by bbs of a different color, the machine immediately starts to produce a widget whose color is determined by the color of the right-most bb. Though correct as far as it goes, this analogy leaves the problem raised in the text untouched. For, unlike in their neurological story in which Bob's decision to steal Anne's car occurs at the same time as the event of P and X hitting N1 at T2, the event of the machine starting to produce a widget occurs *later* than the event of its being hit simultaneously by two or more bbs.

9. Mele and Robb might try another move. Following Fischer (1994, 140), they might argue that the alternative possibility of refraining from the decision to steal Anne's by continuing to deliberate whether or not to do so, is not robust enough for considering Jones blameworthy for his decision to steal the car.
Reply: This move would be implausible for two reasons. First, it would commit them to conceding (contrary to what they claim in their paper) that their example is

not an example of an IRR-situation. Secondly, the defender of PAP might grant their point, but insist that in that case Jones should *not* be held blameworthy for what he did. For if Jones could not have decided otherwise, and the fact that there existed other alternative ways of refraining from the decision to steal the car cannot be appealed to in order to attribute to him the responsibility for his decision to steal the car, then, on balance, it would be unreasonable in those circumstances to expect of Jones to refrain from the decision he made, and, therefore, he should not be held blameworthy for that decision. This reply assumes that there is a conceptual link between an agent's being blameworthy for performing a given act, and it being morally reasonable to expect the agent not have done that act. I defend this assumption in sections 4 and 5.

10. In my discussion of the Mele-Robb example, I have not considered the worry that by neutralizing node N2, P might interfere with Bob's indeterministic decision-making process. For a criticism of their example that addresses this issue, see Kane 1999.

11. That this seems to be her view is strongly suggested by Stump 1999b, section 2 and footnotes 21 and 22; and Stump 1999a. Note that the neural sequence *must* be simultaneous with W(R). Otherwise, if R begins before the occurrence of W(R), then W(R) is causally determined by a,b,c, in which case Stump's story would again fail to describe an IRR-situation. Stump does not seem sufficiently aware of this fact. See Stump 1999b, fn.20.

12. Note that one cannot resist this conclusion by the claim that, because in the counterfactual scenario Jones is forced to decide to vote for a Republican, W(R) occurs in that scenario as well, in which case he would not have avoided making that decision. For the token-decision that Jones makes in that scenario is not identical to W(R), since it occurs after the occurrence of the neural firings x,y,z, that is, at a time which is later than the time at which W(R) occurs in the actual world. Here I am assuming that the (exact) time at which an act or event occurs is essential to it. An even simpler response is to say that, although in the said scenario Jones decides to vote for a Republican candidate, he does *not* decide to do so at T—the exact time at which W(R) occurs in the actual world. Surely it is the avoidability of his deciding *at T* to vote for a Republican candidate that is at issue here, since it is that for which he is held responsible.

13. This power does not, of course, amount to a power to make the alternative decision of voting for a Democratic candidate. But it could be still aptly redescribed as a power to *begin* to make that alternative decision.

14. For a different and illuminating criticism of Stump's example that also addresses other problematic aspects of it, see Goetz 1999a and Goetz 1999b.

15. By an essentially omniscient agent, I mean an agent who is infallible in the sense that it is impossible for him to believe a false proposition, and who is essentially all-knowing in the sense that he cannot fail to believe any true proposition.

16. See Hunt, 1996. For precursors of this example, see Fischer 1986, 55; and Zagzebski 1991, chap.6.

17. A version of this example was suggested to me in discussion by William Alston and Jerome Gellman. The difference between it and the previous example is that its proponent need not assume that God's foreknowing an agent's decision is incompatible with its being avoidable. Thus, he need not see himself committed to the argument for the unavoidability of D(B) employed by Hunt. As I shall argue soon, this difference does not make much of a difference.

18. Put more generally, an event E occurring at a time T is metaphysically necessitated by an event F occurring at time T' iff T' is earlier than T, and the fact that F occurs at T' entails the fact that E occurs at T.

19. Some think that, given God's essential omniscience, the fact that D(B) occurs at T is not only entailed by the fact that God believes at T' that D(B) occurs at T, but that it *also* entails the latter. But this is a mistake. What it entails is merely that the conditional fact that, if T' exists, then God believes at T' that D(B) occurs at T'. For there might be possible worlds in which a time such as T' does not exist.

20. A fact X is nomically necessitated by a temporally prior fact Y just in case X is entailed by the conjunction of Y and some laws of nature, and is not entailed by either conjunct alone.

21. For a constraint on libertarian freedom along precisely these lines, see Alston 1989, 164–165.

22. For an analogous example, see Ginet 1985, 176–177. For other, more complicated counterexamples to 2., see Berofsky 1987, chapter 4.

23. By an "explanatory excuse" I understand an excuse a person makes to deflect the charge that in his acting wrongly, he either acted for reasons which are morally reprehensible (e.g. lying in order to save oneself an embarrassment), or that his act (itself) revealed a lack of concern for morality on his part (e.g. Jones's deciding to accept his friend's offer, being fully aware of the fact that by so doing he would be violating a moral obligation.) Carl Ginet has drawn my attention to the fact that 'excuse' is sometimes also used in another way. For example, as pointed out earlier, 'I was sick' might be an appropriate answer by someone to the question 'What's your excuse for not showing up for work?', although it need not be an appropriate answer in the sense of 'excuse' referred to above. Accepting Ginet's point, I shall distinguish between an explanatory and a justificationary sense of 'excuse' and point out that, in what follows, I shall be using this term only in the former sense.

24. One may obtain a different version of the W-defense if in lieu of pressing the question "what should he have done instead?", one insists on the question "what should he have done to avoid being blameworthy for the act he performed?". These two questions yield different answers in certain cases of unavoidable acts for which the agent may be held derivatively responsible.

25. See Wallace 1994, chapter 4.

26. By 'morally reasonable' I mean morally reasonable for someone who is aware of *all* the relevant moral facts pertaining to S's doing A. Also, like PAP, PAE is not meant apply to cases of derivative responsibility.

27. This argument for PAP differs importantly from the argument for PAP I give in (Widerker 1991). The argument there employs the notion of moral obligation which is not equivalent to the notion of a morally reasonable expectation.

28. See Frankfurt 1975, p.118.

29. Cf. Ginet 1996, 407.

30. I use here the term 'obligation' in the sense of 'can reasonably be expected'.

31. See Frankfurt 1969, 838. This account differs from Frankfurt's official account, according to which an agent is morally responsible for performing a morally wrong act A iff that act is the result of the agent's identifying himself with the desire that moved him to do A. (Frankfurt 1975, 121). F has, however, the advantage of not being open to some standard objections to the official account. For example, unlike the latter, F does not have the consequence that an agent who acted wrongly due to weakness of will is not blameworthy for so acting.

32. We may also refer to the morally negative evaluation captured by F as 'inexcusability'. Note that inexcusability may take on different forms, as the type of moral vice that an agent may display in his acting wrongly may differ from one occasion to another. For a comprehensive typology of this aspect of moral wrongdoing, see Milo 1984.

33. I would like to thank Leonard Angel, Kari Coleman, Stuart Goetz, Bob Kane, Michael Morreau, Charlotte Katzoff, Jerome Gellman, Bill Rowe, and most especially Bob Bunn, Michael McKenna and Carl Ginet, for excellent comments and discussions on earlier versions of this paper.

References

Alston William P. 1989. *Divine and Human Language*. Ithaca: Cornell University Press.

Berofsky Bernard 1987. *Freedom From Necessity*. London: Routledge and Kegan Paul.

Copp David. 1997. Defending the Principle of Alternative Possibilities: "Blameworthiness and Moral Responsibility." *Nous* 31:441–456.

Fischer John Martin 1986. *Moral Responsibility*. Ithaca: Cornell University Press.

Fischer John Martin 1994. *The Metaphysics of Free Will*. Oxford: Blackwell Publishers.

Frankfurt H. 1969. "Alternate Possibilities and Moral Responsibility." Journal of Philosophy 66: 829–39. Reprinted in Fischer 1986.

Frankfurt H. 1975. "Three Concepts of Free Action II." *Proceedings of the Aristotelian Society*. supp. vol.II (1975), 113–25. Reprinted in Fischer 1986.

Frankfurt H. 1983. "What We Are Morally Responsible For." In *How Many Questions*, ed. L. Cauman. New York: Hackett.

Ginet Carl 1985. "Knowledge, Justification, and Reliability. *The Monist* 68: 175–187.

Ginet C. 1990. *On Action*. Cambridge: Cambridge University Press.

Ginet Carl 1996. "In Defense of the Principle of Alternative Possibilities: Why I Don't Find Frankfurt's Argument Convincing." *Philosophical Perspectives* 10: 403–417.

Goetz Stuart 1999a. "Stumping for Widerker." *Faith and Philosophy* 16:83–89.

Goetz Stuart 1999b. "Stump on Libertarianism and Alternative Possibilities" forthcoming.

Hunt David 1996. "Frankfurt Counterexamples: Some Comments on the Widerker-Fischer Debate." *Faith and Philosophy* 13: 395–401.

Kane, Robert 1985. *Free Will and Values*. Albany: SUNY Press.

Kane, Robert 1996. *The Significance of Free Will*.Oxford: Oxford University Press.

Kane, Robert 1999. "Responsibility, Incompatibilism, and Frankfurt-Style Cases." forthcoming.

Kim Jaegwon 1974. "Noncausal Connections." *Nous* 8: 41–52.

Lamb James W. 1993. "Evaluative Compatibilism and the Principle of Alternate Possibilities." *Journal of Philosophy* 90:497–516.

McCann H. 1974. "Volition and Basic Action." *Philosophical Review* 83:451–73.

Mele A. 1992. "Recent Work on Intentional Action." *American Philosophical Quarterly* 29:200–217.

Mele A. 1992. *Springs of Action*. Oxford: Oxford University Press.

Mele Alfred and Robb David 1998. "Rescuing Frankfurt-Style Cases." *Philosophical Review* 107: 97–112.

Milo Ronald D. 1984. *Immorality*. Princeton: Princeton University Press.

Rowe W. L. 1991. *Thomas Reid on Freedom and Morality*. Ithaca: Cornell University Press.

Searle J. 1983 *Intentionality*. Cambridge: Cambridge University Press.

Stump Eleonore 1996. "Libertarian Freedom and the Principle of Alternative Possibilities." In *Faith, Freedom and Rationality*, ed. Daniel Howard-Snyder and Jeff Jordan. (Totowa, N.J.: Rowman and Littlefield

Stump Eleonore 1999a. "Dust, Determinism, and Frankfurt: A Reply to Goetz." forthcoming in *Faith and Philosophy*.

Stump Eleonore 1999b. "Alternative Possibilities and Moral Responsibility: The Flicker of Freedom." *The Journal of Ethics* 3: 299–324.

Van Inwagen P. 1983. *An Essay on Free Will.* Oxford: Oxford University Press.

Wallace R. Jay. 1994. *Responsibility and the Moral Sentiments.* Cambridge: Harvard University Press.

Widerker David 1991. "Frankfurt on "Ought implies Can' and Alternative Possibilities." *Analysis* 51: 222–224.

Widerker David 1995a. "Libertarianism and Frankfurt's Attack on the Principle of Alternate Possibilities." *Philosophical Review* 104: 247–261.

Widerker David 1995b. Libertarian Freedom and the Avoidability of Decisions" *Faith and Philosophy* 12 (1995): 113–118.

Widerker David 1996. "Avoidability and Libertarianism," [together with Charlotte Katzoff] *Faith and Philosophy* 13:415–419.

Zagzebski Linda 1991. *The Dilemma of Freedom and Foreknowledge.* Oxford:Oxford University Press.

Philosophical Perspectives, 14, Action and Freedom, 2000

FREE WILL AND AGENCY AT ITS BEST

Gideon Yaffe
University of Southern California

Some kind of freedom—call it "freedom of action"—is undermined by ropes, chains and other physical constraints. And there is something that all of these constraints have in common—something that makes them all *constraints*: they stand as obstacles to the realization of certain choices.[1] Freedom of action, then, is dependency of conduct on choice; the reason that physical constraints undermine this kind of freedom is that they interfere with such dependency. The question needing to be tackled is this: What more does a full-fledged free agent—an agent who has all the kinds of freedom that we worry about when we worry about "the free will problem"—need beyond this rather limited kind of freedom? Sometimes nothing but fear and apathy, for instance, prevent us from coming to another's rescue; sometimes we are less than full-fledged free agents despite the fact that we are not tied down, our phones lines are not cut. We can be unfree even when nothing interferes with the efficacy of our choices, for things like fear and apathy can perniciously influence what we choose. What we lack in such circumstances is freedom *of will*. But what, if anything, is freedom of will?

This paper argues that two broad strategies for answering this question are mistaken. Many philosophers who have offered substantive theories of freedom of will have followed one or the other of these two strategies. The result is that we need a new approach. Towards the end, I suggest an alternative approach and give some reasons for thinking it promising.

The strategies which I am attacking here, and that which I propose, all depend on a particular conception of what we are doing when we offer an analysis of freedom. In particular, I assume throughout that a choice or action possesses a particular kind of freedom because of something about either what causes it, or the manner through which it is caused. We know, roughly, what feature an action's causal history must exhibit to be an instance of freedom of action: it must be caused by a choice to do it, where the choice is causally crucial: in the absence of the choice the agent would not have so acted. But what must the causal history of a choice be like for the choice to manifest freedom of will?

204 / Gideon Yaffe

What this approach implies is that those with a certain kind of incompatibilist bent are simply not going to be convinced by the view which I propose any more than they are convinced by the views which I attack. That is, there are those who think that the question of an agent's freedom with respect to what she does or chooses turns entirely on the modal limits placed on her potential choice or action by her circumstances or psychology. They see the question of whether or not an agent is free as being the question of whether or not, given relevantly similar circumstances and a relevantly similar psychological state, she "could" have chosen or done otherwise. For theorists of this sort, the central question about freedom is really a modal question turning on the precise modality expressed by the word "could". There are, of course, many senses of "could" under which it is always false that we "could" have done or chosen otherwise than we did given the very same circumstances—if, for instance, the only things that "could" occur are those that did occur—and there are other sense in which it is sometimes true and sometimes false depending on the nature of our circumstances and psychological states. The discussion here simply doesn't speak to those who construe the free will question as, ultimately, a question about the precise modality expressed by the word "could".

Answers to broadly metaphysical questions—such as the question of what it is to possess freedom of will—are often driven by some intuitive, but unsystematic, prior conception of the nature of that which is to be explained. Accounts of the nature of freedom of will have tended to fall into one of two camps, corresponding to two different pictures of what freedom of will is. For some, freedom of will is to be equated with self-expression in choice. According to this picture, the more our choices are *ours*, are grounded in and arise from something important about us, the more we approach freedom of will. For others, freedom of will is to be equated with self-transcendence. The agent who has freedom of will, on this conception, has a will that is responsive to and aimed at those aspects of her circumstances that are of genuine value, that are worthwhile guides of her choice; she is not a slave to herself, but manages to allow her will to express that which is worth expressing.[2]

Self-expression views are aimed at providing accounts of self-*determination* that are consistent with roughly naturalistic metaphysical assumptions. For self-expression theorists, self-determination is to be understood as causation of choice by certain events and states which, because of their relations to one another or to other states and events of the agent, constitute the kind of self that is crucial for moral responsibility, or for other forms of assessment that we might want to levy on an agent in response to a judgment of her freedom. According to such views, it is because her actions or choices express—that is, depend causally upon—deep structures in, or even constitutive of, the self that the agent can be said to have freedom of will.

I use the term "transcendence" to refer to self-transcendence views because for those who believe freedom of will to be equated with self-transcendence—with responsiveness to the evaluative or appropriately reason-giving facts—the ultimate explanation for the claim that a particular agent's choice manifests freedom of will appeals to the fact that her choice is pegged to some fact not about her, but about her environment. Susan Wolf gives an example which might help here.[3] Wolf describes two different agents both of whom answer "Carson City" to the question "What is the capital of Nevada?". The first gives this answer because she has been taught to so answer, the second because, in fact, the capital of Nevada is Carson City. The explanation for the second agent's answer appeals to the truth of the answer; the fact that she gave the answer she did is explained by citing the fact that that is the right answer. Similarly, the choices of the self-transcendent agent can be explained by citing the fact that what she chose was evaluatively optimal; she chooses as she does because what she chooses is best. Since egoistic subjectivism about value is false—what is best for an individual to choose is never a function solely of facts about herself—the choices of the self-transcendent agent are thought to be free not because they arise out of and depend upon aspects of herself (although they may) but, rather, because they arise out of and depend upon those features of her circumstances and psychology on which the value of what she chooses supervenes.

These two traditions of thought on the nature of freedom of will point to two distinct strategies for offering a philosophical analysis of the concept. Those who follow the first, hold self-expression to be both necessary and sufficient for freedom; those who follow the second, hold self-transcendence to be. Substantive theories of freedom of will can be developed by following these strategies and providing criteria which must be satisfied by self-expressive and self-transcendent agents, respectively. But, as I argue here, no matter how these criteria are formulated, both strategies are fundamentally flawed. Neither self-expression nor self-transcendence is either necessary or sufficient for freedom of will. It would be a mistake, however, to simply abandon these strategies entirely, for self-expression and self-transcendence are, somehow, relevant to an analysis of the concept of freedom. I go on to suggest that what this shows, although not definitively, is that a particular assumption about the nature of the concept of freedom of will is false. The debate over the nature of freedom of will has proceeded from the assumption—sometimes explicit sometimes implicit—that freedom of will is a descriptive concept, a concept of metaphysics. But, perhaps this is false. Perhaps, rather, freedom of will is a "thick concept"[4], a concept that is not purely descriptive, but also imputes a certain form of value to that which falls properly under it. To reach this conclusion, I claim, is to draw an inference to the best explanation: there are certain facts which are best explained if freedom of will is a "thick" concept. But more of this later.

My discussion is informed by a distinction between desire and will. On one natural conception of the will—although not the conception that I will be using here—all desires or desiderative attitudes are acts of will. This is to countenance a distinction between beliefs—attitudes with mind-to-world direction of fit—and desires—attitudes with world-to-mind direction of fit[5]—while denying there to be any important difference between willings and desires. On this conception, to want something is to will it. For my purposes here, however, it is important to note subcategories among the generic category of mental states with world-to-mind direction of fit. "Desires", as I will be using the term, are occurrent mental states that motivate us to act in ways useful (relative to our beliefs) for their satisfaction, but which are not governed by the same norms of consistency and coherence that govern willings.[6] It is irrational, for instance, to will both A and not-A, while it is not irrational to desire a state of affairs and at the same time desire that it not occur[7]. While there may be certain norms of rationality that govern desires, they are not the norms of consistency and coherence that govern choices. So, I divide the class of motivational states as follows: All motivational states have a world-to-mind direction of fit. Among those, some are governed by certain standards of rationality such as coherence and consistency and some are not. Those that are are willings, and this class includes a fairly wide range of mental states—choices, volitions, intentions—that may differ from one another but not in ways that are important for our purposes. Those that are not are to be called "desires".

It follows that it is possible not to will, or even to will contrary to, an action that one performs. While we may never act without a motive, we may very well be motivated by a desire rather than a choice, volition or intention. Notice that the word "action" is being used here in a broad sense. Volitional theories of action, for instance, reserve the word "action" for those events or states that are caused by volitions or other willings. There is much that is right about volitional theories, but, I will use the term "action" to refer to any state or event caused appropriately by a motive (although I simply won't give flesh to the word "appropriately" in this formulation) and leave open the possibility that states or events caused appropriately by willings have some important status (perhaps such events are *intentional* or *voluntary* actions).

One final preliminary point. In a number of places I draw on the idea of action performed "for a particular reason". I assume that the relation between a reason, or a mental representation of a reason, on the one hand, and an action performed for that reason, on the other, is causal. To act for a reason is for one's action to be caused in some special way by the feature of the world that is reason-giving, or by one's mental representation of a reason-giving feature, or, perhaps, by both. This is not a substantive theory of what it is to act for a reason, for I have not said what the relevant causal relation is. What is important for my purposes is only that actions performed for reasons have no special features that cannot be countenanced by a fully naturalistic theory of the mental. Just as an action's or choice's freedom is to be found in features of it's causal history, so too the distinctive mark of acting for a reason is to be found in features of the causal relation between the reason (or mental representation of it) and the action performed for the reason.

A Lesson from Standard Compatibilism

In the history of philosophy, at least one figure of towering importance thought that we didn't need a theory of freedom *of will* at all. Hobbes held that freedom of action was both necessary and sufficient for full-fledged freedom.[8] Hobbes was probably wrong. One way of diagnosing his error helps us to see the mistake that is made in equating self-expression with freedom of will. Let's formalize this view as follows:

> *The Standard Compatibilist Thesis*: An agent has full-fledged freedom with respect to action A iff (1) If she chooses to A she will A, and (2) If she does not choose to A, she will not.[9,10]

Even Hobbes encountered the following objection to this view[11]: the truth of conditionals (1) and (2) is not sufficient for freedom. There are unfree agents made unfree not by things like ropes and chains, but, instead, by psychological disorders, coercion, indoctrination, sometimes childhood trauma, and, in certain circumstances, even ignorance of the facts. But these forces undermine freedom not because they are obstacles to the realization of choices, but because they perniciously influence choice. Standard Compatibilism ignores, or dogmatically denies, that this is even possible.[12]

The Standard Compatibilist can respond to this objection by claiming that even the pernicious factors (psychological disorders, coercion, etc.) are obstacles to the realization of our choices and, hence, make the relevant conditionals false. And, this response seems, at first glance, to be satisfactory if, to take one illustrative example, coercive threats lead to action without that action being chosen. Perhaps, the Standard Compatibilist might say, when someone receives a coercive threat, overpowering desires are raised in her which bring her to comply with the threat regardless of what she chooses to do. Her desires control her action, the Standard Compatibilist might insist, thus detaching her will from the causal etiology of her compliant performance. Or, while she may choose to comply with the threat-induced desire, the desire would have, itself, been sufficient to bring about her compliant action regardless of what she chose. This Standard Compatibilist response relies on a seemingly implausible account of coercion, but what, exactly, is wrong with it?

One way to respond to this question is to begin with another: Is coerced action, on the Standard Compatibilist's analysis, intentional action? If not, then, on the Standard Compatibilist's analysis of coercion, coercion undermines freedom by undermining the intentionality, or voluntariness, of the actions it induces. The trouble is that many coerced acts that are rightly described as unfree—acts that are excused with expressions such as "I had no choice, he had a gun to my head"—are intentional. An agent might coolly calculate the results of non-compliance and decide, in the end, that it is better to do as the coercor demands, and, nonetheless, act unfreely. If the force that the coercor applies is sufficient to insure compliant action then the agent is unfree even if the coercor insures compliant *intentional* action. To utilize this response to the Standard Compatibilist is to shift the ground of debate from a question about freedom to a question about intentional action. It remains theoretically open to the Standard Compatibilist to insist that it is possible to act intentionally without one's will playing a crucial role in the causal etiology of action. Thus, the Standard Compatibilist might say, coerced actions are intentional, yet unfree, precisely because they are intentional actions brought about without the participation of the will of the agent. Is there something wrong with the Standard Compatibilist's analysis of coercion even if we grant her the possibility that coerced action, so analyzed, can be intentional action? That is, can we respond to the Standard Compatibilist's analysis of coerced action without shifting the debate to consideration of the nature of intentional action? The answer is "yes".

Start by distinguishing among three things: (1) the behaviors on the part of a manipulator that make it right to say that that individual is engaging in coercion of another, (2) the action that the manipulated performs as a result of and because of the pressures applied by the coercor, and (3) the causal mechanism through which the coercor's behavior succeeds in inducing the compliant actions of the coerced. The Standard Compatibilist provides an explanation for the unfreedom of (2) by appeal to the features of (3); that is, the Standard Compatibilist explains the unfreedom of the coerced conduct not by appeal to the fact that the conduct is coerced but rather by appeal to *the means through which* the coercive pressures are claimed to have their effect: they induce overpowering desires. However, imagine that an agent acts to comply with a coercive threat for the reason that the coercor has provided: I hand over the money precisely so as to avoid being shot. To know that an agent acted for the reasons supplied by the coercive manipulator is to know that the behaviors referred to in (1) cause (2) in some distinctive (undisclosed) way; recall, after all, that that is all there is to acting for a reason. But to know that I acted unfreely in response to coercion it is sufficient to know that the coercive behaviors provided my reason for acting as I did. In order to determine that I am unfree, we don't need to know (3); that is, we don't need to know how, precisely, it came to pass that I complied with the manipulator's demands in order to know that I am unfree. Thus, the Standard Compatibilist offers an explanation for the freedom-undermining force of coercion which is not consistent with an important pattern in our flow of concepts: our move from "acted for the reasons supplied by the manipulator" to "acted unfreely" is not mediated by any further concept such as "acted as a result of over-powering desires".

Notice that it does matter to freedom how coercion causes compliant action. That is, the coercive behaviors must provide the reason for the compliant action, and must, therefore, cause the action in some distinctive way. However, the features of the causal route from coercive pressure to compliant action that the Standard Compatibilist appeals to are not the distinctive features of the route from a reason to action performed for that reason. We often act for a particular reason without being motivated by over-powering desires. The point is that the freedom-undermining force of coercion cannot be explained by appeal to any features of the causal chain from coercive pressure to compliant action not already possessed by that causal route merely by virtue of the fact that it constitutes action for the reasons supplied by the coercion. What this implies is that, likely, the feature of the causal history of coerced acts by virtue of which those acts are unfree will be found merely in the fact that *coercion* is in their causal history and not in the facts about the particular way in which the coercion causes them. So long as it is true that it is sufficient for unfreedom to act for the reasons supplied by the coercor, this must be true, because there is nothing about acting for a reason generally which undermines freedom.

In the discussion so far, much is being built into the idea that the manipulator *supplies* the reasons for the action. We often "supply"—in some sense of "supply"—the reasons for the choices of another without thereby coercing that other: the chef supplies my reasons for choosing to buy the food by cooking it so beautifully; my wife supplies my reasons for choosing to take a trip by being the one that I want to travel with. Further, it is very difficult to specify the precise difference between the way in which a coercor "supplies" reasons for action and the way in which individuals supply such reasons in these cases. But such a specification will be part of an account of the nature of coercion. To coerce someone is to effectively supply her with reasons to act in some special sense of "supply" that I am not specifying here. But when someone else supplies one's reasons for action in the way that is distinctive of coercion, and one chooses in accordance with the reasons so supplied, one chooses without freedom of will. What this means is that the unfreedom which agents experience as a result of coercion comes from the fact that coercion is the source of one's reasons and not from features of the causal route through which those reasons induce compliant choice.

The Standard Compatibilist, then, provides a sufficient condition for the freedom-undermining force of coercion, but doesn't supply the *important* sufficient condition, for her explanation doesn't explain why, in general, coercion undermines freedom whenever the agent acts for the reasons supplied by the coercor's pressures. What this suggests is a very general methodological principle: When providing an explanation for why X undermines freedom, whenever an agent who acts for the reasons that X supplies acts unfreely, we must find a connection between X itself and unfreedom and not a connection merely between regularly found features of the causal sequence from X to action and unfreedom.

So Standard Compatibilism fails, but fails constructively, for its failure points to the need for care when considering how one's theory of full-fledged freedom accounts for the freedom-undermining influence of some particular feature of oneself or one's environment. This methodological lesson will become important in the next section.

Freedom of Will I: The Conditions of Self-Expression

One approach to understanding the nature of freedom of will starts with reflection on what is attractive about the account of freedom of action sketched already. While that account does give an explanation for the fact that ropes and chains undermine freedom, we can still look deeper: why do we take dependence of conduct on the will to constitute *any* form of freedom (even if not all that we take full-fledged freedom to be)? One possible answer—and there is another possible answer to be discussed in the next section—is this: when an agent's conduct depends on her will then part of what happens in the world tracks something about her; to know that an agent had freedom of action when she acted is to see particular occurrences (her bodily movements and certain of their results) as expressive of something about her: what she willed. On the flip side, to know that she had freedom of action with respect to an action that she did not perform is to know that something that was possible failed to happen because of something about her. When we have freedom of action, the way of the world (or at least some of it) is expressive of the state of our wills. The agent who has freedom of action, then, expresses an aspect of herself.

Encouraged by this result, we might turn to the cases of psychological disorder and the rest to see whether, perhaps, what those forces undermine is some other, deeper form of self-expression. And, in fact, it is something like this project that is undertaken by Harry Frankfurt in his widely read paper "Freedom of the Will and the Concept of a Person".[13] It is not enough for an agent's choice—what Frankfurt analyzes as, merely, "effective first order desire"—to be expressed in her conduct for her to be free; deeper facts about her—facts about her reflective attitudes—must be expressed in her choices. Her choices must arise from and depend upon[14] these deep structures in the self, thinks Frankfurt, if she is to have freedom of will. In later work[15], Frankfurt has made further efforts to specify both what structures of the agent need to be expressed in her choices and what relationship her choices must bear to those structures if the agent is to have freedom of will. And similar efforts have been exerted by other theorists as well.[16] But, as I argue in this section, it is neither necessary nor sufficient for the possession of freedom of will to be an agent whose choices are self-expressive.

To see that self-expression is not sufficient for freedom of will, think of the very cases that impugned the case for Standard Compatibilism: the cases of psychological disorder, coercion and indoctrination. An agent who is subjected to certain forms of brainwashing may come out of the treatment a fully integrated and wholly devoted subject, willing, perhaps, to sacrifice all in order to protect any hair on the head of her Leader. When such an agent goes through with it—whatever it is, and it could be *anything*, that is just what makes the very idea of brainwashing so nightmarish—she lacks some kind of freedom...at least, so it seems. It is not freedom of action that she lacks (we can suppose), so she lacks freedom of will. But why? Those who wish to analyze freedom of will as consisting in self-expression in choice must say one of two things in response: (1) the brainwashed don't lack freedom of will (and, hence, since they do not lack freedom of action, they are full-fledged free agents), or (2) the choices of the brainwashed are not self-expressive, or not self-expressive in the right way, or to the degree that they need to be.

Those who take the first route—who deny that the brainwashed lack freedom of will—are denying that it is even possible for someone who possesses the right kind of psyche—who enjoys the specified relationship between deep psychic structures and choices—to lack freedom of will. They hold that it is inconceivable for someone to purposefully induce those structures and relationships with the intention of making the agent choose in a certain way as a result of and in accordance with those structures *and* thereby undermine her freedom of will. We can see what is wrong with this position with a thought-experiment. Imagine that you are a self-expression theorist and you take it to be both necessary and sufficient for freedom of will that an agent's choice bear relation R to psychic structure C. Now imagine that you are given information about a particular case in stages. Stage 1: At the moment, agent S has no inclination or desire to choose to A, nor ought she according to any fair normative standard. Stage 2: Cruella has targeted S and decides to do what it takes to get S to choose to A. Stage 3. Cruella develops a plan of attack and executes it. Stage 4: S chooses to A as a result of Cruella's machinations. Stage 5: Cruella got S to choose to A by causing S to exhibit feature C, which, given the circumstances, was sufficient for S to choose to A and for her choice to bear R to C.

Given the information in Stages 1–4, it seems appropriate to view S as a pawn in Cruella's hands: Cruella aims at nothing but S's making of a choice that S has no reason, prior to Cruella's machinations, to make. And Cruella gets her way. How could this appear to be an instance of freedom of will on S's part? And if it does not, then how could it help to be told *how* Cruella pulled it off, as you are told in Stage 5? Notice that there are various elements of the case as described that might turn out to be important. Perhaps it is important that Cruella *aims* at inducing compliance of the relevant sort and succeeds. That is, perhaps Cruella would not undermine S's freedom of will if she, say, performed actions not intended to induce S's compliance but which happened, nonetheless, to do so. Those who deny that it is possible to undermine an agent's freedom of will through brainwashing that induces the appropriate "mesh" between deep psychic structures and choices must deny that factors such as these are relevant: a choice that comes about as a result of the right kind of psyche exemplifies freedom of will no matter what the source of the relevant psychological configuration.

The trouble with the second possible response—the assertion that those who are the victims of brainwashing are not actually expressing themselves appropriately—can be seen by asking the following question: What aspect of such an agent is failing to be expressed in her compliant choice? Whatever answer is offered—her genuinely reflective acts of identification, her true character, her considered self-conception—those aspects of the agent can, also, be under the control of the brainwasher; if they are, then they too might be expressed in the compliant choice of the agent, for exactly what the brainwasher does is to cause the crucial elements of the agent's psyche to be pointed towards compliant action. We might put this point in terms of a challenge: What is the difference between a fully-integrated and unconflicted agent who has become so through some neutral process of training—an agent, for instance, who has the Aristotelian virtue of bravery—and an agent who is just as unconflicted and devoted to a certain course of conduct as a result of brainwashing? We want to say that the former has freedom of will and the latter does not, but how can we say that within a theory that sees freedom of will as consisting in self-expression in choice?

We might try to answer this challenge by insisting that there is some crucial psychological difference between these two types of agent, a difference which manifests itself as a difference in self-expression. We might say, for instance, that the choices of the brave are available to revision under reflective scrutiny in a way that the choices of the brainwashed are not. Hence, the choices of the brave—in contrast to those of the brainwashed—express not just what the brave are in fact devoted to, but also what they would be devoted to were they to reflect in various ways. The trouble with this response is that it involves violation of the methodological principle described in the previous section. I explain.

We are assuming, at this point, that when an agent makes a choice for the reasons supplied by a process of brainwashing, she lacks freedom of will. The self-expression theorist might explain this by suggesting that brainwashing causes choices that are not available to revision under self-scrutiny; even if the brainwashed were to recognize after self-scrutiny that the potential choice is faulty, she would still choose in that way. This explanation notes a particular feature of the causal sequence from brainwashing to compliant choice: it is rigid; it cannot be changed even as the result of critical examination that finds it to be faulty. But this is not a feature of every causal process from a reason (or a mental representation of a reason) to action for that reason; nor is it a feature which must be possessed by the causal sequence from manipulative behavior to compliant action in order for that manipulative behavior to count as brainwashing; and, yet, whenever agents choose for the reasons supplied by a process of brainwashing, they lack freedom of will. Thus, the explanation picks out a non-crucial fact about a very large set of cases of choice in response to brainwashing and claims it to be the crucial feature.

An example might help here. In the film *The Manchurian Candidate*, a man is brainwashed in such a way that, afterwards, whenever a phone rings in a certain manner, he chooses to do whatever it is that the voice on the other end tells him to do. Let's grant that the process is such that even if he were to reflectively examine the action he is told to do, and even if were to conclude it to be a horrible, unacceptable act, he would still choose to do it. But is this the reason that he is unfree? No. All we need to know in order to know that his responsibility for his choice is severely diminished is to know that he chooses for the reasons supplied to him by the processes of brainwashing that he has undergone. If those are his reasons for choosing as he chose, then we know that he lacks freedom of will when he chooses, regardless of the features of the causal sequence from brainwashing to choice (except those that are required for him to be rightly said to be acting for those reasons).

The problem here is not specific to this particular explanation for the freedom-undermining nature of brainwashing, but is, rather, endemic to *any* explanation that the self-expression theorist might give. The problem is that the self-expression theorist tells us that when the causal chain leading to an agent's choice has feature Y, then that choice is self-expressive. Then, when faced with examples of causal chains leading to choice that have feature Y as a result of the manipulation of a brainwasher, the self-expression theorist insists that, in fact, brainwashing produces choices only through causal processes that *lack* feature Y, and, further, that is why the relevant choices are made without freedom of will. But, unless feature Y is incompatible with the special features of causal sequences by virtue of which those causal sequences are instances of taking as a reason, this response shows too much, for it shows that we aren't always unfree when our choices are made on reasons supplied by brainwashing, but only when they are supplied by brainwashing in a particular way. But this is false for reasons similar to those suggested by the Cruella example above: to know that a manipulator aimed at and succeeded in inducing a choice that the agent had no independent reason to make (the information described in stages 1–4) is to know that the agent's freedom of will is undermined even in the absence of knowledge of the particular means through which the manipulator succeeded in her endeavor.

We can see why self-expression is not even necessary for freedom of will by reflecting on the following case. "The Dutiful" is an agent who reliably chooses in the best possible way, all things considered, given her circumstances. Further, she not only chooses in accord with what is genuinely good, she tracks the good: for each of her possible actions, if that action were the best of her alternatives, she would choose it. The explanation for the fact that she made the choice that she made always appeals to the optimality of that choice. Often, although not always, the Dutiful chooses in a self-sacrificial way. Her particular desires do not take precedence over the desires of others; she chooses as she most desires only when what she most desires accords with what is genuinely best for her to do. Now imagine this person put to the test. Imagine, for instance, that, like Job, everything that she cares about, desires or hopes for is taken away from her, and all she needs to do to get it back is to, say, renounce God (assume this to be a non-optimal act). But she doesn't; she chooses instead to endure her suffering rather than to choose anything other than the best of her possible actions.

Is the choice of the Dutiful self-expressive in the requisite sense? What reason is there to think so? The Dutiful's choice is in conflict with every inclination she has: every desire, every whim, every hope that she has ever held or entertained remains unexpressed, even thwarted, by her choice. We often make choices that fail to be expressive of some of our desires: I choose to work instead of going to the movies not because I don't want to go the movies—I do—but because I need to work. But the case of the Dutiful is different: in certain situations, the entire desiderative side of the Dutiful's psyche plays no role in the production of her choice and, hence, remains unexpressed, unrevealed, by what she chooses. Could an agent whose choices fail to express the entire desiderative side of her psyche be self-expressive? If not, then the case of the Dutiful shows that self-expression of the requisite sort is not necessary for freedom of will.

Again, there are two ways to resist this conclusion: (1) Deny that the Dutiful has freedom of will, or (2) Deny that the choices of the Dutiful fail to be self expressive in the requisite sense. Neither answer is satisfactory.

The trouble with the first of these responses is that there are patterns in our practices that favor the thought that the Dutiful possesses freedom of will. For instance, when faced with two agents each of which has endured the Dutiful's travails where one has chosen as the Dutiful does and the other has given in to the substantial pressures to renounce, whom do we pity and whom do we praise? It is the latter, and not the former, that seems to have been "swept away", or to have not been herself, and the former that seems to have stuck her feet to the ground and not allowed herself to be moved by the forces applied to her. While she labors under substantial pressures to choose otherwise than she does, she does not seem to be under any pressure to choose as she does. How can an agent be unfree when she acts contrary to all of the forces that seem to be pushing on her? It seems that the primary motivation to deny the freedom of will of the Dutiful comes from adherence to an equation between self-expression and freedom and not from examination of the facts.

The trouble with the second response—the insistence that the Dutiful is self-expressive—is as follows: What is it about the Dutiful which is expressed in her choice? Say that the answer to this question is "feature C"—perhaps C is a feature of the Dutiful's character, a deep-seeded evaluative belief, or a disposition to engage in deliberative activities that help her to recognize the good. What about the case forces us to believe that C is expressed by the Dutiful's choice? Well, it seems that the reason to believe C to be expressed is either that it is conceptually impossible to make a choice without expressing feature C, or else that it is conceptually impossible to choose *the good* without expressing feature C.

The former answer can't be right since it implies that it is not possible to choose without expressing oneself in the way that is taken to be necessary for freedom of will. But then this kind of self-expression is an idle condition on freedom of will: no one can lack freedom of will by failing to so express oneself in choice, since it is not possible to both make a choice and so fail. To advocate this response is to return to Standard Compatibilism.

The latter answer—one cannot choose *the good* without expressing feature C—is better, but it is still problematic. The easiest way to make sense of it is to think of feature C as a capacity for recognition of the good together with the power to take the good as one's reason for action. It seems plausible enough that an agent could not really be said to be choosing the good if her choice was not expressive of capacities such as these. To express feature C, on this analysis, is to express something that any agent who chooses the good must express in order to be rightly said to be choosing the good. In a sense, feature C is given with a choice of the good. This suggests that the fact that the Dutiful's choice is self-expressive in this sense is not the crucial fact about the Dutiful that accounts for her freedom of will. The Dutiful is an agent who is self-transcendent. It is possible that an agent is only self-transcendent if in addition to expressing the evaluative facts in her choices, she expresses something about herself in her choices (feature C). But the question is this: which feature of the Dutiful is accounting for her freedom of will, her self-expression or her self-transcendence? If the latter, then self-expression is only necessary for the Dutiful's freedom of will because it is necessary for her self-transcendence.

Still, nothing said so far speaks definitively against this way of resisting the denial of the necessity of self-expression for freedom of will: so far, there is no reason to believe the Dutiful to be a counterexample to the claim that self-expression is necessary since she has freedom of will and is self-expressive in whatever way a self-transcendent agent must be in order to be self-transcendent. However, the trouble with this analysis of the case is that it doesn't allow the self-expression theorist to maintain a consistent account of the nature of the kind of self-expression thought to be necessary for freedom of will. To see this, consider another case: "The Aesthete" always chooses in such a way as to maximize aesthetic value in the world, and is utterly unaware of either moral or prudential value. The Aesthete, for instance, might live in abject poverty so as to fund an elaborate and promising project involving thousands of clones of Paul Cezanne. When asked questions about why she does this, she eloquently extols the virtues of Cezanne's work and complains bitterly of the tragedy of his death at the age of 67—"Ten more years, and who knows what wonders he might have produced!". When asked about the hardships which she endures, and the situation of the baby Cezannes in their hermetically sealed environments, she recounts the facts with interest, but simply doesn't understand why anyone would see those facts as providing any reason—even reasons outweighed by other reasons—to abandon her project.

Let's assume that the Aesthete has freedom of will—on what grounds, after all, could it be denied? The Aesthete is surely self-expressive—a whole range of attitudes and dispositions that are very particular to her are expressed in her choices. But does she express those aspects of herself that are thought to be expressed by the Dutiful? No. The Aesthete exhibits nothing at all to suggest that she even possesses whatever dispositions, attitudes and states are required to recognize and respond to value appropriately. Thus, if the Dutiful is thought to be self-expressive, she is not self-expressive in the same sense as the Aesthete. They have no form of self-expression in common; they don't express the same thing about themselves in their choices nor do they enjoy the same degree of accordance between their choices and other attitudes (the Dutiful, after all, chooses contrary to her desiderative attitudes, the Aesthete in accordance with them).[17] So, either the Dutiful is a counterexample to the claim that self-expression is necessary for freedom of will, or else the Aesthete is.

Freedom of Will II: The Conditions of Self-Transcendence

In the last section I suggested that attempts to cash out freedom of will in terms of self-expression might come about through reflection on what exactly is appealing about the account of freedom of action sketched earlier. Impressed by the fact that an agent who has freedom of action expresses herself in her conduct, we come to think that freedom of will, too, must consist in some form of self-expression. There is, however, another possible moral to glean from the appeal of the account of freedom of action, a moral that leads us towards a self-transcendence view of freedom of will.

As before, we can start with the following question: Even if freedom of action is not all that is involved in full-fledged freedom, why do we take it to capture any sense in which agents can be free? A possible answer to this question begins with a further question: why is it that dependence on the *will* of the agent, rather than on the agent's desires or whims, constitutes freedom of action? Perhaps the answer is that the will, as opposed to desire or whim, is capable of picking out states of affairs as "to be achieved" by virtue of the objective (or at least inter-subjective) value of those states of affairs. In the sense of "desire" and "will" used here, recall, there are certain rationality conditions on willing that do not govern desire. And, we might say, such rationality conditions apply to willing because willing has a point: when functioning correctly, the will aims us towards states of affairs with a force proportionate to their value. The critical phrase in this last formulation is "when functioning correctly": there are, after all, countless examples of choices that fail to aim at what is really, genuinely, valuable. And, this line of thought continues, perhaps this is just what freedom of the will consists in: the right functioning of the will, where the will functions rightly when it leads us to, and is responsive to, the actual value of chosen states of affairs.

Various theorist have reached this conclusion—although not always by quite this route. In contemporary philosophy, views of this sort have been expressed by Robert Nozick, Susan Wolf, Sarah Buss, Paul Benson[18] and in an interestingly different way by John Fischer and Mark Ravizza.[19,20] And this line of thought has a long and venerable tradition: leanings in this direction can be detected in the views of Aquinas, Descartes, Malebranche, Cudworth, Locke and Leibniz, to name a few.[21] To think of freedom of will along these lines is to think of freedom of will as consisting in a kind of self-transcendence. If one's choices are attuned to the evaluative features of one's surroundings, then one's will is guided by something capable of providing a better grounding for choice than can be provided by oneself. This is not to say that the will is not also guided by oneself—one may have an interest, either because of one's desires or wishes or values, to be disposed to choices appropriate to the value of one's circumstances, or, perhaps, as discussed above, it is simply not possible to be responsive to value in one's choices without also responding to the exercise of certain capacities such as capacities for the recognition of the good. In either event, choices that are responsive to value might also be self-expressive, but what makes them instances of the exercise of freedom of will is, rather, that they are attuned to the facts about value, facts that are not reducible to facts about oneself.

As in the case of the conditions of self-expression, satisfaction of the conditions of self-transcendence—whatever they are—is neither necessary nor sufficient for freedom of will. The following case is a counterexample to the necessity claim: "The Egoist" calmly and coolly assesses the value of the features of his circumstances and the likely results of his actions and chooses to act so as to further his own situation and satisfy as many of his own desires as possible, even if that involves trampling on the needs of others or in some other way realizing states of affairs that are intrinsically disvaluable. It seems clear enough that the Egoist possesses (or could possess) freedom of will. Does he transcend himself in his choices? Those who take satisfaction of the conditions of self-transcendence to be necessary for freedom of will are committed to saying "yes". But the claim that the Egoist is self-transcendent is only plausible when an attenuated conception of self-transcendence is invoked, a conception that seems to collapse into little more than an equation between self-transcendence and the necessary conditions of freedom of will. If the determination to satisfy one's own needs at the expense of others counts as self-transcendence, as responsiveness to the evaluative facts, then self-transcendence is just another word for freedom of will.[22]

The argument against the claim that self-transcendence is sufficient for freedom of will is somewhat more complicated. The trouble is that it is possible for agent's dispositions to recognize and respond to value to be activated by a manipulator in order to serve the manipulator's particular ends. This is so in a wide range of cases of coercion. To take a mundane case, if someone holds a gun to your head and thereby induces you to choose to give her money, she does so by making so choosing the best of your options, and thereby activating your ability to recognize which of your options is best and choose accordingly. But she thereby undermines your freedom of will, without undermining your self-transcendence: you recognize which features of your circumstances rightly provide reason for choosing as you do—most notably the manipulator's firm intention to kill you should you heroically refuse—and you choose in a way appropriate to those reason-giving features. Such cases, then, appear to be cases of agents who are self-transcendent, but lack freedom of will.

Just as the self-expression theorist, when faced with cases of brainwashing, felt the need to resist the first analysis of such cases by claiming that, in fact, they do not exemplify self-expression, the self-transcendence theorist will want to resist the natural conclusion to be drawn from coercion cases by claiming that they do not exemplify self-transcendence. A natural way to defend such

218 / Gideon Yaffe

a view is by defining self-transcendence in such a way as to rule out the possibility that the facts about value can be under the control of a manipulator while the agent is still self-transcendent. That is, one might say, to be self-transcendent is not to respond to the evaluative facts as they are, given the actions of a manipulator, but to respond to the evaluative facts as they would be in the absence of the manipulator's manipulations. The trouble with this answer is that it relies on an *ad hoc* distinction between the influence that a manipulator can have on the evaluative facts and the influence that other, quite random, forces can have. I explain.

Imagine a pair of cases: in the first, an agent faces a terrible result if she does not choose to A because a manipulator has promised to bring the terrible result about should she fail to so choose; in the second, the very same terrible result will come about if she fails to choose to A, but the result is assured because of facts quite indifferent to the conduct of the agent. In the first case, for instance, an evil force will cause an agent to be crushed by an avalanche should she choose to take the right fork, while in the second, the avalanche will crush her in just the same way should she make such a choice only because of the precarious position of the snow. According to the line of thought under discussion, if both agents choose to take the left fork for the reasons supplied by the manipulator or the precarious position of the snow, respectively, then the first is not self-transcendent, while the second is. But why? What is it about the influence of another person which takes away the kind of responsiveness to the evaluative facts enjoyed by the second agent?

Perhaps there is an answer to this question, but notice that any answer to it has a very difficult obstacle to overcome: while there might be something freedom-undermining about the influence of another person which could not be duplicated by indifferent forces—perhaps, for instance, the crucial fact is that manipulators, unlike random forces, don't just aim at, but also *track* the compliance of their victims—it isn't clear that any feature of manipulators could be found that isn't present also in cases in which we comply with the wishes of others and thereby reap advantage. To comply with a threat is to be unfree, to comply with an offer is not. The self-transcendence theorist, then, must be able to make both of two distinctions: a distinction between the effect on freedom of will of persons, on the one hand, versus natural forces, on the other; or a distinction between the effect on freedom of will of those who issue threats, on the one hand, and those who issue offers on the other. It isn't clear that a self-transcendence theorist can draw the first distinction without having trouble drawing the second, or draw the second without having trouble drawing the first.

Freedom of Will and the Nature of Evaluative Concepts

So, I take myself to have shown that neither self-expression nor self-transcendence is either necessary or sufficient for freedom of will. But there is something a little peculiar going on. The Dutiful seems to possess freedom of will by virtue of the fact that she is self-transcendent—that would seem to suggest that self-transcendence is sufficient for freedom of will, at least in that case. Similarly, the Egoist seems to possess freedom of will because she is self-expressive, and that would seem to suggest that self-expression is sufficient for freedom of will in her case. Further, in both cases, the relevant feature—self-expression or self-transcendence—seems necessary to the freedom of the individual described: if the Dutiful were to choose against all of her inclinations and desires but, at the same time, to fail to choose what she chooses because of the value of that choice, she would not be free; her choices would be unguided, they would be without satisfactory explanation. Similarly, if the Egoist consistently chose that which furthered her welfare but failed to express anything about herself, she would be, merely, a self-preservationist automata: a creature programmed to pursue her own welfare, but not because of anything deep or important about herself.

What is going on? There are a couple of possibilities: perhaps, we have yet to identify the right feature of agents by virtue of which they are free; or, perhaps, freedom of will must be analyzed as some complicated combination of conjunctions and disjunctions of the conditions of self-expression and the conditions of self-transcendence. Nothing that I've said rules out either of these answers. But there is some reason to think a third answer to be the right one: perhaps freedom of will is a thick evaluative concept.

Consider, first, an uncontroversial example of a thick concept: the concept of pretentiousness in art. We can imagine a series of descriptive features which contribute to, say, a novel's pretentiousness. For instance, if the dialogue in a novel is ponderous—if, that is, characters are frequently making speeches that consist of little more than statements of their philosophical beliefs or their stances on broad moral issues—this might contribute to the novel being pretentious.[23] A novel can be pretentious even if its dialogue is not ponderous and it can have ponderous dialogue and still avoid being pretentious—that is, ponderous dialogue is neither necessary nor sufficient for being a pretentious novel. But, nonetheless, the ponderousness of the dialogue is one of the factors that can be fairly appealed to in an argument that a particular novel is pretentious. Pretentiousness is a "thick concept": it is largely descriptive, but it also imputes to that to which it applies a particular form of disvalue. Determining whether or not the concept of pretentiousness applies to a novel is a matter of evaluatively weighing the novel's descriptive features in order to determine whether or not, taking into consideration the evaluative impact of each of the features, the novel possesses the particular form of disvalue that pretentious novels possess.

Freedom of will, I suggest, is a concept on the model of the concept of pretentiousness. While there are certain descriptive features that agents possess or lack that contribute to their having or lacking freedom of will—in particular, those features that contribute to their being self-expressive or self-transcendent—determining whether or not an agent possesses those features is not enough for determining whether or not the agent has or lacks freedom of will; we must also determine whether or not, by virtue of the possession of the particular combination of relevant descriptive features by the agent, the series of factors that contribute, causally, to the production of the agent's choice possess or lack value.

I am suggesting, then, that the agent who has freedom of will has choices that come about through worthwhile processes, processes possessing a certain kind of value; she approaches, thereby, an aspect of what we might call "agency at its best". If, in a particular circumstance, the attainment of self-transcendence requires the loss of some degree of self-expression, or vice versa, then it may be impossible for an agent to have all of the descriptive features relevant to free-dom of will. But such an agent can still attain freedom of will if, ultimately, by evaluatively weighing the particular degree to which she is self-transcendent at the expense of being self-expressive (or self-expressive at the expense of being self-transcendent) her choice-making processes realize, on balance, the appro-priate form of value. So, an agent has freedom of will when there is positive value to her choice-making mechanism, where the value of that mechanism is assessed by taking into consideration the value of both the degree to which she is self-expressive and the degree to which she is self-transcendent.

This account can be formalized by specifying when it is that a particular feature, F, of an agent's circumstances or psychology, which causally contrib-utes to an agent making the choice that she makes, makes a positive or nega-tive contribution to the agent's freedom of will:

> F, a feature of an agent S's circumstances or psychology, makes a positive (negative) contribution to S's freedom of will iff F's presence contributes more positively (negatively) to S's condition evaluated with respect to S's self-expression or self transcendence than F contributes negatively (posi-tively) to S's condition evaluated with respect to the other trait.[24]

Under this view, we can come to a judgment about an agent's freedom of will by applying this test to the conjunction of all the various factors that contribute causally to her choice. So, an agent possesses freedom of will without qualifi-cation, when F contributes positively to her freedom of will, and F consists of the conjunction of all the relevant features of her circumstances and psychology.[25]

Why should we think this story might be right? The reason is that the con-cept of freedom of will functions in various ways that are best explained if freedom of will is a thick evaluative concept. Notice that we learn a lot about a person when we learn what she takes to undermine freedom and what she takes to be irrelevant to freedom. Political conservatives tend to be unwilling to with-hold responsibility from a person just by virtue of the fact that that person is a victim of childhood abuse, or an addict, because they tend to think that abuse or addiction do not detract from freedom. Political liberals, on the other hand, tend to be willing to take a wider class of appeals as legitimately undermining the appropriateness of moral censure. We might wonder why it is that one's political and moral stances should have any influence at all on one's judgments of freedom or unfreedom. Whether or not an agent is free is not a political issue—although it has political repercussions in particular cases—and so liberals and conservatives shouldn't disagree about who is free and who not; they should disagree only about, say, whether or not an agent needs to be free in order to be justly punished by the state, an argument that might turn on the nature and purpose of punishment by the state, but not on the nature of freedom. If an agent's freedom is like any other descriptive trait of the agent—if the question of whether or not an agent is free has the same status as the question of whether or not the agent was, say, born in Alaska—then disagreements over value should not have an impact on rational assessments of an agent's freedom.

But such disagreements do have an impact on the rational application of the concept of freedom of will. Perhaps this is precisely because whether or not an agent has or lacks freedom of will is, in part, a question of value; answering this question—offering a judgment with respect to an agent's freedom of will—requires offering an assessment of the value or disvalue of the various aspects of her circumstances and psychology which contribute to the production of her choice. There is no reason to expect that such an assessment should, or even could, proceed independently of our evaluative dispositions and attitudes.

It is a commonplace of aesthetic and moral evaluation that the degree of value that we fairly place on that which we are assessing is, in part, a function of what we take to be reasonable to expect from it. It is no fair criticism of a circus that it fails to probe into the nature of the human condition; it is no fair criticism of a small child that she fails to lend support to her parents during their divorce. This fact, I claim, together with the view of freedom I'm suggesting, helps us to explain our intricate intuitions concerning the effect of childhood trauma on the freedom of the adult. A story about the childhood trauma endured by a seemingly wicked person can alter our evaluative tendencies, and thereby alter our judgment about the agent's freedom of will, by influencing our expectations regarding the degree of self-transcendence (or, in some cases, self-expression) that that agent might hope to have.

For instance, imagine that we are given the details of a person's crime and shown that that person knew the evaluative facts and represented them appropriately in her desires, but responded to those facts in a way that seemed to involve the taking of evil for good.[26] Such an agent fails to be self-transcendent in her choices—her choices are inappropriate to the evaluative facts—but there is no reason to think that she is not self-expressive: we can imagine, for instance, that she wholeheartedly and unreservedly does evil, that it is really *her* doing it. Now imagine two different cases. In the first we are given a further story about the loving and supportive environment in which this criminal grew up, and the early penchant that she showed for the infliction of pain that eventually developed into the enraged behavior that has characterized her adulthood. In the second we are given a further story about the terrible abusive circumstances of her upbringing and the prolonged agonies with which she has been inflicted. Given the first agent's early dispositions and tendencies, there is little reason to ever have expected her to get any closer to self-transcendence than she has, and hence the only relevant factors in evaluating the impact of her circumstances and psychology on her freedom of will are their impact on her degree of self-expression. But they have not contributed negatively to her tendency towards self-expression and so we judge her to have freedom of will. Or, to put the point slightly differently, when we see that she was not *turned* into a monster, but began with tendencies in that direction, it seems that the features that led to her criminal choices did not take anything from her, for we cannot reasonably expect her to have better dispositions towards choice in this respect. Neither have the circumstances of the second agent impugned her ability for self-expression: she is a monster and her monstrous qualities are expressed in her criminal choices. But in the case of the second agent, we think that she could have been self-transcendent; we think that she could have responded to value appropriately if only she had not endured the childhood trauma she endured. It starts to seem, then, that in the case of the second agent the abuse she has endured has taken something from her that she very well could have had: a genuine interest in and attraction towards what is actually good, a form of self-transcendence.[27] The circumstances of the second agent, then, seem to have taken freedom of will from her, for the disvalue of the impact of those circumstances, when assessed with respect to self-transcendence, has outweighed their value with respect to self-expression, because, as we learn from the story of her childhood trauma, there was more for her to lose than the first agent ever could. Various pieces of information—in this case information about the childhood histories of agents—effect our evaluative stances by setting baselines for evaluative judgment, and thereby effect our assessments of freedom of will.

Given the diagnosis of our intuitions about childhood trauma that I am offering, it might be objected, genetic flaws that give rise to, say, violent adult behaviors would not detract from freedom of will. But this seems wrong. Wouldn't we be more likely, the objection goes, to think someone's choice to perform a violent act to be made without freedom of will when that choice is the consequence of flaws in genetic make-up? This objection assumes, however, that the self is not something separate from those aspects of oneself that are dictated by one's genetic make-up. If genetic make-up is something that is imposed on the agent, in something analogous to the way in which childhood trauma is imposed on the agent, then our intuitions with regard to its impact on freedom can be analyzed in just the same way as childhood trauma: we will be likely to see it as detracting from freedom of will since it takes something away from the agent that she might have otherwise had (namely self-transcendence). However, if genetic make-up is constitutive of the self—if there is really no meaning to the thought that one is acted on by one's genetic make-up since there is no self to be acted on prior to the having of some genetic make-up— then it is not possible to think of genetic make-up as something that detracts from freedom of will. In this event, it doesn't detract from self-expression and it can only be thought to detract from self-transcendence if we can meaningfully imagine the very same agent as having a different genetic make-up. This is really a point about essential properties: essential properties of agents cannot be meaningfully examined for their impact on freedom of will, since assessments of freedom of will require evaluative comparison between an agent who has and an agent who lacks the relevant property. When the property is essential, this comparison cannot be meaningfully made.

How do we go about weighing the evaluative importance of self-expression and self-transcendence, in a particular case, in order to decide whether or not and to what degree an agent possesses freedom of will? Unfortunately—and this is why this paper offers only a *strategy for developing* a view of freedom of will rather than a full-blooded view of its own—I cannot really answer this question here. (How do we go about weighing, say, ponderousness and breadth of subject matter in determining the pretentiousness of a novel? The answer would require an essay of its own.) I take myself to have provided an account of which features are relevant to the application of the concept of freedom of will, and some reasons for thinking that their relevance is evaluative. But this leaves open the question of how, precisely, they are to be weighed, and without such an account it is impossible to say, in particular cases, which agents have freedom of will and which lack it.

Evaluation often proceeds in front of a background of purposes: when engaging in the kind of evaluation typical of legal thought, for instance, we keep an eye towards maximizing two potentially conflicting goods: the good of society and the good of individual members of the society. This complicated dual interest influences our judgments of legal responsibility.[28] When making certain sorts of aesthetic judgments—those typical in the criticism of art—we enter into the evaluative process with an interest in certain sorts of pleasure that can be found from the engagement with art objects, and which might, for instance, lead us to ignore the social good or evil consequences of the art object. We can expect evaluative judgments to vary in so far as we enter into the evaluative process with varying aims and interests. And, to the degree that this is so, what has been suggested here is that we can expect our judgments with respect to freedom of will to vary with our evaluative purposes and interests. We can expect, for instance, that our judgment that a particular criminal meets or fails to meet *mens rea* criteria in the criminal law to be different from the judgment that we make with respect to the very same agent's freedom of will when we are thinking of moral, rather than legal, responsibility. Depending on our purposes in inquiring about a particular agent's freedom of will, we may weigh self-expression or self-transcendence to different degrees in coming to our all things considered judgment of the value of the impact of the agent's circumstances and psychology on her will. If the rather tentative suggestion being made here is right, then an agent's freedom of will is to be judged by appropriately situated judges rather than metaphysicians.[29]

Notes

1. Sometimes thoughts of this sort are expressed not by appealing to what we choose, but, instead, by appealing to what we want or what we desire. However, as long as we take the will to be a distinctive capacity, different from the capacity for desire

(as I do—see the later remarks in the main text), there are obvious counterexamples to formulations in terms of desires or wants. I express this familiar thought in terms of choice, then, since I take it to be the strongest formulation.

2. For examples of theorists who have followed each of these various directions of thought, see the later sections entitled "Freedom of Will I: The Conditions of Self-Expression" and "Freedom of Will II: The Conditions of Self-Transcendence".

3. See Wolf, *Freedom Within Reason*, p. 72.

4. One of the earliest usages of the term "thick concept" is in Williams, *Ethics and the Limits of Philosophy*, p. 129.

5. It is in this sense that Michael Smith uses the term desire; cf *The Moral Problem*, pp. 7–8. See also G. F. Schueler, *Desire: Its Role in Practical Reason and the Explanation of Action*, especially the introduction and pp. 29–41, for a useful discussion of this and another conception of desire.

6. We sometimes use the term "desire" to refer not to an occurrent mental state but to a disposition to be in a certain occurrent state in certain circumstances. This is what we mean when we say, of the sleeping child, "She want to please her Daddy." We don't think she wants this right this second, but would in certain appropriate circumstances. As I am using the terms, the dispositional state being referred to here is not a desire but merely a disposition to have certain desires.

7. In his excellent book *Intention, Plans, and Practical Reason*, Michael Bratman identifies a series of norms of rationality governing intentions and other acts of will. See, especially, chapter 2.

8. Hobbes' view of freedom is expressed most clearly and explicitly in his essay "Of Liberty and Necessity". Following the publication of this essay, Hobbes engaged in an extensive correspondence over the issues with Bishop Bramhall. Hobbes's essay and much of the correspondence between Hobbes and Bramhall appears in Vere Chappell's *Hobbes and Bramhall on Liberty and Necessity*.

9. This condition could be formulated, with a little ingenuity, in any tense. I use the present tense here only for convenience.

10. Alternatively, the second of these conditional might be formulated as follows: (2') If she chooses to refrain from A, she will refrain from A. What makes (2) preferable to (2') is that we can construct cases in which an agent can only avoid A-ing by making no choice with respect to A. If, for instance, whenever I choose to refrain from tripping, I get so nervous that I trip, then I cannot avoid tripping by choosing to refrain from tripping. But I might, nonetheless be free, in some weak sense, with respect to tripping since I can avoid tripping by thinking of other things and thereby making no choice in favor or against tripping.

11. The objection was posed to Hobbes by Bramhall. See *The English Works of Thomas Hobbes*, v. 5, cf. pp. 40–41. Or Chappell, *Hobbes and Bramhall on Liberty and Necessity*, pp. 43–44. Bramhall puts the objection slightly differently than I do in the main text; but, Bramhall does emphasize that, according to Hobbes' definition of freedom, even creatures such as madmen and children—creatures who have no control over what they choose—are still free.

12. This objection is no different from the objection posed to conditional analyses of "can" by Roderick Chisholm. Chisholm claims that for it to be the case that an agent can do something it must be the case that she can choose to do it, and points out that advocates of the conditional analysis don't require this further condition (see Chisholm, "Human Freedom and the Self", p. 27). In my opinion, Chisholm is simply sensing that it is possible to undermine freedom by tampering with the way

an agent chooses without thereby tampering with the way the agent acts given her choices.

13. It is possible that views of this sort are not so far away from agent-causal theories of the sort that begin with Thomas Reid and continue in the work of Roderick Chisholm and, more recently, Timothy O'Connor and Randolph Clarke. (Reid, *Essays on the Active Powers of Man*, especially Essay IV, chapters 1 and 2; Chisholm, "Human Freedom and the Self"; O'Connor, "Agent Causation" and Clarke, "Toward a Credible Agent-Causal Account of Free Will".) The agent causal theorists do not describe their project as one of unpacking the conditions of self-expression, but, nonetheless, their project can be construed in this way. The agent causalists are concerned that if events or states, rather than agents, are the causes of conduct, then the critical fact about agents by virtue of which they are agents will remain unexpressed in conduct. That is, they take capability for action independent of the causal influence of any particular states or events to be the crucial agency-defining feature and think that choices that are not expressive of this feature—by virtue of being caused by the agent herself—are thus not free. Thus, the Frankfurtian and Reidian projects all aim to capture some sense in which our choices can succeed or fail to be self-expressive. The views differ in that Frankfurt (and those who offer related theories) attempt to capture the relevant sort of self-expression by appealing to certain crucial elements of the agent's psyche—in Frankfurt's original paper he appealed to what he called "second-order volitions"—and the relationship that they bear to other elements such as choices. The agent causal theorists, on the other hand, try to capture the special kind of self-expression by appealing to a special kind of cause: an agent, irreducible to any particular features of the agent.

14. The distinction between Frankfurt's willing addict and a recreational drug-user—someone who is not addicted but acts on a desire to take a drug and has an appropriate higher order attitude in support of that desire—must be made by appeal to dependence between the higher order attitude and the effective first order desire. The recreational drug-user's desire for the drug would not be effective were she not to have the higher order attitude in favor of it; not so for the willing addict. This difference is a difference in self-expression, and thus the degree of self-expression enjoyed by an agent, under Frankfurt's view, is a function, in part, of the counterfactuals which the actual causal sequence leading to choice possesses.

15. See, for instance, Frankfurt's "Identification and Externality", "Identification and Wholeheartedness" and "The Faintest Passion".

16. See, for instance, Friedman, "Autonomy and the Split-Level View", Neely, "Freedom and Desire", Stump, "Sanctification, Hardening of the Heart and Frankfurt's Concept of Free Will", Watson, "Free Agency" and Young, "Autonomy and the 'Inner Self'".

17. It remains open to the self-expression theorist to claim that, despite appearances to the contrary, the Dutiful and the Aesthete have some form of self-expression in common, or to claim that the requisite form of self-expression is disjunctive (an agent must express herself either in the way the Dutiful does or else in the way the Aesthete does, or...), but this further squirming would seem to have diminishing returns in the form of loss of unity in the concept of self-expression.

18. Nozick, *Philosophical Explanations*, pp. 317–362; Wolf, *Freedom Within Reason*, especially chapter 4; Buss, "Autonomy Reconsidered", and Benson, "Freedom and Value".

19. See Fischer, *The Metaphysics of Free Will*, especially chapter 8, and Fischer and Ravizza, *Responsibility and Control: A Theory of Moral Responsibility*. Fischer and Ravizza see the right functioning of the will, to use my terminology, as consisting in choice-producing mechanisms that are "reasons-responsive" in a special sense that they make an effort to define. Their central idea, however, involves thinking of freedom of will as consisting in routes to choice that are grounded in and responsive to features of circumstances that are relevant to making right choices, where "right choices" are just those supported appropriately by reasons. Put in this way, their view does seem to involve something like the strategy that I am discussing.

20. The view expressed in the works of Michael Smith (both by himself and with Jeannette Kennett and Philip Pettit—see Pettit and Smith, "Backgrounding Desire" and "Freedom in Belief and Desire", and Kennett and Smith, "Frog and Toad Lose Control", and Smith, "A Theory of Freedom and Responsibility") probably also belongs in this category. However, Smith et al's insistence that the aspect of their view which sounds like an account of self-transcendence is not rightly called autonomy, but, instead "orthonomy", suggests that they are not thinking of the view in quite the way that I am suggesting.

21. This is obviously not the place for a full discussion of the views of these various figures. A small sampling of texts that might begin to justify my sweeping historical claim here: Aquinas, especially *Summa Theologica* I.q 83, I-II.q 8, I-II.q 10; Descartes, especially the Fourth Meditation, AT VII 57–58; Malebranche, *Treatise on Nature and Grace*, especially Discourse III, sections 8–10; Cudworth, *A Treatise Concerning True and Immutable Morality*, notably pp. 26–27, and *Treatise of Free Will*, especially chapter 8; Locke, *An Essay Concerning Human Understanding*, II.XXI especially II.XXI.48–50; Leibniz, *Theodicy*, especially part I section 45, part II sections 228–235, and part III sections 310 and 319. For a discussion of the role that this line of thought plays in Locke's view of free agency, see my *Liberty Worth the Name: Locke on Free Agency*, especially chapter 1.

22. It might be argued, I suppose, that self-transcendence doesn't require actually choosing rightly, but, rather, choosing in a way that correctly takes into account where the good lies. Under this conception of self-transcendence, even the Egoist can be self-transcendent since he might carefully take into account what it is actually best for him to do and simply decide to do what furthers his own interests. He is responsive to the evaluative facts on this model, he just doesn't respond to them in the ideal way.

This conception of self-transcendence will only seem a viable theoretical option to those who take a strictly non-internalist conception of value properties. That is, those who think that to judge a particular possible one of one's actions to be morally valuable is to be motivated to perform it don't allow for the possibility that one could correctly judge a particular action to be the best of one's options and not be motivated to perform it more strongly than one is motivated to perform any other action. Thus, moral judgment internalists cannot accept the account of self-transcendence under discussion here. However, there may be room for those who reject moral judgment internalism to dispute the claim that the Egoist is a counterexample to the necessity of self-transcendence for freedom.

23. We might worry that the concept of ponderousness is itself a thick concept. Let's assume that it is not. Let's assume, that is, that something like the descriptive definition of ponderousness given in the main text is correct.

24. Notice that it is unclear in the absence of further argument whether or not determinism undermines freedom on this account. In principle, at least, it could be argued that deterministic choice-producing mechanisms possess disvalue, that their effect on self-expression and self-transcendence are, in the end, evaluatively negative. I myself do not know of a satisfying argument to this effect, but I leave it to others to debate the issue. Notice, however, that if it can be shown that the truth of determinism does not undermine the possibility of choice-producing mechanisms that allow either self-expression or self-transcendence, or both, then the theory will turn out to be compatibilist.

25. In "Self Deception and Responsibility for the Self", Stephen White reaches the following conclusion regarding the impact of self-deception on responsibility:

> We must drop the assumption that our practices of ascribing responsibility could have a justification in which discriminations in our ascriptions to different subjects are justified by differences in the intrinsic properties of those subjects' psychologies. (p. 478)

While the suggestion I am making is not as strong as this—for all that has been said, the value of the mechanism through which a person's choice comes about might supervene entirely on "intrinsic properties" of that mechanism—there is some affinity between White's view and the view I am suggesting.

26. An example, perhaps, of such a case is discussed at length by Gary Watson in his enormously thought-provoking article "Responsibility and the Limits of Evil: Variations on a Strawsonian Theme".

27. Some readers may be disturbed by my usages of "could" here. After all, they might say, exactly what we are trying to understand when we give accounts of freedom is in what sense, exactly, alternative scenarios need to be available to agents for freedom. But, the sense of "could" I am invoking is very wan indeed and gets nowhere near amounting to the "could" analyzed by an adequate account of freedom. In particular, there is no reason to think that the agent herself could have done anything to bring it about that she be closer to being self-transcendent; it is simply the case that under different early influences, she would have come to have a different character, and not through any action on her part.

28. See Feinberg, "Problematic Responsibility in Law and Morals" for a marvelous discussion of the ways in which the purposes which we have when assessing legal responsibility differ from those involved in assessing moral responsibility.

29. Thanks to Sarah Buss, Vere Chappell, Phillip Clark, Andrew Eschelman, John Fischer, Paul Hoffman, Elijah Millgram, John Perry, Vance Ricks, Jennifer Rosner, Marleen Rozemond, Kadri Vihvelin, and Gary Watson for comments on this paper or its recent ancestors. Portions of this material were presented to the philosophy departments at the University of California at Irvine and Arizona State University. In both cases I received valuable comments. Special thanks to Michael Bratman for his infinite willingness to re-read, and for always seeing exactly what needs to be fixed.

References

Aquinas, T. [1270] (1945) *Basic Writings of Saint Thomas Aquinas*, Random House, New York.
Benson, P. (1987) "Freedom and Value", in *Journal of Philosophy*, pp. 465–486.

Bratman, M. (1987) *Intention, Plans, and Practical Reason*, Harvard University Press, Cambridge.

Buss, S. (1994) "Autonomy Reconsidered", in *Midwest Studies in Philosophy*, v. 19, pp. 95–121.

Chappell, V. (ed.) (1999) *Hobbes and Bramhall on Liberty and Necessity*, Cambridge University Press, Cambridge.

Chisholm, R. (1964) "Human Freedom and the Self", in Watson, G. (ed) *Free Will*, pp. 24–35, Oxford University Press, Oxford, 1982.

Clarke, R. (1993) "Toward a Credible Agent-Causal Account of Free Will", in O'Connor, T. (ed) *Agents, Causes and Events: Essays on Indeterminism and Free Will*, pp. 201–215, Oxford University Press, New York, 1995.

Cudworth, R. [1731] (1996) *A Treatise Concerning True and Immutable Morality*, Hutton, S. (ed), Cambridge University Press, Cambridge.

Cudworth, R. [1838] (1996) *A Treatise of Freewill*, Hutton, S. (ed), Cambridge University Press, Cambridge.

Descartes, R. (1984) *The Philosophical Writings of Descartes*, v. 1–2, Cottingham, J., Stoothoff, R. and Murdoch, D. (trans.), Cambridge University Press, Cambridge.

Feinberg, J. (1962) "Problematic Responsibility in Law and Morals", in *Doing and Deserving: Essays in the Theory of Responsibility*, pp. 25–37. Princeton University Press, Princeton.

Fischer, J. (1994) *The Metaphysics of Free Will*, Blackwell, Oxford.

Fischer, J. and Ravizza, M. (1998) *Responsibility and Control: A Theory of Moral Responsibility*, Cambridge University Press, Cambridge.

Frankfurt, H. (1971) "Freedom of the Will and the Concept of a Person", in *The Importance of What We Care About*, pp. 11–25. Cambridge University Press, Cambridge.

Frankfurt, H. (1976) "Identification and Externality", in Rorty, A. (ed),*The Identities of Persons*, University of California Press , Berkeley, 1976.

Frankfurt, H. (1987) "Identification and Wholeheartedness", in Fischer, J. M. and Ravizza, M. (eds) *Perspectives on Moral Responsibility*, pp. 170–187. Cornell University Press, Ithaca.

Frankfurt, H. (1992) "The Faintest Passion" in *Proceedings and Addresses of the American Philosophical Association*, v. 66.

Friedman, M. (1986) "Autonomy and the Split-Level View" in *Southern Journal of Philosophy*, v. 24, pp. 19–35.

Hobbes, T. (1646) "Of Liberty and Necessity", in *The English Works of Thomas Hobbes*, v. 4, Scientia Verlag Aalen, Germany.

Hobbes, T. (1648) "The Questions Concerning Liberty, Necessity and Chance, Clearly Stated and Debated Between Dr. Bramhall, Bishop of Derry, and Thomas Hobbes of Malmesbury", in *The English Works of Thomas Hobbes*, v. 5, Scientia Verlag Aalen, Germany.

Kennett, J. and Smith, M. (1996) "Frog and Toad Lose Control", in *Analysis*, v. 56, n. 2, pp. 63–73.

Leibniz, G. W. (1996)*Theodicy*, Huggard, E. M. (trans.), Open Court, La Salle.

Locke, J. [1690] (1975) *An Essay Concerning Human Understanding*, Clarendon Press, Oxford.

Malebranche, N. [1680] (1992) *Treatise on Nature and Grace*, Riley, P. (trans. and ed.), Clarendon Press, Oxford.

Mele, A. (1992) "Recent Work on Intentional Action", in *American Philosophical Quarterly*, v. 29, n. 3, pp. 199–217.

Moore, G. E. (1903) *Principia Ethica*, Cambridge University Press, Cambridge.

Neely, W. (1974) "Freedom and Desire", in *Philosophical Review*, v. 83, pp. 32–54.

Nozick, R. (1981) *Philosophical Explanations*, Harvard University Press, Cambridge.

O'Connor, T. (1995) "Agent Causation", in O'Connor, T. (ed) *Agents, Causes and Events: Essays on Indeterminism and Free Will*, pp. 173–200, Oxford University Press, New York, 1995.

Pettit, P. and Smith, M. (1990) "Backgrounding Desire", in *Philosophical Review*, v. 99, pp. 565–592.

Pettit, P. and Smith, M. (1996) "Freedom in Belief and Desire", in *Journal of Philosophy*, v. 93, pp. 429–449.

Reid, T. (1788) *Essays on the Active Powers of Man*, Lincoln-Rembrandt Publishing, Charlottesville.

Schueler, G. F. (1995) *Desire: Its Role in Practical Reason and the Explanation of Action*, MIT Press, Cambridge.

Smith, M. (1994) *The Moral Problem*, Blackwell, Oxford.

Smith, M. (1997) "A Theory of Freedom and Responsibility", in Cullity, G. and Gaut, B. (eds) *Ethics and Practical Reason*, Oxford University Press, Oxford, 1997.

Stump, E. (1993) "Sanctification, Hardening of the Heart and Frankfurt's Concept of Free Will" in Fischer, J. M. and Ravizza, M. (eds) *Perspectives on Moral Responsibility*, pp. 211–234. Cornell University Press, Ithaca, 1993.

Watson, G. (1975) "Free Agency", in Watson, G. (ed) *Free Will*, pp. 96–110, Oxford University Press, Oxford, 1982.

Watson, G. (1977) "Skepticism about Weakness of Will", in *Philosophical Review*, pp. 316–339.

Watson, G. (1987) "Responsibility and the Limits of Evil: Variations on a Strawsonian Theme", in Fischer, J. M. and Ravizza, M. (eds) *Perspectives on Moral Responsibility*, pp. 119–150. Cornell University Press, Ithaca.

White, S. (1988) "Self Deception and Responsibility for the Self", in McLaughlin, B. P. and Rorty, A. O. (eds) *Perspectives on Self Deception*, pp. 450–484. University of California Press, Berkeley.

Williams, B. (1985) *Ethics and the Limits of Philosophy*, Harvard University Press, Cambridge.

Wolf, S. (1990) *Freedom Within Reason*, Oxford University Press, Oxford.

Yaffe, G. *Liberty Worth the Name: Locke on Free Agency*, forthcoming, Princeton University Press, Princeton.

Young, R. (1980) "Autonomy and the 'Inner Self'" in *American Philosophical Quarterly*, v. 27, pp. 35–43.

DOES LIBERTARIAN FREEDOM REQUIRE
ALTERNATE POSSIBILITIES?

Linda Zagzebski
University of Oklahoma

I

According to causal determinism the chain of causes of an act leads backwards in time to something completely outside the agent. What bothers libertarians is that it seems to follow that something outside the agent is the ultimate cause of the act, what makes it happen. And if what ultimately makes an act happen is what ultimately is responsible for it, then causal determinism seems to imply that no one is ultimately responsible for his acts. Of course, it is a major philosophical challenge to explain what is involved in making something happen and it is sometimes tempting to shift the discussion to something easier to grasp. But whatever digression we take, we should not forget that once we have identified who or what makes an act happen, we have identified who or what is responsible for it, if anything is.

One way to get criteria that insure that an act is not causally determined is to insist that there be no conditions existing just prior to the time of the act that are sufficient for the agent to do the act.[1] That is, the entire history of the world up to but not including the time T at which an act A occurs is compatible both with A's occurring and with A's not occurring. In fact, that condition is often taken to be constitutive of the denial that acts are determined. Call this the Temporal Contingency Principle (TCP):

(TCP) An act A at T is non-determined (temporally contingent) if and only if there is a possible world W that has exactly the same history up to T as the actual world and in which A does not occur at T.

If the condition specified on the right side of TCP is met, A is not determined. A could not be made to happen by anything prior to it if both its happening and its not happening are compatible with everything prior to it. But TCP goes well beyond what is required for A to be causally contingent. Not every event in the temporal history of A is in its causal history. In fact, it is doubtful that any event is such that the entire past history of the world is part of its causal history. Consider what we ask for when we want to know whether two events are related as cause to effect. When someone inquires, "If the money supply increased, would the interest rates go down?", he is not asking whether the rates would go down if *everything* that happened in the past remained the same and the money supply increased since most of what happened in the past has nothing to do with interest rate increases, for instance, the invasion of Poland by the Tatars in 1287.

TCP is too strong. The principle we need instead is something roughly like the following Principle of Causal Contingency (PCC):

(PCC) An act A is non-determined (causally contingent) if and only if there is a possible world W in which all the events in the causal history of A in the actual world occur and in which A does not occur.

Perhaps it will be objected that if an event is causally contingent it has no causal history. Isn't a causally contingent event a break in the causal order? Indeed, it is, but a causally contingent event is not a random event. It is not an event that has no causally explanatory tie to the events preceding it. If the causal history of an event includes all events relevant to explaining what makes it happen, then all events have a causal history even if some events are such that their causal history is not sufficient to fully explain what makes them happen. The scope of the causal history of an event is a difficult question, of course, but the difficulty of the question should not lead us to conclude that the causal history of an event either includes the entire past or nothing at all.

But TCP is tempting for another reason. Unfortunately, we are ignorant of a great deal of the causal history of most events. It is even possible that U.S. interest rate increases in 2000 are causally related to a distant military event in 1287. So even though the attempt to identify causes is an attempt to identify that part of the past that is its causal history, since, as far as we know, *anything* in the past might be in its causal history, we can only be sure that we have included everything in its causal history if we include the entire past. The same point applies to the criterion for causal contingency. TCP rules out the possibility that apparently irrelevant events in the past causally necessitate an act A by requiring that nothing in the past is such that its occurrence rules out the non-occurrence of A. Since the causal history of an event is a subset of its temporal history, we can therefore be sure that we have considered everything causally relevant to the occurrence of a given event only by relating it to the entire past. If an event satisfies TCP it also satisfies PCC. Therefore, TCP is a principle of safety even though it is stronger than is required. Temporal contingency is sufficient for causal contingency, but it is not necessary.

The stronger TCP is tempting because of our ignorance. But perhaps it will be argued that TCP is not too strong since if any event A failed the condition of temporal contingency we would automatically judge that it is causally determined. Suppose that if Poland had not been invaded by the Tatars in 1287 but everything else prior to a particular rise in interest rates remained the same, interest rates would not have risen. Doesn't it follow that the invasion is in the causal history of the movement of interest rates in 2000? No, it does not. To think that it does follow is to think that all counterfactual relations between events imply a relation of temporal modality and that all temporal modalities are causal, and we are in no position to think that. To take an historically important example of a temporal modality that is not causal, consider the fact that it is often thought that divine foreknowledge takes away human free will because of the accidental necessity of past infallible foreknowledge. Accidental necessity is the alleged necessity of the past; presumably, once an event occurs it acquires a form of necessity because there is no longer anything anybody can do about it.[2] If there is past infallible knowledge that A will occur in the future, there is no longer anything anybody can do about either the fact that the foreknowledge occurred or its infallibility. Hence, A cannot but occur. But notice that this argument does not imply that A is causally determined. Therefore, if temporal necessity is a problem for freedom and responsibility it is not because it entails causal necessity. Causal necessity entails temporal necessity but not conversely. Temporal contingency entails causal contingency but not conversely.

Temporal contingency entails that the agent had alternate possibilities at the time of the act. If it is compatible with the entire past history of the world that the agent does either A or not A, then when the agent does A she could have done otherwise. Causal contingency as defined by PCC does not entail alternate possibilities. Again, the foreknowledge example illustrates the point. God's foreknowledge of my act might make it the case that I cannot do otherwise even though God's foreknowledge does not cause my act, and if my act has no other determining causes, it is causally contingent.[3]

In short, temporal contingency entails both causal contingency and alternate possibilities. Causal contingency does not entail alternate possibilities. It should not be surprising, then, if it turns out that a property requiring causal contingency does not require alternate possibilities. Responsibility may be such a property.

II

One way to formulate the libertarian thesis on responsibility given in the first two sentences of this paper is the following:

> (LTR) An agent is morally responsible for her act only if the act is causally contingent.

The thesis that the ability to do otherwise is a requirement for responsibility is given in the following well-known principle:

> (PAP) An agent is morally responsible for her act only if she could have done otherwise.

The reasons for holding PAP are no doubt different for different people, but I want to argue that the desire to defend libertarian freedom, the kind of freedom that requires causal contingency, ought not to be one of them. LTR may be true even if PAP is false. Since causal contingency does not entail alternate possibilities it is possible for an act to be causally contingent even when the agent lacks alternate possibilities. I have already mentioned that divine foreknowledge is one way in which that possibility might be actualized. If alternate possibilities are required for responsibility, then, it cannot be because alternate possibilities are a requirement of causal contingency.

Three decades ago Harry Frankfurt presented a famous argument that was intended to drive a wedge between responsibility and alternate possibilities, and Frankfurt thought he could thereby drive another wedge between responsibility and libertarian freedom.[4] In my judgment he succeeded admirably in breaking apart the conceptual connection between responsibility and alternate possibilities, but he went no distance at all towards supporting determinism.[5] The connection between responsibility and libertarian freedom remains unbroken. On the contrary, I think that a careful look at Frankfurt cases actually supports non-determinism. But let us first review a standard Frankfurt-style case:

> Black, an evil neurosurgeon, wishes to see White dead but is unwilling to do the deed himself. Knowing that Mary Jones also despises White and will have a single good opportunity to kill him, Black inserts a mechanism into Jones's brain that enables Black to monitor and to control Jones's neurological activity. If the activity in Jones's brain suggests that she is on the verge of deciding not to kill White when the opportunity arises, Black's mechanism will intervene and cause Jones to decide to commit the murder. On the other hand, if Jones decides to murder White on her own, the mechanism will not intervene. It will merely monitor but will not affect her neurological function. Now suppose that when the occasion arises, Jones decides to kill White without any "help" from Black's mechanism. In the judgment of Frankfurt and most others, Jones is morally responsible for her act. Nonetheless, it appears that she is unable to do otherwise since if she had attempted to do so, she would have been thwarted by Black's device.[6]

Frankfurt believes that his cases support determinism by falsifying PAP and that they do not presuppose a deterministic universe.[7] Robert Kane and David Widerker have independently argued that F cases do presuppose a deterministic universe and hence cannot be used to support determinism.[8] My position is that F cases do not presuppose determinism but neither do they support it. In this section I will argue that F cases do not presuppose determinism. In section III I will argue that F cases probably succeed in falsifying morally significant versions of PAP, and in section V I will argue that F cases give no support to determinism and arguably support non-determinism.

Kane and Widerker agree with Frankfurt that the denial of PAP is closely connected with determinism. Their disagreement is over the issue of whether

PAP can be falsified independently of falsifing determinism. Since, as I have argued, non-determinism does not entail PAP, it should be possible to falsify PAP without either entailing or presupposing determinism. Frankfurt cases probably succeed in doing that, but even if they do not, the argument of section I should lead us to expect that it is possible to construct cases that do. In this section I want to look at the Kane/Widerker argument that attempts to show that no Frankfurt-style case can falsify PAP without presupposing determinism.

The problem as Kane and Widerker pose it can be put briefly as follows: The Frankfurt machine cannot operate unless it is possible to be a perfect predictor in a non-deterministic universe. It is not possible to be a perfect predictor in a non-deterministic universe. Hence, a Frankfurt machine is impossible. More precisely, consider whatever it is that the agent is responsible for according to the libertarian—an act of will, some other agent-caused event—whatever is the original undetermined cause of her act. The machine cannot intervene before that event in a non-deterministic world because no matter what the prior signs, the event might or might not occur up until the moment it does occur. So the machine cannot tell for sure whether or not to intervene. But the machine cannot intervene after the event since then it is too late to falsify PAP; the agent is already responsible. The most the machine can do is to make her change her mind, and that's not an F case.

One way out of the Kane/Widerker objection proposed recently is that of Alfred Mele and David Robb.[9] Their idea is to postulate two independent causal processes leading up to the act, one deterministic and unconscious, and the other non-deterministic and resulting from conscious deliberation and choice. In their scenario the F-style machine does not simply monitor the agent's neurological activity. It is set to deterministically cause the agent to decide to steal a car at T2. But we are to imagine that he decides on his own to steal the car at T2, the exact moment the deterministic mechanism is set to cause the same decision. Since there are two independent causal sequences in operation in this scheme, there are several possibilities to be considered. The first is the F-style scenario. The deterministic process and the indeterministic process coincide at the moment of decision, T2. Mele and Robb specify that the machine is so designed that in that case the deterministic process ceases operation and the indeterministic process is the one that is effective. The second possibility is that the two processes diverge at T2. Since two contrary choices cannot occur simultaneously, what happens if the agent makes the "wrong" choice at T2? Mele and Robb have thought of this problem and they stipulate that the machine overrides the agent's choice.[10] We need to accept, then, that the machine is designed in such a way that the indeterministic choice overrides the deterministic one when they coincide, but the deterministic choice overrides the indeterministic one when they diverge. This is a stretch, but I would not claim it is impossible.

There are two other possibilities. Since the process of deliberation is also indeterministic, the agent can make his decision prior to T2. Suppose the agent decides on his own before T2 to steal the car. Mele and Robb specify that in that case the deterministic process in place causes him to decide to steal the car again at T2.[11] Suppose instead that the agent decides on his own before T2 not to steal the car. Mele and Robb say that if the device were to issue at T2 in the agent's deciding to steal the car, it would erase any memories that are incompatible with its so issuing.[12] Presumably, then, the machine causes him to change his mind at T2 and to decide to steal the car after all.

These features of the Mele/Robb scenario make it importantly different from more standard F cases. In the latter the agent cannot do otherwise during the entire period of time that the agent is deliberating and making up her mind. The device is set to intervene whenever something in the agent tips off the machine that the "wrong" choice is ahead. That duration is generally assumed to be short, but it is more than an instant. In Mele and Robb's scenario the agent can do otherwise at every moment up to but not including T2. The device is already in operation, leading to a deterministic decision to steal the car at T2 unless the same decision is made indeterministically at T2. Since there is only a single moment at which the agent cannot do otherwise (assuming the description of what happens at T2 is possible), it is not the case that the device insures that a deliberator cannot choose otherwise without making her change her mind. It is only chance that the agent indeterministically makes her decision at T2. She might easily have made it moments earlier, in which case the scenario would not have been an F case. Hence, it is only chance that the scenario turns out to be like Frankfurt's and it is only chance that the Mele/Robb scenario falsifies PAP. That is, it is only chance that in the Mele/Robb scenario the agent is responsible for an act she performed at a moment when she could not do otherwise.

Eleonore Stump has a different approach to answering the Kane/Widerker objection. She argues that if libertarian free choices are correlated with temporally extended neural sequences, an F-style machine can operate in a nondeterministic world by intervening after an initial neural sequence occurs which is a necessary condition for making the choice the machine does not want.[13] As Stewart Goetz has pointed out, it is not clear exactly which processes/events Stump thinks are causally undetermined and which are not, and indeterminacy in this matter can make her description appear vulnerable to the Kane/Widerker objection.[14] But Stump's point seems to be that intervention does not require infallible prediction since all that is required is that it occur after a causally necessary condition for the choice (or other responsible event) has occurred, but before a causally sufficient condition obtains. For example, the process of making a decision might itself be temporally extended and temporally coincide with a neurological sequence. The machine can intervene after the neurological process begins but before it ends. Alternatively, the neurological sequence precipitating intervention might be a causally necessary condition for the choice which occurs subsequently and is causally contingent.[15]

Either option should work. If the process of making the decision has already begun but the outcome is still undetermined, and if the decision cannot be completed without such a beginning, the machine can intervene without needing to perfectly predict the outcome. For the same reason, the machine can intervene after any necessary condition for making the "wrong" choice has occurred. Of course, this means the machine might intervene unnecessarily, but that is not a problem. Stump's description of F cases in an earlier paper suggests this interpretation.[16] In fact, Frankfurt's own description of his principal case suggests this interpretation as well:

> Suppose someone—Black, let us say—wants Jones₄ to perform a certain action. Black is prepared to go to considerable lengths to get his way, but he prefers to avoid showing his hand unnecessarily. So he waits until Jones₄ is about to make up his mind what to do, and he does nothing unless it is clear to him (Black is an excellent judge of such things) that Jones₄ is going to decide to do something *other* than what he wants him to do.[17]

Presumably, even if Black is an excellent judge of what Jones is about to do, he is not infallible. He can infallibly identify neither causally necessary nor causally sufficient conditions for Jones' choice. But the case requires that he be infallible only with respect to identifying a causally necessary condition. This is a bit more than Frankfurt has a right to claim about the case, but it is considerably less than Widerker and Kane suppose is required. The fact that most commentators on F cases have posed them in terms of an infallibly predictive device has no doubt misdirected subsequent discussion. All that F cases require is the capacity to identify a causally necessary condition for a non-determined choice in advance of the choice, and that is in principle possible in a non-deterministic world.

The best description of a case of this kind I know of is given by Derk Pereboom.[18] In Pereboom's case the machine is set to make the agent decide to declare an illegal tax deduction if he does not do so on his own. The agent's psychology is such that a causally necessary condition for him to decide not to commit the illegal act is that a moral reason occur to him with a certain force. All the machine need do is intervene just after such a moral reason occurs to the agent with the given force. The machine can thereby make it the case that the agent cannot do otherwise even in a non-determined universe. What makes Pereboom's case especially promising is that many libertarians will agree that thinking of a moral reason is a causally necessary condition for choosing the morally right thing in many circumstances. Such a view not only does not presuppose determinism, but it is likely to be part of a typical libertarian account of what usually happens in cases of moral temptation. I conclude that the description of standard F cases does not presuppose determinism.

III

Some libertarian defenders of PAP contend that the agent in Frankfurt cases does have ethically important alternate possibilities, alternate possibilities entailed by her responsibility, even though she does not have the alternative of doing otherwise. Consequently, a number of variations of PAP have been proposed and defended against Frankfurt-style examples. It is obvious that some libertarians defend PAP only because they believe that libertarian freedom requires alternate possibilities. Since they are convinced by F cases that PAP is false, they then feel compelled to look around for some variation of PAP that is true and that can withstand Frankfurt's attack. Otherwise, they think, they will be forced to give up belief in libertarian freedom. But if the argument I have given that causal contingency does not entail alternate possibilities is convincing, it may be sufficient to take away the principal motive of some libertarians for finding a true version of PAP. So for them I need not say anything more.

Other libertarians may accept my position that PAP is not entailed by causal contingency and yet continue to maintain that PAP is entailed by libertarian freedom since there is more *in* libertarian freedom than causal contingency. This position requires an argument going from a substantive account of the nature of libertarian freedom to the consequence that the agent has alternate possibilities. What would such an argument look like?

Determinism and its denial are theses about the causes of an act, what makes it happen, whereas PAP is a thesis about what the agent might have caused instead. Libertarians are not committed to a single position on the process whereby an agent causes her act, but there is agreement that the chain of causes of a free act ends in the agent. There is nothing outside the agent that is ultimately the cause of her act. One way in which this position has been explicated is via the concept of agent causation. According to this view the cause of an act for which the agent is responsible is the agent herself, not an event of any kind, not even the event of her exercising her agency. From this point of view agency is a kind of power. Thomas Reid contended that it is essentially a two-way power. An agent does not have the power to cause an act unless she also has the power not to:

> Power to produce any effect implies power not to produce it. We can conceive no way in which power may be determined to one of these rather than the other, in a being that has no will.
>
> Whatever is the effect of active power must be something that is contingent. Contingent existence is that which depended upon the power and will of its cause.[19]

Here Reid ties the possession of alternate possibilities to agent causation itself and he seems to be inferring the contingency of an act from the fact that it arises in a situation in which the agent had the power not to perform the act.[20] So on Reid's view agent causation is partially constituted by the possession of alternate possibilities. Here, then, is an argument connecting a form of the libertarian position on freedom with alternate possibilities. The argument is that agent causation entails alternate possibilities, not because causal contingency entails alternate possibilities, but because the power of agency itself demands it. Let us call this Reid's principle:

(RP) An act A is agent-caused by S only if S had the power not to agent-cause A.

RP can be used to defend a form of PAP. The argument would go as follows:

(1) An agent S is morally responsible for an act A only if S agent-causes A.

(2) S agent-causes A only if S had the power not to agent-cause A. (RP)

Therefore,

(3) An agent S is morally responsible for an act A only if S had the power not to agent-cause A.

(3) is a form of PAP. A version of PAP very similar to (3) has been defended by Edward Wierenga as a response to F cases. Wierenga's version is the following:

(PAPC) Necessarily, for every person S and act of will A such that S causes A, S is morally responsible for performing A only if S could have refrained from causing A.[21]

It is clear from Wierenga's discussion that he has agent causation in mind.[22] A similar defense of alternate possibilities has been given more recently by Michael McKenna, who argues that in F cases it is up to the agent whether or not her act puts her stamp upon the world.[23] McKenna does not specifically mention agent causation either, but his discussion of the power of an agent to make the act her own or not is clearly similar in spirit to the views of Reid and Wierenga.

Wierenga claims that even in F cases S could have refrained from causing A. If S makes A happen, then it was open to her to make it happen or not to make it happen. But it seems to me that even though it was open that she not make A happen, it was not open *to her* not to make A happen. It was open to the machine to make her make A happen. Of course in that case S would have exercised the power not to do A if the machine hadn't intervened. But as it turned out, the machine intervened before she could exercise that power. The most she can do is to fail to will, but even then it is the machine that makes it happen that she fails to will. *She* can't do anything to avoid being responsible for the act. The machine does it for her.

It appears, then, that "could have refrained" in PAPC does not refer to a power that S has. It is true that either the act is agent-caused or an act of the same type is machine-caused. It is also true that in most descriptions of F cases the machine's operation depends upon what the agent does.[24] But even then it is not up to the agent whether or not the machine operates. It is only because of what she *would have done* that the machine goes into operation. If the machine operates, it is before she can exercise an alternate power. In Pereboom's example the machine does operate because of what the agent actually does—thinking of a certain moral reason. But having a moral thought is not exercising the right kind of power for attributing moral responsibility if indeed it is exercising a power at all. Again, the machine operates before she is in a position to exercise any contrary power.

McKenna makes another move in an attempt to preserve the idea that the agent in F cases retains a two-way power. He says an agent can have a power even though she is unable to exercise it. I have said that in F cases the machine takes away the agent's ability to exercise the power to choose otherwise. Might it still be the case that she has the power to choose otherwise even though the machine prevents her from exercising it?[25]

I am inclined to think we should be as suspicious of unexercisable powers as of imperceptible trees. But although I think that doubt is in order, I actually agree with McKenna that there are powers one can have without being able to exercise them at every moment at which the power is possessed. The power to perform such complex activities as playing a Schubert Impromptu, making bread, or writing one's will is not compromised by the fact that a piano, kitchen equipment, or writing materials is not available at this moment. The fact that I cannot exercise the power right now does not detract in any significant way from my present possession of the power since it is not the kind of power that requires continuous exercisability. These activities take some time to perform and, in the case of making bread, the time it takes is discontinuous. The fact that I cannot initiate the process at this moment is of no consequence. In contrast, if my eyes are now bandaged shut, I do not now have the power to open my eyes. The power to open my eyes is the kind of power I need to be able to exercise now if I possess it now. That is probably because opening my eyes is a basic act or very close to a basic act, whereas playing an Impromptu and making bread are far from basic acts. My conjecture is that the possession of a power at T and the ability to exercise it at T split apart only for some acts that are clearly not basic acts. One does not at T have the power to perform a basic act unless one also possesses at T the ability to exercise that power. The power to refrain from choosing an act is like the power to open my eyes and unlike the power to make bread. Choosing and refraining from choosing are basic acts and if my conjecture is right then, like opening my eyes, they are possessed at T only when I can exercise them at T.

In any case, even if I am wrong in this conjecture and an agent can possess the power to refrain from choosing in F cases without having the ability to exercise that power, what is gained is not very helpful to the defender of (3) or PAPC. What is the point of insisting that an agent is responsible for her act A only if she has the power to agent-cause A, but the power need not be exercisable? An unexercisable power is a pretty thin reed upon which to hang moral responsibility. What McKenna may be trying to point to is a deeper, more enduring property of the agent that is possessed even in some situations in which she cannot do otherwise. I have argued that her status as a libertarian agent can remain even in such cases and is that deeper property.

I conclude that PAPC is false because it is false that *the agent* could have refrained from causing A. If S refrains from causing A, the designer of the machine is the cause of S's not causing A. S cannot exercise a power to refrain because she can never complete the act of deciding to make what the designer of the machine considers the wrong choice. And if she cannot exercise the power to refrain she does not have the power to refrain. She fails to exercise agent causation, but failure to exercise agent causation is not the same thing as exercising agent-refraining. It is not open to her to make it not happen, although it is open that she not make it happen.

McKenna says he's willing to concede that the agent does not have it within her power to do otherwise. Nevertheless, he says she could have avoided the particular thing that she did.[26] Now my remarks above imply that there is a sense in which this is true. Even though *she* can't avoid agent-causing her act, the state of affairs of her agent-causing her act is avoidable. It is not avoidable through the exercise of her own power, although it is avoidable because of something about her or something she does. Since the most we have a right to say in F cases is that her agent-causing A is avoidable, and since she does agent-cause A in F cases, the strongest principle we can affirm is not (2) but (2′):

(2′) S agent-causes A only if S's agent-causing A is avoidable.

And we can conclude, not (3), but (3′):

(3′) An agent S is morally responsible for an act A only if S's agent-causing A is avoidable.

(3′) does affirm an alternate possibility of a weak kind. But the avoidability of S's agent-causing A in (3′) amounts to nothing more than that it might not happen, and that does not add anything to the thesis that it is causally contingent. The avoidability is not due to a power that S has, although it is due to a power she would have had and exercised if the machine had not intervened.

Another approach to connecting alternate possibilities and responsibility focuses on the conditions under which an agent is blameworthy. Michael Otsuka argues that an agent is blameworthy only if there is something she could have voluntarily done instead that would have rendered her entirely blameless.[27] The advantage of Otsuka's proposal is that he does not make it a requirement for blameworthiness for performing an act of a given type that the agent could have refrained from performing an act of the type for which she is blameworthy.[28] But she must have had an option open to her that gives her a way out of blame. Now if the machine intervenes after a necessary condition for the choice the machine is designed to prevent, the intervention is too early to satisfy Otsuka's requirement. Suppose that we use a case like Pereboom's in which the precipitating event is a moral thought which is necessary but not sufficient for the agent to make the decision the machine wants to prevent. If the thought is a kind that always occurs involuntarily, there is nothing the agent could have done before the intervention that would have rendered her blameless, and yet we think she is to blame if the machine does not need to intervene. If the agent could have entertained the thought voluntarily, then it is true that there is something she could have done that would have precipitated the action of the machine, thereby rendering her blameless, but her blamelessness would have little to do with what she did. Surely, when the machine does not need to intervene and in ordinary situations in which there is no machine in existence we do not blame her because she could have had such a thought. She is to blame because her act was the result of a libertarian free choice, not because she might have had a moral thought which would have been necessary but not sufficient for deciding not to commit the act. Having a moral thought is not exercising the kind of power relevent to her blameworthiness. Otsuka is right that her blameworthiness is avoidable, but its avoidability is not due to her own power. Like the other defenders of alternate possibilities, he can affirm (3'), but he cannot attribute any significant form of two-way power to the agent.

In short, the challenge facing defenders of any version of PAP is that the version defended not only must not be falsified by F examples, but it has to be motivated. The problem is that the motivation is likely to go through an account of agency that utilizes something like (2). However, F cases can be interpreted as counterexamples to (2) as well as to most versions of PAP. On the other hand, (2') can be supported and used to conclude (3'), but that tells us no more than that a responsible act must be avoidable, not that the agent must have been able to do something to avoid it. Hence, even though I think it is right to focus on agent causation in identifying the ground of responsibility, it is probably wrong to think of the power of agent causation as involving alternate powers. Even though there almost always *are* alternate powers of some sort in cases of agent causation, it is doubtful that they are an intrinsic part of the power of agency itself.

IV

I have claimed it is likely that no significant version of PAP can be devised that is not falsified by Frankfurt-style counterexamples. I have also argued that it is likely that successful versions of F cases can be devised that do not require that the machine be a perfect predictor of the agent's choices, contra Kane and Widerker. Nonetheless, my real reaction to F cases does not depend upon their being literal counterexamples to PAP. The beauty of these thought experiments is that they force us to confront what it is in a situation in virtue of which we judge the agent responsible. What we see in an F situation, I believe, is that we *don't care* what Black's mechanism is capable of doing because it doesn't actually do anything at all. And since the lack of alternate possibilities is tied to what the mechanism is capable of doing rather than to what it actually does, we see that we don't care whether or not the agent has alternate possibilities. Either way she is responsible. Suppose that Wierenga, McKenna, Otsuka, and others are right in thinking that she does, in fact, have alternate possibilities of some kind in Frankfurt situations. Since the point of the F cases is to show us the irrelevance of the mechanism, it does not matter how far the power of the mechanism actually goes. There is no doubt that the mechanism has *some* significant power of constraint on the agent. There are some alternate possibilities which she normally possesses in a non-deterministic world which she does not possess on the machine. But the intuition of most people who hear of F cases is that the machine has no effect at all on her level of responsibility or on that for which she is responsible.

What the F cases do is to make us think about responsibility in a novel way, a way that calls our attention to the difference between the features of a responsibility situation that are salient and those that are not. What we see is that Black's machine plays no role in our judgment about Jones's responsibility. We do not evaluate Jones any differently with the machine than without it, nor would we evaluate Jones any differently if, *per impossibile* (perhaps), the machine became a perfect predictor. Nor need we work to identify the respect in which the agent retains an alternative since our judgment of her responsibility does not depend upon the success of that search, nor do we attribute responsibility to her in any different way once we think we have identified the precise sense in which she has alternate possibilities.

V

The intuition that the agent is responsible in F cases does not refute the libertarian thesis LTR, nor does it falsify (3′). Whatever reason the libertarian has for thinking a person agent-causes his act in an ordinary non-Frankfurt-style situation applies just as well to a Frankfurt situation, and if the former act is causally contingent, so is the latter. The avoidability of the one is the same as the other. This means that F cases do not refute the libertarian position. Furthermore, they do not give any support to determinism. That is because a certain kind of libertarian will say that the reason why the agent is responsible in F cases is that she agent-causes the act and agent-causation requires that the act be causally contingent. Notice that this point is not the same as the first. The first and weaker point is simply that the libertarian is not forced to give up LTR when she accepts that the agent is responsible in F cases. Libertarianism is compatible with the rejection of PAP. The second and stronger point is that she will accept that the agent is responsible in F cases *for libertarian reasons*. She accepts F cases because the libertarian condition still obtains in those cases. She can reject PAP, then, because doing so has no effect on the deeper libertarian intuition operative in these cases. Of course, the determinist will see F cases differently, but that is just because the determinist and the non-determinist see every case differently. The point is that F cases do not give the libertarian any more reason to accept determinism than ordinary cases do.

But the libertarian can go farther. She can capitalize on F cases to support non-determinism. Ironically, one of Frankfurt's own remarks provides the argument. Frankfurt says:

> Even though the person was unable to do otherwise...it may not be the case that he acted as he did *because* he could not have done otherwise. Now if someone had no alternative to performing a certain action but did not do it because he was unable to do otherwise, then he would have performed exactly the same action even if he *could* have done otherwise. The circumstances that made it impossible for him to do otherwise could have been subtracted from the situation without affecting what happened or why it happened in any way. Whatever it was that actually led the person to do what he did, or that made him do it, would have led him to do it or made him do it even if it had been possible for him to do something else instead.[29]

In a deterministic world the agent's act is caused by events outside the agent, so in one clear sense of "because," the act occurs because of those events. He acts because he could not do otherwise. Hence, he does not satisfy the condition for responsibility in the passage just quoted. Frankfurt remarks that it is important that there is no morally relevant difference between the situation in which the agent has alternate possibilities and one in which they have been eliminated by a Frankfurt-type mechanism. This means that the comparison of the F situation with one in which the agent *can* do otherwise is important to the intuition that the agent is responsible on Frankfurt's own account. He says that the circumstances that make it the case that the agent could not have done otherwise could have been subtracted from the situation without affecting what happened or why it happened in any way. But notice that this implies that what the agent would have done *if* he had been able to do otherwise is relevant to his responsibility in the actual situation since the subtraction of the conditions that make it the case that he cannot do otherwise turns the situation into one in which he *can* do otherwise. A curious feature of Frankfurt's point here is that as a determinist he cannot claim that a possible world in which the agent can do otherwise is close to the actual world, so the comparison of the actual situation with one in which he can do otherwise is a comparison of the actual world with a very distant world, one in which the basic structure of natural law differs from that which actually obtains.

On the page following the passage just quoted Frankfurt offers an amendment to his claim and a new principle of alternate possibilities which he can support: "a person is not morally responsible for what he has done if he did it *only because* he could not have done otherwise." [emphasis added].[30] Notice that this is not simply a clarification or innocuous addition to the passage quoted above; it is a different and weaker position. To say that an agent is not responsible for an act if he did it only because he could not have done otherwise leaves open the possibility that when he is responsible he did the act *partly* because he could not have done otherwise. In that case, if the circumstances that make it the case that the agent could not have done otherwise were subtracted from the situation, it presumably *would* affect what happened or why it happened in some way, contrary to what Frankfurt says in the quoted passage. As a determinist, Frankfurt must countenance dependence of the agent's act on the conditions that make it the case that he cannot do otherwise since on his view those conditions are the cause of the act. But it is worth noting that this position requires a partial retraction of his claim that in a responsibility situation the conditions that make it the case that the agent cannot do otherwise are irrelevant to why he did what he did.

Libertarians will make a different judgment. We think that Frankfurt was right in his point that the agent is responsible because what he does in an F situation is relevantly similar to what he would have done if he been able to do otherwise. But it is also important that Black's meddling is a quirk that in the normal course of events would not have entered the picture at all. The point could be put as follows: It is only an accident that Black exists, and if he had not existed the agent would have had alternate possibilities. And if he had had alternate possibilities he would have done the very same thing in the same way. He is, therefore, just as responsible as he would have been if he had had alternate possibilities. To say otherwise is to permit the agent too great a degree of positive moral luck. He can't get off the moral hook *that* easily.

Therefore, we get the conclusion Frankfurt wants precisely because of our interest in what would have happened if Jones had been able to do otherwise, along with our inclination to think that but for the short-lived existence of an inoperative device, Jones would have actually been able to do otherwise. If the universe is causally determined, however, the second condition is not satisfied and the first is logically problematic since any proposition of the form *If Jones had been able to do otherwise, then...* has an antecedent that contradicts the laws of nature in such a world.

At the beginning of this paper I remarked that it is tempting to bypass the difficult concept of what it is to make an act happen and to take various digressions. There is nothing wrong with digressions as long as they illuminate our target concept and we eventually get back to it. Talk of counterfactual conditions for the attribution of responsibility is a digression. It can help illuminate the idea of causing or making something happen, but eventually we have to get back to the idea those conditions aimed to elucidate, and that is the idea of causing an act, making it happen. Once we have identified who or what makes an act happen we have identified the potential bearer of responsibility for it. In Frankfurt cases in a non-deterministic world the agent makes her act happen in as ultimate a sense as you like; in a deterministic world it is not the agent that ultimately makes her act happen. Frankfurt cases do nothing to lead us to rescind the view that this is a significant difference. What they do show is that PAP is a false path. The presence of alternate possibilities may be a reliable sign of the presence of the agency needed for responsibility, but it is not necessary for it.

I suspect that the moral of Frankfurt cases can be generalized to apply to many properties that have counterfactual conditions for their application. If I am right that such conditions are usually proposed because they are a sign of what we think is really important, it can happen that they fail because of the presence of a counterfactual manipulator even when the target property still obtains. For example, several well-known definitions of knowledge include counterfactual conditions. In another place I have argued that epistemic Frankfurt-style cases show that these conditions can fail for reasons parallel to the reasons for the failure of PAP.[31] In general, what might have happened is often a good indication of what *did* happen, but it is not essential to it.[32] PAP is a thesis about what might have happened; causal determinism and non-determinism are theses about what did happen.

Notes

1. I use "act" for the event for which an agent is primarily responsible. It may be an act of will, an overt act, or even a firing of neurons, provided that it is the kind of event for which we attribute responsibility to the agent in the basic sense.
2. The term "accidentally necessary" comes from Ockham's use of the idea of necessity *per accidens*, a form of temporal necessity. The necessity is said to be "accidental" because the event it is not necessary at all times but only after the event occurs. See *Predestination, God's Foreknowledge, and Future Contingents*, trans. by Marilyn McCord Adams and Norman Kretzmann (Indianapolis: Hackett, 1969).
3. I made this point in *The Dilemma of Freedom and Foreknowledge* (Oxford University Press, 1991), p. 119, and in "Foreknowledge and Freedom," *Companion to Philosophy of Religion*, edited by Philip L. Quinn and Charles Taliaferro (Blackwell, 1997). For a recent proponent of this position see David Hunt, "On Augustine's Way Out," *Faith and Philosophy* 16, #1 (January 1999), and "Moral Responsibility and Unavoidable Action," forthcoming in *Philosophical Studies*.
4. Harry Frankfurt, "Alternate Possibilities and Moral Responsibility," Journal of *Philosophy* 66 (December 1969), pp. 828–839; reprinted in *Moral Responsibility*, edited by John Martin Fischer (Ithaca, N.Y.: Cornell University Press, 1986), pp. 143–152. Subsequent page references will be taken from the Fischer reprint.
5. I have argued this before in *The Dilemma of Freedom and Foreknowledge*, chap. 6.
6. This adaptation of Frankfurt's example using a neurological device is similar to some of the cases described by John Martin Fischer. An early use of this type of example appears in "Responsibility and Control," *Journal of Philosophy* 89 (January 1982), pp. 24–40.
7. "Alternate Possibilities and Moral Responsibility," in Fischer, p. 149, note 3. Frankfurt does not conclude the truth of determinism in this paper, but he thinks that PAP is the only thing standing in the way of the acceptance of the compatibility of determinism and responsibility. It can then be argued that once compatibilism is accepted, there is nothing blocking the acceptance of determinism.
8. Robert Kane, *The Significance of Free Will* (N.Y.: Oxford University Press, 1996); David Widerker, "Libertarianism and Frankfurt's Attack on the Principle of Alternate Possibilities," *Philosophical Review* 104 (April 1995), pp. 247–261, and "Libertarian Freedom and the Avoidability of Decisions," *Faith and Philosophy* 12 (January 1995).

9. "Rescuing Frankfurt-Style Cases," *Philosophical Review* vol. 107, #1 (January 1998), pp. 97–112.
10. P. 103.
11. Mele and Robb, footnote 11.
12. *ibid.*
13. Eleonore Stump, "Libertarian Freedom and the Principle of Alternate Possibilities," in *Faith, Freedom, and Rationality*, edited by Jeff Jordan and Daniel Howard-Snyder (Lanham, Md: Rowman and Littlefield, 1996), pp. 73–88.
14. "Stumping for Widerker," *Faith and Philosophy*, vol. 16, #1 (January 1999), pp. 83–89.
15. This interpretation of Stump is confirmed in "Dust, Determinism, and Frankfurt: A Reply to Goetz," *Faith and Philosophy* 16, #3 (July 1999), pp. 413–422. In this paper Stump makes her position clearer. She argues that all it takes to falsify PAP is a device that interrupts the neural sequence correlated with an act of will after it begins but before it ends. The precise nature of the relationship between the act of will and the agent's brain states does not matter for the argument, and it is even possible that they are identical. This scenario falsifies PAP, but it does not require that an act of will is determined, even if it is identical with a neurological event. Stump maintains that Aquinas also rejected both PAP and causal determinism.
16. See Eleonore Stump, "Intellect, Will, and the Principle of Alternate Possibilities," in *Christian Theism and the Problems of Philosophy*, edited by Michael D. Beaty (University of Notre Dame Press, 1990). In this paper Stump describes an episode from Dostoevsky's *The Possessed* in which Verkhovensky is prepared to intervene with a surgical procedure to insure that Fedya murders the Lebyatkins if there is "any chance" that he won't do so when offered a bribe (p. 255). This implies that the intervention would occur after a causally necessary but insufficient condition for deciding not to commit the murder has occurred. Of course, Verkhovensky is not in a position in identify causally necessary conditions with 100% accuracy, but the point is sound since we can easily imagine how someone could identify a causally necessary condition in a non-deterministic universe.
17. "Alternate Possibilities and Moral Responsibility," pp. 148–149.
18. "Alternate Possibilities and Causal Histories," this volume.
19. "Of Active Power in General," Essay 1 of *Essays on the Active Power of the Mind* (MIT Press, 1969), p. 35.
20. In fact, Reid thought that the idea of a cause derives from that of a power and concluded that in the strict sense only conscious beings are causes. See "Of the Liberty of Moral Agents," chap. 2, "Of the Words Cause and Effect, Action and Active Power," in *Essays on the Active Powers of the Human Mind*, (MIT Press, 1969), pp. 267ff. What is especially interesting about this view is that it makes agency and the possession of alternate possibilities the prior idea. Causation and contingency are derivative.
21. Edward Wierenga, *The Nature of God: An Inquiry into Divine Attributes* (Ithaca: Cornell University Press, 1989), p. 85. An earlier version of the same type of response is given by Margery Bedford Naylor in "Frankfurt on the Principle of Alternate Possibilities," *Philosophical Studies* 46 (1984), pp. 249–258.
22. Wierenga says his view is similar to that of Reid in the footnote on p. 85.
23. Michael McKenna, "Alternate Possibilities and the Failure of the Counterexample Strategy," *Journal of Social Philosophy*, vol. 28, #3 (Winter 1997), p. 75.

24. An exception is causal over-determination scenarios in which the machine is set to cause a certain choice but the agent causes the same choice by her own power at the same time.

25. McKenna, p. 81.

26. McKenna, p. 77.

27. Michael Otsuka, "Incompatibilism and the Avoidability of Blame," *Ethics* 108 (July 1998), pp. 685–701.

28. Otsuka makes this explicit on p. 690.

29. Frankfurt, pp. 150–151.

30. Frankfurt, p. 152.

31. In "Must Knowers Be Agents?", presented at conference on Virtue and Duty in Epistemology, Santa Barbara, Calif, Nov. 13, 1999; forthcoming in *Virtue Epistemology*, Oxford University Press.

32. I am grateful to David Hunt, Andrew Eshleman, and Daniel Speak for comments on an earlier draft of this paper.

Philosophical Perspectives, 14, Action and Freedom, 2000

VALUING AND THE WILL

Michael E. Bratman
Stanford University

I. Valuing

In "Free Agency" Gary Watson argued that an account of free agency needs to distinguish what a person wants or desires—what a person is to some extent moved to do—from what a person values.[1] One may desire things one does not value—one example Watson gives is that of a "squash player who, while suffering an ignominious defeat, desires to smash his opponent in the face with the raquet."[2] And even when one values what one desires the motivational strength of the desire may not correspond to the extent to which one values what the desire is for.

What is it to value something? Watson notes that it at least involves wanting it: "to value is also to want".[3] But it involves more than this. When Watson tries in this paper to say what more it involves he tends to identify valuing with judging good.[4] He then goes on, in a tentative way, to offer a gloss on the idea of a person's values, a gloss that highlights a connection with one's reflective conception of a good life:

> an agent's values consist in those principles and ends which he—in a cool and non-self-deceptive moment—articulates as definitive of the good, fulfilling and defensible life.[5]

In a later essay Watson continues to hold that "valuing cannot be reduced to desiring (at any level)" but grants that his earlier gloss on an agent's values "is altogether too rationalistic".[6] He writes:

> For one thing, it conflates valuing with judging good. Notoriously, judging good has no invariable connection with motivation... . One can in an important sense fail to value what one judges valuable.[7]

I think Watson was right on a number of counts. He was right to emphasize the centrality to our understanding of human agency (including especially forms of free agency and self-determination) of some notion of valuing. He was right to insist that to value is not merely to want, though valuing does involve wanting. And he was, I think, right later to note the need for a distinction between valuing and judging good. That said, we are still without a more detailed story about the nature of valuing.

I want to sketch such a story. My proposal draws on several recent papers of mine.[8] In these papers I try to bring together into a single framework structures emphasized by, on the one hand, hierarchical theories of our agency and, on the other hand, what I have called a planning theory of intention.[9] My account of an agent's valuing tries to draw on this proposed synthesis in a way that is responsive to the cited points of agreement with Watson and that highlights connections between a person's valuings and (what we might reasonably call) that person's will.[10]

It will be useful to develop my proposal about valuing by exploiting certain Gricean ideas about, as he called it, "method in philosophical psychology".[11] So let me begin by saying what those ideas are.

II. Gricean creature construction

In his 1975 presidential address to the American Philosophical Association, Paul Grice sketched an approach to philosophical psychology that he labeled "creature construction". The idea, briefly, is

> to construct (in imagination, of course) according to certain principles of construction, a type of creature, or rather a sequence of types of creature, to serve as a model (or models) for actual creatures.[12]

Grice calls his creatures "pirots" and writes:

> The general idea is to develop sequentially the psychological theory for different brands of pirot, and to compare what one thus generates with the psychological concepts we apply to suitably related actual creatures...[13]

I find this methodology useful for present purposes.[14] I think that by proceeding with a process of broadly Gricean creature construction we can gain some insight into a number of theories and debates in the philosophy of action. We can, in particular, learn something important about valuing and its relation to the will.

Let me make some brief remarks about how I will proceed. My aim is to see a number of different models of agency as reasonable stages in a sequence of creature constructions. At each stage in the sequence I will try to identify an issue or problem that suggests some sort of modest addition to or extension of the earlier design.[15] The result will be a series of "just so stories". And this may give us pause. How does such a series of possible constructions tell us something about our own actual agency? Part of the answer is that the methodology depends on our arriving at a model of agency that recognizably applies to us—to adult human agents in a broadly modern world. We have a number of more or less articulated ideas about central features of our agency—what I have called "core" features of our agency.[16] A series of Gricean creatures is illuminating about our actual agency only if the series arrives at a model that does justice to these—or at least to many of these—core features. I hasten to add, though, that such a series need not be a unique route to a model of these core features; it need only be one intelligible route in which the steps along the way build appropriately on their antecedents.

But why not simply describe the final model of agency? Why bother with prior stages in the sequence of constructed creatures? The answer is that such a construction can help clarify how complex elements of our agency build on but differ from less complex elements. I think this is in particular helpful when we come to valuing. The model I arrive at in the end involves, as already indicated, a merger of hierarchical and planning structures. By seeing this model as an outcome of a sequence of constructed creatures we are in a position to identify different conceptions of valuing, and to clarify their relations to each other.[17]

III. Desires, considered desires, and deliberation

I will begin considerably further along a "sequence of types of creature" than does Grice. Let us suppose that *Creature 1* has both beliefs about its world and various desires concerning different possible states in that world, including different possible acts it might perform. These desires need not be organized in any systematic way, and may well come into conflict in particular cases. When there is conflict, Creature 1 is moved to act by its strongest desire (or cluster of desires) at the time of action.

Creature 1 is pushed and pulled by its desires. It is an agent in only a minimal sense. Behavioral outputs are as much attributable to the particular desires which were, on the occasion, strongest, as they are to an agent in any important sense different from those desires.

In search of more robust forms of agency, let us consider a creature who is more reflective about its desires. It acts only after it has considered what it desires in light of its beliefs, including beliefs about what relevant experiences are like. Sometimes such consideration changes what it desires. Perhaps it begins with a desire to fly to a distant land; yet, after consideration of what such an experience is really like, it comes to desire not to take the trip.

David Gauthier calls desires that pass such a test of reflection "considered".[18] Let us follow him in doing so. And let us construct a second creature, *Creature 2*. Creature 2 acts on the basis of its beliefs and *considered* desires. Because its desires are considered it differs from Creature 1.[19] But it remains like Creature 1 in a basic way: its desires and beliefs at the time of action determine what it intentionally does (or, anyway, tries to do) then.

Creature 2's intentional efforts depend on the motivational strength of its considered desires at the time of action.[20] So far we have been seeing the process by which conflicting considered desires motivate action as a broadly causal process, a process that reveals motivational strength. But a creature—call it *Creature 3*—might itself try to weigh considerations provided by such conflicting desires in deliberation about the pros and cons of various alternatives. In the simplest case, such weighing treats each of the things desired as a prima facie justifying end. In the face of conflict it weighs such desired ends, where the weights correspond to the motivational strength of the associated, considered desire.[21] The outcome of such deliberation will match the outcome of the causal, motivational processes envisaged in our description of Creature 2. But in the process of weighing the desired ends are treated as justifying, and the deliberation tracks that.

Creature 3, then, has this capacity for a kind of deliberation in the face of conflicting desires. In this respect it goes beyond Creature 2. But since the weights it invokes in such deliberation correspond to the motivational strength of the relevant considered desires (though perhaps not to the motivational strength of non-considered desires), the resultant activities will match those of a corresponding Creature 2 (all of whose desires, we are assuming, are considered). Each will act in ways that reveal the motivational strength of considered desires at the time of action, but for Creature 3 it will also be true that in some (though not all) cases it acts on the basis of how it weighs the ends favored by its conflicting, considered desires.

IV. Planning agents

It is time to note that many of Creature 3's considered desires will concern matters that cannot be achieved simply by action at a single time. It may, for example, want to nurture a vegetable garden, or to build a house. Such matters will require organized and coordinated action that extends over time. What it does now will depend not only on what it now desires but also on what it now expects it will do later given what it does now. It needs a way of settling now what it will do later given what it does now.

The point is even clearer when we remind ourselves, what we have so far ignored, that Creature 3 is not alone. It is, we may assume, one of some number of such creatures; and in many cases it needs to coordinate what it does with what others do so as to achieve ends desired by all participants, itself included. It needs others to be able reliably to predict what it will do later given what is done now.

There are, then, substantial pressures for mechanisms that support coordination and organization, both within the life of a particular creature, and across the lives of a number of interacting creatures. Such mechanisms, further, need to respect basic limits we can expect to characterize the psychology of such creatures.[22] We can expect such creatures to have limited resources of time and attention for complex reasoning,[23] and to be limited in what they know about themselves and their world. We need to add to the design of Creature 3 structures that support coordination, intra-personal and inter-personal, in ways compatible with these limits.

A plausible strategy here would be to add capacities to settle in advance on complex but partial plans of action.[24] A creature who can settle in advance on partial plans of action, fill them in as time goes by and as need be, and follow through in the normal course of events, is thereby in a better position to satisfy needs for coordination given basic cognitive limits. So let us add such planning structures to the structures of considered desires and beliefs characteristic of Creature 3. *Creature 4*, then, is a planning agent.

Creature 4's plans are plans for its own actions. Given their role in coordination, such plans will normally need to satisfy demands for consistency and coherence. They also will normally need to be stable, to be resistant to being easily reconsidered and abandoned. Otherwise such plans would not play their needed role in organized activity. Further, in having such plans our creature will need to be able to think of itself as the agent of actions at different times, of actions now and later. It will need to be able to think of itself as an agent who persists over time, one who begins and eventually completes temporally extended projects.

Creature 3, at any moment of choice, asks only what present action is best supported by its current beliefs and considered desires. Creature 4, in contrast, also has available plans of action settled on earlier. On some occasions of action Creature 4 can simply continue with what it had earlier planned to do rather than step back and reconsider what present action is best supported by its current beliefs and considered desires. This is what is involved in having stable plans of action. In constructing Creature 4 we need to characterize this stability.

In the basic case of interest Creature 4 has a prior plan to act in certain ways in its present circumstance, a prior plan formed on the basis, in part, of earlier beliefs about what its now-present circumstances would be. It is now faced with new information about its present circumstances, information that it did not anticipate when it formed its prior plan. When should it reconsider its prior plan in light of this new information? How stable should its plan be in the face of such new information?

These are questions about how to design the newly introduced planning structures. We want our answer to involve a modest extension from structures already present. One way to do this is to tie our account of plan stability directly to the creature's limits. We distinguish two different cases. There are, first, cases in which there is a present option that is known by the creature to be clearly favored by its present, relevant beliefs and considered desires. In such a case it will simply do what it now knows to be favored by those present beliefs and desires. In a second case it is not clear to the creature what the outcome would be of reconsideration of its prior plan in light of its new information. Now, there are costs of time and attention to stopping always to reconsider a prior plan in light of such new information. To the extent that a strategy of always reconsidering would make one less predictable to cognitively limited agents like oneself, there are further costs tied to needs for coordination. These costs are magnified for a creature whose various plans are interwoven so that a change in one element can have significant ripple effects that will need to be considered. So let us suppose that the general strategies Creature 4 has for responding in such a case to new information about its circumstances are sensitive to these kinds of costs. Its strategies are designed so that by following them a limited creature with basic needs for coordination will tend to promote, in the long run, the satisfaction of its considered desires and preferences. We can suppose that in some instances of the second kind of case this will mean that Creature 4 follows through with a prior plan even though, had it explicitly reconsidered in light of its present considered desires and relevant beliefs, it would have acted differently.[25]

Creature 4 is a somewhat sophisticated planning agent. But it has a problem. It can expect that its desires and preferences, though considered, may well change over time in ways that tend to undermine its efforts at organizing and coordinating its activities over time. Perhaps in many cases this is due to the kind of temporal discounting emphasized by (among others) George Ainslie.[26] So, for example, Creature 4 may have a plan to exercise every day. This plan may be grounded in its considered preference for exercising every day over never exercising. Its problem, though, is that each day, when faced with exercising then, it tends (even after full consideration) to prefer a sequence of not exercising on the present day but exercising all days in the future, to a uniform sequence of exercising each day, the present day included. At the end of the day it returns to its earlier considered preference in favor of exercising on each and every day. Nevertheless, its plan or policy[27] of exercising every day will be in trouble. Each day, when it comes time to exercise, it will prefer—and this will be a considered preference—not exercising that day.

Though Creature 4, unlike Creature 3, has the capacity to settle on prior plans or policies concerning exercise, this capacity does not yet help in such a case. This is not, after all, a case in which it is unclear at the time of action what would be the result of reconsideration, in light of new information, of the prior plan to exercise today. It is patently clear to the agent, at exercise time on each day, that it presently prefers not to exercise on the present day, though this considered preference will, it knows, change back later in the day. So Creature 4 will systematically undermine its prior exercise plan or policy.

Such cases of temptation, driven perhaps by temporal discounting, are likely to be quite common. Indeed, as Ainslie would emphasize, it seems an important fact about agents like us that such temptations systematically arise even when desires are considered. We can better equip our creatures for this fact about their own psychologies by providing for prior plans and policies that are stable in ways stronger than that envisaged in the construction of Creature 4.

How? Well, a planning agent sees itself as an agent who persists through time. In planning it is planning for its own future. Built into the capacity and disposition to be a planning agent is a commitment to giving some sort of significance to how it itself will in the future see its present actions. This suggests that we construct a creature whose plans are stable in the following, further way: there is a tendency to stick with a prior plan, despite a present and considered preference to the contrary, when it knows that it would later regret abandoning the plan and would later welcome having stuck with the plan despite its now-present preference. The stability of this creature's plans is shaped in part by such a (other things equal) no-regret principle.[28]

In the temptation cases highlighted by Ainslie, Creature 4 acts on its present preference; but in acting in this way it thereby frustrates a present and continuing preference for a uniform series of temptation-resisting actions over a uniform series of actions of giving in to temptation. To counteract this tendency to frustrate this present and continuing preference we build in a structure of plan stability that gives anticipated future regret a role in present plan-or-policy execution. This modification in the stability of the creature's prior plans and policies is grounded in commitments to some extent implicit in the planning structures already present in Creature 4. And, without going into details, I think it is clear how plans and policies that were stable in this further way might help in cases of temptation. A creature whose plans were stable in ways in part shaped by such a no-regret principle would be more likely than Creature 4 to resist temporary temptations. So let us build such a principle into the stability of the plans of *Creature 5*. Creature 5 is, like Creatures 3 and 4, an agent with considered desires and preferences, and an agent who deliberates in light of those considered desires and preferences. Creature 5 is, like Creature 4, a planning agent. But the stability of Creature 5's plans and policies is not derived solely from facts about its limits of time, attention, and the like. It is also grounded in the central concerns of a planning agent with its own future, concerns that lend special significance to anticipated future regret.

V. Hierarchy

Creature 5's desires and preferences are considered. Nevertheless, these desires and preferences sometimes change over time in ways that lead to problems about temptation and, more generally, to various forms of cross-temporal incoherence. Such changes may well lead to conflict with prior plans and policies. That was why we strengthened the stability of the plans and polices of Creature 5 by adding a (other things equal) no-regret principle. But these tensions between prior plans and policies, on the one hand, and present, considered desires and preferences, on the other hand, also elicit pressure to reflect further on those desires and preferences themselves. Given the tension between these preferences and prior plans and policies there is reason to give the creature the ability to reflect further and to ask itself whether it really wants a given desire or preference to play the cited roles in its agency.[29]

Does this question really differ from the question that already arose in the construction of Creature 2, the question whether a desire would survive consideration in light of relevant beliefs? It seems that it does. A desire to smoke might in fact survive consideration even though it is a desire the creature, on reflection, would rather not have and would rather did not shape its deliberation and action.[30] In that sense it may still be a desire the creature does not reflectively support or endorse. So there is reason to add to our creature sufficient resources to arrive at its own reflective endorsements or rejections of its desires.

How should we understand such resources? In an important series of papers Harry Frankfurt has argued, roughly, that the relevant resources are primarily resources for arriving at higher-order desires: a desire concerning one's desire to smoke, for example.[31] More specifically, they are resources for arriving at higher order desires concerning which first-order desires are effectively to control one's action, and in that sense be one's "will".[32] So let us add to Creature 5 the capacity and disposition to arrive at such hierarchies of higher-order desires concerning it's "will". This gives us a new creature, *Creature 6.*

VI. Merging hierarchical and planning structures: part one

There is, however, a problem with Creature 6, one that has been much discussed. It is not clear why a higher-order desire—even a higher-order desire that a certain desire be one's "will"—is not simply one more desire in the pool of desires. Why does it have authority to constitute or ensure the *agent*'s (that is, the *creature*'s) endorsement or rejection of a first-order desire?[33] Applied to Creature 6 this is the question of whether, by virtue solely of its hierarchies of desires, it really does succeed in taking its own stand of endorsement or rejection of various first-order desires. Since it was the ability to take its own stand that we were trying to provide in the move to Creature 6, we need some response to this challenge.

A successful response will need to introduce further structure; but we will want to see whether that further structure need involve only a modest extension from features that are already present in Creature 6. Now, Creature 6 is both a hierarchical and a planning agent. Perhaps there are resources implicit in the planning structures that can be used to supplement the hierarchical structures in a way that addresses the cited problem of authority.

Indeed, I think there are. As a planning agent Creature 6 has plans and policies concerning its actions. It is a short step to plans and policies concerning the functioning of its own desires. In particular, it is a short step to policies in favor of or against relevant functioning of relevant desires. Such policies, I think, help provide a plausible solution to the authority problem.

How? Let me briefly rehearse an argument for this that I have developed elsewhere.[34] The basic point is that Creature 6 is not merely a time-slice agent. It is, rather, and understands itself to be, a temporally persisting planning agent, one who begins, continues, and completes temporally extended projects. On a broadly Lockean view, its persistence over time consists in relevant psychological continuities (for example, the persistence of attitudes of belief and intention) and connections (for example, memory of a past event, or the later intentional execution of an intention formed earlier).[35] Certain attitudes have as a primary role the constitution and support of such Lockean continuities and connections. In particular, policies that favor or reject various desires have it as their role to constitute and support various continuities both of ordinary desires and of the policies themselves. Such policies also have it as their role to support various connections across time, as when one self-consciously follows through with a previously formed policy. So such policies have it as their role to help constitute and support the temporally extended structure of agency, as that structure is understood on a broadly Lockean approach. Indeed, it is in part by way of supporting and constituting such Lockean ties that such policies play their role of supporting broad forms of cross-temporal coordination and organization of motivation and action. For this reason such policies are not merely additional wiggles in the psychic stew. Instead, these policies have a claim to help determine where the agent—that is, the temporally persisting agent—stands with respect to its desires. Or so it seems to me reasonable to say.

Let us then give *Creature 7* such higher-order policies. Creature 7 has the capacity to take a stand with respect to its desires by arriving at relevant higher-order policies concerning the functioning of those desires over time. Creature 7 exhibits a merger of hierarchical and planning structures. Like Creature 6 it is reflective in ways that involve higher-order pro- and con-attitudes concerning its lower-order desires. But the higher-order attitudes of Creature 7 specifically include higher-order policies.[36] We understand such policies by appeal to the planning theory; and we ground their authority in their connection to the temporally extended structure of agency.

VII. Merging hierarchical and planning structures: part two

Creature 7 takes a stand concerning its desires by way of higher-order policies concerning relevant functioning of those desires. What functioning? Since we are seeking continuity with Creature 6 let us suppose that for Creature 7 these policies concern which desires are effectively to motivate, are to be one's "will" in Frankfurt's technical sense.

This brings us to a problem, however. Recall Creatures 3–5. They weigh conflicting ends for which they have conflicting, considered desires. They assign weights to those desired ends, weights that correspond to the motivational strengths of the considered desires. Creature 7 goes beyond Creatures 3–5 in part because Creature 7 has higher-order policies that favor or challenge motivational roles of its considered desires. When Creature 7 engages in deliberative weighing of conflicting, desired ends it seems that the assigned weights should reflect the policies that determine where it stands with respect to relevant desires. But the policies we have so far appealed to—policies concerning what desires are to be one's will (in Frankfurt's technical sense of "will")—do not quite address this concern. The problem is that one can in certain cases have policies concerning which desires are to motivate and yet these not be policies that accord what those desires are for a corresponding justifying role in deliberation.[37] My policy may be to allow a certain desire to motivate as a way of letting off steam, or because I find such a motivational process itself to be charming; but I need not thereby have a policy of treating what is desired as a justifying end in deliberation. It is one thing to favor a state of affairs that involves a desire and an action motivated by that desire; it is another thing to favor treating the included desire as providing a justifying end.[38] In being limited to higher-order policies that concern solely which desire is to motivate, Creature 7 seems not yet fully to have the capacity to take a stand concerning how he will treat his desires as reason-providing in deliberation.

A solution is to give our creature—call it *Creature 8*—the capacity to arrive at policies that express its commitment to being motivated by a desire *by way of its treatment of that desire as providing, in deliberation, a justifying end for action*.[39] Creature 8 has policies of treating (or not treating) certain desires as providing justifying ends—as, in this way, reason-providing—in motivationally effective deliberation.[40]

Creature 8, like Creature 7, brings together both hierarchical and planning structures. Unlike Creature 7, though, Creature 8 has higher-order policies that concern not only the motivational role of its desires, but also its treatment of its desires as reason-providing in motivationally effective deliberation.[41] These are policies concerning what weight, if any, is to be given to desired ends in motivationally effective deliberation. Following a discussion of related matters by Robert Nozick we can say that such policies involve a "commitment to make future decisions in accordance with the weights it establishes..."[42]

Let us call such policies *self-governing* policies. Now such a creature might have self-governing policies that conflict with and challenge each other. This would introduce complexities I want to put to one side here. So I will suppose that Creature 8's self-governing policies are mutually compatible and do not challenge each other.[43]

The grounds on which Creature 8 arrives at (and on occasion revises) such self-governing policies will be many and varied. We can see these policies as crystallizing complex pressures and concerns, some of which are grounded in other policies or desires.[44] These self-governing policies may be tentative and will normally not be immune to change. Nevertheless, given their role in the creature's temporally extended agency, we can say, roughly, that for the creature to be in control is for such policies to be in control.

Now, in describing Creature 8 we have focused on cases in which its first-order desires precede its formation of relevant higher-order self-governing policies. But we may suppose that Creature 8's capacity to arrive at new self-governing policies also includes the capacity to arrive, on reflection, at a new package of self-governing policy and associated first-order desire. For example, Creature 8 might, as a result of a powerful personal experience of helplessness, newly come both to desire to help others and to have a policy of treating that desire as reason-providing. Indeed, Creature 8 might thereby arrive at a new first-order *policy* of helping others, together with a higher-order policy of treating that first-order policy as reason-providing. (A first-order policy is it-self a kind of first-order desire, in the broadly generic sense of "desire" I am using here.) In such a case the creature may arrive at a reflexive policy to help others by way of treating this very policy of helping others as setting a justify-ing end for deliberation.[45]

My pursuit of Gricean creature construction stops here, at least for now.[46] Creature 8 is an agent with considered desires and beliefs, stable plans and policies, and higher-order self-governing policies some of which may be reflex-ive in the way just highlighted. In these respects our model of Creature 8 seems to me to capture important core features of *our* agency.

This much in hand, it is time to return to our query about the nature of valuing.

VIII. Models of valuing

Begin by asking at what point in our series of constructed creatures some-thing like valuing can be discerned. The answer, I take it, is: Creature 3. Crea-ture 3's desires are considered; and it treats what those considered desires are for as justifying ends in deliberation. It would be natural to say that Creature 3 values what it, after consideration, desires, and it values such things to the ex-tent that, after consideration, it desires them.[47] Such valuing involves wanting, but is more than that, as Watson wanted.

Valuing in this sense continues to be present in Creatures 4 and 5. What is added in the construction of those creatures is not a new structure of valuing, but rather a structure of more-or-less stable plans built on top of the same struc-ture of valuing. For example, the story about regret in our discussion of Crea-ture 5 led to a change not in the basic account of valuing but, instead, in the account of the stability of plans and policies.

Note, however, that once we introduce hierarchical structures—as we did with Creatures 6–8—these matters begin to change. Consider, in particular, Creature 8. Creature 8 has certain higher-order planning structures, including higher-order self-governing policies concerning its treatment of its own de-sires (including its own first-order policies) as reason-providing. These higher-order planning structures, in contrast with the planning structures introduced with Creatures 4 and 5, are not simply built on top of a separate structure of valuing. Instead, these higher-order planning structures themselves feed back to and help shape what such a creature can plausibly be said to value. I pro-ceed to explain.

Suppose Creature 8 has a considered (though temporary) preference in fa-vor of not exercising today. But suppose it has a higher-order policy that dis-counts the weight of this preferred end in deliberation, given its conflict with its considered preference for regular exercise over regular non-exercise. Sup-pose that this policy is not in conflict with some other self-governing policy of that creature. And suppose this creature deliberates about whether to go to the gym today. What weight will it assign to exercise: the weight associated with its considered (though temporary) preference in favor of not exercising today? or the weight associated with its self-governing policy? Given the authority of such a self-governing policy to speak for the agent—an authority grounded in ties to Lockean conditions of persistence of the agent over time—I think that it is this policy-determined weight that will be relevant to Creature 8's deliberation about what to do now. It is when this policy is effective and its policy-determined weight is operative in deliberation that we can say not only that there is a deliberative process but also that the agent is deliberating and the deliberation is its own.

If we ask what Creature 8 values in this case, the answer seems to be: what it values is constituted in part by its higher-order self-governing policies.[48] In particular, it values exercise over non-exercise even right now, and even given that it has a considered (though temporary) preference to the contrary. Unlike Creatures 3–5, what Creature 8 now values is not simply a matter of its present, considered desires and preferences. It is in part a function of its higher-order self-governing policies. The introduction of these self-governing policies has changed the structure of its valuing.

This points toward a story about one important kind of valuing for a creature as complex as Creature 8. Roughly speaking, such an agent values X (in the relevant sense) when it has a desire for X (a desire that may itself be a first-order policy) and a self-governing policy in favor of treating that desire as providing an end that is justifying (perhaps to a certain, specified degree) in motivationally effective deliberation.

Now, this model of Creature 8 seems in relevant respects to be a (partial) model of us. So we arrive at the conjecture that one important kind of valuing of which we are capable involves, in the cited ways, both our first-order desires and our higher-order self-governing policies. In an important sub-class of cases our valuing involves reflexive policies that are both first-order policies of action and higher-order policies to treat the first-order policy as reason-providing in motivationally effective deliberation.[49]

This may seem odd. Valuing seems normally to be a first-order attitude. One values honesty, say. The proposal is that an important kind of valuing involves higher-order policies. Does this mean that, strictly speaking, what one values (in this sense) is itself a desire—not honesty, say, but a desire for honesty? No it does not. What I value in the present case is honesty; but, on the theory, my valuing honesty in part consists in certain higher-order self-governing policies.

Could one have a policy of treating, say, helping others as a justifying end in motivationally effective deliberation, and yet still not have a first-order desire in favor of helping others? I think the answer is yes. However, actually to treat helping others in this way in motivationally effective deliberation will, I think, involve some such first-order desire (in the broadly generic sense of "desire"). In the absence of such a desire, then, the cited policy will involve a commitment to coming to have the desire.[50] Should we say that such a higher-order policy, in the absence of the first-order desire, suffices for valuing? Well, it is not by itself a kind of valuing characteristic of self-determined activity, for that requires valuing that really does control action. But we might still say that this is a kind of (somewhat attenuated) valuing, related in indicated ways to the motivationally more robust valuing I have highlighted.[51]

IX. Valuing and the will

Our proposal ties an important kind of reflective valuing to the will of an agent whose agency is temporally extended. Intentions, plans, and policies were initially introduced on top of prior structures of considered desires. Those structures of considered desires were, at these preliminary stages, structures of valuings. Intentions and the like were introduced in response to pressures for coordination in the pursuit of what was, in that sense, valued. Such intentions involve a commitment to action, and so could reasonably be said to constitute structures of the will. Once such structures of the will were on the scene, there was pressure for them to include reflection on the very desires which grounded the introduction of those structures in the first place. Such pressure led us to Creature 7, and then to Creature 8. Given their ties to the temporally extended structure of agency, these structures fed back into the determination of what the agent values. This led us to our conclusion: the agent's reflective valuing involves a kind of higher-order willing.[52]

Notes

1. Gary Watson, "Free Agency," *Journal of Philosophy* 72 (1975):205–220.
2. Ibid., p. 210.
3. Ibid., p. 215
4. Ibid., p. 212
5. Ibid., p. 215
6. "Free Action and Free Will," *Mind* (1987): 145–172, at p. 150.
7. Ibid. See also Michael Stocker, "Desiring the Bad: An Essay in Moral Psychology," *Journal of Philosophy* (1979): 738–753.
8. "Identification, Decision, and Treating as a Reason," *Philosophical Topics* (1996):1–18 [reprinted in my *Faces of Intention: Selected Essays on Intention and Agency* (New York: Cambridge University Press, 1999)]; "Reflection, Planning, and Temporally Extended Agency," *The Philosophical Review* (forthcoming); and "Hierarchy, Circularity, and Double Reduction," unpublished manuscript.
9. For central discussions of hierarchical theories see Harry Frankfurt *The Importance of What We Care About* (New York: Cambridge University Press, 1988). For my presentation of the planning theory see *Intention, Plans, and Practical Reason* (Cambridge, Mass.: Harvard University Press, 1987; reissued by CSLI Publications, 1999) and *Faces of Intention*.
10. As I note in "Reflection, Planning, and Temporally Extended Agency," I see the planning theory of intention as a modest theory of the will.
11. Paul Grice, "Method in Philosophical Psychology (From the Banal to the Bizarre)" (Presidential Address) in *Proceedings and Addresses of the American Philosophical Association* (1974–75): 23–53.

262 / Michael E. Bratman

12. Ibid., p. 37
13. Ibid., p. 37
14. Here I take myself to be in agreement with a number of other philosophers. One
example is John Perry, who endorses this Gricean methodology in his "Perception,
Action, and the Structure of Believing," in his *The Problem of the Essential Indexical and Other Essays* (New York: Oxford University Press, 1992): 121–149, at
pp. 121–122. (See also his paper with David Israel, "Fodor and Psychological Explanations" in *The Problem of the Essential Indexical*: 301–321, at p. 306.) Another
example is J. David Velleman, who points to a methodology that is Gricean in spirit
in his "Introduction" to his *The Possibility of Practical Reason* (Oxford University
Press, forthcoming). Velleman's discussion helped rekindle my thinking about the
15. So I will try to respect Grice's "supposition that the psychological theory for a given
type is an extension of, and includes, the psychological theory of its predecessor-
16. In my "Reflection, Planning, and Temporally Extended Agency".
17. I see my remarks here about the significance of creature constructions as in the
spirit of Grice's remarks in "Method in Philosophical Psychology" at p. 37. Let me
add that, as will become clear below, this methodology also helps me to articulate
relations between several different ideas about planning agency that I have dis-
18. David Gauthier, *Morals by Agreement* (New York: Oxford University Press, 1986),
pp. 29–33. Gauthier suggests (p. 30) that certain forms of inexperience preclude
having a considered desire even if one fully reflects in light of beliefs one does
have. This is a complexity I will put to one side here. Thanks to Sergio Tenenbaum
19. To be more realistic we might limit ourselves to saying that Creature 2 has the capacity to make the transition from unconsidered to considered desires but does not
always do this. But it will keep the discussion more manageable to simplify and to
20. See Alfred R. Mele, "Motivational Strength," *Nous* 32 (1998): 23–36.
21. I do not say this is a principle that Creature 3 itself appeals to in its deliberation.
The connection between weights in deliberation and motivational strength is a structural feature of Creature 3's psychology, not a principle the creature itself cites in
22. Cp. Grice's remarks about the role of the "Engineer" in creature construction in
"Method in Philosophical Psychology," at p. 38.
23. This is a general point of Herbert Simon. See, e.g., his *Reason in Human Affairs*
(Stanford: Stanford University Press, 1983).
24. This is a theme of my *Intention, Plans, and Practical Reason*.
25. See *Intention, Plans, and Practical Reason*, chap. 5, and my "Planning and the
Stability of Intention," *Minds and Machines* 2 (1992): 1–16.
26. See his *Picoeconomics: The Strategic Interaction of Successive Motivational States
within the Person* (New York: Cambridge University Press, 1992). I discuss Ainslie's views in my "Planning and Temptation," in Larry May, Marilyn Friedman,
and Andy Clark, eds., *Mind and Morals: Essays on Ethics and Cognitive Science*
(Cambridge, Mass.: Bradford/MIT Press, 1995): 293–310 (reprinted in my *Faces
of Intention*). See also David Gauthier, "Resolute Choice and Rational Delibera-

27. I see policies as intentions that are general in relevant respects. See my *Intention, Plans, and Practical Reason*, at pp. 87–91, and my "Intention and Personal Policies," *Philosophical Perspectives* 3 (1989): 443–469.
28. This is, roughly, a view of plan stability I develop in "Toxin, Temptation, and the Stability of Intention," in Jules Coleman and Christopher Morris, eds., *Rational Commitment and Social Justice: Essays for Gregory S. Kavka* (New York: Cambridge University Press, 1998) [reprinted in my *Faces of Intention*]. In that paper I also discuss alternative models of stability proposed by David Gauthier and Edward McClennen.
29. The significance of a version of this question has been a major theme in work of Harry Frankfurt. See esp. his *The Importance of What We Care About*.
30. Cf. Gauthier: "Some persons prefer to smoke—and their preference may be fully considered and all too experienced—and yet they prefer to prefer not to smoke." *Morals by Agreement*, at p. 32.
31. See esp. his *The Importance of What We Care About*.
32. "Freedom of the Will and the Concept of a Person," in *The Importance of What We Care About*, p. 14.
33. See Watson, "Free Agency", pp. 217–219. Frankfurt's most recent response is in his "The Faintest Passion," (Presidential Address) *Proceedings and Addresses of the American Philosophical Association* 66 (1992): 5–16, reprinted in his *Necessity, Volition, and Love* (New York: Cambridge University Press, 1999): 95–107 .
34. "Reflection, Planning, and Temporally Extended Agency".
35. I will simply take such a broadly Lockean view for granted in the present context. The terminology of connections and continuities comes from Derek Parfit, *Reasons and Persons* (New York: Oxford University Press, 1984), 204–209. I note a divergence in my use of these terms in my "Reflection, Planning, and Temporally Extended Agency".
36. So the psychology of Creature 7 continues to have the hierarchical structure of pro-attitudes introduced with Creature 6. The difference is that the higher-order pro-attitudes of Creature 6 were simply characterized as desires in a broad, generic sense, and no appeal was made to the distinctive species of pro-attitude constituted by plan-like attitudes. That is the sense in which, following Grice, the psychology of Creature 7 is an "extension of" the psychology of Creature 6.
37. For related discussions see J. David Velleman, "The Guise of the Good," *Nous* 26 (1992): 3–26, esp. 3–7; Michael Smith, *The Moral Problem*, (Oxford: Blackwell, 1994): 131–136.
38. I make this point also in "Hierarchy, Circularity, and Double Reduction."
39. I try to say more about what it is for an agent to treat a desire as, in the relevant sense, reason-providing in my "Hierarchy, Circularity, and Double Reduction". A consequence of my view there is that such treatment involves an intention or policy in favor of relevant functioning of the desire. This means that a policy of treating a desire as reason-providing is higher-order in two ways: first, it concerns the desire; second, it concerns a mode of treatment that itself involves an intention or policy.
40. See my "Identification, Decision, and Treating as a Reason," and my "Reflection, Planning, and Temporally Extended Agency". Somewhat related ideas can be found in Rachel Cohon, "Internalism about Reasons for Action," *Pacific Philosophical Quarterly* 74 (1993): 265–288; Allan Gibbard, *Wise Choices, Apt Feelings* (Cambridge, Mass.: Harvard University Press, 1990), at p. 163; T. M. Scanlon, *What We Owe to Each Other* (Cambridge, Mass.: Harvard University Press, 1998), chap. 1;

and Christine Korsgaard, *The Sources of Normativity* (Cambridge: Cambridge University Press, 1996), esp. chap. 3.

41. In this way Creature 8 involves, as Grice would want, an "extension" of structures already present in Creature 7.

42. Robert Nozick, *Philosophical Explanations* (Cambridge, Mass.: Harvard University Press, 1981), at p. 297.

43. In terminology drawn from Frankfurt, "The Faintest Passion," we can say that the creature in such a case is "satisfied" with its self-governing policies. I develop the idea of satisfaction in a way that is a bit different from Frankfurt's version in my "Reflection, Planning, and Temporally Extended Agency". In this latter essay I also note—a further, important complication I will not discuss here—the need also to introduce what I call "quasi-policies".

44. This may be in the spirit of Charles Taylor's remarks about our efforts to arrive at "articulations" of our "largely inarticulated sense of what is of decisive importance." See his "Responsibility for Self," reprinted in Gary Watson, ed., *Free Will* (New York: Oxford University Press, 1982), at pp. 122–123.

45. Keith Lehrer discusses a related (but different) idea of a reflexive higher-order preference. See his *Self-Trust: A Study of Reason, Knowledge, and Autonomy* (New York: Oxford University Press, 1997), pp. 110–112.

46. Further discussion would need more fully to address issues raised by various kinds of conflict. We might, in addition, also go on to consider what happens when our creatures join with each other to form *shared* intentions, plans, and policies. I discuss some of the issues raised by this possibility in a quartet of papers on shared agency included in my *Faces of Intention*. It might be that the story I go on to tell here about valuing could usefully be extended (using resources from my account of shared intention) to creatures who systematically join with each other in shared intentions and policies, at times thereby arriving at shared values. But that is an issue for another occasion.

47. Cp. Gauthier: "[v]alue is a measure of considered preference." (*Morals by Agreement*, at p. 33) Michael Smith criticizes Gauthier's view about valuing in his *The Moral Problem*, at pp. 141–142. But his criticism simply assumes, contrary to Watson's proposal, that valuing need not involve wanting. [Gilbert Harman makes a related point in response to Smith in his "Desired desires," in R. G. Frey and C. W. Morris, eds., *Value, Welfare, and Morality* (New York: Cambridge University Press, 1993):138–57, at p. 150.] My reason for providing, below, a different model of valuing is different from Smith's, and is compatible with Watson's constraint that valuing involves wanting.

48. Another philosopher who has pointed in the direction of a connection between valuing and policies is David Copp. Copp claims that one's "values" consist, roughly, in policies concerning the course of one's life. Copp, though, does not focus on the kinds of higher-order policies that have been my concern here. See David Copp, *Morality, Normativity & Society* (New York: Oxford University Press, 1995) esp. pp. 177–178. It was Copp, too, who first suggested to me that my account of identification in my "Identification, Decision, and Treating as a Reason" might yield an account of valuing. Gilbert Harman, in a helpful conversation, also once suggested that he might favor some sort of close connection between valuing and policies.

49. Michael Smith has argued against a hierarchical account of valuing, sketched by David Lewis, according to which "valuing is just desiring to desire." [David Lewis, "Dispositional Theories of Value," *Proceedings of the Aristotelian Society* suppl.

vol. (1989):113–137, at p. 115.] Smith's main criticism is, in effect, that Lewis does not solve the authority problem for hierarchical theories. I agree with this criticism of Lewis's account. But if I am right that appeal to planning structures helps solve the authority problem then Smith's objections to Lewis need not apply to my account. See Michael Smith, *The Moral Problem*, at pp. 142–147.

50. Here I depart from Frankfurt's decision to consider only higher-order desires concerning first-order desires one already has. See "Freedom of the Will and the Concept of a Person," in *The Importance of What We Care About*, pp. 15–16.

51. In this paragraph I am indebted to conversation with Fred Schueler and Sergio Tenenbaum.

52. Thanks to Lori Gruen, Agnieszka Jaworska, Keith Lehrer, Elijah Millgram, Peter Railton, Fred Schueler, Sergio Tenenbaum, J. David Velleman, Gideon Yaffe, and audiences at the University of Michigan and the University of New Mexico. Many of the ideas in this essay come from work done while I was a Fellow at The Center for Advanced Study in the Behavioral Sciences. I am grateful for financial support provided by The Andrew W. Mellon Foundation.

Philosophical Perspectives, 14, Action and Freedom, 2000

THE EPISTEMIC REQUIREMENTS FOR MORAL RESPONSIBILITY

Carl Ginet
Cornell University

In this paper I will use the term "action" to mean a person's (voluntarily and intentionally) moving their body in a certain way and thereby bringing about a certain consequence. For example, Herman moves his arm and hand and thereby causes a car door to close on Sammy's fingers. And I will use the term "omission" to mean a person's failing to prevent some event because they did *not* move their body in a certain way at a certain time, that is, had they moved in that way at that time, their movement would have prevented the event; let us call this event the consequence of the omission. For example, Herman fails to push a certain button on the dashboard before exiting his car, and, if he had pushed that button then, his doing so would have closed the sunroof and thereby prevented the rain from soaking the interior of his car. (These are, I realize, somewhat artificial meanings for the terms "action" and "omission", not in complete conformity with their ordinary use.)

What is required for a person to be morally responsible for such an action or omission (or for the consequence involved in the action or omission)? Let us restrict our attention to actions or omissions in which the consequence is undeserved harm to someone, to their person or to their interests, and ask a more restricted question: What is required for a person to be morally *blameworthy* for a *harmful* action or omission?

I will assume here that one thing required is that the agent could have avoided the action or omission. I will call this the "could-have-done-otherwise condition," or "CDO condition" for short. This assumption is controversial. (Harry Frankfurt has put forward a type of example which, as he and many others see it, shows that being able to avoid a harmful action or omission is not required for being morally responsible for it. Some who are persuaded by Frankfurt-type examples suggest that, instead of the CDO condition, some would-have-done-otherwise-if condition is what is necessary.[1]) I'll not defend my assumption here. The question I want to pursue in this paper is this: assuming that the CDO condition is necessary for being blameworthy for a harmful action, what else is necessary?[2] (My answer to this question, or some adaptation of it, might well prove to be equally satisfactory if we were to replace the CDO condition with some would-have-done-otherwise-if condition, but I'll not explore that possibility.)

I

We need to state the CDO condition more exactly. We are considering actions where at a certain time t1 a person S moves their body in a certain way M and thereby causes a harmful consequence of a certain sort H, and omissions where at a certain time t1 S does *not* move in a certain way M and thereby fails to prevent a certain sort of harmful consequence H. The specification of the CDO condition that may first come to mind is something like the following.

> (A) For actions: until t1 it was open to S not to make movement M then or any other movement that would bring about H;
> for omissions: until t1 it was open to S to make movement M then or some other movement that would prevent H.

But this is, unfortunately, too simple. It fails to cover cases where, although at t1 it was no longer open to S to make (or not to make) M at t1, at some earlier time it was open to S to act (or not to act) in some way such that, *had* S so acted (or not so acted) at that earlier time, it *would* have been open to S until t1 to make (or not to make) M at t1. For example, Frank sets off on a walk at 7:00pm and is a mile from home at 7:30pm when he suddenly remembers that he promised his family to record a certain TV program that begins at 7:30. Despite his being unable at 7:30 to turn on the TV and VCR, Frank can properly be held accountable for failing to do so and, if he had no outweighing good reason for bringing it about that he was unable to do so, he can be held blameworthy for this failure.

In order to cover cases of this sort we must state the CDO condition necessary for S's being blameworthy for an action or omission in the following, more complex way:

> *For actions*: At some time t0 not later than t1, either (i) S acted in a certain way W such that it was open to S at t0 not to act in way W then and, had S not acted in way W then, it would have been open to S at t1 not to make M or any other movement then that would bring about H, or (ii) S did not at t0 act in a certain way W such that it was open to S to act in way W then and, had S acted in way W then, it would have been open to S at t1 not to make M or any other movement then that would bring about H.
> *For omissions*: At some time t0, not later than t1, either (i) S acted in a certain way W such that it was open to S at t0 not to act in way W then and, had S not acted in way W then, it would have been open to S at t1 to make M or some other movement then that would have prevented H, or

(ii) S did not at t0 act in a certain way W such that it was open to her to act in way W then and, had S acted in way W then, it would have been open to S at t1 to make M or some other movement then that would have prevented H.

II

Let us first consider the restricted class of cases that satisfy condition (A) above—that is, actions where S had it open to her *at t1* not to make M or any other movement that would cause H, and omissions where S had it open to her *at t1* to make movement M or some other movement that would prevent H. In such cases I will say that the CDO condition is satisfied *at t1*.[3]

S's harmful action may satisfy the CDO condition at t1 but still not be one for which S deserves blame, if at t1 S did not know that then making movement M would bring about H *and* S's failure to know this was not itself blameworthy. For example, Simon enters the hotel room he has just checked into and flips what appears to be, and what he takes to be, an ordinary light switch, but, to his surprise and consternation, the flipping of the switch sets off a loud fire alarm. It seems that, because he did not know that his flipping the switch would have this unfortunate consequence, it would be wrong to feel indignant with him for bringing about that consequence.

Similarly, S's harmful omission may satisfy the CDO condition at t1 but still not be one for which S deserves blame, if at t1 S did not know that then making movement M would prevent H and S's failure to know this was not itself blameworthy. Herb did not unlock the back door before leaving for work, and therefore later that day the plumber was unable to get in to repair the furnace and left a note saying that he would not be able to come again until next week. But Herb did not know that the plumber was scheduled to come that day—his wife made the appointment and forgot to tell him—so Herb cannot be justly reproached for not making the movements that would have prevented the postponement of the furnace repairs.

Should we say, then, that, when an action (or omission) satisfies the CDO condition at t1, S is blameworthy for bringing about harm H by making movement M at t1 (or for failing to prevent harm H by making movement M at t1) only if it is also the case that at t1 S knew that making movement M would bring about H (or knew that making M would prevent H)? No, this would be to require S to know too much. Even though Herman, when he pushed the car door, did not know that he would thereby close the door on Sammy's fingers, we are right to feel some indignation towards Herman for causing Sammy's pain and injury, *if* Herman knew that Sammy was still emerging from the car and that there was a possibility that Sammy would put his fingers where the door could close on them. George tossed a rock over the edge of a cliff, which struck and injured someone on the trail below. Even though he did not know that it *would* hit someone, we are surely right to reproach George for a reckless act, if he knew that there were or might well be people on the trail below and therefore knew that his tossed rock *might* hit someone. Such examples suggest that we should not require for blameworthiness more than that at t1 S knew that making movement M would *or might* cause H.

It will be convenient to use the verb "know" and cognate terms in a special restricted sense. I'll mark such uses with an asterisk (*). Let us stipulate that "at t1 S knew* that..." implies that at t1 S *actively* believed (the truth) that... To say that George knew* that there might be people on the trail below when he tossed his rock is to imply, not only that he then believed this truth, but also that this consideration had not then slipped his mind: he was then sufficiently aware of this possibility that it would *not* be correct to say that he threw the rock only because he failed to recall (to think of) the possibility of people below. He threw the rock while aware that it might hit someone below. This does not entail that he *intended* that it hit someone; he may not have cared whether it did or even have hoped that it would not.

S must, of course, (and usually will) have had justification for believing that causing H (or harm of that sort) by moving in way M was a non-negligible possibility. (In the case of George's throwing the rock over the cliff, his beliefs would give him such justification if they merely lacked any basis for thinking that the area below was very unlikely to have any people in it.) It is not quite enough, however, to require only that S have some justification or other for believing this: S must have a justification for believing it that is not also a reason for believing a *false* proposition as to *how* her making movement M would or might cause H. Melanie shoots her gun and thereby causes the death of her enemy, fully intending to do so. Her belief as she pulled the trigger that by firing the gun she would cause her enemy's death was correct and justified, for she is an expert marksman and just an hour ago she checked the operation of her gun and loaded it. But what happened was this: the bullet she fired was deflected by a flying bird; nevertheless the firing of the gun caused the death of her enemy because the sound of the shot startled a passing driver and caused him to lose control of his car which struck and killed her enemy. Here I am disinclined to regard Melanie as blameworthy *for the death of her enemy* (though she is, of course, to be blamed for acting with the intent of killing him). She seems no more culpable for that consequence than she would have been had she aimed her shot harmlessly into the sky and unintentionally caused her enemy's death in a similar way. What negates blameworthiness for the harmful consequence in both cases is that the justification Melanie has for her true belief that her firing the gun will cause the death of her enemy is also a justification for a *false* belief as to *how* it will bring about that consequence.

Let us say of justification that has this unfortunate property that it is not *proper* justification. And let us stipulate further that "at t1 S knew* that moving in way M then would or might cause a consequence of sort H" implies, not only that at t1 S actively believed this truth, but also that S had proper justification for this belief.

Should we say, then, with respect to a harmful action, that what is additionally necessary when the CDO condition is satisfied at t1, is this: at t1 S knew* that moving in way M then would or might cause a consequence of sort H? No. This is still to require more than is necessary.

A person may be blameworthy for a harmful action, even if they fail to realize that their movement will bring about a harm, if the failure to realize this is itself something for which the person is blameworthy. Consider a revised version of our example of Simon and the switch that set off a fire alarm. Suppose that the switch did *not* look at all like an ordinary light switch—the whole thing was red, much larger than a typical light switch, and located fairly high up on the wall. Moreover, immediately below it in large white letters on a red background were the words "FIRE ALARM". Simon is a normal adult whose native language is English and he has been about in the world enough to know about the typical appearance of light switches and about fire alarms. But so intent was he on finding a light switch that he somehow failed to notice the words "FIRE ALARM", or to take in the significance of the conspicuous differences between the switch he pulled and a typical light switch, and thought that the switch he flipped would just turn on a light. As Simon himself later confessed in making profuse apologies, his failure to notice or heed those things was inexcusable. A certain amount of indignation towards him, for his causing the alarm to go off, would be deserved (though, of course, not as much as if he had intentionally set it off).

Similar observations hold for cases of harmful omissions. Consider a revised version of the case of Herb's not unlocking the back door. When Herb comes down to make his breakfast, there is a note by the coffeemaker from his wife. Herb puts the note aside without reading it, telling himself that he will read it as soon as he's poured his juice and coffee. But he starts thinking about something else and forgets the note. The note reads, "Herb, Before you leave please unlock the back door so that the plumber can get in to fix the furnace." Herb goes off to work without unlocking the back door. Even though Herb didn't know* as he was leaving for work that, if he then unlocked the back door, he would prevent the plumber's being locked out, his wife would be justified in reproaching him for failing to prevent this, given that his failure to read her note before leaving was blameworthy.

It is clear that failure to realize that one's action or omission would or might have the harmful consequence can itself be culpable: the belief one lacked is a belief one *should* have had. And that being so, even if it is only because of that failure that one commits the harmful action or omission (i.e., one would not have done so had one known* at the time that it might have the harmful consequence), one is blameworthy for the harmful consequence.

So we can say that, when the CDO condition is satisfied at t1 (the time of making, or omitting to make, the relevant bodily movement), what is further required in order for S to be blameworthy for the harmful action or omission is the following disjunctive condition: at t1, either S knew* that moving in way

M would or might bring about the harm H (or, in the case of an omission, S knew* that moving in way M would or might prevent H) or S should have known* this.

III

Let me here digress briefly to note an interesting question that arises about cases, like that of George's throwing a rock over the cliff, where the agent knew* or should have known* that his act (or omission) *might* have a certain sort of harmful consequence. Imagine two such cases which differ only in that in one the agent's act (or omission) *does* have the sort of harmful consequence he knew* or should have known* it might have, but in the other it does *not*. With respect to all other relevant circumstances, particularly with respect to the agent's mental state at the time of his potentially harmful act (or omission), the cases are exactly alike. The interesting question is this: Does the *un*lucky agent (the one whose action (or omission) does have the harmful consequence) deserve *more blame* for his action (or omission) than the lucky agent deserves for his?

Thomas Nagel (1979) and Bernard Williams (1981) have argued that our actual practice of moral assessment implies an affirmative answer to this question; our moral reactions in such cases show that we do take the degree of blame an agent deserves to depend on sheer luck. Against this view, Brian Rosebury (1995) has made a convincing case that examples that may seem to support it do not actually do so. (Rosebury's discussion covers cases where the agent neither knew* nor should have known* that her action (or omission) might have a harmful consequence, as well as the cases we are concerned with here, where the agent knew* or should have known* this.)

In some such examples, Rosebury argues, what is being described as observers' expressing or feeling a greater degree of moral condemnation toward the unlucky action (or its agent's feeling a greater degree of self-reproach) is being misdescribed, that it is actually some other feeling or attitude, such as dismay or regret or sadness. This may be the appropriate thing to say, for instance, about Herman's feelings after closing the car door on Sammy's fingers as compared with Hermione's feelings after narrowly missing closing the door on Sammy's fingers: Herman of course feels a great deal worse than Hermione did, but the additional negative feeling, insofar as it is rational and appropriate, is keen regret and dismay at having caused an injury rather than more severe self-reproach or heavier guilt.

But there are cases where our greater negative feeling towards the unlucky agent really is moral blame. About these Rosebury argues that our attitude does not reflect what would be our considered judgment were we to take adequate account of the agent's epistemic responsibilities and limitations at the time of his action. So, for example, Sammy's mother may initially be inclined to condemn Herman a good deal more strongly for his carelessness when he slams the car door on Sammy's fingers than the mild reproach she felt towards Hermione for her earlier car-door slamming that luckily missed Sammy's fingers. But when she reflects that Hermione was as heedless as Herman and that Herman had as much excuse for being heedless as Hermione had—both were preoccupied with what they were about to do after getting out of the car—the mother's feelings of indignation towards the two of them should tend to equalize. Or I might be initially inclined to feel greater outrage at a midnight bombing of a shop that killed people than at one that did not kill or injure anyone. But after realizing that in neither case did the bomber intend to kill people (in both they hoped that no one would be around when the bomb exploded) and that in both cases the bomber knew* there was a non-negligible chance that the bomb would kill people, I become as outraged at the action of the "lucky" bomber as I am at the action of the "unlucky" bomber.

IV

Returning now to our investigation of the epistemic requirements for blameworthiness, can we find something general and informative to say about what sort of circumstance will make true the judgment that at t1 S *should* have known* that his action (or omission) would or might have a harmful consequence of sort H (in a case where at t1 S did *not* know* this)? We can, I think, say this: S's failure to know* must have been a consequence of some earlier action or omission concerning which S then knew* or should have known* that it would or might lead to such an unfortunate failure of knowledge* as S in fact suffered at t1 (Holly Smith calls this the "benight*ing*" action or omission). That is: at some time t0 earlier than t1, either S acted in a certain way W that brought about his failure to know* at t1, which was responsible for his harmful act (or omission) then, and at t0 S knew* or should have known* that his so acting then would or might lead (risked leading) to that sort of failure to know*, or S omitted to act in a certain way W such that S's acting in way W at t0 would have prevented his failure to know* at t1 and at t0 S knew* or should have known* that his so acting then would or might prevent that sort of failure to know*. Let's call the harmful act (or omission) at t1, which occurred because of S's knowledge* failure at t1, the "benight*ed*" act (or omission).

For example, Simon's failure to realize that the switch he was flipping was an alarm switch was (in one version of the example) culpable because, in the period between the time when the switch first caught his eye and the time he flipped it, he could and should have stopped to think what its unusual location and appearance might mean and to attend more closely to the letters on the plaque below it, actions which would have made him realize what the switch was and prevented his flipping it. Herb's failure to realize that by omitting to unlock the back door before he left he was preventing the plumber from fixing the furnace that day was blameworthy (in one version of the example) because he could and should have avoided this failure by reading the note by the coffeepot before laying it aside (or by putting it somewhere he could not avoid seeing it later). Or consider another, rather different example, where S knows* that there is a sort of action he could take that would prevent a certain harm but S fails to know* *which* specific sort of action it is (and is blameworthy for this failure): Herb neglected to memorize the combination to the lock on his locker at the fitness center (or to take a copy of it with him), and so when he and his partner return to the locker after their squash game, he does not know* what manipulations of the lock would open the locker, manipulations which he could then carry out if only he knew* what they were (and, of course, if he had opened the locker then, he would have prevented much inconvenience for himself and his squash partner).

Those were examples, of a benighted act and benighted omissions, where what did the benighting was a prior omission. One would expect that blameworthy failure to know* would typically come about through a prior omission. It is hard to think of realistic examples where what brings it about is a prior action. Here are some unrealistic examples, which are variations on the example of Herb's failure to leave the back door unlocked. Suppose that Herb's wife told him before she left the house that he should unlock the back door before he leaves so that the plumber can get in. Right after his wife leaves, Herb takes a certain drug in order to enjoy the hour's worth of euphoria it induces on his train ride to work, but he knows that this drug also induces memory lapses; and, sure enough, because of the drug he forgets to unlock the back door. He is blameworthy for this forgetting because he could and should have avoided the drug-taking that induced it. Or suppose that normally Herb and his wife keep both back and front doors unlocked while they are home, and so what Herb's wife tells him is to *not* lock the back door before he leaves. Again, Herb takes the drug with the result that, while locking the back door, he fails to recall that by doing this he will be preventing the furnace from being fixed that day.

Suppose that at t0 S did *not* know* but *should have* known* that his act then would or might bring about the relevant sort of subsequent failure to know* that occurred at t1 (or that the act he omitted at t0 would or might prevent the relevant sort of subsequent failure to know* that occurred at t1). Then the blameworthiness of this knowledge* failure at t0 must be owing to a fact of just the same form as was required to make the knowledge* failure at t1 blameworthy—that is, a prior blameworthy act (or omission), at t-minus-1 earlier than t0, that is benighting with respect to the benighted act (or omission) at t0. For example, before Horace leaves for work his wife tells him to telephone her before he comes home from work in order to find out whether he needs to do a certain errand on the way home; before leaving for work (t-minus-1) Horace neglects to write a reminder to do call his wife in his daily diary, so that as he leaves work for home (t0) he fails to recall that he should do this, and so on the way home (t1) he fails to know* that he should do the errand.

There is thus the possibility of a prior *sequence* of blameworthy benighting acts (or omissions), each member of which leads to a subsequent blameworthy benighted act (or omission), that eventually comes to the benighted act (or omission) at t1. Such a prior sequence cannot, however, go back forever, given that S's life does not go back forever. The sequence cannot be such that it has no beginning, such that each member is an act (or omission) that is benighted by a preceding benighting act (or omission). It must begin with a blameworthy act (or omission) that is not benighted, where S knowingly* brings about (or omits to prevent) the harm that consists of a subsequent benighted act (or omission). As Michael Zimmerman (1997, p. 417) says, "culpability for ignorant behavior must be rooted in culpability that involves no ignorance".

V

Let's now take stock. We've established that, given that the CDO condition is satisfied at t1, what more is necessary for S to be blameworthy for his harmful act (or omission) at t1 is the following:

(K) either (i) S knew* at t1 that his moving in way M then would or might bring about (or, in the case of omission, prevent) a harm of sort H, or (ii) S did not then know* this but there is a sequence of one or more prior acts (or omissions) that ends with the act (or omission) at t1 and is such that (a) each member before this last member benights the subsequent member, (b) the first (earliest) member of the sequence was *not* a benighted act (or omission)—at the time S knew* that her act (or omission) would or might lead to the sort of harm it in fact led to, namely, the benighted act (or omission) that is the next member of the sequence—and (c) at the time of each benighted act (or omission) in the sequence S should have known* (was blameworthy for not knowing*) that it would or might lead to the sort of benighted act (or omission) that it in fact led to in the next member of the sequence.

It's time now to consider the case where the CDO condition is not satisfied at t1 but only at some earlier time t0. That is, at t1 it was *not* open to S not to make movement M then (or, in the case of omission, to make M then), but at t0 earlier than t1 either (i) S acted in a certain way W such that it was open to S at t0 not to act in way W then and, had S not acted in way W then, it would have been open to S at t1 not to make M or any other movement then that would bring about H (or, in the case of omission, it would have been open to S at t1 to make M or some other movement that would prevent H), or (ii) S did not at t0 act in a certain way W such that it was open to S to act in way W then and, had S acted in way W then, it would have been open to S at t1 not to make M or any other movement then that would bring about H (or, in the case of omission, it would have been open to S at t1 to make M or some other movement that would prevent H).

In such cases, which satisfy the CDO condition only earlier than t1, what more is necessary for S to be blameworthy for her harmful act (or omission) at t1? To answer this we need only apply the K condition formulated above, but take t0 in such a case to be the time referred to in the K condition as t1, the acting (or omitting to act) in way W at t0 in such a case to be what is designated in the K condition as the harmful act at t1, and the benighted harmful act (or omission) at t1 in such a case to be what is designated in the K condition as the harmful *consequence* H of the harmful act (or omission) at t1.

So, for example, Sheldon and his children arrived at the amusement park at t1; Sheldon was unable at t1 to pay the fee necessary to gain admittance, because at an earlier time t0 he had omitted to put money in his wallet, something he could have done then. Sheldon may still be blameworthy for his omitting to pay the admission fee at t1, even though he could not then have done so. Whether he is, I suggest, depends on whether his omitting to put money in his wallet satisfies the K condition, with t1 in it taken to be the time of that omission, moving in way M taken to be whatever movements would have put the money in his wallet, and the harm H that would have been prevented taken to be the subsequent unavoidable failure to pay the entrance fees. And an analogous point holds when a prior avoidable omission renders unavoidable a later action (rather than omission) and when a prior avoidable action (rather than omission) renders unavoidable a later omission or action. We simply take t1 to be the time of the prior action or omission and that action or omission to be what satisfies the CDO condition at its time, take its harmful consequence to be the subsequent unavoidable harmful action or omission, and then apply the K condition to determine whether S is blameworthy for that harmful consequence.

We are now in a position to formulate a general statement of a necessary condition for blameworthiness, which includes the CDO condition and the further, epistemic requirements that we have been investigating in this paper.

S is blameworthy for bringing about (or failing to prevent) harm H by moving (or omitting to move) in way M at t1 only if: [*the CDO condition*] at some time t0, not later than t1, either (i) S acted in a certain way W such that it was open to S at t0 not to act in way W then and, had S not acted in way W then, it would have been open to S at t1 not to make (or to make) M or any (some) other movement then that would bring about (prevent) H, or (ii) S did not at t0 act in a certain way W such that it was open to S at t0 to act in way W then and, had S acted in way W then, S would have had it open to her at t1 not to make (or to make) M or any (some) other movement then that would bring about (prevent) H; and [*the epistemic condition*] either (i) S knew* at t0 that her acting (or omitting to act) in way W would or might bring about (or, in the case of omission, prevent) a harmful act (or omission) of the sort S subsequently committed at t1, or (ii) S did not at t0 know* this but there is a sequence of one or more acts (or omissions) that ends with the act (or omission) at t0 and is such that (a) each member before this last member benights the subsequent member, (b) the first (earliest) member of the sequence was *not* a benighted act (or omission)—at the time of it S knew* that it would or might lead to the sort of harm it in fact led to, namely, the benighted act (or omission) that is the next member of the sequence, and (c) at the time of each benighted act (or omission) in the sequence S should have known* (was blameworthy for not knowing*) that it would or might lead to the sort of benighted act (or omission) that it in fact led to in the next member of the sequence.

I venture to suggest that this two-part necessary condition is also sufficient for S's being blameworthy for her harmful act (or omission).

Notes

1. The most well worked out suggestion of this sort that I know of is in Fischer and Ravizza 1998.
2. I've gained much insight on this topic from Holly Smith 1983.
3. Actions in this restricted class satisfy part (i) of the more general condition for actions when t0 = t1 and acting-in-way-W = making-movement-M; and omissions in this restricted class satisfy part (ii) of the more general condition for omissions when t0 = t1 and acting-in-way-W = making-movement-M.

References

Fischer, John and Ravizza, Mark, 1998, *Responsibility and Control*, Cambridge University Press.

Smith, Holly, 1983, "Culpable Ignorance", *The Philosophical Review* 97, p. 543–571.

Nagel, Thomas, 1976, "Moral Luck", *Proceedings of the Aristotelian Society* Supp. Vol. 50; reprinted in revised form in Nagel 1979.

Nagel, Thomas, 1979, "Moral Luck", in *Mortal Questions*, Cambridge University Press.

Rosebury, Brian, 1995, "Moral Responsibility and 'Moral Luck'", *The Philosophical Review* 104, pp. 499–524.

Williams, Bernard, 1976, "Moral Luck", *Proceedings of the Aristotelian Society* Supp. Vol. 50; reprinted in revised form in Williams 1981.

Williams, Bernard, 1981, "Moral Luck", in *Moral Luck*, Cambridge University Press.

Zimmerman, Michael J., 1997, "Moral Responsibility and Ignorance", *Ethics* 107, pp. 410–426.

Philosophical Perspectives, 14, Action and Freedom, 2000

GOAL-DIRECTED ACTION: TELEOLOGICAL EXPLANATIONS, CAUSAL THEORIES, AND DEVIANCE

Alfred R. Mele
Davidson College

Teleological explanations of human actions are explanations in terms of aims, goals, or purposes of human agents. According to a familiar *causal* approach to analyzing and explaining human action, our actions are, essentially, events (and sometimes states, perhaps) that are suitably caused by appropriate mental items, or neural realizations of those items.[1] Causalists traditionally appeal, in part, to such goal-representing states as desires and intentions (or their neural realizers) in their explanations of human actions, and they take acceptable teleological explanations of our actions to be causal explanations. Some proponents of the view that human actions are explained teleologically resist this.[2] They regard the causal approach as a *rival*. I dub this position "anticausalist teleologism," or *AT*, for short. I favor the causal approach, but I will not directly argue for it here. My aim is more modest. I will develop a serious problem for *AT* that strongly suggests that teleologists need causalism; and I will rebut a style of objection to the project of providing a causal analysis of acting in pursuit of a goal that recently resurfaced in the literature on teleological explanations of action, a style of objection featuring a certain kind of causal deviance.

1. Davidson's Challenge and Two Unsuccessful Replies

The idea that our actions are to be explained, causally, in terms of mental states or events is at least as old as Aristotle.[3] The first major source of its revival in contemporary action theory was Donald Davidson's "Actions, Reasons, and Causes" (1963). There, in addition to rebutting various arguments against the causal approach, Davidson raised the following challenge to noncausalists about action-explanation: If you hold that when we act intentionally we act for reasons, provide an account of the reasons *for which* we act that does not treat (our having) those reasons as figuring in the causation of the relevant behavior (or, one might add, as realized in physical causes of the behavior)! The challenge is particularly acute when an agent has more than one reason for *A*-ing but *A*-s only for some of them. Here is an illustration that I offered elsewhere:

> Al has a pair of reasons for mowing his lawn this morning. First, he wants to mow it this week and he believes that this morning is the most convenient time. Second, Al has an urge to repay his neighbor for the rude awakening he suffered recently when she turned on her mower at the crack of dawn and he believes that his mowing his lawn this morning would constitute suitable repayment. As it happens, Al mows his lawn this morning only for one of these reasons. In virtue of what is it true that he mowed his lawn for this reason, and not the other, if not that this reason (or his having it), and not the other, played a suitable causal role in his mowing his lawn? (Mele 1997a, p. 240)

A general version of this question may be framed as follows: In virtue of what is it true that a person acted in pursuit of a particular goal? No proponent of *AT*, as far as I know, has offered a plausible, informative answer to this question. In the present section, I criticize a pair of anticausalist teleologist attempts to answer it.

Currently, the most detailed defense of *AT* and reply to the Davidsonian challenge is found in an intriguing book by George Wilson (1989).[4] In the book's final chapter, "Irreducibility Again, and Rivalry," Wilson offers a statement of his teleological alternative to causalism as illustrated in a discussion of a man who climbs a ladder to fetch his hat:

> the teleological alternative informs us that the man's desire to retrieve his hat is relevant to explaining why he went up the ladder in virtue of the fact that *this* was a desire he went up the ladder in order to satisfy. He went up the ladder for the *conscious* purpose of satisfying his desire to retrieve his hat. But then, this is just the fact that his movements up the ladder were intended to promote the satisfaction of this desire. It is these teleological truths about the man that support the claims that
>
> > He went up the ladder because he wanted to retrieve his hat
>
> and
>
> > He went up the ladder because he (thereby) intended to satisfy his desire to get his hat. (pp. 287–88)

As Wilson notes (pp. 215–16), causalists who accept "teleological descriptions" of the sort present in this passage take them to be descriptions of causally relevant items. For example, that the man went up the ladder *in order to* satisfy his desire to get his hat is understood as a matter of that desire's (or a realizing state's) playing a suitable causal role.[5] Naturally, Wilson rejects this idea.

An apparent problem for Wilson's view may be introduced by way of the following variant of his illustration.[6] Suppose that a man, Norm, left not only his hat on the roof, but also a tool kit and a basket of bricks. He wants to fetch each, he knows he cannot get them all at once, and as he starts up the ladder he is undecided about what to retrieve this time. When he is about half way up the ladder, Norm forms an intention to get the bricks on the current trip and moves the rest of the way up with that intention.

If Norm "went up the ladder [the rest of the way] because he (thereby) intended to satisfy his desire to get" the bricks, in virtue of what is that true? Wilson's answer in the passage I quoted is that "his movements [the rest of the way] up the ladder were *intended* to promote the satisfaction of this desire." But imagine that although these movements were indeed intended to promote this, Norm's so intending (and its physical realizer) played no causal role in the production of the movements. Imagine that once Norm decided to get the bricks, his body moved as it did only because random Q signals from Mars just then started providing exactly the right input to his muscles and, even so, it seemed to Norm that he was moving himself up the ladder in just the way he had been doing. (The Q signals struck Norm just when bizarre Z rays from Venus prevented events in his brain from causing muscle contractions and the like.) In that event, it is false that Norm *climbed* the rest of the way up the ladder. Although his body continued to move up the ladder as it had been, and although he *intended of his movements* that they "promote the satisfaction of [his] desire," Norm was no longer the agent of the movements.

More important for present purposes, even though there is a reading of 'Norm went up the ladder' on which the sentence is true, it is *false* that "he went [the rest of the way] up the ladder because he wanted to retrieve [the bricks]," and false as well that "he went [the rest of the way] up the ladder because he (thereby) intended to satisfy his desire to get [the bricks]."[7] Rather, Norm went the rest of the way up the ladder because the Q signals provided certain input to his muscles.

This case admittedly is a strange one. Even so, it lays bare a point that might otherwise be hidden. Our bodily motions might coincide with our desires or intentions, and even result in our getting what we want or what we intend to get (or what we intend our motions to promote), without those motions being *explained* by the desires or intentions. The challenge for Wilson, in part, is to get want-to-behavior and intention-to-behavior explanation into the picture while not relying on want-to-behavior and intention-to-behavior *causation* (or causation by neural realizations of pertinent mental items). The present case apparently shows that he fails to do this in our passage.

One might counter that, since Norm was not the *agent* of the movements or motions in question, they were not *his* movements, and hence were not movements of the sort with which Wilson is concerned in our passage. Two observations are in order. First, if the correct diagnosis of Norm's not being the agent of the movements is that a pertinent desire or intention of his (or an associated realizing state) did not play an appropriate causal role in the production of those movements, then causalism is vindicated. Second, Wilson adopts a very broad conception of action according to which the "movements" on the ladder were, indeed, performed by Norm (e.g., "A man performs a convulsive and spasmodic movement when he clutches and cannot loose a live electric wire, and someone undergoing an epileptic seizure may perform a series of wild and wholly uncontrollable movements" [p. 49]). Wilson regards the broadness of his conception of action as a virtue, and the broad conception figures significantly in his attack on causalism, in some examples of causal deviance (see, e.g., pp. 271–73).

Wilson may claim that, in my case, Norm's movements up the ladder were not, in fact, "intended to promote the satisfaction of" his desire to get the bricks (cf. Wilson 1997, pp. 69-70). In a chapter on intention in action, he writes: "If an agent has intended of her behavior *b* that it *A*, then not only was that behavior directed at *A*-ing, but it was *sentiently* and often *consciously* directed at *A*-ing" (1989, p. 146).[8] He adds that "sentient direction...entails that the mechanisms of the agent's bodily control, as exercised in the performance of *b*, were systematically and selectively responsive to the agent's perception of her environment." So, since Norm did not exercise his mechanisms of bodily control in performing the relevant movements, Wilson can say that those movements were not *intended by* Norm to promote the satisfaction of his desire to get the bricks.

In spinning my story, I assumed that Norm's intending of his movements up the ladder that they promote the satisfaction of his desire to get the bricks is sufficient for those movements' being intended by him to promote this. But Wilson can reply that this assumption reveals a mistaken conception of intention. I seem to be presupposing that Norm's intention is an *attitude*. And Wilson rejects the idea that intentions are attitudes (e.g., 1989, p. 229).

If intentions are not attitudes, what are they? Wilson says that "intentions in actions are very special *properties* of the actions that exhibit them" (pp. 222–23) and that "'Being intended to achieve such-and-such' is, if one likes, a 'mentalistic' or 'psychological' property of behavior" (p. 292).[9] He also tells us that "the concept of 'sentient directionality'...is the same as the concept of 'intention in action'" (pp. 146–47). Wilson's view, I think, is that an agent's intending movements of his to promote the satisfaction of his desire to get *x* is precisely his sentiently directing those movements at promoting the satisfaction of that desire. He says that the fact that "the man went up the ladder for the *conscious* purpose of satisfying his desire to retrieve his hat" is the same fact as that "his movements up the ladder were *intended* to promote the satisfaction of this desire" (p. 288). And the latter fact, apparently, is supposed to be the same fact as that the man sentiently directed his movements up the ladder at promoting satisfaction of this desire. Now this one fact, described in three different ways, is alleged to "support" the claims that "He went up the ladder because he wanted to retrieve his hat" and "He went up the ladder because he (thereby) intended to satisfy his desire to get his hat," and, therefore, to support the claim that "the man's desire to retrieve his hat is relevant to explaining why he went up the ladder." But why aren't the claims that are supposed to be supported by the fact that is described in three different ways simply further descriptions of the same fact? The answer, I suppose, lies in the occurrence of the word 'because' in these claims.

Notice that from the fact that the man "went up the ladder because he wanted to retrieve his hat" we cannot safely infer that he performed an action. In a variant of Norm's case, malicious Martians take control of Norm's body and cause it to move up the ladder by zapping his feet with levitation rays and his hands with comparable motion controllers because they know he wants to get his hat. His wanting to get his hat figures importantly in the causal sequence that results in his going up the ladder; thus, it is true that he went up the ladder *because* he wanted to retrieve his hat. Even so, it is the Martians who control Norm's body, not Norm. The same point could be made about the fact that the man "went up the ladder because he (thereby) intended to satisfy his desire to get his hat," if "he (thereby) intended" were merely to signal the presence of an intending attitude. The real work here is done by the notion of sentient direction that Wilson wants to capture in such expressions as "he (thereby) intended." And, I think, we can fairly read the second "because" claim as follows: 'The man went up the ladder because, at the time, he was sentiently directing his movements at satisfying his desire to get his hat.'

Causalists will want to interpret an agent's sentiently directing his movements at the satisfaction of a certain desire in a way that accords the desire (or its neural realizer) a causal role; and I must confess that I cannot find in Wilson's book a clear—and clearly—noncausal account of what it is for a movement to be sentiently directed at the satisfaction of a desire. Wilson says that facts of the following kind "about the context of the action, about the agent's perception of that context, and about the agent's sentient relations to his own movements...make it true that he intended of those movements that they promote his getting back his hat [read: make it true that those movements were *sentiently directed* by him at promoting his getting back his hat]":

> [1] The man, wondering where his hat is, sees it on the roof, fetches the ladder, and immediately begins his climb. [2] Moreover, the man is aware of performing these movements up the ladder and knows, at least roughly, at each stage what he is about to do next. [3] Also, in performing these movements, he is prepared to adjust or modulate his behavior were it to appear to him that the location of his hat has changed. [4] Again, at each stage of his activity, were the question to arise, the man would judge that he was performing those movements as a means of retrieving his hat. (p. 290)

But is this enough?

Two observations are in order before this question can properly be answered. The first concerns the second sentence of the passage just quoted. What knowledge is attributed to the man there? Not the knowledge that he is about to perform a sentiently directed movement of a certain kind, if sentient direction is a notion that this passage is supposed to explicate. However, this does not block the supposition that the man knows, in some sense, that he is about to perform a movement of his left hand onto the next rung, for example, in Wilson's broad sense of "perform a movement."

Second, Wilson claims that "to try to [A] is (roughly and for the pertinent range of cases) to perform an action that is intended to [A]" (p. 270). Brief attention to trying will prove useful. Suppressing the qualification for a moment, Wilson's claim amounts, for him, to the assertion that to try to A is to perform an action that is sentiently directed by the agent at A-ing. Regarding the following plausible proposition, there is no need to worry about limiting the range of cases: (T1) if one is doing something that one is sentiently directing at A-ing, then one is trying to A, in an utterly familiar, unexacting sense of "trying." Although people may often reserve attributions of trying for instances in which an agent makes a considerable or special effort, this is a matter of conversational implicature and does not mark a conceptual truth about trying.[10] A blindfolded, anesthetized man who reports that he has raised his arm as requested, quite properly responds to the information that his arm is strapped to his side by observing that, in any case, he *tried* to move it—even though, encountering no felt resistance, he made no *special* effort to move it.[11] And when, just now, I typed the words "just now," I tried to do that even though I easily typed the words. Now, T1 entails (T2) that one who is not trying to A, even in the unexacting sense of 'trying' identified, is not sentiently directing one's bodily motions at A-ing. T2 is very plausible indeed, as is the following, related proposition: (T3) one who is not trying to do anything at all, even in the unexacting sense of 'trying,' is not sentiently directing one's bodily motions at anything.

In the following case, as I will explain, although Norm is not, during a certain time, trying to do anything, even in the unexacting sense of 'trying' that I identified, he nevertheless satisfies all four of the conditions in the quotation at issue during that time. The moral is that these conditions are insufficient for a person's sentiently directing "movements" of his at the time. Their insufficiency follows from the details of the case and the platitude that an agent who is not trying (even in the unexacting sense) to do anything is not sentiently directing his bodily motions at anything.

Norm has learned that, on rare occasions, after he embarks on a relatively routinized activity (e.g., tying his shoes, climbing a ladder), Martians take control of his body and initiate and sustain the next several movements in the chain while making it seem to him that he is acting normally.[12] He is not sure how they do this, but he has excellent reason to believe that they are even more skilled at this than he is at moving his own body, as, in fact, they are. (The Martians have given Norm numerous demonstrations involving other people.) The Martians have made a thorough study of Norm's patterns of peripheral bodily motion when he engages in various routine activities. Their aim was to make it seem to him that he is acting while preventing him from even *trying* to act by selectively shutting down portions of his brain. To move his body, they zap him in the belly with M-rays that control the relevant muscles and joints. When they intervene, they wait for Norm to begin a routine activity, read his mind to make sure that he plans to do what they think he is doing (e.g., tie his shoes, or climb to the top of a ladder), and then zap him for a while—unless the mind-reading team sees him abandon or modify his plan. When the team notices something of this sort, the Martians stop interfering and control immediately reverts to Norm.

A while ago, Norm started climbing a ladder to fetch his hat. When he reached the midway point, the Martians took over. Although they controlled Norm's next several movements while preventing him from trying to do anything, they would have relinquished control to him if his plan had changed (e.g., in light of a belief that the location of his hat had changed).

Return to facts 1 through 4. Fact 1 obtains in this case. What about fact 2? It is no less true that Norm performs his next several movements than that the man who clutches the live electric wire performs convulsive and spasmodic movements. And the *awareness* of performing movements mentioned in fact 2 is no problem. The wire clutcher can be aware of bodily "performances" of his that are caused by the electrical current, and Norm can be aware of bodily "performances" of his that are caused by M-rays. Norm also satisfies a "knowledge" condition of the sort I identified. If Wilson is right in thinking that an ordinary ladder climber knows, in some sense, that he is about to perform a movement of his left hand onto the next rung, Norm can know this too. What he does not know is whether he will perform the movement on his own or in the alternative way. But that gives him no weaker grounds for knowledge than the ordinary agent has, given that the subject matter is the performance of movements in Wilson's broad sense and given what Norm knows about the Martians' expertise. Fact 3 also obtains. Norm is prepared to adjust or modulate his behavior, and we may even suppose that he is *able* to do so. Although the Martians in fact initiated and controlled Norm's next several movements up the ladder while preventing him from trying to do anything, they would not have done so if his plans had changed. Fact 4 obtains as well. In Wilson's sense of "perform a movement," Norm believes that he is performing his movements "as a means of retrieving his hat." (Norm does not believe that the Martians are controlling his behavior at the time. After all, he realizes that they very rarely do so.)

Even though these facts obtain, Norm does not sentiently direct his next several movements up the ladder at getting his hat, since he is not sentiently directing these movements at all. As I mentioned earlier, Wilson maintains that one's sentiently directing a bodily movement that one performs entails one's exercising one's mechanisms of bodily control in performing that movement. However, Norm did not exercise these mechanisms in his performance of the movements at issue. Indeed, he did not make even a minimal effort to perform these movements; owing to the Martian intervention, he made no effort at all—

that is, did not try—to do anything at the time. And it is a platitude that one who did not try to do anything at all during a time t did not sentiently direct his bodily motions during t.

It might be suggested that although Norm did not directly move his body during the time at issue, he sentiently directed his bodily motions in something like the way that his sister Norma sentiently directed motions of her body when she orally guided blindfolded colleagues who were carrying her across an obstacle-filled room as part of a race staged by her law firm to promote team-work. If Norma succeeded, she may be said to have brought it about that she got across the room, and her bringing this about is an action. Notice, however, that there is something that she was trying to do at the time. For example, she was trying to guide her teammates. By hypothesis, there is nothing that Norm was trying to do at the relevant time, for the Martians blocked brain activity required for trying. And this is a crucial difference between the two cases. The claim that Norma sentiently directed motions of her body at some goal at the time is consistent with $T3$; the comparable claim about Norm is not.[13]

Now, what is it to exercise one's mechanisms of bodily control in perform-ing a movement that is sentiently directed specifically at promoting one's re-trieving one's hat? Again, causalists will favor an answer that features a desire or intention to get one's hat, or some event of intention-formation or intention-acquisition, or some realizing state or event, as a cause of the exercise. And, again, Wilson has failed to provide a noncausalist alternative to this sort of answer. He has not answered the question—a crucial one for teleologists—raised in the introduction to this section: In virtue of what is it true that a per-son acted in pursuit of a particular goal?[14] Thus, he has not successfully met the Davidsonian challenge.[15]

Scott Sehon attempts to answer this challenge (1994). Under the heading "Defusing the Davidsonian Challenge," he argues that a teleologist can appeal to counterfactuals to "distinguish between reasons an agent acted on and rea-sons the agent had but did not act on" (p. 67). Sehon invites us to imagine that Heidi "lifts a heavy book up to the top of a bookshelf" while having the fol-lowing pair of desires: "a desire to put the book where it belongs and a desire to strengthen her biceps." He assumes that only one of these desires "provides the reason why Heidi lifted the book," and he asks which one does so. Sehon reports that this question, "as viewed from the teleological theory, looks roughly like this: toward which outcome did Heidi direct her behavior, that the book was put away or that her biceps were strengthened?" The correct answer, he contends, depends on what counterfactuals of a certain kind are true of Heidi at the time. If the book had belonged on the bottom shelf, would she have put it there, or would she have placed it on the top shelf? If something more suitable for the purposes of exercising her biceps had been present, would she have lifted it, or would she have lifted the book? And so on.

Suppose that the counterfactual test indicates that Heidi's goal was that the book be returned to its proper place. Even so, one will not know in virtue of what it is true that Heidi directed her behavior toward that goal until one knows in virtue of what it is true that Heidi directed her behavior. We can apply Sehon's counterfactual test to a case in which Martians who wished to deceive Heidi into believing that she was acting manipulated her muscles in order to make her bodily motions fit the intention she had at the time to return the book to its proper place while preventing her from even trying to return it, and we would get the result that Heidi directed her behavior toward the book's being returned there. But, of course, that result would be false, since Heidi was not directing her behavior—that is, acting—at all in this case. Rather, the Martians were controlling the motions of her body.

True counterfactuals are true in virtue of something or other. Their truth is grounded in something factual. If Heidi was executing—that is, acting on—an intention to return the book to its proper place, then, other things being equal, we should expect such counterfactuals as the following to be true: if Heidi had believed that the book belonged on the bottom shelf, she would have placed it there; if Heidi had believed that the book's proper place was the middle shelf, she would have put it there. But if these counterfactuals are true for the reasons we expect them to be, their truth is grounded in part in Heidi's *acting* with the intention of putting the book where it belongs; their truth does not explain what it is for Heidi to be acting with this intention.

One moral of the objections I have raised to Wilson's and Sehon's attempted answers to the Davidsonian challenge is clear. Unless desires, intentions, or their physical realizers play a causal role in the production of a person's bodily motions, and not simply the causal role of providing information about goals to mischievous Martians, there is the threat (as in my Martian chronicles) that the person is not acting at all, much less acting in pursuit of the goal(s) that the desire or intention specifies. Partly because teleologists have not offered an acceptable account of what it is to *act*, or to "direct" one's bodily motions, they have not offered an acceptable account of what it is to act for the sake of a particular goal.

2. Causalism and Primary Deviance

Causalists claim to have a solution to this problem. They offer a causal account of human action in terms of mental items—items such as beliefs, desires, intentions, and associated events (e.g., acquiring an intention to A straightway)—or their physical realizers. If an account of this kind is correct, the stage is set for a causal account of what it is for a human being to act for a particular goal in the same terms. In this section, I will introduce an objection that some teleologists have raised against the possibility of a successful causal account of acting in pursuit of a particular goal, an objection featuring causal deviance. First, a word about causalism is in order.

As I have explained elsewhere, a familiar causal approach to understanding and explaining action—I will call it *CA*—treats actions as analogous to money and sunburns in a noteworthy respect.[16] The piece of paper with which Norm purchased his hat is a genuine U.S. dollar bill partly in virtue of its having been produced (in the right way) by the U.S. Treasury Department. The burn on his back is a sunburn partly in virtue of its having been produced by exposure to the sun's rays. A duplicate bill that Norm produced with plates and paper stolen from the Treasury Department is a counterfeit dollar bill, not a genuine one. And a burn that looks and feels just like the one on his back is not a sunburn, if it was produced by exposure to a heat lamp rather than the sun. Similarly, according to CA, a certain event occurring at t is Norm's raising his right hand at t—an action—partly in virtue of its having been produced "in the right way" by certain mental items (or their neural realizations). An event someone else covertly produces by remote control—one including a visually indistinguishable rising of Norm's right hand not produced by an intention or desire of Norm's, or an associated mental event (or, again, pertinent realizations)—is not a raising of Norm's right hand by Norm, even if it feels to Norm as though he is raising his hand.

No plausible version of CA identifies actions with *non-actional* events caused in the right way (cf. Brand 1984, ch. 1).[17] That would be analogous to identifying genuine U.S. dollar bills with pieces of printed paper that are not genuine U.S. dollar bills and are produced in the right way by the U.S. Treasury Department; and so identifying genuine U.S. dollar bills would be absurd. To say that an event E is an action partly in virtue of its having been produced in "the right way" is not to say that E is a non-actional event—any more than to say that a piece of printed paper P is a genuine U.S. dollar bill partly in virtue of its having been produced in the right way is to say that P is not a genuine U.S. dollar bill.

Several distinct kinds of causal deviance that are relevant to attempted causal analyses of *intentional* action have received attention in the literature.[18] One kind—what I elsewhere termed "primary" deviance (Mele 1992b, p. 209)—has a special relevance for the project of constructing a causal analysis of action itself. Here is a well-known illustration:

> A climber might want to rid himself of the weight and danger of holding another man on a rope, and he might know that by loosening his hold on the rope he could rid himself of the weight and danger. This belief and want might so unnerve him as to cause him to loosen his hold [unintentionally]. (Davidson 1980, p. 79)

Given the prominence of intention in the recent causalist literature, a reformulation of this example in terms of intention is in order: a climber intends to rid himself of the danger of holding another man on a rope by loosening his hold, and this intention so unnerves him as to cause him to loosen his hold unintentionally.

Some causal theorists who have assessed cases of this kind as attempted counterexamples to a causal account of what it is for an action to be intentional have dismissed them on the grounds that they are not cases of action at all (Brand 1984, p. 18; Thalberg 1984): the agent's being unnerved consists at least partly in his losing control over his hands, with the result that his grip loosens; he does not perform an action of loosening his grip. If this diagnosis is correct, primary deviance may pose a problem for the project of constructing a causal analysis of action, and, hence, for a related project regarding acting for the sake of a particular goal. Consider the following simple-minded analysis of action: A is an action performed by S if and only if S intended to A, that intention was a cause of X, and X is a bodily motion of a kind involved in some actual or possible A-ing. In the present case, let X be the climber's relevant finger and hand motions. The problem is evident.[19]

In a recent paper, appealing to primary causal deviance, Scott Sehon suggested that no amount of refinement will yield an acceptable causal analysis of teleological locutions like 'S performed action A in order to B' and that teleological explanations of action are "irreducible" to causal explanations (1997). Rather than offer a causal analysis here, I will construct a case in which a teleological explanation of a particular action is an explanation of precisely the kind that causal theorists have offered and then develop a moral about primary causal deviance.

3. A Myth About Simple Agents

Epimetheus longed for a new kind of agent, something between god and beast. So he created what he called "man," some female and some male; they looked very much like young adult human beings today. However, man was utterly inactive, and the entire race would soon have become extinct if Epimetheus's brother, Prometheus, had not spied him crying in the midst of his new beings. "What's the problem?" Prometheus asked. "I created these beautiful beings to play with, and now they won't do anything at all," Epimetheus replied. Prometheus gently chided his brother. "Well, of course they won't," he said. "At least they won't do things of the sort you have in mind. You haven't given them any desires; they have nothing to motivate them. They'll need some beliefs too, so that they'll have some idea how to go about satisfying their desires. And intentions would also help." Prometheus then launched into an explanation of the differences among various kinds of behavior, including tropistic behavior of the sort found in marigolds and mosquitoes and intentional behavior, but his brother quickly lost interest. "Fix them for me, Prometheus," Epimetheus pleaded. Prometheus thought that it would be better to let the race die out and then allow evolution to take its course, but he consented nonetheless.

Two points need to be made before the next part of the story is told. The first concerns Prometheus's conception of action. As I mentioned earlier, Wilson adopts a very broad conception of performing a movement—and hence of overt action—according to which "A man performs a convulsive and spasmodic movement when he clutches and cannot loose a live electric wire" (1989, p. 49). Neither Prometheus nor Epimetheus count this as action. Give a comatose man a strong and lengthy electric shock and his body will jerk about convulsively and spasmodically for some time, but the comatose man is not acting, or performing bodily movements. The sustained jolt of electricity, not the comatose man, is moving the man's body. The same is true of the unfortunate man who cannot let go of the live wire. To be sure, there is a sense of "action" in which even acids, waves, and wind act, but this is not the sense that concerns Prometheus and his brother. Nor are they concerned with tropistic "actions": for example, plants bending—or ticks climbing—toward the light.

The second point is that the part of story that I am about to tell is metaphysically more complicated than I will make it out to be. Prometheus, in thinking about how to turn "man" into an agent, was guided by a psychological theory and by biological expertise. He had no definite metaphysical opinion about the precise connection between beliefs, intentions, and the like, on the one hand, and the physical states that realize them, on the other. To simplify the story, I will tell it largely in psychological language, but some readers may prefer to interpret the psycho-causal assertions as assertions about the physical realizers of psychological events and states.

Prometheus's initial concern was overt action (i.e., action essentially involving peripheral bodily motion), and he was a bottom-up designer. In his planning, he started with overt action, as he conceived of it, and worked up. He wanted overt actions to be causally initiated by acquisitions of what he called *proximal* intentions—intentions to A straightaway. (Intentions, as he conceived of them, are executive attitudes toward plans, plans being the representational content of intentions.)[20] So Prometheus reconfigured the human brain and body with this end in view. In the newly configured beings, the acquisition of a proximal intention would initiate the sending of a "command" signal to what he called the "Promethean motor cortex" (*PMC*). The signal would specify the kind of action to be performed straightaway and it would be transformed in the *PMC* into specific fine-grained executive signals to specific muscles. For example, the acquisition of a proximal intention gently to touch the tip of one's nose with the tip of one's right index finger would initiate the sending of an appropriate command signal to the *PMC*, where it would be transformed into specific motor signals—executive signals with the function of initiating muscular motion—to the appropriate muscles. (Like some philosophers of action, Prometheus took overt actions to begin in the brain.)[21] The motor signals would "command" the muscles to move in certain ways. In the case of intentions that are for movements and not also for what Prometheus called "agent-external results" (e.g., raising one's right hand, as opposed to touching a branch—or one's nose—with one's right hand), the signals would command the muscles to move in ways such that the completion of the movement would ensure satisfaction of the intention. In the case of intentions that include agent-external results (e.g., an intention to pick up an apple with one's right hand), the signals would command the relevant muscles to move in ways appropriate to the satisfaction of the intention.

The new design also was such that Promethean agents engage in overt action *only if* the acquisition of a proximal intention plays this initiating role. The neural architecture of Promethean agents was such that only the command signals initiated by the acquisition of a proximal intention would be transformed in the *PMC* into motor signals. Furthermore, the *PMC* would produce motor signals only by transforming command signals; and in the absence of motor signals produced by the *PMC*, a Promethean agent was in no position to act overtly. The biological design of Promethean agents included no alternative route to overt action.

The clever Prometheus also assigned a causal role to the *persistence* or continued presence of a proximal intention. Such persistence would causally sustain the signaling process, and, hence, the relevant bodily motions, until the agent either came to believe that achievement of the (final) goal represented in his intention was ensured or instead came to believe that continuing his present course of action was not worth the trouble.[22] An agent's coming to hold the latter belief would extinguish the intention. Prometheus's design also ensured that the dissolution of a proximal intention would put an end to associated action, unless the action had gone too far to be halted.

Prometheus was particularly proud of his use of intentions in the causal *guidance* of human action sustained by a persisting intention.[23] In the case of intentions that incorporate plans with more than a single "node," receipt of feedback indicating that one's body is moving according to plan and that one's bodily motions are getting one closer to one's goal would promote the occurrence of motions called for by the next portion of one's plan. Feedback indicating that things are veering off course would foster corrections of bodily motions, the standard for corrections being provided by the plan embedded in the agent's persisting intention. Even in the case of relatively simple actions like unclenching one's right fist, persisting intentions played a guiding role in Prometheus's agents. Within a few milliseconds of acquiring a proximal intention to unclench his fist, an agent would begin exhibiting motions called for by his intention, and he would stop exhibiting such motions upon receiving feedback indicating that the fist is unclenched. Prometheus designed human agents in such a way that their "directing" their on-going bodily motions required that persisting intentions of theirs be playing a guiding role. No other way of endowing them with self-direction occurred to him.

Incidentally, the subtle Prometheus understood a phenomenon that he called "direct ballistic continuation."[24] Consider an ordinary case of snapping one's fingers. An agent embarking on a conventional right-handed finger-snapping with his palm facing up presses his thumb and middle finger firmly together and then, maintaining the pressure, simultaneously slides the thumb to the right and the finger downward. After a certain point, the agent is no longer in control of the process. The finger whips downward, thumping into his palm next to his thumb, and the thumb slides off to the right. Here we have direct ballistic continuation of motions that had been guided. Prometheus regarded the ballistic motions I just described as part of the agent's action of snapping his fingers.

Prometheus gave little thought to the question whether any overt actions are properly regarded as continuing beyond the agent's bodily motions. If Abel throws a rock at a rat and hits the rat with that rock, thereby killing it, does his action of killing the rat end when the rock leaves his hand, when the rat dies, or at some other point? Prometheus viewed this question as distinctly philosophical; he took it to lie beyond the expertise of a biological engineer like himself. However, he did design human agents in such a way that what he called "agents' contributions" to their overt actions ended with the termination of their *guided* bodily motions.

In Prometheus's opinion, intentions were well-suited for the causal function of guiding action, since they incorporate action-plans. Furthermore, given the executive nature of intention, their acquisition, he thought, would be an ideal causal initiator of action and their continued presence would nicely causally sustain actions. (Naturally, some fine tuning was required.) Prometheus devised some ways for agents to acquire, and even actively to form, intentions on the basis of practical thinking. But that part of the story need not be told for present purposes. Nor, fortunately, need the story about how he instilled free will into human beings be recounted here.

Predictably, Prometheus's agents were very clumsy at first, but as time passed they learned to do some relatively simple things. Eventually, they learned to do some truly great things. However, the simpler things are what concern me now.

One day, as part of a test, Prometheus asked a young woman named Eve whether she could gently move her right hand upward in order to touch, with the tip of her index finger alone, the golden pear that was growing on a branch a few inches over her head. Eve indicated that she would try, having acquired an intention to do just that. She gently reached up with her right hand until she saw the tip of her index finger come into contact with the pear, and then she stopped. "Excellent," Prometheus exclaimed. He added, "You can put your hand down now. Later, whenever you feel like touching that pear again, just reach up and touch it as you did this time." A few minutes later, Eve did so. Confident of success on that occasion, Eve had the bold intention of touching the pear with the tip of her right index finger rather than the more modest intention of *trying* to do this.

The following assertions (among others) about Eve certainly seem true.

1. Eve raised her right hand until her index finger came into contact with the pear.
2. Eve raised her right hand in order to touch the pear.

Now, teleologists allege that "teleological explanations explain by specifying an action's goal or purpose; for example, when we say that Jackie went to the kitchen in order to get a glass of wine, we thereby specify the state of affairs at which her action was directed" (Sehon 1997, p. 195). But in virtue of what is it true that a person acted in pursuit of a particular goal? Wilson and Sehon have failed to answer this question successfully, as I argued in Section 1. Nor have they given us the wherewithal to answer the following question about Eve: In virtue of what is it true that Eve acted in pursuit of the goal of touching the pear?

Can *CA* do any better? According to *CA*, again, actions are, essentially, events (and perhaps sometimes states) that are suitably caused by appropriate mental items (or the physical realizations of those items). Given the way Prometheus designed Eve as an agent, and suppressing reference to physical realizations, *CA* suggests that Eve's second action of raising her right hand until the tip of her index finger came into contact with the pear is a certain series of events that was causally initiated by her acquisition of an intention to touch the pear with the tip of her index finger, causally sustained by the continued presence of that intention, and causally guided by that persisting intention.[25] The series includes command signals, bodily motions, and the finger's coming into contact with the pear. *CA* suggests as well that, on this occasion, the fact that the action at issue was initiated, sustained, and guided in the way just mentioned is sufficient for the truth of the assertion that Eve raised her right hand *in order to* touch the pear. And both suggestions apparently contain what teleologists allege to be a teleological explanation of Eve's action of raising her right hand, since the suggestions include a specification of that action's goal or purpose—namely, that Eve touch the pear with the tip of her right index finger.

4. Handling Primary Deviance

If these suggestions are correct, then there are informative, conceptually sufficient conditions—conditions that are *causal* in nature—both for (1) an event's being an action and for (2) an event's being an action performed in pursuit of a particular goal. If there are such conditions, causalists are in much better shape than anticausalist teleologists. For, as I have argued, such teleologists have not provided informative sufficient conditions for either (1) or (2). It merits emphasis here that informative, conceptually sufficient anticausalist conditions for (2) are precisely what the Davidsonian challenge summarized in Section 1 calls for.

Should the causalist suggestions at issue be accepted? According to anticausalist teleologists, the answer is *no*. Sehon (1997) contends that reflection on causal deviance of the sort at work in cases like that of Davidson's climber justifies this negative answer (cf. Wilson 1989, ch. 9). As it happens, this climber is one of Prometheus's agents, a fellow named Clem. Can causalists identify something of a causal nature in virtue of which it is false that Clem performed the action of loosening his grip on the rope and false that he loosened his grip in order to "rid himself of the...danger" posed by continuing to hold the rope?

Yes, they can, as I will explain. Since Davidson's case is sketchy, several versions need to be considered.

Version 1. Clem's acquiring the intention—intention N—to rid himself of the danger of holding his climbing partner on his rope by loosening his hold does not initiate the sending of motor signals to appropriate muscles. Instead it unnerves Clem, with the result that he loses control over his hands. His grip loosens and the rope slips from his hands.

Here, Clem does not perform the action of loosening his grip; for Promethean agents are designed in such a way that they can perform overt actions only in cases in which the acquisition of a proximal intention initiates the sending of motor signals to appropriate muscles. And, of course, if Clem does not perform this action at all, he does not perform it in pursuit of a goal.

It might be claimed that there is no difference between *motor signals* that initiate bodily motions and *nervousness* that initiates bodily motions. In Promethean agents, this is false. In his creatures, motor signals carry instructions to muscles, whereas nervousness contains no such instructions. Moreover, in his agents, what Prometheus called the "motor control system"—a biological system constituted by the Promethean motor cortex and associated areas of the brain—plays an indispensable role in the production of overt action whereas bodily motion directly produced by nervousness is produced independently of this system.[26] In Prometheus's beings, direct causation of bodily motion by nervousness is quite distinct from direct causation of bodily motion by motor signals.

Version 2. Clem's acquiring intention N initiates the sending of appropriate motor signals. Those signals do not reach his muscles. Instead, they unnerve him, with the result that he loses both his grip on the rope and his intention.

Given that Clem is a Promethean agent, he performs the action of loosening his grip on the rope only if a relevant intention of his sustains the pertinent motions of his body. But the relevant intention is extinguished before the pertinent bodily motions occur. So, again, Clem does not perform the action of loosening his grip and therefore does not perform this action in pursuit of a goal.

Version 3. Again, Clem's acquiring intention N initiates the sending of appropriate motor signals, which signals do not reach his muscles. Again, the signals unnerve Clem, with the result that he loses his grip on the rope. However, intention N is not extinguished when it initiates the signals. In fact, its continued presence causally sustains the nervousness that results in Clem's temporary loss of control over the motions of his hands (cf. Mele 1992a, pp. 202–3).

If Clem is not "directing" his hand motions (to use a teleologist's term), he is not performing the action of loosening his grip on the rope. As a Promethean agent, Clem's directing the motions of his hands requires that a relevant intention of his be playing a guiding role in the production of his hand motions. But no intention of Clem's is playing this role; his nervousness prevents that by temporarily depriving him of control over the motions of his hands. So, once again, Clem is not performing the action of loosening his grip; *a fortiori*, he is not performing this action in pursuit of a goal.

Version 4. Clem's acquiring intention *N* initiates the sending of appropriate motor signals. This time, those signals reach their targeted muscles, and he begins to loosen his grip on the rope. His fingers start moving. This unnerves him, with the result that he loses his grip on the rope (cf. Mele 1992a, pp. 202–3; Sehon 1997, pp. 201–2). In beginning to loosen his grip he does not yet loosen it sufficiently for the rope to unravel from his hand; the nervousness that results in his losing his grip plays an intervening causal role. And the continued presence of intention *N* causally sustains the nervousness that results in Clem's temporary loss of control over the motions of his hands.

Although there was a time at which Clem was beginning to loosen his hold on the rope—and doing this in pursuit of the goal of ridding himself of his dangerous burden—he does not perform the action of dropping his partner, nor the action of loosening his hold enough to drop his partner. Nor, *a fortiori*, does he perform either of these actions in pursuit of a goal. Given his construction as a Promethean agent, Clem is not capable of contributing to the continuation of an overt action of his once his relevant bodily motions are not being guided by an intention of his. This itself does not entail that, after becoming unnerved, Clem is no longer performing the action of loosening his hold; for, in some cases, direct ballistic continuations of motions that had been guided may be parts of actions, as in the finger-snapping example. However, the nervousness-produced motions of Clem's hands are not direct ballistic continuations of his previous motions. After all, they are produced by the nervousness that his beginning to loosen his grip causes. Even if they are, in some sense, continuations of earlier motions, they are not direct ballistic continuations. So, in short, Clem's performance of the action of loosening his hold is terminated too soon for him to have performed the action of dropping his partner, or the action of loosening his hold enough to drop his partner.[27]

Now, my Promethean myth is a myth. One feature of the neural architecture of Promethean agents is that the PMC produces motor signals only by transforming command signals that are initiated by the acquisition of a proximal intention. This is a somewhat magical feature. In principle, a counterfeit of such a signal—for example, a counterfeit signal produced by direct electronic stimulation of the brain and not by the acquisition of a proximal intention—might be transformed into motor signals. But my crucial claim in this connection is that Promethean agents are designed in such a way that they can perform overt actions only in cases in which the acquisition of a proximal intention initiates the sending of motor signals to appropriate muscles. The possibility of counterfeit command signals undermines this claim only if there are cases in which such a signal, and not the acquisition of a proximal intention, initiates an overt *action*. Are there such cases? If a neuroscientist stimulates a Promethean agent's brain in such a way as to send a "command" signal to the PMC, which is then translated into motor signals, and he does not produce the signals by producing an intention, then, intuitively, the agent does not act. Rather, he is manipulated in such a way that his body mimics action.[28] The same implication, I submit, will emerge in any attempted counterexample of the style at issue.[29]

Suppose that a neuroscientist produces a proximal *intention* in a Promethean agent by direct stimulation of the agent's brain and that the acquisition of this intention initiates bodily movement in the normal way. Suppose also that the persisting intention plays the sustaining and guiding roles that I described. The agent certainly has been manipulated, but I see no good reason to deny that he has been manipulated into performing an action. There is a difference between (1) Mr. X causing Mr. Y's body to move without causing Y to move his body and (2) Mr. X causing Y to move Y's body. The first case involving neuroscientific intervention is an instance of (1), I have suggested. The second case, intuitively, is an instance of (2).

Early in this section, I asked whether causalists can identify something of a causal nature in virtue of which it is false (in versions of the case in which this *is* false) that Clem, a Promethean agent, performed the action of loosening his grip on the rope and false that he loosened his grip in order to "rid himself of the danger" posed by continuing to hold the rope. The answer certainly seems to be *yes*. As far as I can tell, my Promethean myth, stripped of its magical feature, is coherent. And even though the story is a relatively simple one, it provides the basis for a causal diagnosis of ways in which primary causal deviance blocks action in an agent of a certain kind. The mix of causal initiation, sustaining, and guiding that I have been describing seems to do the trick in a Promethean agent.

To be sure, anticausalists will wish to develop counterexamples to the claim that this mix is conceptually sufficient, in a Promethean agent, for action. I see no way of producing a conclusive proof of this sufficiency, and I welcome attempted counterexamples. If the attempted counterexamples fail, or instead motivate useful refinement of the mix, I obviously would regard that as good news. A counterexample that showed that *no* causalist mix would do the trick in a Promethean agent would be bad news for causalists, but I doubt that one is forthcoming.

Elsewhere, Paul Moser and I offered a causal analysis of what it is for someone to *A* intentionally, given that his *A*-ing is an action (Mele and Moser 1994). We did not offer an analysis of action. Nor, as I said, will I do that here. That task is complicated by, among other things, the existence of several alternative live options about the *individuation* of actions; the fact that there are purely mental actions, as well as overt actions with goals that are changes in the external world (e.g., that my car be functioning again by noon) and overt actions with goals that include nothing external to the agent's body (e.g., the goal that one unclench one's right fist); the apparent need for a distinction between basic and nonbasic actions; and tricky issues about the connection between mental events and states, on the one hand, and what realizes them, on the other. Obviously, these issues are beyond the scope of the present paper.

Equally obviously, most of these issues must be addressed as well by anticausalist teleologists in search of an acceptable account of action and of acting in pursuit of a particular goal. I have shown that neither Wilson nor Sehon has offered an adequate account—or even informative conceptually sufficient conditions—of either of these things, and I have done this in a way that strongly suggests that it will be very difficult to avoid causalism in producing satisfactory accounts, or satisfactory statements of conceptually sufficient conditions. I have shown, as well, that, in the case of at least one kind of agent, causalists can handle the problem allegedly posed by representative instances of primary causal deviance for the project of providing a causal analysis of acting in pursuit of a particular goal.[30]

Notes

1. See Goldman 1970, Thalberg 1977, Thomson 1977, Davidson 1980, Hornsby 1980, Brand 1984, Bishop 1989, Mele 1992a. In connection with the parenthetical clause about states, consider a child playing hide-and-seek who remains perfectly still for several minutes because she wants not to be found. Her intentionally remaining perfectly still for this period is naturally viewed as an action. On the causal approach, her remaining motionless at the time—a *state*—might be an action in virtue of its causal history.
2. See, e.g., Taylor 1966, Wilson 1989 and 1997, and Sehon 1994 and 1997.
3. See, e.g., *Nicomachean Ethics* 1139a31–32: "the origin of action—its efficient, not its final cause—is choice, and that of choice is desire and reasoning with a view to an end."
4. After summarizing Davidson's challenge (pp. 168–70), Wilson complains that anticausalists have left us pretty much in the dark about the connection between reasons and actions and he remarks that "without some more positive identification of the putatively noncausal connection in question, the nature of this linking remains mysterious" (p. 171).
5. See Alvin Goldman's treatment of "*in order to* explanations" (1970, pp. 77–78).
6. The following case first appeared in Mele 1992a, pp. 248–49. In my discussion of Wilson's position there, I neglected to consider a significant reply that is open to Wilson. That reply will be taken up shortly.
7. In this paragraph and the next two, I borrow from Mele 1992a, pp. 249–50.
8. In Mele 1992a, I failed to treat this assertion and its kind as *definitional* assertions when criticizing Wilson's position. However, as I will argue shortly, the assertion does not help Wilson. (Here and elsewhere in this paper, I have substituted my preferred variables for Wilson's.)
9. Notice that this preserves the apparent synonymy of 'Norm's movements M were intended by him to N' and 'Norm intended of his movements M that they N'.
10. See Adams and Mele 1992, p. 325; Armstrong 1980, p.71; McCann 1975, pp. 425–27; McGinn 1982, pp. 86–87.
11. See James 1981, pp. 1101–3. For discussion of a case of this kind, see Adams and Mele 1992, pp. 324–31.
12. Some of the details of this case were prompted by an objection Helen Beebee raised to an earlier version.

13. Consider a case that may seem to be a problematic for *T3*. Helen has agreed to play a sledding game in which, after seating themselves in a circular sled at the top of a snowy slope and grasping straps to hold themselves in place, contestants are spun around several times and given a solid push. Their objective is to guide the sled through the narrow opening between a pair of bright orange poles twenty yards down the hill. When Helen comes out of her spin. She notices that the sled is heading straight toward the opening. She is prepared to alter the course of the sled, if necessary (by leaning), and she keeps her eyes fixed on the poles. As luck would have it, Helen does not need to alter the sled's course. She does nothing more than continue to grasp the straps and keep her eyes on the poles. Amazingly, the ride was so smooth that Helen did not need to move any part of her body, including her head and her eyes.

Did Helen sentiently direct the motion of her body down the slope at promoting her sled's traveling between the poles, or was she too "passive" on this occasion for that to be so? Notice that a parallel question can be asked about trying. Did Helen try to get the sled to travel between the poles, or was she too "passive" for that to be so? Undoubtedly, intuitions will vary. But should it turn out that the judgment is warranted that Helen's motion down the hill was sentiently directed by her at the pertinent goal, I conjecture that the warranting considerations would count no less strongly in favor of the judgment that Helen *tried* to achieve this goal. Not only is sentiently directing motion at a goal something that we do, but it involves effort— effort directed at achieving the goal.

14. It might be suggested that Wilson should add an anti-intervention condition to the four conditions he offers. But if the addition of such a condition would contribute to conceptually sufficient conditions for an agent's sentiently directing his movements at a goal because the relevant kinds of intervention prevent the obtaining of normal causal connections between mental items or their neural realizers and bodily motions, to add the condition would be to admit defeat.

15. For other criticisms of Wilson's attempt to meet the Davidsonian challenge, see Roth 1999, section 3.

16. In the remainder of this paragraph, I borrow from Mele 1997a, p. 232.

17. In this paragraph, I borrow from Mele 1997b, p. 136.

18. For a taxonomy, see Mele 1992b, pp. 208 and 210.

19. There are, of course, other problems with the simple-minded analysis. For example, there are purely mental actions, such as adding a collection of numbers in one's head.

20. For elaboration of this view, see Mele 1992a, chs. 8–11.

21. See Brand 1984, p. 20; Mele 1992a, pp. 201–2.

22. On sustaining roles of intentions, see Brand 1984, p. 175; Thalberg 1984; Bishop 1989, pp. 167–71; Mele 1992a, pp. 130–31, 180–84, 192–94.

23. On the guiding role of intentions, see Brand 1984, Part IV; Thalberg 1984, pp. 257–59; Bishop 1989, pp. 167–72; Mele 1992a, pp. 136–37, 220–23.

24. For a useful discussion of ballistic bodily movements, see Sheridan 1984, pp. 50–54.

25. Recall that on the first occasion, Eve's intention was to *try* to touch the pear with her index finger. On a distinction between intending to *A* and intending to try to *A*, see Mele 1992a, pp. 132–35 and 146–50.

26. On the motor cortex and motor signals, see Georgopoulos 1995 and Porter and Lemon 1993. Of course, I am not claiming that actual human agents function exactly like Promethean agents.

27. Two additional points about nervousness are in order. First, nervousness does not always block action. Indeed, it sometimes contributes to the performance of an action (see Mele 1992a, pp. 243–44). The second point concerns a case in which Clem knows that he frequently loses control over crucial parts of his body when he tries to execute frightening proximal intentions. Wanting to bring about Don's death in a way that will seem accidental, he hits upon the following plan. He will invite Don to climb a mountain with him and form the intention at a suitable time to try to let go of the support rope; his forming that intention, he predicts, will initiate an attempt to let go of the rope that will cause him to lose control over his hands, with the result that Don falls to his death. Clem climbs the mountain with this plan. At a certain time, he forms the intention to try to let go of the rope, and things happen just as he predicted. Did Clem perform the action of letting go of the rope? No, for he lost control over his hands; they were moving, but he was not moving them. However, on the assumption that forming an intention (as opposed to merely acquiring one) is an action (see Mele 1999a), in executing his master plan Clem did perform the actions of bringing it about that he lost control over his hands, bringing it about that his grip on the rope loosened, bringing it about that the rope fell from his hands, bringing it about that Don fell to his death, and so on. (For discussion of a related case, see Mele 1995, pp. 413–14.)

28. Wilder Penfield writes: "When I have caused a conscious patient to move his hand by applying an electrode to the motor cortex of one hemisphere I have often asked him about it. Invariably his response was: 'I didn't do that. You did.' When I caused him to vocalize, he said, 'I didn't make that sound. You pulled it out of me'" (1975, p. 76).

29. Setting aside artificial cases, notice that the neural architecture of a particular kind of being may be such that mere desires, say, are not equipped to send command signals, even if there are possible beings in which action is (sometimes) initiated by proximal desire acquisition rather than by proximal intention acquisition.

30. For responses to other alleged problems raised by anticausalist teleologists, see Mele 1992a, ch. 13 and 1999b. Drafts of this paper were presented at The Australian National University, Monash University, the University of Auckland, Southern Methodist University, and the University of Texas at Austin. For helpful discussion or written comments, I am grateful to John Bishop, Randy Clarke, Doug Ehring, Mark Heller, Jennifer Hornsby, Karen Jones, Corey Juhl, Vera Koffman, Mike Martin, Mike Ridge, Abe Roth, Fred Schueler, Scott Sehon, David Sosa, Steve Sverdlik, George Wilson, Nicole Wyatt, and especially Helen Beebee. The criticism of Wilson's position in Section 1 derives partly from a paper I presented at an author-meets-critics session on Wilson 1989 at the 1996 meeting of the Pacific Division of the American Philosophical Association.

References

Adams, F., and Mele, A. 1992. "The Intention/Volition Debate." *Canadian Journal of Philosophy* 22: 323–38.

Aristotle. *Nicomachean Ethics.* In W. Ross, ed. *Works of Aristotle*, Vol. 9. London: Oxford University Press, 1915.

Armstrong, D. 1980. "Acting and Trying." In D. Armstrong, *The Nature of Mind.* Ithaca: Cornell University Press.

Bishop, J. 1989. *Natural Agency.* Cambridge: Cambridge University Press.

Brand, M. 1984. *Intending and Acting*. Cambridge: MIT Press.

Davidson, D. 1980. *Essays on Actions and Events*. Oxford: Clarendon Press.

————. 1963. "Actions, Reasons, and Causes." *Journal of Philosophy* 60: 685–700. Reprinted in Davidson 1980.

Georgopoulos, A. 1995. "Motor Cortex and Cognitive Processing." In M. Gazzaniga, ed. *The Cognitive Neurosciences*. Cambridge: MIT Press.

Goldman, A. 1970. *A Theory of Human Action*. Englewood Cliffs, NJ: Prentice-Hall.

Hornsby, J. 1980. *Actions*. London: Routledge & Kegan Paul.

James, W. 1981. *The Principles of Psychology*, vol. 2. Cambridge: Harvard University Press.

McCann, H. 1975. "Trying, Paralysis, and Volition." *Review of Metaphysics* 28: 425–27.

McGinn, C. 1982. *The Character of Mind*. Oxford: Oxford University Press.

Mele, A. 1999a. "Deciding to Act." *Philosophical Studies*.

————. 1999b. "Is There a Place for Intention in an Analysis of Intentional Action?" *Philosophia* 27: 563–75.

————. 1997a. "Agency and Mental Action." *Philosophical Perspectives* 11: 231–49.

————. 1997b. "Passive Action." In G. Holmström-Hintikka and R. Tuomela, eds. *Contemporary Action Theory*, vol. 1. Dordrecht: Kluwer.

————. 1995. "Motivation: Essentially Motivation-Constituting Attitudes." *Philosophical Review* 104: 387–423.

————. 1992a. *Springs of Action: Understanding Intentional Behavior*. New York: Oxford University Press.

————. 1992b. "Recent Work on Intentional Action." *American Philosophical Quarterly* 29:199–217.

Mele, A. and Moser, P. 1994. "Intentional Action." *Noûs* 28 (1994): 39–68.

Penfield, W. 1975. *The Mystery of the Mind*. Princeton: Princeton University Press.

Porter, R. and Lemon, R. 1993. *Corticospinal Function and Voluntary Movement*. Oxford: Clarendon Press.

Roth, A. 1999. "Reasons Explanations of Actions: Causal, Singular, and Situational." *Philosophy and Phenomenological Research* (forthcoming).

Sehon, S. 1997. "Deviant Causal Chains and the Irreducibility of Teleological Explanation." *Pacific Philosophical Quarterly* 78: 195–213.

————. 1994. "Teleology and the Nature of Mental States." *American Philosophical Quarterly* 31: 63–72.

Sheridan, M. 1984. "Planning and Controlling Simple Movements." In M. Smyth and A. Wing, eds. *The Psychology of Human Movement*. London: Academic Press, pp. 47–82.

Taylor, R. 1966. *Action and Purpose*. Englewood Cliffs: Prentice-Hall.

Thalberg, I. 1984. "Do Our Intentions Cause Our Intentional Actions?" *American Philosophical Quarterly* 21: 249–60.

————. 1977. *Perception, Emotion, and Action*. Oxford: Basil Blackwell.

Thomson, J. 1977. *Acts and Other Events*. Ithaca: Cornell University Press.

Wilson, G. 1997. "Reasons as Causes for Action." In G. Holmström-Hintikka and R. Tuomela, eds. *Contemporary Action Theory*, vol. 1. Dordrecht: Kluwer, pp. 65–82.

————. 1989. *The Intentionality of Human Action*. Stanford: Stanford University Press.

Philosophical Perspectives, 14, Action and Freedom, 2000

RESPONSIBILITY IN CASES OF MULTIPLE PERSONALITY DISORDER

Walter Sinnott-Armstrong
Dartmouth College

Stephen Behnke
Division of Medical Ethics, Harvard Medical School

Multiple Personality Disorder (MPD), now also known as Dissociative Identity Disorder, raises many questions about the nature of persons, the goals of treatment, the suggestibility of patients, and the reliability of defendant reports of their own mental states. These issues become crucial when courts need to decide whether or not to punish a person with MPD who has committed a crime. This paper will explore that issue and propose a test of when people with MPD should be held criminally responsible.

1 Diagnostic Criteria of MPD

Many people are unfamiliar with Multiple Personality Disorder, so we begin by quoting its diagnostic criteria in DSM IV:

A. The presence of two or more distinct identities or personality states (each with its own relatively enduring pattern of perceiving, relating to, and thinking about the environment and self).
B. At least two of these identities or personality states recurrently take control of the person's behavior.
C. Inability to recall important personal information that is too extensive to be explained by ordinary forgetfulness.
D. The disturbance is not due to direct physiological effects of a substance (e.g. blackouts or chaotic behavior during Alcohol Intoxication) or a general medical condition (e.g. complex partial seizures).
Note: In children, the symptoms are not attributable to imaginary playmates or other fantasy play.

There is wide disagreement about how many people really meet these criteria and, thus, about how many people really have MPD. However, we will assume for the sake of argument that some people do have MPD, and that some of them commit crimes. The theoretical issues remain basically the same regardless of how common MPD really is.

2 Cases of MPD

This mental illness varies in important ways from case to case. Here we will focus on three brief case studies. In each, the facts are in question, but we present the facts as claimed by the defense, so that we can determine whether those facts, if established, would be enough to remove criminal responsibility.

The Grimsley Case (1982): Robin Grimsley received a report of a lump in her breast. This psychological trauma, according to Grimsley, "caused her to dissociate into the personality of Jennifer, who is impulsive, angry, fearful, and anxious. Jennifer has a drinking problem." On this day, Jennifer drank, drove, and was charged with driving under the influence of alcohol. In her defense, Grimsley "contend[ed] that when she is Jennifer, Robin is unaware of what is going on, has no control over Jennifer's actions, and no memory of what Jennifer did later on when she is restored to the primary personality of Robin." Ms. Grimsley had been previously diagnosed with MPD and had been in psychotherapy since 1977. Nonetheless, the court held Grimsley responsible on the grounds that "There was only one person driving the car and only one person accused of drunken driving. It is immaterial whether she was in one state of consciousness or another, so long as in the personality then controlling her behavior, she was conscious and her actions were a product of her own volition. The evidence failed to indicate that Jennifer was unconscious or otherwise acting involuntarily."[1]

The Denny-Shaffer Case (1993): Denny-Shaffer took a baby out of a hospital and transported him across state lines to Texas. She then called her boyfriend at work and told him that she had had his baby in his bed. She had taken blood and a placenta from the hospital in order to be able to convince him that she really did have the baby there. Over the next few weeks, she took care of the baby and showed him to several people, including her family. However, she was finally caught and convicted of kidnapping an infant and transporting him across state lines. Her defense was that her host alter, named Bridget, was unconscious and not aware of the kidnapping for all or part of those weeks, so she could not have prevented the crime.

The court held "There is evidence for the defendant plainly sufficient to support inferences by the trier of fact that Denny-Shaffer suffers from a severe mental defect or disease [MPD]; that at the time of the abduction, her dominant or host personality was not in control so as to cause commission of the offense, and was not aware that an alter personality or personalities were the cognizant parties controlling the physical actions; that as a result of the defendant's severe mental disease or defect, the host or dominant personality was unable to appreciate the nature and quality or wrongfulness of the conduct which the alter or alters controlled; and that the defendant had proven these facts by clear and convincing evidence."[2] On this basis, the courts found Denny-Shaffer not guilty.

The Woods Case: "John and Sally had dated for over a year and had been sexually intimate. She had given him considerable emotional and intellectual support and was apparently the one mutual love experience of his life. Sally was also the only person he had ever told about having 'different people' inside him." One of the alters inside Woods was Ron, who was "aggressive and verbally limited." "Ron indicated that on the day of the murder he saw a suspicious footprint in Sally's carpet that made him think she was seeing another man. He heard John ask about this, and Sally replied that she would sleep with whomever she wanted." "After this exchange between John and Sally, Ron saw John 'die'. He believes that Sally had 'killed' John by the things she had said to him... . Ron...felt that he had to try to bring John 'back'. Meanwhile, he also knew that Sally was 'far away' from them with the devil and he had to bring her back too. In order to accomplish this, he had to 'loose the evilness from her and stop the words from coming out.' He felt that if Sally spoke any more, she would not only have killed John, she would have 'taken him with her'. It was to this end that he stuffed Sally's underpants into her mouth, since that was where the evil was coming from. He also shook her to bring her to where they were." "John apparently then cleaned the room and left town for several days. Phone records indicate that during that time he called newspapers and funeral homes to check on whether Sally was dead. He was picked up by the police when he returned to town. At first he denied the crime. After several days and a long session of non-recorded questioning, he confessed."[3] Woods was later diagnosed with MPD.

Such cases raise many questions. One initial question is verbal: How should we describe the actors in these cases? Some psychiatrists refer to different people, others to different personalities, and still others to different personality states or mental states. It will be crucial below to determine whether, for example, Robin is the same person as Jennifer, so we do not want to prejudge that issue in our terminology. We will also need to use the word "personality" in its more common sense to refer to character or personality traits that are or explain the general ways in which people tend to act or feel or think. To avoid confusions, then, we will use the technical term "alter" to describe Robin and Jennifer as well as their analogs in other cases.

It will be important to remember that this terminology is just another way of talking about a collection or group of mental states or processes. When we say that one alter is in control at a time, all this means is that some mental states within a certain group determine what is done at that time. The alter, even when in control, need not be an entity any more than a mood is.

3 Responsibility

With this terminology in place, we can ask more substantive questions. One question is metaphysical: Are the separate alters distinct persons? Another question is practical: What should the courts do with these people? Our main goal is to answer this practical question for the courts, but it is important to see how these questions are related.

Courts must choose between three main options: prison (possibly with psychiatric help) or forced confinement in a mental institution (possibly with bars) or freedom (possibly with mandated periodic treatment). There might not seem to be a great deal of difference between the first two options. However, punishment in prison involves an element of condemnation and blame that is lacking from forced confinement in a mental institution. That is why responsibility is required before punishment in prison. It might be socially useful to punish these people, because it incapacitates a potential criminal and also because it deters faking. It might even be therapeutically useful to punish these people, if punishment will make them accept their responsibility and pull their lives together. Nonetheless, to punish any person in order to achieve such a social goal when that person was not responsible would be seriously unjust according to standards accepted throughout the history of our society and most other societies. Punishment of innocent people is seen as one of the worst kinds of injustice.

Usually people are responsible only for what they do. That is why, if I commit a crime, it would be unfair to punish you, since you are a separate person, and you did not commit any crime. There are exceptions. Maybe you helped me prepare to commit the crime. Maybe you could have stopped me, but you didn't, because you wanted me to commit the crime. Still, because I am a separate person, if you did not help me and could not stop me, then you are not responsible for my crimes, so it would be unjust to punish you for my crime. Almost everyone accepts this principle or something very much like it.

Similar restrictions apply to involuntary commitment. To hold someone against their will in a mental institution when that person is not dangerous to self or others is widely seen as horrendous. If you were thrown into a locked mental ward because some other person is dangerous, then you would have a grave complaint. A dangerous person need not be responsible in order for confinement to be acceptable, but at least the person who is confined has to be dangerous. It is not enough if a different person is dangerous.

Thus, a court's choice cannot be separated completely from metaphysical questions of personal identity. Courts have to decide which person did the crime and whether that person is responsible before they can determine whether to punish or commit that person.

These issues of personal identity and responsibility are especially difficult and crucial in cases of MPD. If different alters are different persons, then to punish one who did not commit the crime would be to punish an innocent person. In the Grimsley case, for example, Robin could complain that she is being forced to live in jail and is thereby punished for something that a different person (Jennifer) did, and which Robin could not have prevented. We might have to inflict such punishment on Robin for lack of any better alternative, but we would have to see such punishment as involving an element of terrible injustice to an innocent person.

As Saks argues,[4] the situation then seems like that of Siamese twins, one of whom spontaneously grabs a gun and shoots someone without the other twin being able to stop the crime. It would be unjust to put both Siamese twins in jail, since one is innocent. It is not clear what the courts should do in such a case, but to put both twins in jail would involve a serious element of injustice. A similar element of injustice would occur if we punish a person with multiple personality disorder and *if* each of the alters were a distinct person like a Siamese twin with little or no control over the one who committed the crime.

In contrast, such punishment is not unjust in this way if different alters are instead just different parts or aspects of a single person. On this model, it is neither Robin nor Jennifer who did the crime and is punished. It is Grimsley, the person of whom Robin and Jennifer are just parts or aspects. This total person, Grimsley, can be held responsible for what one part of her did, just as anyone can be held responsible for what one temporal part of them did, e.g., for what that part of them that existed last Monday did on last Monday. The punishment might be unjust on other grounds, but one could not argue simply that an innocent person is being punished if different alters are not different people.

This makes it crucial to determine whether the alters in a case of MPD really are different persons in a relevant way. If so, punishment would be wrong. If not, punishment might be justified.

4 Problems for Multiplicity of Persons

Several psychologists and philosophers, including Elyn Saks[5] and Jennifer Radden,[6] claim that alters in a case of MPD are distinct persons. However, this hypothesis seems to lead quickly to absurd consequences: If different alters were different persons, we should allow them to vote separately, to marry different spouses, and so on. After all, we do and should allow Siamese twins to vote and marry separately, so the same would apply to people with MPD if that analogy held, and if distinct alters were distinct persons. Moreover, if someone has ten alters, may they claim nine dependents on a tax form? Who should file the form? If a female with MPD has a child, which alter is the mother? If another alter takes the child on a trip without permission, is that kidnapping? Is it adultery if alters switch during sex or robbery if alters switch during a bank withdrawal? Can one alter sue another? Even to raise such issues reveals serious problems for the multiple-persons view.

Defenders of the multiple-persons view might respond that we can treat the alters as the same person for the purposes of voting and marriage but as different people when it comes to depriving them of freedom. However, if one of the alters is extremely violent and unpredictable, and if we may not deprive the other alters of freedom simply because of what one alter did, then we also may not commit them jointly to a secure mental hospital. We would have to let them all go free or else admit a serious injustice. That implication seems absurd, but it is hard to avoid if the separate alters are seen as separate persons.

Finally, the treatment of choice in such cases attempts to get these alters to fuse. This often means that one alter simply goes out of existence. If each alter really did constitute a different person, then it would not be at all clear why such fusion and disappearance is desirable. Why is it better to have only one person in a body instead of several? Moreover, to cause one alter to disappear out of existence permanently would seem like murder. What would justify a psychiatrist in causing one alter to cease existing for the sake of another alter if the former alter really were a separate person? That would be as wrong as killing one Siamese twin just to benefit the other twin.

Defenders of the multiple-persons view might still respond that what counts as a person for the sake of criminal responsibility is different from what counts as a person in all of these other contexts. Sometimes we do need to use different concepts in different areas. However, the absurdity of treating different alters as different persons puts a heavy burden of proof on anyone who claims that the alters should be treated as different persons for the sake of criminal responsibility. If each of these alters does not have a separate and equal right to existence, to vote, to marry, and so on, why would each have a separate and equal right not to be jailed for what another alter did? Such a position seems arbitrary and implausible. One would need a very strong argument to defend the claim that personhood relevant to criminal responsibility is so different from personhood in all other areas.

5 Arguments for Multiplicity of Persons

What arguments could be given for the multiple-persons view? One common move is to apply something like Daniel Dennett's criteria of personhood.[7] Dennett claims roughly that a person is rational, the subject of intentional predicates, a moral object, a moral subject or agent, a language-user, and the possessor of a special kind of consciousness (or self-consciousness). Each alter seems to have these characteristics in at least some cases of MPD. In the Grimsley case, for example, both Robin and Jennifer use language, are self-conscious, make rational choices and form rational beliefs (which is an intentional predicate), have rights (including not to be hurt), and have duties as moral agents (including not to lie). One might conclude that each alter is a separate person in those cases.

This argument fails because all of these observations can be explained easily by someone who denies that Robin and Jennifer are separate persons. Compare a normal person without MPD named Norm. That part of Norm that consists of Norm's life on a certain day (or when he is in a certain mood) can be called NormPart. NormPart uses language and is self-conscious and rational, insofar as Norm uses language and is self-conscious and rational on that particular day (or when he is in that particular mood). NormPart also has a right not to be hurt and a duty not to lie insofar as Norm has those rights and duties on that particular day (or when he is in that particular mood). All of these characteristics of persons can be ascribed to NormPart, because they can be ascribed to Norm during the time when that part of Norm exists.

Now compare this with alters in a case of MPD. If alters are parts of a person instead of separate persons, then they can meet all of Dennett's criteria of persons simply because the persons of whom they are parts have those properties during the times when those alters are in control of the person. Even if different alters exist at the same time, they perform different individual acts, and each act can be ascribed to a particular alter (so that alter can be said to make that rational choice) only because the person of whom that alter is a part does that act. In some such way, those theorists who claim that different alters are parts of the same person can explain why we ascribe Dennett's criteria when we do, and they can explain this just as well as those theorists who claim that different alters are different persons. Thus, Dennett's criteria do not favor one view of individuation over the other.

More technically, the problem with this argument is that it confuses different contrast classes. Dennett's criteria are intended to distinguish a person from a non-person, such as an object, plant, or lower animal. Dennett never intended his criteria to be used to distinguish one person from another, that is, to individuate persons. Moreover, Dennett's criteria are ill-suited for individuation. Suppose all we know is that Mark Twain is a rational, self-conscious language user and a moral object and subject; and so is Samuel Clemens. This tells us that Mark is a person, and Sam is a person. It does not tell us whether or not Mark and Sam are the same person. "Mark" might be a nom-de-plum for "Sam", in which case Mark is the same person as Sam. This person might go by the name "Mark" in some contexts at some times (such as when writing) but by the name "Sam" in other contexts at other times (such as when dining). Similarly, if "Robin" and "Jennifer" are just different names for different parts of a single person's life, then each can fully meet Dennett's criteria but still be the same person. So even if Dennett's tests show that each alter is or is part of a person as opposed to a plant, these criteria cannot show that these alters are different persons as opposed to parts of the same person.

6 Personal Identity

To argue for or against personal identity, a different kind of criterion is needed. In particular, one would need a necessary condition of personal identity in order to argue that two alters are or are parts of different persons. A *necessary* condition of personal identity is simply some relation between X and Y such that, whenever X and Y do not stand in that relation, X is *not* the same person as Y. In contrast, a *sufficient* condition of personal identity is a relation between X and Y such that, whenever X and Y stand in that relation, X *is* the same person as Y.

We will propose a sufficient condition of personal identity to show that different alters in cases of MPD are or are parts of the same person. This strategy will not settle the philosophical issues around personal identity or MPD. Indeed, part of our point is that one need not settle those issues to defend criminal punishment in cases of MPD against objections based on personal identity.

Many criteria of personal identity have been proposed. Here we will discuss criteria that focus on the body, brain, memory, personality, projects, awareness, and control. These criteria could, of course, be conjoined and disjoined. One such combination of criteria will be crucial to our argument.

6.1 Body and Brain

In real life, we usually determine whether the person next to us is the same person as the one we married by looking at the shape of her body or at least face. Of course, the shape of a person's body and face can change radically over the years or suddenly as a result of some injury. Large parts of the body can be amputated or transplanted. The possibility of such partial changes in one's body show that complete bodily identity is not necessary for personal identity, but identity between bodies as wholes (which does not require identity of all body parts) still might be necessary. In any case, complete bodily identity and even a continuous chain of stages linking the body of the person we married to the person next to us still seems sufficient for personal identity in the real world.

Science fiction raises doubts. Since John Locke,[8] the bodily criterion of personal identity has been rejected by most philosophers on the basis of examples where minds switch bodies. Suppose a Prince and a Cobbler go to sleep in the same castle. In the morning the Prince's mind is in the Cobbler's body, and the Cobbler's mind is in the Prince's body. Locke and his followers take it as obvious that the person who was the Prince is now identical with the Prince's mind in the Cobbler's body, not the Cobbler's mind in the Prince's body. This is supposed to show that the identity of a person depends on the mind rather than the body.

Such examples seem less unrealistic when one considers the possibility of a brain transplant. In Shoemaker's example,[9] while performing two brain transplants at once (just to show off?), a surgeon inadvertently puts Brown's brain in Robinson's body, thereby producing a combination called Brownson, which has all of Brown's memories, personality traits, and so on. The surgeon also puts Robinson's brain in Brown's body, but that combination dies. Shoemaker and his followers think it is obvious that Brown is the same person as Brownson. This is, again, supposed to show that personal identity follows the mind rather than the body.

However, it is crucial that Brownson has Brown's brain, even though Brownson has no more of Brown's body. As Bernard Gert argues,[10] if Robinson were hypnotized in such a way that Robinson's body took on all of Brown's memories, personality traits, and other mental features, then nobody would say that the result was identical with Brown, especially if Brown still existed with all of the same memories, personality traits, and other mental features. So brain identity still seems necessary for personal identity.

It also seems sufficient. This is clearest when brain transfer follows hypnosis:

>...prior to brain transfer between Brown and Robinson, Brown had been hypnotized and told that he was Robinson. He then makes memory claims to be Robinson and assumes the personality and character of Robinson. Thus, prior to the brain transfer, Brown has the psychological features of Robinson. If, while in this state, Brown's brain is put in Robinson's body, we would have a person who would have Robinson's body, Brown's brain, and Robinson's psychological features. Yet I should want to say that this person is really Brown.

This person would not be Brown if any mental features were necessary for personal identity, since the body with Brown's brain has none of Brown's mental features. Thus, if the resulting person really is Brown, then mental features do not seem necessary, and brain identity seems sufficient for personal identity.

Why is it sufficient? The answer seems to be that the brain is that part of the body that is associated with psychological features. (It would be more precise to refer to only part of the brain, but we will speak of the brain as a whole for simplicity.) If the heart were the seat of the mind, then heart identity might determine personal identity. What determines personal identity is the identity of whatever organ (or set of organs or part of an organ) is associated with mental properties. Since this organ in real humans is the brain, we will talk simply about brain identity.

Admittedly, if the brain is frozen until it ceases to function, then there is no person at all, so there cannot be the same person. Nonetheless, if the same brain is functioning, then it is the same person, even if the brain is not functioning in the same way. Since our brains function very differently when we are asleep or drunk or hypnotized or suffering from Alzheimer's, but we are still the same persons, personal identity cannot require the same brain function even if it does require some brain function.

What about Locke's case? Now that we realize that it matters how the cobbler's body came by the prince's mind, we need to ask what happened overnight. If the cobbler was hypnotized, and so was the prince, then we would not say that the prince is now the cobbler with the prince's mind. If an evil surgeon switched the brains of the prince and the cobbler, then we would say that the cobbler with the prince's mind (and brain) was the prince, but that would cause no trouble for the brain criterion. The only case that would cause trouble for the brain criterion would be if the mind switched bodies without the brain and then if personal identity followed the mind. But that is impossible according to many views of mind, including most varieties of physicalism. One would suppose that Locke's example is possible only if one thinks that the mind is a separate substance independent of the body and brain. Since such views of the mind are questionable, so is Locke's argument against the brain criterion.

This criterion is easy to apply to cases of MPD. Different alters in a case of MPD inhabit the same body completely. That body has a single brain. It is not even split as in split-brain patients. Some evidence suggests that different alters use different parts of the brain or that the brain displays different patterns of activity when different alters are in control. But there are also some differences between the patterns of activity when a single person is in different moods or stages of life, or when asleep or drunk. These normal differences might not be as extreme as in cases of MPD, but they still show that, even if the brain functions differently when different alters are in control, this alone cannot undermine our conclusion that these alters must be (parts of) the same person if brain identity is sufficient for personal identity.

6.2 Memory

Many philosophers continue to reject the brain criterion on the basis of examples like Locke's. The most common alternative focuses on memory. This criterion also has some basis in everyday life. Even if you cannot recognize your old friend, Joe, because he was burned beyond recognition, you might still be able to identify your old friend by recalling certain memories. Admittedly, as every lover of spy fiction knows, I might be able to recall that Joe jumped off a diving board with you on September 17 twenty years ago, even if I am not Joe. What I cannot do unless I am Joe is remember *having* the experience of jumping off the diving board with you alone that time. And only you can remember having the experience of jumping off the board with Joe that fateful time. We will call such memories of having experiences *experiential memories*.

Experiential memories can fade just like other memories. I might not be able to remember jumping off the board. A person can even suffer complete amnesia and lose all previous experiential memories. That would not show that he was not the same person as he was before the amnesia. He would still have the same parents, children, social security number, and so on, even if his character or personality did change. Consequently, experiential memories are not necessary for personal identity, and no lack of experiential memory can be used to argue *against* personal identity.

That is important here, because the experiential memories of people with MPD are radically disconnected. If a connected chain of experiential memories were necessary for personal identity, then alters in a case of MPD would be different people. But so would people with amnesia, dissociative fugue, and blackouts during intoxication or after hypnosis, as well as many of us. Since that is implausible, disconnection among experiential memories cannot be used to show lack of personal identity in cases of MPD or anywhere else.

Experiential memories still might provide a sufficient condition of personal identity. Suppose that on Wednesday Ron remembers having his experience of eating breakfast on Monday although Ron does not remember any experience on Tuesday. Then on Thursday Ron also remembers having the same experience on Monday, although Ron does not remember having any experience on Tuesday or Wednesday. Despite the disconnections among his memories, the fact that his experiential memories on Wednesday and Thursday are memories of having the same experience on Monday seems to be enough to show that the person who had that experiential memory on Wednesday is the same as the person who had the experiential memory on Thursday. More generally, when X and Y have memories of having at least one common experience, then their memories will be said to converge. A single pair of convergent experiential memories seems sufficient for personal identity.

This criterion can be extended if identity is transitive, so that, if X is identical with Y, and Y is identical with Z, then X is identical with Z. Suppose that each day Ron remembers the preceding day but nothing before. On Friday Ron remembers eating breakfast on Thursday but not on Wednesday, on Thursday Ron remembers eating breakfast on Wednesday but not on Tuesday, and so on. Ron's experiential memory chain shows that Ron on Friday is the same person as Ron on Thursday, Ron on Thursday is the same person as Ron on Wednesday, and so on. By transitivity, it follows that Ron on Friday is the same person as Ron on Wednesday, and so on. These identities hold even if no experiential memory is shared on Friday and Tuesday. More generally, we can say that two experiential memory chains converge when each chain contains one of a pair of convergent experiential memories. Such convergence between experiential memory chains seems to be sufficient for personal identity, even between times when there are no current convergent memories.

It does not matter whether my experiential memory is distorted in some ways, but it is not enough to have *an* experiential memory of eating toast for breakfast on Monday at 8:00 a.m., since different people can eat the same thing at the same time and later remember having *an* experience of eating toast for breakfast on Monday at 8:00 a.m. What different people cannot do, on this theory, is remember (or have memory chains that converge on a memory of) having exactly the same experience of eating breakfast on Monday. This test of personal identity, thus, rests on some test of experience identity.

This reliance creates problems when we distinguish numerical identity from exact phenomenological similarity. Two experiences are exactly similar phenomenologically when they do not differ in any detail that is observable or introspectable by the person having the experiences. Such experiences still might not be numerically identical, as is shown by science fiction. Possibly through hypnosis, Ron can have an experience of eating breakfast on Monday that is exactly like Don's in all detectable respects. Each sees the same people, dishes, and decorations from the same angles, so each of their heads would seem to have been in the same place at the same time looking in the same direction. Each also experiences the same flavors, smells, sounds, and feelings in exactly the same order. Later Ron and Don can have experiential memories that are exactly similar phenomenologically, and they can reliably describe them to me.

Nonetheless, if Ron and Don are now standing next to each other with different brains and personalities, they cannot be the same person. So exact phenomenological similarity is not enough for personal identity. What would be sufficient is that the remembered experiences be numerically identical. That seems to require that the same person had them. But then we need to know whether Ron and Don were the same person while they had the experience before we can know whether they remember having numerically the same experience and, thus, before we can use memories to determine personal identity at a later time.

This problem of circularity has led many philosophers to abandon memory as a criterion of personal identity. It still suffices for personal identity that a chain of experiential memories converges on numerically the same experience. However, this cannot provide a general criterion of personal identity because it cannot be applied without assumptions about personal identity at the time of the remembered experience.

Luckily, those assumptions seem plausible in cases of MPD. Suppose Mel is born in 1990, goes to school for the first time 1995, then develops MPD in 1996. If each of Mel's alters has an experiential memory of something that happened to him during the first day of school or of any other experience before developing MPD, then there should be no doubt that these experiential memories are memories of numerically the same experience. The reason is that there was clearly only one person at the time of the experiences that are remembered. Since numerical identity of persons and experiences is not in doubt at that earlier time, the later memories seem sufficient for personal identity at the later time, when personal identity is at issue.

Moreover, even if such memories are rejected as a criterion of personal identity, they can still be evidence. It is only in science fiction that different people have phenomenologically exactly similar experiential memories. Consequently, the fact that Mel's alters share some phenomenologically exactly similar experiential memories in 1990 is at least very strong evidence that these alters are (parts of) the same person.

Admittedly, Mel is fictional, too. To apply the memory test to real cases is harder. In the Grimsley case, for example, it is not obvious whether Robin and Jennifer remember having any common experience. Luckily, no common experiential memory is necessary. It would be enough if their chains of experiential memories converge, that is, include some memory of having the same experience. But that is hard to prove as well. We cannot rely on current reports, even if sincere, since the shared experiential memory in the chain need not be accessible at the current time. So personal identity will be hard to prove from memories on the record.

Nonetheless, it seems likely that Robin's chain of experiential memories and Jennifer's chain of experiential memories converge on at least one shared memory of the same experience. Both do remember being told about the lump in her (!) breast. In addition, each is probably linked to many experiential memories, possibly of experiences in childhood before the onset of MPD, when there was definitely only one person. Most likely, each alter can or could remember going to school or to a friend's house, or having been scared when their parents fought or angry when a sibling hurt them, or something else. It is possible that no such convergence ever existed, but this seems unlikely.

Moreover, even if none of their current memories are links in convergent chains, it seems even more likely that that Robin and Jennifer could have such memories after therapy. If they would then be the same person, and if each is the same person then as they are now, they must be the same person now. So it seems very unlikely that they are not the same person by the memory criterion, even if their identity is hard to prove.

Similar remarks seem to apply to every actual case of MPD. It is possible that, when MPD arises, a new person appears with no memories of the past and no actual or potential convergence with the other person who shares the same body. But there is little or no evidence for this in actual cases, and the opposite seems much more plausible, at least in the cases above.

What if no converging chain did exist? Then we could not use this sufficient condition of personal identity to argue that these alters are the same person. That still would not imply that the alters are different people, because convergent memory chains are not necessary for personal identity, as we argued above. In any case, there is reason to believe that such convergent memory chains do exist in many cases of MPD, so that is reason to believe that these alters are (parts of) the same person, if this is a sufficient criterion of personal identity.

6.3 Conjunction

Doubts remain about whether either brain identity or a convergent experiential memory chain is sufficient for personal identity. One might still wonder whether a convergent memory chain is enough when the memories in the chain occur in or are associated with separate bodies. One also might wonder whether complete brain identity or even whole body identity is enough when memories are not linked, as in Locke's prince and cobbler switch.

Luckily, neither criterion alone need be defended by opponents of the multiple-persons view of MPD. Even if neither brain nor memory alone suffices, it does seem clearly sufficient for personal identity that, for example, a person named "Liz" and a person named "Beth" share complete bodily identity (including complete brain identity) in conjunction with a (multiply) convergent experiential memory chain, and nobody else now or ever has any exactly phenomenologically similar experiential memories. When all of this comes together, there is no reason to doubt that Liz and Beth are the same person.

That is what happens in cases of MPD. In the Grimsley case, Robin and Jennifer share the same body completely, including the same brain. It seems very likely that their experiential memory chains converge at many points. And nobody else has any experiential memories that are phenomenologically exactly similar to theirs. This seems sufficient for their personal identity. At the very least, it is strong evidence that Robin and Jennifer are (parts of) the same person. The same argument could be given in all other real cases of MPD. This refutes any multiple-persons view of MPD.

6.4 Personality

Defenders of a multiple-persons view will respond that something more is necessary for personal identity. If so, the conjunctive criterion is not sufficient. If the added necessary condition is not met in cases of MPD, this would show that alters in cases of MPD are not (parts of) the same person.

One condition that is often claimed to be necessary is continuity or similarity of personality (or character). In this context, one's personality is something like that set of values or dispositions that constitutes or explains why one acts, feels, and thinks in the general ways that one does. On this view, X is the same person as Y only when X's personality is sufficiently similar to that of Y. Something like this seems to lie behind much common talk, such as when someone says to her degenerate spouse, "You are not the person I married," meaning that the spouse's personality has changed dramatically.

This criterion won't work in law. Suppose Joe is a heroine addict who undergoes a religious conversion to fundamentalism. His character or personality changes almost totally. We would and should still let him inherit what his grandfather left him in a valid will. We would and should still find him guilty for crimes that he committed before his conversion (even if we reduced or commuted his sentence). The same applies to people with manic depression or bipolar disorder, who change dramatically without any external cause. If a continuous personality were required for personal identity, and if personal identity were required for punishment, then one could escape punishment by changing one's personality after committing a crime; but criminals who plan such an escape should not be let off. Moreover, one main purpose of criminal law is deterrence (even if limited by guilt), but I can fear future punishment even if I know that I will have a different personality by the time I am punished. Finally, personality can vary in degrees but criminal law needs an on-off criterion as a necessary condition of guilt, since courts cannot declare anyone partly guilty, at least in our system. For all of these reasons, continuity of personality does not seem necessary for the kind of personal identity that is necessary for criminal responsibility, which is our topic here.

6.5 Projects

The vague idea of personality could be made more precise if one's personality is constituted or determined by one's projects and how they should fit together. That idea might lead to a test like that suggested by Carol Rovane:

> an individual person exists when there is a set of intentional episodes such that: (1) these intentional episodes stand in suitable rational relations so as to afford the

possibility of carrying out sustained coordinated activities; (2) the set includes commitment to particular unifying projects whose execution involves the very sorts of sustained coordinated activities made possible by (1); and (3) the commitment to carrying out these unifying projects brings in train a commitment to achieving overall rational unity within the set.[11]

This analysis implies that an alter is an individual person if and only if its intentional episodes (beliefs, emotions, and so on) meet conditions (1)-(3). It also suggests that two alters are not parts of the same individual person if and only if either suitable relations do not hold between the intentional episodes of the alters or they do not share any unifying project or they are not committed to achieving rational unity between their projects.

This test does not seem sufficient for personal identity. My wife and I carry out sustained coordinated activities that make it possible for us to execute our shared projects of raising our children and maintaining our personal relationship. We are committed to achieving overall rational unity within and between our projects. Nonetheless, my wife and I are still separate persons. Rovane does countenance group persons, but my wife and I do not seem to be parts of a group person, at least in any way relevant to criminal law. Moreover, the part of Norm that exists on Monday and the part of Norm that exists on Tuesday might each meet Rovane's three conditions if Norm needs both days to complete a certain project. However, neither the part of Norm that exists on Monday nor the conjunctive part of Norm that exists through Monday and Tuesday is an individual person who is distinct from Norm. If Rovane's conditions were sufficient, they would yield so many persons that we wouldn't know which one to hold responsible.

More important here, Rovane's three conditions are not necessary for personal identity over time. Even if no shared project or commitment unifies what I was at age six with me now, I am still the same person now as I was at age six. Rovane's criteria might seem to work better within a short time period, but consider a man with extreme manic depression. Sometimes he is suicidal, and sometimes he thinks that he is a great artist. When he is manic, he sees no value in suicide. When he is depressed, he sees no value in his art. In neither phase is he actually committed to rational unity within this set of projects, nor is he able to sustain coordinated activities through both phases. Still, neither phase by itself is a person, and the man is the same person in both phases, because he meets the body and memory conditions. If he commits a crime while manic, then we may legitimately hold him responsible and punish him while he is depressed. So unifying projects cannot be necessary for any kind of personal identity that is crucial to criminal responsibility.

Rovane might respond that such objections misinterpret commitment as a psychological state, whereas her notion of commitment is normative.[12] In the normative sense, intentional episodes are committed to overall rational unity if and only if they are subject to criticism as irrational to the extent that they fail to achieve overall rational unity among their projects, regardless of whether they actually accept this commitment. Manic-depressive moods are then not distinct persons because they need to unify projects in different moods in order to be rational, but alters in MPD might still be distinct persons if they need not unify their projects to be rational. However, this move to normative commitments cannot undermine our claim that alters in a case of MPD are parts of the same person. Alters in a case of MPD are subject to criticism for lacking rational unity. If they were not, then it would be hard to see why they need to be cured or may be required to undergo treatment. Maybe sometimes unification should not be sought, as Rovane argues. We do not always hold alters to their commitments by criticizing them for lacking unity. Nonetheless, in the above cases and others that involve crimes, it seems irrational for one alter to interfere with the projects of another alter in some situations where such interference need not be irrational for a distinct person. After all, the alters still share the same body and brain, as well as convergent memories. Consequently, alters do seem to be parts of the same person even on this normative interpretation of Rovane's view.

6.6 Awareness and Control

One thing that might seem to distinguish MPD from manic depression is a lack of awareness between phases. Alters might then count as different people if X is the same person as Y only when X is aware of what Y does. Awareness does seem relevant to criminal law insofar as X cannot control what Y does or prevent Y from committing a crime if X is not aware that Y is committing a crime. One could also move directly to the issue of control by holding that X is the same person as Y only when X is able to control what Y does.

When we apply such tests to our cases, the alters come out different persons. In the Grimsley case, Jennifer is not always aware of what Robin does, and vice-versa. Moreover, Jennifer cannot stop Robin from doing certain things, even when she is aware of what Robin is doing. In the Woods case, John and Donnie often can't know what Ron is doing or control Ron. In the Denny-Shaffer case, Bridget is not aware of or able to stop the other alter's crime. So these different alters are all different persons if either awareness or control is necessary for personal identity.

Alters are sometimes reported to have a kind of co-consciousness. One alter might be aware of what the other is thinking even if nothing is said out loud. However, nothing like this is essential to or happening at the time of the crimes in our cases. Such co-consciousness also does not enable one alter to control actions by another. So each alter still seems to lack the kind of awareness and control that might seem necessary for criminal responsibility.

However, neither awareness nor control is necessary for personal identity at least over time. I cannot control what I did yesterday, since it is past. I might not be aware of it, if I do not now remember doing it. But that does not mean that I am not the person who did it, or that I cannot be punished for doing it. The same goes for control over the future. Even if even if I am not able on

Monday to control what I eat for dinner on Tuesday, and even if I am not aware of what I will eat, much less aware of eating it, that still does not show that I am not the same person on both days. Thus, personal identity can hold over time without either awareness or control.

Alters in a case of MPD seem analogous in relevant respects to different parts of a single person's consciousness at different times. If each alter is aware of and can control what it does at a certain time, but is unaware of and cannot control what the other alter does at a different time, then the alters are related much like temporal parts of a single person when one temporal part is aware of and can control what it does at a certain time, but is unaware of and cannot control what another temporal part does at a different time. Thus, if awareness and control are not necessary for personal identity over time, this is a reason to believe that awareness and control are also not necessary for personal identity between alters.

One might respond that this analogy is irrelevant, because it matters that alters can exist consciously at the same time in some cases. However, it is not clear why this matters or destroys the analogy to temporal parts of a single person. It is true that we do not hold someone responsible for what he cannot control at the time when he does it, but an alter who commits a crime in a case of MPD often can control what she does at the time when she does it. In the Denny-Shaffer case, the alter who took the baby could have stopped herself from taking the baby. The other alter, Bridget, who became conscious later, could not then change the past. But none of us can change what our past selves did. If lack of control over past selves removed criminal responsibility, then all criminals would go free. So lack of control over a past alter also should not remove criminal responsibility.

Opponents might still object that one alter should not be held responsible for what another alter did when the former could not control the latter, any more than one person should be held responsible for what another person does when the former cannot control the latter. But this response blatantly assumes that different alters are or are like different persons. That begs the question here, which is precisely whether alters are or are like different persons. It makes sense to deny such criminal responsibility in cases of MPD if one assumes that different alters are different persons, but we need an independent reason to show that they really are different persons. No criterion of awareness and control can show the lack of personal identity among alters, because that criterion itself remains suspect at best.

6.7 Skepticism about Personal Identity

One final position is skeptical. Under the influence of powerful arguments by Hume[13] and Parfit,[14] many contemporary philosophers believe that the concept of absolute personal identity is incoherent, so we should stop asking whether X and Y are or are not the same person. We will not assess this surprising claim here.

All we need to say here is that, if the notion of absolute personal identity is as incoherent as skeptics claim, then it cannot be used to argue against punishing people with MPD when one alter commits a crime. Incoherence in a concept makes it useless for arguments and shows that it is not necessary for criminal responsibility.

Moreover, even if no natural bundles of states make a person, we still might need to bundle some alters or other mental states together artificially for our purposes. The law constructs artificial categories in many areas, as skeptics can and should admit. The criminal law's concept of a person would just be one more and one that is unavoidably artificial, if skeptics are correct. Since in a case of MPD we cannot punish or even involuntarily commit one alter without the others, the bundles to be used in criminal law seem obvious. For practical reasons, we have to treat all alters that share the same body as if they are parts or aspects of the same person. This would be objectionable if the alters really were different people. But no objection on that basis could be raised if absolute personal identity is incoherent. Thus, skepticism about personal identity cannot stand in the way of punishing a person with MPD. It might even support it.

7 Insanity

We have argued that alters in a case of MPD are (parts of) the same person in any way that is required for criminal responsibility. This removes one reason not to punish people with MPD. But it does not imply that punishment is always appropriate. Punishment still might be wrong on other grounds. Sometimes it is. We will argue that a person with MPD should be punished if and only if the alter in control at the time of the crime meets the applicable standards of criminal sanity (assuming, throughout, the actus reus and mens rea apart from sanity).

7.1 Which alter?

Why count only the alter in control? To see why, imagine someone with an intermittent psychosis or delusion. This person commits a crime. Is this person responsible? That depends. If this person committed the crime when not undergoing any psychotic episode, then there is no reason not to hold this person criminally responsible. It seems irrelevant that he is psychotic at other times before and after the crime. Conversely, if he is so deluded at the time of the crime that he thought he was squeezing a lemon when he was really squeezing his victim's neck, then he is not responsible, regardless of whether his delusion disappeared later and earlier. The same point applies if someone is intermittently drunk or hypnotized. What matters is his mental state at the time of the crime.

This is recognized in almost all legal formulations of an insanity defense. The classic M'Naghten rule excuses only for lack of knowledge "at the time of committing the act".[15] The more recent Model Penal Code excuses only for disabilities "at the time of such conduct".[16] According to these and almost all other laws, then, we should hold a person with MPD criminally responsible if and only if he meets the relevant standards of criminal sanity at the time of the crime. We argued above that alters in cases of MPD are analogous to temporal parts of a normal person. This suggests that the agent at the time of the crime is the alter in control at that time. The crucial legal question then must be whether that alter at that time meets the relevant standards of insanity.

This focus also makes sense if one considers the main purpose of punishment to be deterrence. A person with MPD will be deterred if and only if the threat of punishment will prevent him from committing a crime. Fear of punishment in an alter that is unconscious or not in control at a time *cannot* deter the person from committing the crime at that time (unless that fear leaks into the alter that is in control). Fear in the alter that is in control can prevent crime in this way, if that alter meets the relevant standards of sanity. Consequently, this purpose of punishment is served best by making each alter aware that the whole person will be held responsible if the alter in control at the time of the crime meets the relevant standards of sanity.

The converse "only if" is more problematic, since there are exceptions to the general rule against punishing people who lack control at the time of the crime. If a driver can foretell that she will fall asleep at the wheel and then become dangerous, that driver ought to stop driving and can be held responsible for a collision, even if she is asleep and hence unable to prevent the collision at the time when it occurs. Analogously, if a person is aware that she will lose control mentally and become dangerous, and if she could take steps to reduce this danger but does not do so, then it seems fair and would serve the purpose of deterrence to hold her responsible for what she does after she loses control. This exception applies to people with MPD if one alter knows that another alter is dangerous and could prevent that dangerous alter from taking over or could arrange circumstances in which that dangerous alter would not be as dangerous, such as by seeking treatment or consenting to commitment. In these circumstances, the innocuous alter may be held responsible for failing to take such steps to prevent danger and for the foreseeable effects of that failure on later times, including later acts by other alters. However, the innocuous alter is still responsible only if the innocuous alter was in control and did meet the relevant standards of sanity at the time of the failure. Thus, this apparent exception actually supports the rule that a person with MPD may be held responsible for an act (or failure to act) and its foreseeable consequences if and only if the alter in control at the time of that act (or failure) is sane by the relevant standards.

An opposing test was proposed in the Denny-Shaffer case. The court there held that a person with MPD is responsible only if the dominant or host personality or alter was aware of and able to prevent the crime. This might make sense if one assumes that alters in a case of MPD are like separate persons, and the host alter is the leader of the group. But we already argued against the assumption of separate persons. Moreover, the analogy to temporal parts of the same person suggests the opposite. If I am usually kind and gentle, but I get in an angry mood and commit a crime one day at 7:00 p.m., then whether I am responsible for that crime depends on whether my anger made me out of control at 7:00 p.m. My responsibility does not depend on whether the personality in control at 7:00 p.m. was my more common personality. It does not even matter if I often or usually get angry in the evening, unless I could foretell and prevent or prevent any danger from my anger. The fact that one mood or alter is dominant in the sense of being more common does not excuse the same person for crimes done while in other moods or by other alters.

7.2 What is Criminal Insanity?

To this extent, we agree with the court in the Grimsley case, which held that a defendant is criminally responsible "so long as in the personality then controlling her behavior, [the defendant] was conscious and her actions were a product of her own volition." The proper focus is on the alter in control at the time. However, the Grimsley court did not articulate the right test for whether that controlling alter is criminally responsible.

It is clearly not enough that the controlling alter "was conscious". Every defendant who is excused by the insanity defense was conscious at the time of the crime. Nor is it enough for criminal responsibility that "her actions were a product of her own volition". Any defendant acting under a compulsion (such as a kleptomaniac) or a delusion (such as that he is squeezing a lemon) still has a volition that causes her act, so her act is intentional. The defendant still does not seem criminally responsible if she had no control over that volition (if her will was not free) or if she formed her volition or intention only because she was misled by beliefs over which she had no control.

These conditions for criminal responsibility are formulated in the legal standard of insanity of the Model Penal Code:

> A person is not responsible for criminal conduct if at the time of such conduct as a result of mental disease or defect he lacks substantial capacity either to appreciate the criminality (or wrongfulness) of his conduct or to conform his conduct to the requirements of the law.

An important qualification is added later:

> the terms "mental disease or defect" do not include any abnormality manifested only by repeated criminal or otherwise anti-social conduct.

Let us assume that this standard is morally acceptable and adopted by the jurisdiction in question. Then our view is that a person with MPD should be held criminally responsible if and only if the alter in charge at the time of the crime did not lack substantial capacity to appreciate the wrongfulness of his conduct or to conform his conduct to the requirements of the law.

The relevant notion of capacity can be explained in terms of responsiveness to reasons. A person has the *capacity to conform* to law if and only if he will conform to law if there are adequate reasons for him to conform to law and he is able to be aware of these reasons. The reasons are *adequate* if awareness of the reasons would make it irrational for him not to conform to law. A person is *able to be aware* of such reasons if he would be aware of such reasons if they were presented to him in an appropriate way.

For example, sleepwalkers are unaware of what is going on around them. Someone who kills while sleepwalking would still kill even if a police officer stepped out into full view and said, "Stop or I'll shoot" (assuming that the police officer did not wake up the sleepwalker). The presence of the police officer is an adequate reason not to try to commit the crime, since it would be irrational to try to commit the crime while aware of such circumstances. However, the sleepwalker is unable (while asleep) to be aware of these reasons, because he would not become aware of the police officer's presence even if the police officer stepped into full view. The sleepwalker will commit the crime anyway, thus showing that he is not responsive to reasons and hence lacks capacity to conform to law.

A similar analysis works for capacity to appreciate the wrongfulness of an act, but here the relevant reasons are reasons to believe. Suppose that Joy believes that her sister is the devil attacking her.[17] To kill the devil when the devil is trying to kill you would not be wrong. It would be self-defense. Now suppose that no evidence could convince Joy that her sister is not the devil attacking her. Since this belief is not responsive to reasons, neither are Joy's beliefs that her act is necessary for self-defense and that it is not (morally or legally) wrong for her to kill her sister. Thus, Joy lacks the capacity to appreciate the wrongfulness of her conduct.

The notion of capacity might be understood in other ways, and many details remain to be worked out.[18] However, something like this account of capacity as responsiveness to reasons seems appropriate here because one main point of punishment is to provide reasons not to commit crimes. Punishment deters by making it irrational to try to commit a crime in most circumstances. This purpose of punishment makes it appropriate not to punish people who could not be deterred thorough no fault of their own. That is the condition captured by the Model Penal Code when supplemented by an account of capacity as reasons responsiveness.

7.3 Conclusions

This test also illuminates our cases studies. In our view, Woods is not guilty because Ron, who was the alter in control at the time of the crime, was so deluded that he thought that he had to kill Sally in order to protect his own life as well as the life of another alter, John. Since self-defense and defense of others is a legal and moral justification for killing, the controlling alter, Ron, believed that he was justified and so was not doing anything wrong. This belief was not responsive to the evidence, if nobody could have convinced him otherwise. It is not completely clear that Ron's belief was incorrigible in this way, but it does seem so, as long as we continue to assume the defense's version of the facts. It follows that Ron, who was the controlling alter, lacked substantial capacity to believe otherwise and, thus, to appreciate the wrongfulness of his conduct. That is why we think that Woods should be excused from criminal responsibility and found not guilty by reason of insanity (although he should still be committed to a mental institution because he is dangerous to others).

Contrast the Denny-Shaffer case. Here the controlling alter seems to have known that her act of kidnapping was both morally and legally wrong, as evidenced by the fact that she hid it from everyone else and never claimed to have any adequate justification for her act. Neither alter was delusional, unless one counts it as a delusion that one alter believed that she would get away with her crime (as most criminals believe). The controlling alter also seems to have had the capacity to conform her conduct to law, as suggested by her long and careful planning, the skill and patience with which she committed the crime, and so on. Her timid dominant alter also wanted a child, so the alter who kidnapped the baby merely added the courage needed to carry it off. None of this proves that the kidnapping alter had the capacity to conform to law, but it is evidence; and the defense never denied that the kidnapping alter had the capacity to conform to law. The defense argued only that one alter could not control the other alter's conduct. We already saw why that defense is not sufficient, since each alter still could control her own conduct. This makes Denny-Shaffer crucially different from Woods, and also from sleepwalkers and other cases of criminal insanity. That is why it makes sense to hold Denny-Shaffer responsible by our test.

The MPC test is not so easy to apply to the acting alter in other cases, such as the Grimsley case, partly because crucial facts are not clear. Was Jennifer so drunk that she lost control of what she was doing, including whether and how she drove a car? If not, Grimsley should be held guilty. If so, maybe she should still be held guilty if she could control whether she got that drunk. But maybe not, if Jennifer was extremely compulsive or deluded into thinking that her drinking was neither dangerous nor illegal. It seems to us that she was probably responsible for driving, since there was no independent evidence of any such compulsion or delusion. But the facts of this case are not completely clear on such crucial matters. In any case, it is often hard to get adequate evidence of insanity even in cases apart from MPD. MPD does not make it any harder to apply most tests of criminal insanity, so there is no reason not to apply those legal tests to MPD whenever they are used for other defendants.

Our test of responsibility in cases of MPD does not answer all of the questions, and it will be hard to apply in many cases. Still, our test fits the purpose of punishment and avoids any absurd results. This makes it better than any current alternative, so we conclude that it should be adopted, at least until a better alternative comes along.[19]

Notes

1. *State v. Grimsley*, 447 N.E. 2d at 1076.
2. *U. S. v. Denny-Shaffer*, 2 F.3d 999 (10th Cir. 1993) at 1016.
3. As described by Judith Armstrong, "The Case of Mr. Woods", manuscript pp. 2, 4, 5, 11, 12, and 2. The internal quotations are from interviews with Woods.
4. Elyn R. Saks, "Multiple Personality Disorder and Criminal Responsibility" (manuscript)
5. "Multiple Personality Disorder and Criminal Responsibility", and (with Stephen Behnke) *Jekyll on Trial: Multiple Personality Disorder and Criminal Law* (1997)
6. Jennifer Radden, *Divided Minds and Successive Selves: Ethical Issues in Disorders of Identity and Personality* (Cambridge, Mass.: M.I.T. Press, 1996).
7. Daniel Dennett, "Conditions of Personhood", in *The Identities of Persons*, ed. A. O. Rorty (Berkeley; University of California Press, 1976), pp. 175–196 at 177–178. Quoted by Saks, "Multiple Personality Disorder and Criminal Responsibility".
8. John Locke, *An Essay Concerning Human Understanding* (New York; Dover, 1959), Book II, Chapter 27, p. 457. Originally published in 1690.
9. Sydney Shoemaker, *Self-Knowledge and Self-Identity* (Ithaca; Cornell University Press, 1963), pp. 23 ff.
10. Bernard Gert, "Personal Identity and the Body", *Dialogue* X, 3 (1971), pp. 458–478. The following quotation is from p. 472. For a more recent defense of a bodily criterion, see Eric Olson, *The Human Animal; Personal Identity Without Psychology* (New York; Oxford University Press, 1997).
11. Carole Rovane, *The Bounds of Agency* (Princeton; Princeton University Press, 1998), p. 174.
12. We are indebted to Isaac Levi for pressing this response.
13. David Hume, *A Treatise of Human Nature*, ed. L. A. Selby-Bigge (Oxford; Clarendon Press, 1973), Book I, Part IV, Section VI. Originally published in 1739.
14. Derek Parfit, *Reasons and Persons* (Oxford; Clarendon Press, 1984)
15. *Regina v. M'Naghten*, 8 Eng.. Rep 718 (1843)
16. *Model Penal Code* (Philadelphia; American Law Institute, 1956), Tentative Draft no. 4, Art. 2, Sec. 4.01, p. 27. The full test is quoted below from this page. For a defense of the MPC rule, see Walter Sinnott-Armstrong, "Insanity *vs.* Irrationality", *Public Affairs Quarterly* vol. 1, no. 3 (July 1987), pp. 1–21.
17. Our example derives loosely from the case of Joy Baker discussed by Richard Bonnie in "The Moral Basis of the Insanity Defense," *ABA Journal*, vol. 69 (1983).
18. For some more details, see Bernard Gert and Timothy Duggan, "Free Will as the Ability to Will", *Nous* 13 (1979), pp. 197–217.
19. For helpful comments on drafts, we thank Bernie Gert, Eric Steinhart, and Kathleen Wallace.

324

Philosophical Perspectives, 14, Action and Freedom, 2000

THE SURVIVAL OF THE SENTIENT

Peter Unger
New York University

1. Introduction: Ourselves and Sentient Others

In this quite modestly ambitious essay, I'll generally just assume that, for the most part, our "scientifically informed" commonsense view of the world is true. Just as it is with such unthinking things as planets, plates and, I suppose, plants, too, so it also is with all earthly thinking beings, from people to pigs and pigeons; each occupies a region of space, however large or small, in which all are spatially related to each other. Or, at least, so it is with the bodies of these beings. And, even as each of these *ordinary entities* extends through some space, so, also, each endures through some time. In line with that, each ordinary entity is at least very largely, and is perhaps entirely, an *enduring physical* entity (which allows that many might have certain properties that aren't purely physical properties.) Further, each ordinary enduring entity is a *physically complex* entity: Not only is each composed of parts, but many of these parts, whether or not absolutely all of them, are themselves enduring physical entities, and many of *them* also are such physically complex continuing entities.

When an ordinary entity undergoes a significant change, then, at least generally, this change will involve changes concerning that entity's constituting physical parts, whether it be a rearrangement of (some of) these parts, or a loss of parts, or a gain of parts, or whatever. Often, the entity will still exist even after the change occurs. As we may well suppose, this happens when, from two strokes of an ax, an ordinary log loses just a chip of wood. As we may then say, such a change conforms with the log's "persistence conditions." Somewhat less often, such an ordinary entity undergoes a change that means an end to it: When a bomb's explosion makes our log become just so many widely scattered motes of dust, the log will no longer exist. Such a momentous change *doesn't* conform with the log's persistence conditions.

Insofar as we may learn which changes involving a particular log conform with its persistence conditions, and which do not, we might learn a fair amount about what it is for a physically complex enduring entity to be that log. Perhaps pretty similarly, insofar as we may learn which changes involving *you* conform with *your persistence conditions,* and also which do not, we might learn a fair amount about what it is for a physically complex enduring entity to be *you;* and, presumably in parallel, we might learn what it is for *another* such complex entity to be *me.*

This learning is clearly a possibility for us, I'll suggest, should materialism be true, and should a weak form of dualism be true, where some concrete individuals, at least, have not only physical properties, but also some nonphysical mental properties. And, it may also be possible, I'll suggest, should the truth lie, instead, with a more substantial dualism, rather like Descartes' view, but one allowing, perhaps, there to be nonphysical minds that aren't personal minds, as with porcine minds, and canine, and feline.

Whatever the metaphysic we might favor, when inquiring into our persistence conditions we should seek to appreciate what's involved in a *philosophically adequate concept of ourselves.* As I'll even now suggest, such an adequate concept must be well suited for engagement with our central prudential thoughts and concerns, with what, in my *Identity, Consciousness and Value* (henceforth ICV), I called our *(broad) egocentric values.*[1] And, it must be well suited for engagement with our morality. Our appreciation of that may help us see, better than I saw in ICV, that an adequate concept of ourselves must be a psychological conception, perhaps the concept of a being who'll exist when, and only when, his mind does. This may be so *whatever* worldview may be true, whether materialistic, or dualistic, or idealistic, or what-have-you.[2]

A prompting cause of the present effort is the appearance of Eric Olson's valuable (1997) book, *The Human Animal: Personal Identity without Psychology* (henceforth THA). Using the label "The Psychological Approach" very broadly, Olson has it cover all the views on which our persistence is tied to the continuation of our psychology. In opposition to all such views, he forcefully advocates a Biological Approach:

> In place of the Psychological Approach I propose a radically nonpsychological account of our identity. What it takes for us to persist through time is...biological continuity: one survives just in case one's purely animal functions—metabolism, the capacity to breathe and circulate one's blood, and the like—continue. I would put biology in place of psychology, and one's biological life in place of one's mind, in determining what it takes for us to persist: a biological approach to personal identity.[3]

In much of what follows, I'll be arguing that, with the Biological Approach, there can't possibly be any philosophically adequate view of our existence or persistence: As any conception of ourselves that's a biological concept isn't (primarily) a mental conception, it won't comport well with central prudential thoughts and concerns, and also with our moral thinking. Even as either failure shows the inadequacy of a Biological Approach to ourselves, with both there's an overwhelming case for a Psychological Approach.

In parallel, I'll argue that it's only a Psychological Approach, and not a Biological Approach, that's adequate for those *nonpersonal* sentient beings whom, in the normal course of events, will be found with typical living animals: Even if they be subpersonal entities, still, a philosophically adequate concept of such nonpersonal beings my feline pet, Felix, and your canine pet, Oscar, must closely parallel an adequate concept of ourselves.

Toward the essay's end, I'll float an extremely general thought about our commonsense metaphysic, about our ordinary ontology: Though this ontology recognizes many entities whose mentality is essential to their very existence, it recognizes *none* whose biology is truly essential. Perhaps there are *no ordinary entities*, I'll conjecture, for which the Biological Approach provides an adequate account.

2. Questions of Strict Survival, Vegetable Cases and Transplant Cases

After the book's Introduction, the body of *The Human Animal* (THA) begins with this paragraph:

> The topic of this book is our identity through time. What does it take for you and me to persist from one time to another? What sort of changes could one survive, and what would bring one's existence to an end? What makes it the case that some past or future being, rather than another, is you or I? (7)

As an early step in advocating a Biological answer to these opening questions, in the book's first section Olson presents a relevantly puzzling pair of cases. Apparently favoring the Biological Approach, there's first a "Vegetable Case;" and, apparently favoring the Psychological Approach, there's then a "Transplant Case."[4]

To do justice to the intriguing Vegetable Case, I quote Olson at some considerable length:

> Imagine that you fall into what physiologists call a persistent vegetative state. As a result of temporary heart failure, your brain is deprived of oxygen for ten minutes-...by which time the neurons of your cerebral cortex have died of anoxia. Because thought and consciousness are impossible unless the cortex is intact, and because brain cells do not regenerate, your higher mental functions are irretrievably lost. You will never again be able to remember the past, or plan for the future, or hear a loved one's voice, or be consciously aware of anything at all, ...
>
> The subcortical parts of the brain, however, ... are more resistant to damage from lack of blood that the cerebrum is, and they sometimes hold out and continue functioning even when the cerebrum has been destroyed. Those...sustain your "vegetative" functions such as respiration, circulation, digestion, and metabolism. Let us suppose that this happens to you... . The result is a human animal that is as much like you as anything could be without having a mind.

> The animal is not comatose. Coma is a sleep-like state; but a human vegetable has periods in which... . It can respond to light and sound, but not in a purposeful way; it can move its eyes, but cannot follow objects consistently with them... .
>
> Neither is the animal "brain-dead," for those parts of its brain that maintain its vegetative functions remain fully intact... . The patient (sic) is very much alive, at least in the biological sense in which oysters and oak trees are alive.
>
> How can we be sure that the patient (sic) in this state has really lost all cognitive functions? ...there may be room for doubt. So imagine that you lapse into a persistent vegetative state *and* that as a result your higher cognitive functions are destroyed *and* that the loss is permanent. (THA, 7–8)
>
> ...My question in the Vegetable Case is whether the human animal that results when the cerebrum is destroyed is strictly and literally you, or whether it is no more you than a statue erected after your death would be you. Do you come to be a human vegetable, or do you cease to exist... ? (THA, 9)

Both among people and within folks, there are conflicting responses to the Vegetable Case. Of most interest for Olson, there's the reaction that, even at the Case's end, you'll still exist (albeit as a "human vegetable.")

When confronting a relevantly similar case right on the heels of the Vegetable example, we'll be pretty primed to respond to it, too, along a similarly Biological line.[5] And, it's right on those heels that Olson offers us his Transplant Case:

> ...Imagine that an ingenious surgeon removes your cerebrum...and implants it into another head. ... Your cerebrum comes to be connected to that human being in just the way that it was once connected to the rest of you. ...; and so it is able to function properly inside its new head just as it once functioned inside yours.
>
> The result is a human being who is psychologically more or less exactly like you. ... On the other hand, she does not remember anything that happened to the person into whose head your cerebrum was implanted, nor does she acquire anything of that person's character (at least at first).
>
> The puzzle, as you have no doubt guessed, is what happens to you in this story (call it the "Transplant Case"). Are you the biologically living but empty-headed human being that has inherited your vegetative functions? Or are you the person who ends up with your cerebrum and your memories? (Or has the operation simply brought your existence to an end?) (THA, 9–10)

(Now, for such a Transplant Case to be most instructive, what's extracted from [the head of] the body must be fit for subserving what's central to mentality. But, as science seems to show, your upper brain, by itself, can't subserve conscious experience; rather, there must be some neural interaction between your upper and your lower brain. So, the presented example will be suppositionally enhanced; as may be safely done in the current context, we suppose this scientific appearance misleading and, in fact, your cerebrum's sufficient to subserve all your mentality.) Even though it's presented right after the Vegetable Case, most respond to the Transplant Case by thinking you are "the person who ends up with your cerebrum and your memories."[6]

With our responsive tendencies to Olson's two main cases being such a perplexingly messy batch of proclivities, there's much reason to think hard about the examples. What's more, we have yet more reason to think hard when we ponder passages in W. R. Carter's valuable recent (1990) paper, "Why Personal Identity is Animal Identity," which boldly begins:

> We start with two felines, Felix and Jefferson, say, who are treated by the same veterinarian. A bizarre surgical blunder occurs and Felix's brain winds up in Jefferson's head. The resulting cat, call him Felixson, *looks* for all the world like Jefferson but *behaves* exactly like Felix (and not at all like Jefferson). The situation is complicated by the fact that Felix's debrained body is provided with enough transplanted tissue [tissue that does not come from Jefferson] so that it continues to live and function in feline-like ways. (Let's call this cat Felixless.) We are confronted here by certain questions of feline identity. To my way of thinking, these questions have rather obvious answers. It is true that Felixless is (=) Felix. Accordingly, it is false that Felixson is (=) Felix. My guess is that this assessment of the matter will encounter little, if any, serious resistance. This is surprising (to me), since many people take an entirely different view of a similar situation involving human rather than feline subjects.[7]

As we'll eventually see, the questions Carter thinks "have rather obvious answers" are actually subtly difficult questions. Now, we'll see these related words from Carter's paper:

> ...a psychological continuity account of feline identity looks so utterly implausible. Why is this? Well, perhaps it is because it is clear (isn't it) that cats are (attributively) *animals*. ... Since the term "Felix" refers to the animal..., and the term "Felixless" refers to the animal..., there is no denying that Felix is identical with Felixless. Accordingly, Felix is not identical with Felixson... . And why should the situation be different when we turn from feline identity to personal identity?

With at least some force, Carter *challenges* the thought that, in the Transplant Case, you are the being who ends up with your mentality, even as he *provides at least some* plausibility for the idea that (before getting new brain tissue) *you are* the (temporarily) mindless being that's inherited your vegetative functions, much as you (permanently) might be in the Vegetable Case.

Much more than favoring any particular Approach to ourselves, this section supports this importantly more general proposition: Whatever the right approach to the general conditions for the existence and persistence of Peter Unger, the personal sentient being, it will be, in all essentials, the same as the right approach for Felix Unger, the *nonpersonal* sentient being.

3. Thoughts and Concerns about Particular Sentient Beings: Avoiding Great Pain

Whatever else you may be, you must certainly be whatever it is that you think about when you think about *yourself*; if you're not *that*, you're nothing at

330 / Peter Unger

all. Likewise, you must be whatever it is you *care* about when you care about *yourself.* On a most natural and central reading of these sentences, both are, of course, quite platitudinous. Yet, the second sentence, concerning your concern for yourself, might serve as a helpful reminder and guide, helpful toward our appreciating our deepest beliefs about ourselves. For, it may help us bear in mind these related sentences: When you truly care about yourself, then, whatever else may concern you, you must certainly care, and care very greatly, that *you'll not experience protracted excruciating pain;* when just *that* concern of yours is quite fully in force, it's from a *strictly egoistic* perspective that your concern flows. Conversely, and maybe most instructively, if there's someone that, from a strictly egoistic perspective, you *don't* care whether she'll experience such horrible great pain, then, as far as you can tell or believe, *that* person *isn't you.*

A concept of ourselves that comports well with these points concerning self-concern might be a philosophically adequate conception, as with, perhaps, a concept that's central to a Psychological Approach. By contrast, any concept that comports *poorly* with them, as with, perhaps, concepts central to a Biological Approach, can't be an adequate concept of ourselves.

The sensible thoughts just proposed may be sensibly generalized from us people to all sorts of sentient beings: So, flowing from a concern *for Oscar,* there might be no concern on your part whether a certain canine sentient being will feel great pain. But, then, as far as you can tell or believe, *that* sentient being *isn't* Oscar. And, any concept that comports poorly with *this* point, as *might* be true of any central to a Biological Approach, can't then be a philosophically adequate concept of Oscar, or of any canine sentient being.

Guided by this section's reflections, I'll look to use a "philosophical tool" first employed in ICV, the Avoidance of Future Great Pain Test.[8] Eventually, I'll apply it to Olson's Vegetable Case, or to a most suitable enlargement of that example, and to Carter's Feline Transplant Case, or to a most suitable enlargement of that related example. By the time all that's done, few should be friends of a Biological Approach to the existence and persistence of any sentient beings, ourselves included, and many should favor a Psychological Approach. First, let's look at a case where it's easy to observe the test to be quite well employed.

To begin, suppose that, for no good reason, a bad surgeon replaces your heart with an artificial blood-pumper. About the person who has only such a plastic "heart," our central question is this: Is the person emerging from this operation *you*? For a most convincing answer to the question, we may employ our Test: With the choice flowing fully from your purely egoistic concern, will you choose to (have yourself) suffer *considerable pain* right before the operation takes place, if your *not* taking the bad hit up front will mean that, soon after the procedure's over, the person emerging from the operation then will suffer *far greater pain*? Yes; of course, you will. This response indicates that, as your strongest beliefs run, *you'll be* that person. Now, I'll try to use our Test to make progress with this essay's philosophically far more interesting questions.

Following Sydney Shoemaker's early work on the subject, in recent decades the literature on personal identity has seen many cases where there's the exchange of two people's bodies.[9] Much as was done in ICV, let's consider such a case involving you and, not someone qualitatively quite unlike you, but, rather, your precisely similar twin.[10] At this case's end, do *you* still exist? And, if so, *who are you*? Toward answering these questions reasonably, we may employ the Avoidance of Future Great Pain Test. Indeed, we may employ it twice over.

First, about the person who ends up with your original brain and a new body, we ask this question: With the choice flowing fully from your purely egoistic concern, will you choose to (have yourself) suffer considerable pain right before this case's wild processes begin if your *not* taking the bad hit up front will mean that, soon after all its processes are complete, the person then with your brain, and thus with your mind, will suffer *far greater pain*? Yes, of course, you will. Though not completely conclusive, this strongly indicates that, as we most deeply believe, throughout this case you're the person with your brain.[11]

Second, and yet more tellingly, we ask the parallel question: With the choice flowing fully from your purely egoistic concern, will you choose to (have yourself) suffer considerable pain right before this case's wild processes begin if your *not* taking the bad hit up front will mean that, soon after all its processes are complete, the person then with your body, but with your twin's mentally productive brain, then will suffer *far greater pain*? Not at all; from an egoistic basis, that's a *poor* choice. Though this response might not be absolutely decisive, it's quite conclusive enough. So, we conclude, well enough, that *you haven't even the slightest belief that here you're the being (with your healthy old body) who's inherited your vegetative biological functioning.*

At least as regards our commonsense view of ourselves, about the general conditions of our existence and persistence, this negative response may be indicating a very bad fate for the Biological Approach, in any of its versions. As well, it may also be indicating doom for any view on which the survival of our *bodies* is central to our own survival.

With parallel moves, we may see some indications that a Biological Approach might be no better for canine sentient beings than it is for personal sentient beings: We may see this with a slight variant on the case just considered, in which each occurrence of you is replaced by Oscar, each occurrence of your precise twin is replaced by an occurrence of his twin, and so on. About the canine being who ends up with Oscar's original brain and a new body, we ask this question: With the choice flowing fully from your *concern for Oscar*, will you choose to have him suffer considerable pain right before this case's wild processes begin if *his not* taking the bad hit up front will mean that, toward the end, the being then with his brain, and his mentality, will suffer *far greater pain*? Yes, of course, you will. And, this strongly indicates that, as we most deeply believe, here he'll be the being with his brain. Second, and again far more tellingly, we ask the parallel question: With the choice flowing fully from your *concern for him*, will you have him suffer *considerable pain* near the start if *his not* taking the bad hit up front will mean that, toward the end, the being then with his body, but not his mind, then will suffer *far greater pain*? Not at all. So, again well enough, we can conclude that *you haven't even the slightest belief that Oscar is the being (with his healthy old canine body) who has inherited Oscar's vegetative biological functioning.*

4. Can There Be an ENORMOUS Separation of Strict Survival and Relevant Concern?

For clear thinking about (our deepest beliefs about) the conditions of our existence and persistence, the points observed in the preceding section are, I think, of great importance: Where there is a being that's the proper object of your full-fledged egoistic concern, just there you yourself will be. And, most crucially, where there's no such "properly protected" being, there's no being that's you. But, some able philosophers have even so much as denied that importance, and many, I think, may fail to appreciate it.[12] Why?

In recent thinking about the relation between our transtemporal identity and our egoistic concern, there's much confusion engendered, I believe, from encounters with some salient and seductive hypothetical examples. Most salient among them may be a certain physically robust case of "symmetrical fission." Toward dispelling the confusion, and toward furthering clarity, let's now most thoughtfully encounter just such an example.

Suppose, now, that each half of your brain can do all that the whole does, as far as subserving mentality goes (and, we may now add, as far as sustaining biology goes.) Further, suppose that, when we extract your brain from your body, and we nicely slice your brain in two, we'll have two new people, each relevantly just like you were right before this two-sided fission occurs. (Each of them may then be given a new body, each precisely like the old was at the time of extraction.) Further still, we'll agree that you're not either of the two who are so new.

From a rational concern for yourself, how much should you care about each of the two resulting people? Well, as we've agreed, neither is you; so, from just that concern, you shouldn't care a fig. But, then, closely related to your purely egoistic concern, you might have other rational attitudes that are quite small and natural extensions of self-concern. And, then, we may ask: Flowing from at least some few of these related concernful attitudes, how much should you care about one of your fission descendants?

As it has seemed to many philosophers, you should care just as much as, even in the ordinary case of your own day to day survival, you today should care for yourself tomorrow. And, as it has seemed to some of these many, the salient lesson to be learned from that first thought is this second proposition: Questions regarding someone's strict survival can come apart from questions regarding his egoistic concern, and also his closely related concerns, quite *as far as you please.*

Even should all of the prior paragraph hold true, a thought that seems nearly as absurd as it's extravagant, there still might be no reason whatever to think that these questions can come apart so enormously that, from concerns much like purely egoistic attitudes, it may be natural, or rational, for us to care about beings with whom we have no substantial mental connection. But, what's needed to give some plausibility to the Biological Approach is precisely some reason to think just that. And, as it certainly seems, the prospects here are as bleak as can be.

Suppose that, flowing from your own egoistic concern, or even from any relevantly small extension thereof, you haven't even the least concern whether a certain being will experience terrible pain. Well, while that being might then be a certain horse, perhaps somewhere in Australia, or even a certain person, perhaps a young girl in Africa, one thing of which we can be quite confident is that, as far as you know or believe, *that* being *isn't you.* Perfectly parallel points hold for other sentient beings: Suppose that, flowing from your concern for *Oscar,* you haven't even the least concern whether a certain being will experience terrible pain. Now, while that being might then be the President of France, we can be quite certain that, as far as you know or believe, *that* being *isn't Oscar.*

5. A Complementary Pain Test Confirms Our Avoidance of Great Pain Test

Because we're hardly omniscient, and we're not even close to being perfectly logical or rational, it's good to see that, as a check on our results with the Avoidance of Great Pain Test, we may appropriately employ a logically related test, even a *complementary* test, and observe the results that then obtain. Just so, we'll now look to apply, most relevantly, a philosophical tool that may well be called the *Sparing from* Future Great Pain Test.[13]

So, let's return to consider the body-exchange (or, as the Biological Approach would have it, the brain-exchange) between Oscar and his precisely similar twin. As we've supposed, at this case's end there'll be one canine being with Oscar's original brain and mind, though little of his biological structures and processes, and there'll be another with another canine being's original brain-based mentality, and a great deal of Oscar's biological structures and their continuing processes. About all of that, you've never had even the least choice or influence.

In application to such a nicely relevant case, our Sparing from Future Great Pain Test directs that, always to be flowing (as closely as possible) from your concern for Oscar, your choice is to be just this choice: Shortly after awakening from the operations just envisioned, one of the two canine beings will experience much excruciating pain and the other will be spared from feeling even any pain at all. You are to choose, perhaps even before the operations are performed, which of the resulting beings suffers such great pain and which of the canines is spared. Very rationally, you will choose for the canine with Oscar's original brain, and Oscar's canine mind, to be spared, and for the torture to go to the other resulting canine. For, your reasoning, evidently, is every bit as appropriate as it's simple: The former canine is Oscar, the being about whom you're here so especially concerned; the latter is another sentient being.[14]

With simple variations, we may strengthen the probative value of our Sparing Test. For example, we may suppose that your choice is between (1) sparing the being with Oscar's old brain the infliction of severe pain for a certain significant period and letting the being with his old body suffer *far more* severe pain for a *far greater* period and (2) sparing the being with his old body that *far worse* severe pain and letting the one with his old brain suffer that *far less bad* pain. With the concern being for Oscar, this great imbalance of pain makes no difference; just as surely as before, you choose (1), sparing the one with Oscar's brain-based mind. So, this now seems very clear: It's just that canine being that, as far as you really believe, is actually Oscar.

Now, if we were perfectly logical and rational, it would be a foregone conclusion that these responses with the Sparing Test would comport with those previously elicited with our Avoidance Test. But, of course, we're not perfectly logical or rational. So, while the observed agreement was at least somewhat to be expected, it wasn't a foregone conclusion. Thus, the results obtained with our truly complementary test confirm those obtained with our previous philosophical tool. So, in our inquiry, we'll employ them both.

6. Clear Moral Thinking about Particular Sentient Beings

Early on, I said that, just as much as for engagement with our central prudential thoughts and concerns, a philosophically adequate concept of ourselves must be well suited for engagement with our morality. In a brief treatment of the issue, I'll show why that should be so.

As the progress of our project suggests strongly, many of our moral thoughts regarding you and me will regard, just as well, Oscar and Felix. Then, at a bare minimum, an adequate concept of ourselves must engage morality in the way that's well done, as well, by a philosophically adequate concept of a particular sentient being.

Suppose that I've solemnly promised *you*, a moral agent, to look out for (the well-being of) your son, Al, who's another moral agent, and also to look out for (the well-being of) your sentient canine pet, Oscar, who's not a moral agent. Then, in the normal run of things, I'll have incurred a moral obligation, first, to look out for Al, and, second, to look out for Oscar. Let's focus on this second obligation.

Going philosophically hypothetical, suppose that some dastardly super-scientists have produced a precise duplicate of Oscar, one Oscarnew, and, shortly thereafter, they've taken Oscar's brain and nicely placed it in Oscarnew's debrained body, and vice versa, with the philosophically expected result. Finally, we suppose that they force, on me, this instance of our Sparing Test. I must choose between (1) having terrible pain inflicted on the being with Oscar's original brain—still subserving Oscar's mind—in Oscarnew's original body and sparing from pain the being with Oscarnew's brain—still subserving Oscarnew's mind—in Oscar's body and (2) having terrible pain inflicted on the being with Oscarnew's brain in Oscar's body and sparing the being with Oscar's brain in Oscarnew's body. Flowing from my obligation to keep my promise to you, what should I do? As we deeply believe, I morally must choose (2) over (1). What does that suggest? Contrary to the Biological Approach, it suggest that, as we deeply believe, Oscar will be where his original brain is still subserving his mind.

As it is here with Oscar, so it is with Al. And, so it will be with us, too. As with any sentient beings, a philosophically adequate concept of ourselves, one well suited for engagement with morality, must be, primarily and essentially, a psychological conception. So, as those suitably sensitive to moral matters should agree, a Psychological Approach is very far superior to a Biological Approach even for the likes of Oscar and Felix, let alone for you and me.

7. Properly Painful Problems with Human Vegetables, and with Feline Vegetables

As I'm suspecting, by now most will indeed agree that, at least for such personal sentient beings as ourselves, a Psychological Approach is quite as appropriate as a Biological Approach is irrelevant. But, even if there's very widespread agreement on the matter, it's still well worth resolving, I think, some problems, or puzzlement, whose treatment we've deferred. Among this unfinished business, perhaps the most salient task is to provide a satisfactory treatment for Olson's intriguing Vegetable Case. Anyhow, to that task, we'll now turn.

As with other examples relevant to our central topic, for a treatment that's revealing we should use one of our Pain Tests. But, as a being in persistent vegetative state hasn't any capacity to feel any pain, how can we apply even our Avoidance of Pain Test? Initially at least, that seems a tall order. As things turn out, the job may be done rather well.

Toward that end, we make these suppositions: Within the next month, you'll have just such a horrible temporary heart failure that, as your brain will be deprived of oxygen for ten minutes, your cerebral cortex will die of anoxia; consequently, you'll "become a human vegetable." As you also know, there'll then be extracted, from the head of the "vegetative animal," its dead (upper) brain. And, into the continuously living "debrained body," there'll be well implanted a suitable living (upper) brain: Perhaps even coming into existence via a "statistical miracle," but, in any case, this will be a brain made of matter quite distinct from any that ever served toward constituting you. At the same time, this implant will be precisely similar to your (upper) brain, as it was when last it subserved your mentality. By the end of this sequence, there'll be a person with your original body, who's inherited your biology, though there'll be nobody who's inherited your mentality. While this person's mind will be precisely similar to yours, in its last moments of existence, it will be a numerically different normal mind. As with anyone with a normal mind, this person can certainly suffer terrible pain.

With such suitable suppositions made, there's an Aptly Enlarged Vegetable Case. And, with this Enlarged Case, there's ready to hand, I think, a revealing employment of our Avoidance of Future Great Pain Test: From your egoistic concerns, at the beginning you are to choose between (1) your suffering some significant pain, before a human vegetable's in the situation, so that, near the sequence's end, the person with the new (upper) brain suffers no pain at all and (2) your suffering no early pain and having it that, near the end, that person suffers terrible torture. Rationally, you choose (2) over (1). This choice shows that, as far as you know or believe, you *won't* be the entity that's inherited your biology.

It's still a "logical possibility," let's agree, that, after the anoxia but before the implantation of a new living upper brain, you were an insensate human vegetable. Then, just with that vegetable's receiving just such a new brain, you ceased to exist. But, really, is any of that even the least bit plausible? Are we really to believe that, though it's possible for you to come to have *no* mind, what's impossible is for such a mindless *you* to survive your coming to *have a mind*? Such a suggestion as that, I'll suggest, is quite an absurd idea.

From Human Vegetable Cases, there's really no case to be made for a Biological Approach to *ourselves*. And, from Feline Vegetable Cases, as may happen with my sentient Felix, there's nothing to be gained for a Biological Approach to *nonpersonal sentient* beings, as an Aptly Enlarged Feline Vegetable Case can help us easily see.

Sensibly, we may extrapolate from our recent experiences: The more we're free from confusions about sentient beings, saliently including ourselves, the less there'll even seem to be said for a Biological Approach to beings that must have minds.[15] Nor will there seem anything significantly favoring a "Bodily Approach" to ourselves, or to nonpersonal mental others. Now, without going hypothetical in a way that's utterly wild, it may be impossible to take a case with a *completely dead* human, wholly devoid of life as well as mind, and to enlarge it so that our Pain Tests can be revealingly applied. But, so what: If a *living* mindless human body won't ever be one of us, and won't even ever subserve one of us, a *dead* mindless body will hardly do better. And, again, what's true of you and me also holds for Oscar and Felix.

By this point, we've seen more than enough, I think, to do a good job with what may be the sole remaining salient piece of unfinished business, namely, the provision of a satisfactory treatment for Carter's Feline Transplant Case. For, what does this case involve, if not a feline vegetable, an insensate Felix-less obtained from the sentient Felix, by the extraction of that feline being's (upper) brain? According to Carter, though he has no mentality at all, still Felix-less is (=) Felix, because the mindless entity's inherited the biology that supported, or subserved, the sentient being. But, Felixless really isn't Felix, as our recent reasoning revealed.

We've just taken good care of what might well be called "the harder of the two main halves" of Carter's Transplant Case. The easier half concerns what we are to make of Carter's Felixson, a feline being who results from transplanting Felix's brain into the debrained body resulting from extracting a feline brain from one Jefferson; at the case's start, this Jefferson is another normal feline sentient being, who's wholly distinct from Felix. In either of two ways, our Avoidance Test can show that (as far as we know or believe) Felixson is Felix (and he's not Jefferson.) To the most energetic reader, I leave all that as an exercise.

8. People and Seople

On our "scientifically informed" commonsense view of things, your psychology is realized in, or it's at least subserved by, your brain: If there's someone else who's physically precisely similar to you, then *his* mentality will be realized only in *his* brain and *yours* will be subserved only by *yours*. There will be this numerical difference of the two mentalities, of the two minds, even if the distinct brains that subserve the two are precisely similar in every detail. And, if your mentality ceases to exist, then you yourself will cease to exist, even though your "duplicate" may continue to exist.

Equally on this commonsense view, though quite completely against the "vivisectionist" view of Descartes, the brain of Oscar, your beloved canine pet, realizes *Oscar's* psychology, or at least it subserves the mentality of that canine sentient being: If there's a canine who's physically precisely similar to Oscar, and wholly distinct from Oscar, there will be a numerical difference of the two minds, even if the canine mentalities are qualitatively quite the same. And, if his mentality ceases to exist, then Oscar himself will cease to exist, even though his "duplicate" may continue to exist.

Now, even while our commonsense view has these parallels be quite deep commonalities, our common language might lack a sortal common noun that serves nicely to highlight them for us, so that, for such central issues as this essay's main questions, we're prompted to take an essentially parallel approach to all sentient beings, us people being just some among many. In what's meant to be a sensibly progressive spirit, let me introduce a new English sortal noun, "serson," whose meaning is the same as the phrase "*sentient being*," and whose most colloquial plural is "seople." (As well as having such new nouns, we may have correlative new words, saliently including new quantifier words. For example, even if "everyone" doesn't include, in its proper reference, Oscar and Felix, we may have "everyane"—pronounced EVERYWANE—properly include them, just as properly as it will include you and me.)

With these terms, we may progressively express propositions that, even as they concern our main topics, feature centrally in our commonsense view of things: Every earthly serson, and not just every earthly person, has both a body and a mind. And, while it's *not* true that an earthly serson will exist just exactly in case her body exists, it *is* true that any serson at all, whether earthly or not, will exist when, and only when, her mind exists. Following from the foregoing, some such sentences as these should be treated more as commonplace thoughts than contentious ideas, both by materialists and by commonsensical dualists: If there's only a barely developed organic body extant, and there's not yet any mind even so much as barely subserved by the body, as with an early fetus, then, in such a mentally insignificant situation, there's really no serson existing, neither personal nor even nonpersonal. [In ICV I left it as an open question whether there might have been an (earlier) time when I wasn't a person and, even, when I lacked all capacity for thought and feeling. (5–6) In THA Olson argues that, given my book's main views, there's no good way for me to have us people, or any seople, be (identical with) any such wholly mindless things. (81–85) Agreeing now with Olson, in the present essay I no longer leave that question open; on my present position, a more complete view, I never was any mindless early fetus, nor was sentient Oscar ever any mindless canine fetus.] By contrast with such wholly mindless early episodes, if there's a more developed body that's subserving a mind, even a quite rudimentary mind, then there'll be a serson. And, if it comes to pass that there's only our serson's body extant, with the mind no longer existing, then this serson will no longer exist.

When a serson is alive and well, what's the relation between the serson himself and, on the other hand, his body?

On what I take to be a pretty appealing substantial dualist view, but a view that might be at least as troubling as it's appealing, a serson's body will causally support, and subserve, the serson's immaterial mind. What's more, and what may be metaphysically even a bit more basic, just when providing just such support, the serson's body will support the immaterial being that's the serson himself. Further, Oscar won't have any spatial extension and, perhaps, that immaterial being won't even have any spatial location. In ways we might never well understand, immaterial Oscar may be, nonetheless, quite directly affected by, and he may quite directly affect, certain physical entities, perhaps certain parts of a certain brain.

On what I take to be a pretty appealing materialist view, but perhaps also a view as troubling as it's appealing, a serson and his body will be spatially coincident entities; with each in the very same space as the other at the very same time, the very same matter will serve to constitute each of the two distinct material entities. So, even as Oscar may now be alive and well, he and his body will be different material complexes, though each is composed of exactly the same matter, and each occupies precisely the same space. On a pretty commonsensical materialist view, a rather plausible reckoning of such ordinary entities will have that be so, even if, perhaps, that reckoning is hardly free of difficulties. How, or why, will that be so? As with you and me, Oscar's *persistence conditions* differ from those of his body. To see what that rather technical sentence says, I'll aim to display its main implications, in the next section, while providing the sentence with intuitive support.

9. A Serson and His Body Are Distinct Entities

Even if it subserves mentality, as it now does, your brain is just one of several salient organs in your body that, together with various other bodily parts, serve to constitute the body as a whole. Accordingly, whether your body's dead or alive, in this regard, at least, the relation between your brain and your body is very like that between your heart and your body, and very like that obtaining between your liver and that whole human body. It's no surprise, then, that, if any single one of these organs is removed from the bodily whole, and then is even annihilated, your body will still exist. Of course, the same holds for other serson's bodies, as with Oscar's.

Along with some philosophically familiar thoughts, and some ideas here previously presented, those intuitive propositions suggest a certain pair of cases. While each example is but a slight variant on the other, the lesson that one suggests is, in an obvious way, quite the opposite of, and quite a nice complement of, the lesson we may learn from the other.

Continuing to employ the suppositions that have served us so well so far, we'll start with the Brain Explosion Case: Right out of sentient Oscar's skull, some strangely fanatical scientists remove his (upper) brain, and they place it in the philosophically familiar stimulatory vat. While in this vat, that living brain will subserve just as rich a stream of conscious experience as ever it did when in the serson's head. At the same time, and still lying on a laboratory table, (the rest of) Oscar's body, as it's placed on a highly effective life-support system, remains alive, though it can't, of course, subserve mentality.[16] For a while all is pretty peaceful, until an exploding bomb destroys the brain in the vat, the vat itself, and even the building in which the vat is housed. In this explosion, the matter that served to compose Oscar's brain is so utterly wrenched apart, and the tiny bits are so fully intermingled with so much other dust from the explosion, that there's not even any significant chance of anything like a relevant reversal ever occurring. Meanwhile, (the rest of) your canine serson's body remains intact, and even alive.

At the end of this Brain Explosion Case, Oscar, the salient serson, no longer exists. (On a materialistic metaphysic, and on plausible forms of dualism, that will be so.) At the same time, Oscar's body continues to exist. On the most relevant understanding of the terms employed, it's most reasonable to accept both sentences. So, Oscar's body can survive the termination of Oscar himself.

It's time to turn to the complementary example, the Body Explosion Case. From the example's start right up to the time when "all is pretty peaceful," things are just as in the previous case, with Oscar's brain in a vat in one area and, at a distance, his living body on a lab table. Then, an exploding bomb destroys (the rest of) the body on the table, the table itself, and the whole lab building. In this explosion, the matter that served to compose (the rest of) Oscar's body is so utterly wrenched apart, and the tiny bits so fully intermingled with so much other dust, that there's not even any significant chance of anything like a relevant reversal. Meanwhile, your canine serson's brain continues to subserve his mind.

At the end of this Body Explosion Case, the salient serson's body no longer exists. At the same time, Oscar himself continues to exist. On the most relevant understanding of our terms, Oscar can survive the termination of Oscar's body.

Now, if Oscar could survive the cessation of his body, but Oscar's body couldn't survive Oscar's own cessation, then, while we should think the two were different, we might well think that, while Oscar himself was a genuine entity, his body had some lesser ontological status. And, in such an event, perhaps we shouldn't think that, with Oscar and his body, we have two distinct entities. But, as we saw just before, Oscar's body *can* survive Oscar's own cessation, just as Oscar can survive his body's cessation. So, apparently, we do quite well to think that, inasmuch as each has persistence conditions so utterly different from the other's, sentient Oscar is one being and, though spatially and materially coincident with him, Oscar's body is quite another entity. Apparently and intuitively, even if we should accept a most materialistic version of our commonsense metaphysic, we should think that much to be true.

Finessing Questions about Materially Coincident Entities

At least to my mind, sometimes it's puzzling, to put the point mildly, how there could be two quite different entities each composed of the very same matter, in the very same space, at the very same time, and not just one entity that we may think of in two quite different ways. But, for two related reasons, this paper's not the place to dwell on any such puzzle.

First, and as was stated at its outset, we're here just assuming that, for the most part, our "scientifically informed" commonsense view of the world is true. And, in dwelling on our puzzle, we might well be calling into question what's here our working hypothesis, rather than seeing what work we can do within the compass of what seems the accepted view.

Second, and as is familiar in philosophy, the puzzle about the possibility of materially coincident entities is a quite general puzzle, hardly peculiar to questions about embodied seople and their bodies: In illustration, consider a certain ball, we'll call it "Barry," and a certain spherical piece of brass, we'll call it "Patty," each composed of the very same brass, in the very same place, throughout all the time of their existence. (The brazen alloy first comes to exist in the very form in which it composes Patty and Barry and, later, it ceases to exist suddenly, suddenly composing neither.) Yet, even as Barry and Patty have quite different persistence conditions, there are here, it seems, two quite distinct entities. So, on the one side, if the brass were forced through a wire extruder, that brass would come to compose a long thin brass wire and no ball at all. In such an event, it seems, we'd have the same *piece* of brass as before, and Patty would still exist, but Barry wouldn't exist. And, on the other side, we might have gradually replaced our ball's brass, bit by tiny bit, by congruous bits of gold, widely scattering all our brass. In such a very different event, it seems, we'd have the same *ball* as before, and Barry would still exist, but our piece of brass, our Patty, wouldn't still exist.

As is proper with this quite modestly ambitious essay, we leave for other inquiries such a general problem as the puzzle about the possibility of materially coincident entities. As is also proper, we set aside other puzzles, more or less related, that may similarly seem to call into question, more or less effectively, our commonsense view of the world.

10. Reference and Existence, Appearance and Reality

For what's really a very bad reason, many of my paper's points might be denied by philosophers, perhaps especially by materialists, who may be unduly impressed by what sometimes seem plain expressions of common sense in ordinary discourse. For example, after my mind no longer exists and there's only my living body in a vegetative state, someone may point at what's in that state and say, apparently with complete propriety, "There's Peter Unger." Doesn't that serve to indicate that, even if my mind no longer exists, I can still exist? And, isn't that a strong point in favor of a Biological Approach to my existence and persistence?

Well, quite the same may be done, apparently, when there's only my dead body in the situation. So, such apparently ordinary and proper episodes won't provide any strong points, it seems clear, in favor of a Biological Approach to me. But, then, mightn't they provide a strong point in favor of a Bodily Approach to my existence and persistence, on which I may still exist not only without my mind, or any mind, but also without my biological life, or any such life? No; it does not.

Very often, we refer to one entity, conveniently, obliquely and indirectly, by more directly referring to another, with which the first is, especially in the context of the current discourse, readily associated. Now, sometimes the discrepancy between the two referents is blatantly obvious. This happens when we say of a bus driver that she's over fifteen feet high, and unable to get through a certain tunnel, referring not only to her but, less directly and more truthfully, to the bus that she drives. Now, when the discrepancies are that blatant, there's little tendency to take our direct remark, about the driver herself, to be a literal statement that's really true; rather, it's only some implied statements, like the statement that a certain bus is over fifteen feet high, that we take to be true.

Other times, however, the discrepancy is less blatant. That happens, I'll suggest, with (standard uses of) sentences like "As Uncle Joe is dead, we should get him off the floor and out of the house, so that we can put some nice big potted plant right where he is" and "As Oscar is dead, we should get him off the floor and out of the house, so that we can put some nice big potted plant right where he is." Though not so blatantly obvious, in these sentence's closing clauses there's reference to more than just the relevant seople themselves; rather indirectly, there may be a reference to the seople's bodies, or to their remains, or to both of the foregoing, or to yet something else that's fit for spatial removal. And, while the standardly expressed statement about the moving of the seople themselves might not be true, there may then be such suitable implied statements, about the moving of their bodies, and about the moving of their remains, that are perfectly true. And, the discrepancy just stressed will be made yet more evident when we observe such closely related sentences as "Billions of years after Uncle Joe's death, he'll be interstellar dust" and "Billions of years after Oscar's death, he'll be interstellar dust."

What is more, paralleling the "apparent facts of reference" regarding ourselves, there are such apparent facts regarding our bodies. Thus, after I'm dead, you may point at my corpse and say "There's Peter Unger's body;" and, not only may what you say be in perfect conversational order, but, as well, it may be perfectly true. Now, a sentence like "Billions of years after it decays, Unger's body will be interstellar dust" also looks to be in perfect order. But, when standardly uttering such an orderly sentence, will you be saying what's true? Of course, not.

Now, suppose that, after I die, my corpse is placed in a spaceship and, when the ship is somewhere between Mars and Jupiter, the spaceship explodes, along with all its salient contents, including my body. Pointing at an apt place between Mars and Jupiter, when night next comes you may say "There's Peter Unger's body;" and, what you say may be in perfect conversational order. But, is what you say really true; does my body really still exist? Not a chance. By contrast, it might well be that my *remains* still exist and, mainly between Mars and Jupiter, they're widely scattered.

Over a wide range of referential discourse, what may first look to be plain facts may come to look, much more realistically, to be nothing factual at all.

11. Seople (Conceptually) Can Survive the Loss of Their Biological Lives

Absent sufficient psychological continuity, biological continuity isn't sufficient for the continued existence of sentient beings, neither people, like you and me, nor nonpersonal seople like Oscar and Felix. But, is biological continuity *necessary* for our survival? Well, insofar as it's needed for subserving the serson's mind it may be necessary. But, then, this biology's needed only causally, or quasi-causally; it's not most basically necessary, as the persistence of the serson's mind is necessary, for the survival of the sentient being.

As a philosophically adequate concept of the sentient canine who is Oscar centers on his sentience, it follows that the concept won't place any biological requirements on Oscar, provided only that there's no entailment from his sentience to anything biological. And, as it certainly seems, there isn't any such entailment. To confirm this appearance, it may be useful to reflect on an example that's just an adaptation, to the canine situation, of a case concerning people that, perhaps a bit too timidly, I offered in ICV. (122) So, suppose that very gradually, over the course of a year, the neurons of Oscar's brain are replaced by inorganic entities, but always in such a way that, from one day to the next, there's precious little effect on his thought and feeling. (If the supposed proposition conflicts with actual natural laws, then, suppose that there's a change in the laws so that, in consequence, there's no longer any conflict.) During the year, there's a serson whose brain, partly natural and organic, and partly artificial and inorganic, continues to subserve Oscar's mind, including his conscious thoughts and feelings. By the end of this year, there's a serson whose entirely inorganic brain, we're supposing, still subserves the nonpersonal mind of sentient Oscar. Finally, suppose that this mentally productive brain is transplanted into a suitable inorganic "canine" body, so that the nonbiological whole is able to engage with his environment, and experience this active engagement, just as effectively, and just as vividly, as the original organic Oscar ever did.

From your concern for Oscar himself, supposing that also to continue, you choose lesser early pain for Oscar, even though he's then organic, rather than much greater later pain to be inflicted on the inorganic being we've just been supposing. As this indicates, we take this later being to be the very same sentient being that was sentient Oscar at the case's start; though he's no longer biologically alive, your nonpersonal serson survives.

12. Are There ANY Ordinary Entities that CAN'T Survive Losing Their Biological Lives?

On our ordinary metaphysic, many of the things we recognize are in fact alive; they all share the property of *being alive*, we may say, where that property's understood to be a purely biological attribute, a property without any psychological implications. And, among these living entities, there are many that, so far as we know and believe, haven't even the least capacity for thought or experience. These insensate ordinary entities include many organisms, as with a tree outside my window that we may conveniently call *Trudy*, as well as many that are far from ever being organisms, as with a skin cell of yours that we may call *Sylvia*.

As has happened with ever so many trees, some day Trudy will die. When that happens, we may agree, Trudy will no longer be alive; but, will Trudy no longer exist? On our commonsense metaphysic, at least, it seems that Trudy may still exist, even as, on this common view, there may exist, on earth right now, very many dead trees that were once alive. (Now, when a dead tree undergoes a great deal of decay, and almost all its matter becomes widely dispersed, then, in the typical case, at least, the tree will no longer exist. So, should *all that* happen to Trudy, and not just the cessation of her (biological) life, then Trudy will no longer exist. And, should an exploding bomb blow our living Trudy sky high, as we lately imagined happened with Oscar's living body, then, again, Trudy will no longer exist. But, then, apparently, it will not be simply by ending Trudy's (biological) life that the bomb will end Trudy's existence.) Perhaps it might be that, on our common metaphysic, Trudy's being alive isn't essential to Trudy's existence, no more than it's essential to the continued existence of Oscar's body that it remain alive.

As has happened with ever so many cells, some day Sylvia will die. When that happens, Sylvia will no longer be alive, we may agree; but, will Sylvia no longer exist? Perhaps it might be that, on our commonsense metaphysic, Sylvia will still exist, even as it seems that, on your feet right now, there really are many dead cells that were once alive.

Without having confidence in the proposed propositions, I've suggested some thoughts for the serious consideration of contemporary philosophers. Continuing to assume our commonsense metaphysic is generally correct, I'll just as neutrally propose a few further propositions.

First, there's this quite general statement: With *being alive* not essential even for the likes of Trudy and Sylvia, there *aren't any* ordinary things, or things (of a sort) ordinarily recognized by us, for which having that property is crucial to their existence.

Second, and more cautiously, there's this more specific statement: It's not essential to the continued existence of any *animals* that they continue to be alive.

For the moment, let's suppose that this second proposition is true. Then, even if it may be easy to distinguish conceptually between sentient Oscar and his body, it might be impossible to distinguish between Oscar's body, which might also bear Oscar's name, and a certain canine animal, which might *also* be an Oscar. So, then, it just might be that, while there's one Oscar who's so much as a sentient being, there's another, materially coincident with him, that's both a canine animal and a canine body. On the other hand, it may still be possible to distinguish between Oscar the canine body and Oscar the canine animal, even if, as we're supposing, neither need be alive. Then, there'll be (at least) three materially coincident Oscars, the serson, the animal and the body. Sometimes inclined even toward this somewhat suspicious last alternative, I leave further thinking on these matters to future investigations.

13. Maintaining an Adequate Philosophical Perspective on Ourselves

When attempting ambitious philosophical work, we may fail to maintain an adequate philosophical perspective: For example, we may come to think that, when properly concerned for ourselves, what we should be most concerned for are certain bodies, or animals, or organisms, that may have not even the least capacity for any thought or feeling at all. Far from bettering our understanding of ourselves, we've then quite lost sight of ourselves. To better our understanding, we must, at the very least, maintain an adequate philosophical perspective on ourselves. And, for that, we must continue to think of ourselves as being, most essentially, thinking and feeling individuals.[17]

Notes

1. In ICV, see pages 212–217. Henceforth, ICV's numbers will be (bracketed) in the text.
2. Owing largely to considerations concerning agency and the will, I'm now far more inclined toward a substantial dualism than when I wrote ICV and when, a couple of years later, I replied to a prominent dualist, Richard Swinburne, in a Book Symposium on ICV; see Swinburne (1992) and Unger (1992). Detailing these considerations would be the work of another essay, much longer than the present paper. Due to the complex considerations, I'm now *at least somewhat* more inclined toward *any* view on which I'm not wholly constituted of parts each ontologically more basic than myself. So, it's important to me now that, for the most part, this paper's thoughts comport well with very many metaphysical conceptions.
3. THA, pages 16–17. [As with ICV, often THA's page numbers will be (bracketed) in the text.] Though failing to notice the intriguingly allied work of W. R. Carter, Olson does usefully observe on page 19 that, in recent decades, such a biological view, or a position much like his, has been advocated by at least these other able authors: Michael Ayers, Paul F. Snowdon, Judith J. Thomson, Bernard A. O. Williams, and Peter van Inwagen. Yet, on that very page, Olson says, "The Biological Approach has been strangely neglected in the literature (sic) on personal identity." If, along with the five philosophers he there notes, we count Olson himself, who'd already published several papers to this effect, and Carter, with even more such papers then published, we find at least seven able and active advocates in the recent literature. (Mentions of their relevant works constitute most of the present paper's References.) By my standards, this Approach has been *very* strangely neglected!
4. The Vegetable Case is first presented on pages 7–9, the Transplant Case on 9–11.
5. Here, I may well rehearse these words from page 92 of my (1996): "Long examined by psychologists, but longer ignored by philosophers, the response someone makes to a given example can be greatly influenced by (her memory of) responses made to cases previously encountered. And, since folks want their responses to seem consistent, often the influence is greatest when the present case seems "essentially the same" as the just previous example."
6. Though it seems recently to have gone into a great and welcome decline, at least for several decades and right up through the 1980s, all too many philosophers have championed the view that, when thinking about hypothetical cases that are more than just quite modestly hypothetical, we'll be (almost) doomed to promote far more confusion than philosophical insight. Toward showing the prominence of that protracted pessimism, on page 200 of his (1984) *Reasons and Persons*, Derek Parfit presents this passage from W. V. Quine (1972): "The method of science fiction has its uses in philosophy, but...I wonder whether the limits of the method are properly heeded. To seek what is "logically required" for sameness of person under unprecedented circumstances is to suggest that words have some logical force beyond what our past needs have invested them with." But, such very wholesale pessimism has no real basis. Indeed, soon after offering the quote from Quine, Parfit makes quite a good case for the truth that there's at least as much to be lost from a great aversion to using far-fetched cases as from a dogged reliance on such examples.
   Let me close this note with the observation that in my (1996) I give a great deal of thought, and space, to making the case that, though very far from always,

quite often our responses to cases, including even actual cases, do more toward engendering confusion than providing instruction. So, I'm no friend of an *uncritical reliance* on cases, not even on *actual* cases.

7. For the quoted opening passage, Carter (1990) has two notes; the first just specifies salient ways in which Felix and Jefferson are qualitatively different, and the second just says what I've above place in [square brackets]. Right after the quoted material, Carter places in display a quote from page 78 of Sydney Shoemaker's contribution to Sydney Shoemaker and Richard Swinburne (1984), rightly acknowledges Shoemaker's seminal influence for our topics.

8. In ICV, it's first used in section 10 of chapter 1. Much later, in "How Presumptive Tests for Survival Beliefs May be Improved," which is section 5 of chapter 7, the avoidance of future great pain test is refined. But, for most of what's to be done in the present essay, the refinements are more distracting than enlightening.

9. For the exchange case that starts this flurry of examples, see pages 23–25 of Shoemaker (1963). As he plainly realizes that case is very naturally regarded as a materially robust version of a famous case in Locke. Indeed, just before presenting his own example, on page 22 Shoemaker quotes Locke's remark that "should the soul of a prince, carrying with it the consciousness of the prince's past life, enter and inform the body of a cobbler, as soon deserted of his own soul, every one sees that he would be the same person with the prince, accountable only for the prince's actions," appending a footnote for Locke: *Essay*, I, 457. (In a footnote on his page 14, Shoemaker cites Locke's *Essay*.)

10. On page 103 of ICV, there's an exchange case that's thus qualitatively symmetrical. In some notable respects, the qualitative symmetry provides a useful purification.

11. What I've just been saying *doesn't* imply that, throughout all conceivable cases, or even all nomologically possible cases, you will be wherever your mentally productive brain will be. Indeed, in ICV there's an entire section, section 6 of chapter 5, that's devoted to providing argument for the contrary view, those arguments providing an affirmative answer to the section's interrogative title, "Might We Survive Brain Replacements and even Brain Exchanges?"

12. In section IV, chapter 3 of THA, Olson conspicuously denies this.

13. In ICV I used this test rather rarely. Thus, till now, it's been anonymous.

14. Though the examples are pretty far-fetched, it's very clear, and it's perfectly determinate, what is the truth of the salient matters in these cases. Indeed, the salient matters are very nearly as clear as with cases of *heart*-exchange: When there's the exchange of hearts between you and a qualitatively identical other person, it's extremely clear, and of course perfectly determinate, who's who throughout and, in later stages, who's acquiring which heart. And, that's hardly any clearer right now than it was years before the first (successful) heart transplant operation, when it was (already) very clear, and perfectly determinate, who'd survive in the event of such a (successful) operation.

15. As our treatment of Vegetable cases also shows, there's also precious little to be gained from hybrid approaches that feature biological continuity as an even reasonably central element. For example, we might consider a "closest continuer" view according to which, whenever suitable psychology is present, the mentality dictates the conditions of our survival, but, when it's absent, biological continuity might suffice for our survival. What we just said for the Biological Approach itself, we may say, apparently with equal justice, for such hybrid approaches: The more we're

free from confusions about our existence and persistence, the less there'll even seem to be said for them. For the main point of this note, I'm grateful to Kit Fine.

16. When the serson's active brain is way over there and (the rest of) his healthy body is right nearby here, is the serson simply over there, a quite cohesive entity, or he is partly there and partly here, a rather scattered entity? And, what of his body? In this essay, I mean to leave open what are the answers to these questions.

   As I'm inclined to believe, the serson himself is, in the envisaged situation, a quite cohesive entity that's just where his mentally productive brain is, way over there. As I'm also inclined to think, the body is also quite cohesive, but it's right nearby here, not at all where the brain is. But, to support these inclinations, at all well, rather complex arguments may be requited. So, in this essay, I set them both aside.

17. Many people have been helpful toward getting this paper to be more useful and less riddled with error. Very helpful indeed have been David Barnett, John Carroll, W. R. Carter, John Gibbons, John Heil, Peter Kung, Jeff McMahan, Michael Lockwood, Eric Olson, Michael Rea, Sydney Shoemaker and, most especially, Mark Bajakian and Kit Fine. To such helpful sentient beings, I'm duly grateful and thankful.

References

Ayers, Michael. 1990. *Locke*, Vol.2. London: Routledge.

Carter, William R. 1980. "Once and Future Persons," *American Philosophical Quarterly* 17: 61–66.

―――――. 1982. "Do Zygotes Become People?" *Mind* XCI: 77–95.

―――――. 1988. "Our Bodies, Our Selves," *Australasian Journal of Philosophy* 66: 308–319.

―――――. 1990. "Why Personal Identity Is Animal Identity," *LOGOS* 11: 71–81.

―――――. 1992. Review of *Identity, Consciousness and Value. Ethics* 102: 849–851.

Locke, John. 1894. *An Essay Concerning Human Understanding*, ed. Fraser. Oxford University Press.

Olson, Eric T. 1994. "Is Psychology Relevant to Personal Identity," *Australasian Journal of Philosophy* 72: 173–186.

―――――. 1995. "Human People or Human Animals?" *Philosophical Studies* 80: 159–181.

―――――. 1997. "Was I Ever a Fetus?" *Philosophy and Phenomenological Research* LVII: 95–110.

―――――. 1997. *The Human Animal: Personal Identity without Psychology*. Oxford University Press.

Parfit, Derek. 1984. *Reasons and Persons*. Oxford University Press.

Quine, W. V. 1972. Review of Milton K. Munitz, ed. *Identity and Individuation, Journal of Philosophy* LXIX: 488–497.

Shoemaker, Sydney. 1963. *Self-Knowledge and Self-Identity*. Cornell University Press.

―――――. 1984 *"Personal Identity: A Materialist's Account,"* in S. Shoemaker and R. Swinburne, *Personal Identity*. Basil Blackwell.

―――――. 1992. "Unger's Psychological Continuity Theory," *Philosophy and Phenomenological Research* LII: 139–143.

―――――. 1997. "Self and Substance," *Philosophical Perspectives* 11: 283–304.

―――――. 1999. "Self, Body and Coincidence," *Proceedings of the Aristotelian Society*, Supplementary Volume, LXXIII, forthcoming.

Snowdon, Paul F. 1990. "Persons, Animals and Ourselves," in *The Person and the Human Mind*, ed. Christopher Gill. Oxford University Press.

―――――. 1991. "Personal Identity and Brain Transplants," in *Human Beings*, ed. David Cockburn. Cambridge University Press.

―――――. 1995. "Persons, Animals and Bodies," in *The Body and the Self*, eds. J. L. Bermudez, A. Marcel and N. Eilan. The MIT Press.

_____. 1996. "Persons and Personal Identity," in *Essays for David Wiggins: Identity, Truth and Value*, eds. S. Lovibond and S. G. Williams. Basil Blackwell.

Swinburne, Richard. 1984. "Personal Identity: The Dualist Theory," in S. Shoemaker and R. Swinburne, *Personal Identity*. Basil Blackwell.

_____. 1992. "Discussion of Peter Unger's *Identity, Consciousness and Value*," *Philosophy and Phenomenological Research* LII: 149–152.

Thomson, Judith Jarvis. 1987. "Ruminations on an Account of Personal Identity," in *On Being and Saying: Essays for Richard Cartwright*, ed. J. J. Thomson. The MIT Press.

Unger, Peter. 1990. *Identity, Consciousness and Value*. Oxford University Press.

_____. 1992. "Reply to Reviewers," *Philosophy and Phenomenological Research* LII: 159–176.

_____. 1996. *Living High and Letting Die*. Oxford University Press.

van Inwagen, Peter. 1980. "Philosophers and the Words 'Human Body'," in *Time and Cause*, ed. P. van Inwagen. Reidel.

_____. 1990. *Material Beings*. Cornell University Press.

_____. 1992. "Critical Study of Peter Unger's *Identity, Consciousness and Value*," *Nous* XXVII: 373–379.

Williams, Bernard. 1970. "Are Persons Bodies?" in *The Philosophy of the Body*, ed. S. Spicker. Reprinted in Williams, *Problems of the Self*, Cambridge University Press, 1973.

FROM SELF PSYCHOLOGY TO MORAL PHILOSOPHY[1]

J. David Velleman
University of Michigan

Prescott Lecky's *Self-Consistency* was published in 1945, four years after the author's death, at the age of 48.[2] Subtitled *A Theory of Personality*, the book defended a simple but startling thesis:[3]

> We propose to apprehend all psychological phenomena as illustrations of the single principle of unity or self-consistency. We conceive of the personality as an organization of values which are felt to be consistent with one another. Behavior expresses the effort to maintain the integrity and unity of the organization.

Lecky regarded self-consistency as the object of a cognitive or epistemic motive from which all other motives are derived.[4] "The subject must feel that he lives in a stable and intelligible environment," Lecky wrote: "In a world which is incomprehensible, no one can feel secure."[5] The subject therefore constructs an organized conception of his world—an "organization of experience into an integrated whole"—and this organization just *is* his personality, because the effort to maintain its consistency is what gives shape to his thought and behavior.[6]

Central to the personality, so conceived, is the subject's conception of himself. "The most constant factor in the individual's experience," according to Lecky, "is himself and the interpretation of his own meaning; the kind of person he is, the place which he occupies in the world, appear to represent the center or nucleus of the personality."[7] Because the subject's world-view is thus centered on his self-view, his efforts to maintain coherence in the one are centered on maintaining coherence in the other. "Any idea entering the system which is inconsistent with the individual's conception of himself cannot be assimilated but instead gives rise to an inconsistency which must be removed as promptly as possible."[8]

If a person is to maintain consistency in his self-conception, he has to *be* consistent—to think and behave in ways that lend themselves to a coherent representation. That's why the person's conception of his world, and especially of himself, can play the functional role of his personality: it organizes his thought and behavior into a unified whole. Lecky offered the following illustration of how this process works.[9]

> Let us take the case of an intelligent student who is deficient, say, in spelling. In almost every instance poor spellers have been tutored and practiced in spelling over long periods without improvement. For some reason such a student has a special handicap in learning how to spell, though not in learning the other subjects which are usually considered more difficult. This deficiency is not due to a lack of ability, but rather to an active resistance which prevents him from learning how to spell in spite of the extra instruction. The resistance arises from the fact that at some time in the past the suggestion that he is a poor speller was accepted and incorporated into his definition of himself, and is now an integral part of his total personality. ... His difficulty is thus explained as a special instance of the general principle that a person can only be true to himself. If he defines himself as a poor speller, the misspelling of a certain proportion of the words which he uses becomes for him a moral issue. He misspells words for the same reason that he refuses to be a thief. That is, he must endeavor to behave in a manner consistent with his conception of himself.

I regard this as one of the most remarkable passages in twentieth-century moral psychology. On the one hand, it offers an explanation for a pathology that has become especially significant to us—the pathology of being defeated by a negative self-conception. We now look for this particular form of self-defeat not only in children's failure to learn spelling but also, for example, in the perpetuation of racial and sexual stereotypes that are internalized by their victims.[10] On the other hand, this passage also offers, in capsule form, a theory of moral motivation. It says that a person refrains from stealing because he cannot assimilate stealing into his self-conception.

What's remarkable about the passage is that it attributes self-defeat and moral behavior to one and the same motive. A child fails to learn as if on principle, while thieving is, as it were, against his stereotype; or, rather, acting on principle and acting to type are both manifestations of one and the same drive, to maintain a coherent self-conception. Could the question *Why be moral* be so closely related to *Why Johnny can't spell*?

Clearly, Lecky overstated his hypothesis in the passage quoted above. Many psychological factors may go into causing a particular person to spell badly or to refrain from stealing: a self-consistency motive is unlikely to be the only cause or even the primary cause of such behavior. But I would like to believe that this motive can figure among the causes, in roughly the manner described by Lecky; and so I would like to believe that the quoted passage is merely exaggerated rather than false.

My reasons for *wanting* to believe this don't amount to reasons for *believing* it, because they are philosophical rather than empirical. I have presented these reasons elsewhere, in arguing that various philosophical problems about agency can be resolved by the assumption that agents have a motive for doing what makes sense to them.[11] People's having such a motive, I claim, would account for their being autonomous, acting for reasons, having an open future, and thus satisfying our concept of an agent. As a philosopher of action, then, I hope that Lecky is right.

I think that my arguments may be of philosophical interest even if Lecky is wrong, since they show our concept of agency to be realizable, whether or not it is realized in human beings.[12] But experience has taught me that philosophers aren't interested in an account of purely possible agents, and that they tend to regard my account as no more than that, because they find its motivational assumption implausible. Philosophers are generally unwilling to believe that people have a motive for doing what they understand.

I have therefore decided to venture out of the philosophical armchair in order to examine the empirical evidence, as gathered by psychologists aiming to prove or disprove motivational conjectures like mine. By and large, this evidence is indirect in relation to my account of agency, since it is drawn from cases in which the relevant motive has been forced into the open by the manipulations of an experimenter. The resulting evidence doesn't tend to show the mechanism of agency humming along in accordance with my specifications; it tends to show the knocks and shudders that such a mechanism emits when put under stress. But we often learn about the normal workings of things by subjecting them to abnormal conditions; and viewed in this light, various programs of psychological research offer indirect support to my account of agency. I'll begin by reviewing the relevant research, leaving its relevance to my account of agency for the final section of the paper.

Cognitive Dissonance

The largest and most well-known program of research on cognitive motivation is the theory of cognitive dissonance. In the classic demonstration of dissonance, by Festinger and Carlsmith (1959), subjects performed an extremely tedious task and then were asked to tell the next subject that the task was enjoyable. Some were offered $1 by the experimenter for performing this service; others were offered $20. Those who received only $1 for saying the task was enjoyable subsequently came to believe that it *was* enjoyable, whereas those who had received $20 continued to believe that it was tedious. Festinger and Carlsmith hypothesized that the subjects who received only $1 experienced greater "dissonance" between their attitudes and their behavior, and altered their opinion in order to reduce this dissonance.

The effect reported by Festinger and Carlsmith has been replicated hundreds if not thousands of times, but its interpretation remains controversial. Festinger and Carlsmith did not clearly explain their dissonance hypothesis, and others have proposed alternative hypotheses to account for their results.[13]

Aronson's version of the dissonance hypothesis

The clearest version of the dissonance hypothesis was proposed by Elliot Aronson (1968).[14] Aronson argued that the subjects' cognition of their behavior was at odds with what they would expect themselves to have done under the circumstances. What they would expect themselves to have done, having found the task boring, is to say that it was boring; but they found it boring and said that it was interesting. Their cognition of what they had done therefore clashed with the expectation that would naturally follow from their cognition of the circumstances. The subjects changed their opinion of the task, according to Aronson, so that they could change their cognition of the circumstances, rendering it consistent with their cognition of what they had done.

The hypothesis that Aronson thus framed in terms of expectations can also be framed in terms of explanations. Just as the subjects' cognition of having found the task boring would lead to an expectation at odds with their having said that it was interesting, so it would leave them at a loss to explain why they had said that it was interesting. Finding their behavior inexplicable and finding it contrary to expectation would be two aspects of the same cognitive predicament. And changing their opinion of the task would resolve the predicament under either description, by rendering their behavior both explicable and predictable under the circumstances as re-conceived.

This hypothesis relies on two assumptions that are not explicitly stated either by Aronson or by Festinger and Carlsmith. The first assumption, pointed out by Kelley (1967), is that *none* of the subjects knew the full explanation of their behavior.[15]

The pressure that induced these subjects to lie was covert: it was the pressure exerted by the experimental setting and the authority conferred by that setting on the experimenter. People are notoriously unaware of how powerful such pressure can be.[16] Hence the subjects in Festinger and Carlsmith's experiment didn't know why they lied. One group of subjects were offered an explanation designed to seem adequate to them, while the others were offered an explanation designed to seem inadequate. In all probability, $20 would not have been sufficient to induce most of the subjects to lie if it had been offered by a stranger with no authority; but $20 was sufficient for the subjects *to believe* that it had been a sufficient inducement for them, whereas $1 was not. Hence some of the subjects but not others were supplied with what seemed like an adequate explanation of their behavior, or an adequate basis on which to expect it.

The second assumption required by the dissonance hypothesis is that the subjects who changed their opinion also deceived themselves about having changed it. The awareness of having retroactively come to believe what they had already said would not have provided them with an explanation of why they had said it, or with a basis on which their saying it could have been expected. The premise required to explain or predict their behavior was that they had believed what they were saying at the time, as they said it. In retroactively coming to believe what they had said, then, they must also have come to believe, falsely, that they had believed it all along.

As supplemented by these assumptions, the dissonance hypothesis says that when people cannot identify the forces that have shaped their behavior, they conjure up forces to make it seem intelligible and predictable—if necessary, by retroactively forming a motivationally relevant attitude and projecting it back in time.[17] This maneuver would appear to be motivated by the subjects' desire for explanatory and predictive coherence in their self-conceptions, a motive of the sort postulated by Lecky. Hence the results of forced-compliance experiments, as explained by the dissonance hypothesis, appear to support Lecky's theory of self-consistency.

A rival explanation: self-perception

Daryl Bem (1972) has argued that subjects who seem to be motivated by cognitive dissonance are merely interpreting their own behavior as if they were external observers:

> Just as an outside observer might ask himself, "What must this man's attitude be if he is willing to behave in this fashion in this situation?" so too, the subject implicitly asks himself, "What must my attitude be if I am willing to behave in this fashion in this situation?" Thus the subject who receives $1 discards the monetary inducement as the major motivating factor for his behavior and infers that it must reflect his actual attitude; he infers that he must have actually enjoyed the tasks. The subject who receives $20 notes that his behavior is adequately accounted for by the monetary inducement, and hence he cannot extract from the behavior any information relevant to his actual opinions; he is in the same situation as a control subject insofar as information about his attitude is concerned. (pp. 16–17)

In this "self-perception explanation," Bem says, "there is no aversive motivational pressure postulated." As described by Nisbett and Valins (1972), "Bem's reinterpretation of dissonance phenomena avoids the use of any motivational concept," and so "the two positions appear to be at a logical impasse": dissonance theory attributes the subjects' change of attitude to "a motivated process" whereas Bem attributes it to "a passive, inferential process."[18]

Subsequent research has shown that the correct explanation for dissonance phenomena is indeed motivational.[19] But I do not want to interpret this research as discrediting Bem's explanation in terms of self-perception. Bem's only mistake, I believe, is in claiming that his self-perception explanation doesn't depend on any motivational postulate. In fact, his self-perception theory postulates the same motive as cognitive-dissonance theory; and so the two theories give coordinate explanations that are mutually reinforcing.[20]

Bem's thesis is that a person often comes to know about his own attitudes in much the same way as we do when observing him from the outside. Bem's formulation of the thesis suggests that a person receives his self-knowledge passively, as if by a process of sensory perception. But this suggestion is superfluous to the thesis—and, indeed, incompatible with Bem's defense of it.

To be sure, our knowledge of a person's attitudes is often obtained by a process that is quasi-perceptual. That is, hearing a person's vocalizations is often inseparable from hearing them as the assertion of a particular proposition, and seeing his bodily movements is often inseparable from seeing them as an effort to attain a particular end. On other occasions, however, we hear a person's voice without hearing what he's saying, or we see his movements without seeing what he's doing; and what he is saying or doing are then matters that we have to figure out.

On the latter occasions, detecting the attitudes behind a person's behavior requires a process that is not passive and perceptual but active and intellectual: it requires a process of interpretive inquiry. We will not undertake that process unless we have the requisite motives. If the meaning of someone's vocalizations or movements doesn't impress itself upon us immediately, we won't bother to figure it out unless we want to—that is, unless we want to understand what he is saying or doing, or to anticipate what he's likely to say and do next. On such occasions, interpretation is an activity that must be motivated.

Unfortunately, social psychologists tend to speak of all interpretation as perceptual, as in the phrases "self-perception," "interpersonal perception," "social perception," and the like. This usage highlights the cases in which interpretation is passive and receptive rather than active and motivated. Even though Bem denies that one is automatically given a knowledge of one's attitudes, he calls the process of acquiring such knowledge "self-perception," and so he is naturally interpreted as describing a process that is passive. The possibility that self-perception might be a motivated activity therefore goes unnoticed.

Yet Bem himself implicitly concedes this possibility, when he says that an observer "might ask himself, 'What must this man's attitude be if he is willing to behave in this fashion in this situation?'" This question expresses the observer's desire to understand and anticipate, a desire without which he wouldn't ask the question or, having asked it, would let it go unanswered. Bem's thesis is that the subject "implicitly asks himself" the same question about himself, because a knowledge of his attitudes is not automatically given to him any more than it is to an observer. To portray the subject as asking this question is to acknowledge that he doesn't passively perceive his own attitudes but must sometimes actively inquire into them. It is therefore to acknowledge a motive for self-inquiry.

Now, an interest in explanation and prediction is the basis of all consistency motivation, according to Lecky. Consistency isn't desired for its own sake; it's desired as the form of the predictable and the intelligible, by a creature who "must feel that he lives in a stable and intelligible environment." Inconsistency isn't intrinsically disturbing; it's disturbing because it stymies comprehension, and "[i]n a world which is incomprehensible, no one can feel secure."[21] A desire for consistency in one's self-conception thus arises, according to Lecky, from the desire to understand and be able to anticipate oneself—the very desire expressed by the question that Bem attributes to the self-interpreting subject.

Hence the motive implicitly conceded by Bem is the same motive that is explicitly postulated by Lecky, the desire for self-knowledge. Bem should not deny the existence of this cognitive motive, since his own theory presupposes it.

Lecky's insight was that the desire for self-knowledge can drive either of two, coordinate processes. If we want to understand what we do, we can either figure out why we've done things, after we've done them, or we can make sure that we don't do things unless we already know why. The latter process entails doing only what we are aware of having motives or other dispositions to do; and so it amounts to the process of being true to ourselves by acting in accordance with our self-conceptions, the self-consistency process described by Lecky. The former process entails interpreting our behavior after the fact: it is the self-perception process described by Bem. Self-consistency and self-perception are thus two phases of a single activity—the practical and intellectual phases of self-interpretation.

Note that dissonance-reduction lies on the intellectual side of this contrast. When a subject experiences cognitive dissonance, it's too late for him to make his behavior consistent with his self-conception; he has to adjust his self-conception to fit his behavior, which is in the past. Bem and Aronson are thus describing one and the same process, of fitting an interpretive hypothesis to past behavior.

In Aronson's story, the subject begins with an interpretation that doesn't fit—namely, that he believed the experimental task to be tedious—and the resulting discomfort moves him to frame a new hypothesis, that he believed the task to be fun. In Bem's story, the subject appears to have no initial interpretation, and so he isn't motivated by any discomfort. But he is still motivated by a desire for an interpretation that fits his behavior, the desire whose frustration caused the initial discomfort in Aronson's version. The only point of disagreement between Aronson and Bem is whether the subject was dissatisfied with one interpretation before being moved to frame an interpretation that satisfied him.[22]

Thus, the dissonance theorist and the self-perception theorist aren't at a "logical impasse": they are in fact comrades in arms. Both are describing a process of self-interpretation, motivated by a desire for self-knowledge.[23]

If the differences between dissonance theory and self-perception theory are so small, why do their proponents believe that they yield different predictions, and that they are consequently supported by different experimental results?[24] The answer, I think, is that each theory isolates and simplifies one aspect of a large and complicated reality. The reality behind both theories is the holistic process of fitting an interpretation to behavior—a process that is complicated, in the first-personal case, by the possibility of working in the opposite direction, by fitting one's behavior to an interpretation. Each theory treats a single aspect of this process as if it were the whole, thus obscuring the fact that they are, as it were, different ends of the same elephant.[25]

I have already explained how self-perception theorists focus on the case of automatic, passive self-understanding, neglecting cases in which self-understanding is attained through active self-inquiry, motivated partly by the discomforts of reflective ignorance and incomprehension. The corresponding fault among dissonance theorists is a tendency to focus on individual inconsistencies of particular kinds, neglecting the overall cognitive goals in relation to which inconsistency is undesirable, in the first place. The narrow focus of either theory allows its proponents to state specific algorithms—an algorithm for attributing attitudes, in the one case, and an algorithm for computing total dissonance, in the other. These algorithms do yield conflicting predictions, which would be confirmed by different experimental outcomes. But the algorithms are radically underdetermined by the theories to which they have been attached, and in both cases they are implausible. Attributing attitudes and eliminating inconsistencies are two aspects of the overall process of making sense of the world, a process that has not been and probably cannot be reduced to an algorithm.

Consider an experiment by Snyder and Ebbesen (1972), billed as "a test of dissonance theory versus self-perception theory."[26] This experiment modified a standard dissonance protocol by making salient to the subject either his initial attitude, or the behavior inconsistent with that attitude, or both. Snyder and Ebbesen claimed that making the subject's attitude salient to him ought to increase his awareness of dissonance between it and his behavior, thereby increasing his tendency to alter the attitude, if dissonance theory were correct; whereas if self-perception theory were correct, making the subject's attitude salient ought to discourage him from attributing a different attitude to himself. Snyder and Ebbesen reported that their results favored self-perception theory in this respect.

But the "prediction" that Snyder and Ebbesen derived from dissonance theory depends on a very narrow view of the circumstances. To be sure, if the subject's belief that a task was tedious is made salient to him, then he will be more aware of its inconsistency with his statement that the task was interesting.[27] But his initial belief would also be inconsistent with a subsequent *belief* that the task was interesting, and this potential inconsistency will also be impressed on him by the salience of the former belief. Once he is made aware of believing that the task was tedious, he cannot come to believe that it was interesting without acknowledging that he has changed his mind, for no apparent reason. Thus, even as the discomfort associated with his initial belief is intensified, so is the discomfort to be expected from the alternative.

What, then, does dissonance theory predict that the subject will do? Surely, the theory cannot make a definite prediction in a case so under-described. What the subject will do depends on circumstances that will vary from one subject to another, since he will seek the most coherent view of the situation *all things considered*. Among the things he'll have to consider will be such questions as what the task was, specifically, and how offensive to his personal tastes; whether he is the sort of person to lie, or the sort of person to be unsure of what he likes; whether he identifies with the experimenter or with his fellow subjects; and so on. If dissonance theorists think that they have an algorithm for predicting how such questions will be resolved, they are mistaken. But their critics are also mistaken if they think that the failure of some particular algorithm entails the failure of the theory.

Another rival explanation: self-enhancement

I have now argued that self-perception theory tacitly presupposes the same cognitive motive that is explicitly postulated by dissonance theory, and that these theories can appear to yield conflicting predictions only if formulated with more precision than their shared theoretical basis can support. But self-perception theory is not the only attempt to re-interpret the evidence gathered in dissonance research. Others have explained that evidence by postulating motives that clearly aren't cognitive.

According to dissonance theory, the Festinger-Carlsmith subjects came to believe what they had said in order to escape a specifically cognitive predicament, of being unable to explain their behavior, or of finding it contrary to expectation. But they might instead have come to believe what they had said in order to escape the appearance of having been irrational, in having said it for no good reason. In that case, their change of mind would have aimed to rationalize their past behavior rather than to remedy their current state of reflective ignorance or incomprehension; and it would thus have aimed at removing not a cognitive problem but a threat to their self-esteem as rational agents. The effects of forced compliance have therefore been taken by other psychologists to indicate a motive for attaining a favorable view of oneself rather than for maintaining consistency with one's actual self-view—a motive of self-enhancement rather than self-consistency.[28]

Of course, dissonance theory is not committed to denying the influence of the former motive. Everyone prefers not to look foolish, and this preference may well be implicated the forced-compliance phenomena. Dissonance theory is merely committed to asserting the influence of an additional motive, a motive to avoid that which is inexplicable or contrary to expectation. But if the phenomena cited in support of dissonance theory can be completely explained by a desire not to look foolish, then the theory will have lost most of its empirical support.

Attribution Effects

A number of experimenters claim to have found dissonance effects that cannot be explained as instances of self-enhancement.[29] But I am less interested in dissonance *per se* than in the cognitive motive for reducing it—a motive that, as we have seen, can drive not only dissonance-reduction but self-perception and other attributional processes as well. I therefore prefer to draw further evidence from phenomena that don't clearly involve dissonance but turn out to involve the same cognitive motive.

Self-verification

One such phenomenon has been explored by William B. Swann, Jr., under the label "self-verification."[30] Swann has shown that people tend to seek, credit, and retain feedback that confirms their actual self-conception, even if that conception is negative. Thus, for example, people tend to choose and feel committed to partners who view them as they view themselves, for better or worse.[31] When interacting with someone who appears to view them differently, they tend to behave in ways designed to bring him around to their view, even if it is unflattering.[32] They also lend more credence to his feedback about them, and are more likely to remember that feedback, if it confirms their conception of themselves, favorable or unfavorable.[33]

Because these tendencies are associated with negative as well as positive self-conceptions, they cannot be explained by a desire for self-enhancement.[34] Yet they don't exactly confirm the Leckian hypothesis. What Swann and his colleagues have found are biases in people's collection and interpretation of feedback from others. These biases may well be motivated by a self-consistency motive such as Lecky postulated. But Lecky hypothesized that this motive would lead people to confirm their self-conceptions directly, by behaving in ways that verified those conceptions. Lecky's hypothesis was that people who think of themselves as poor spellers would not just choose friends who think of them as poor spellers, too, but would actually tend to spell poorly in order to be true to themselves. Swann's research does not demonstrate a tendency toward such direct, behavioral self-verification.

There is ample evidence for behavioral self-verification of positive self-views, especially in children. This evidence is less than conclusive, because it can be explained, at least in part, by a motive for self-enhancement; but it is nevertheless worth reviewing, since it coincides in interesting respects with Lecky's views.

Miller, Brickman, and Bolen (1975) compared attribution and persuasion as means of modifying the behavior of elementary school pupils. In one experiment, they compared the littering behavior of children who had repeatedly been told that they *ought to be* tidy (persuasion) with that of children who had repeatedly been told that they *were* tidy (attribution). Both groups decreased their rate of littering, in comparison with both their own prior rate and that of a control group that was offered no messages on the subject. But the effects of attribution were significantly greater and lasted significantly longer than those of persuasion. Children who had been told that they were tidy showed a sharp and lasting decrease in their rate of littering, whereas children who had been told that they ought to be tidy showed only a moderate decrease in littering and then returned to littering at the same rate as the control group. In another experiment, the same researchers found a similar difference in the effect of attribution and persuasion on children's performance in arithmetic. Children told that they *were* skillful and highly motivated in arithmetic showed a greater and more long-lasting improvement than children told that they *ought to be* skillful or motivated.

These experiments compared favorable attributions with injunctions, which did not have a similarly favorable tone and might even have been interpreted by the children as presupposing an unfavorable attribution instead. (Why would teacher exhort us to be tidy if we weren't in fact untidy?) Perhaps, then, the experiments demonstrated, not an interesting motivational difference between attributions and injunctions, but an utterly unsurprising difference between positive and negative reinforcement. Grusec and Redler (1980) sought to rule out this alternative explanation by comparing favorable attributions with equally reinforcing praise offered for the same behavior. Children who had won marbles in a game were induced to deposit some of them in a collection bowl for poor children, whereupon they were either praised for doing so (reinforcement), told that their doing so showed that they liked to help others (attribution), or given no feedback at all (control). The children were then left to play the marble game on their own, while an experimenter observed through a one-way mirror to record how many marbles they placed in the collection bowl. Finally, the children were given colored pencils as a reward for their participation in the experiment and told that they could deposit some of them in a box for classmates who had not participated. Among 8-year-olds, the treatments were equally effective in increasing donations of marbles, but only attribution increased the donation of pencils. The 8-year-olds generalized their increased helpfulness to a new situation only if they had heard themselves described as helpful. These results were confirmed in subsequent sessions with the same children.[35]

Grusec and Redler gathered additional, developmental evidence by repeating the marble-and-pencil experiment with older and younger children. Neither treatment had any effect on 5- and 6-year-olds, while they were equally effective on the 10-year-olds. Grusec and Redler hypothesized that the former subjects were too young to understand the implications of trait attributions, whereas the latter were sufficiently mature to extend the attributions on their own, without hearing them from the experimenters.

This developmental hypothesis was subsequently bolstered by research applying Freedman and Fraser's (1966) "foot-in-the-door" technique to children in the same range of ages. Eisenberg *et al.* (1987, 1989) rewarded children with prize coupons for participating in an experiment and then induced some of them to donate part of their winnings to the poor. By eliciting this first donation, the experimenters had gotten a "foot in the door," designed to help them elicit further sharing behavior. Eisenberg *et al.* found that children were susceptible to this technique only if they were old enough to demonstrate an understanding of trait stability; and then their susceptibility was correlated with an independent measurement of their motivation toward self-consistency. These results suggest that the technique depended on the children's motivation to behave in accordance with self-attributions of helpfulness or generosity induced by their first donation.[36]

All of these experiments seem to show subjects being true to themselves by behaving in ways that verify self-attributions. Indeed, some of the experiments seem to confirm Lecky's claim that such behavioral self-verification accounts for moral behavior, while others seem to confirm his corresponding claim about academic performance. Hence attribution research with children is at least consistent with Lecky's views on the connection between being a bad speller and not being a thief.

Unfortunately, these findings involve the attribution of positive traits, and so they can in principle be explained by a motive of self-enhancement.[37] The children who heard themselves described as tidy or helpful may have come to regard tidy or helpful behavior as a way of earning that favorable description rather than as a way of making sense to themselves in light of it. Of course, a self-enhancement motive would not necessarily account for the difference in effectiveness between attribution and praise, or for the observed correlations with the development of trait-based self-understanding or with independently measured levels of motivation for self-consistency. But these phenomena may be too subtle to determine a choice between rival explanations.

What would confirm the existence of a cognitive motive is evidence that people tend to verify self-conceptions that don't enhance their self-esteem. Some researchers have therefore attempted to demonstrate a tendency to confirm negative self-conceptions.

In the classic experiment of this type, Aronson and Carlsmith (1962) asked subjects to identify the pictures of schizophrenics from among pictures that had in fact been randomly cut from a Harvard yearbook. Since subjects had no grounds for questioning the feedback they received about their rate of success, that feedback could be manipulated by the experimenters. Some subjects were led to believe that they were being consistently successful or unsuccessful; others were led to believe that they were scoring a long string of failures followed by a short string of successes, or a long string of successes followed by a short string of failures. All subjects were then given an opportunity to re-do the last set of items, on which some of them had seemed to take a turn for the better or the worse. Those who had seemed to take such a turn changed more of their answers, even if the turn they had taken was for the better. They thus appeared to prefer scoring consistently poorly to scoring inconsistently—as if trying to confirm the self-conception that they had formed during their initial string of failures.

Unfortunately, efforts to duplicate this result have met with only intermittent success.[38] One possible explanation, proposed by Swann (1986), is that most of the attempts at duplication have tested the effects of artificially induced self-conceptions about one's ability at a previously unfamiliar task. Yet the tendency to verify a self-conception appears to depend on the degree of certainty with which that conception is held.[39] Hence these experiments may not have induced self-conceptions with the degree of certainty required to produce an observable effect. And, indeed, the most persuasive replication of Aronson and Carlsmith's result was in subjects who had been found to hold negative overall self-views with relative certainty.[40] For these subjects, success was inconsistent not only with an immediately prior series of failures but with a well-entrenched conception of themselves. Even so, this line of research cannot be regarded as clearly demonstrating the presence of self-consistency motivation.

Self-attribution of emotion

The research summarized in the previous section is inconclusive partly because it focuses on self-conceptions of personal traits. These traits are often conceived in evaluative terms, and so attributing them to oneself often yields a self-conception that is clearly favorable or clearly unfavorable. A tendency to verify favorable self-conceptions can always be explained by a motive of self-enhancement; and whatever cognitive motive there is to verify self-conceptions may not be sufficiently strong to prevail reliably over the desire to falsify them when they are unfavorable. Hence the self-attribution of personal traits is unlikely to produce clear evidence of self-consistency motivation. A more likely source of such evidence is the self-attribution of motives or emotions, which—unlike traits of character—are often evaluatively neutral.

In the classic experiment on such attributions, Schacter and Singer (1962) recruited subjects for an experiment billed as testing the effects of a vitamin on vision. Two thirds of the subjects were injected with adrenaline, labeled as the vitamin; one third were injected with a saline solution but told it was the vitamin as well. One of the adrenaline-injected groups was informed that the drug would cause symptoms of arousal—trembling hands, racing heart, and so on. The others were not warned of any side effects.

Each of the subjects then moved on to the next activity, at which he was ostensibly joined by a fellow subject, who was in fact a confederate of the experimenters. For half of each group, the confederate became increasingly angry at the next activity; for the other half, the confederate became giddy and playful. The experimenters then observed the extent to which the subjects were influenced by the confederates' behavior. Those who had received a placebo, and those who had received adrenaline and been warned of its side effects, were influenced significantly less than those who had received adrenaline without being warned. The latter group showed a marked tendency to behave as if they were angry or giddy, depending on how their fellow subjects were behaving.

Schacter and Singer hypothesized that the subjects in this group interpreted their arousal as anger or euphoria, according to the suggestion provided by their fellow subjects, and then enacted the emotion that they had attributed to themselves. So interpreted, the experiment showed that people have a tendency to behave in accordance with the motives that they *believe* themselves to have—which would be a tendency toward self-consistency.[41]

The Schacter-Singer results have repeatedly been called into question on methodological grounds.[42] But the underlying hypothesis has been confirmed in experiments of a significantly different design.

Zillman, Johnson, and Day (1974) arranged for subjects to be angered by someone and then to engage in vigorous exercise. Some of the subjects were given an opportunity to retaliate against their provoker shortly after exercising; others were given the same opportunity after a longer interval. The latter group retaliated more intensely than the former. Zillman and his colleagues hypothesized that the subjects' retaliation expressed the degree of anger that they perceived themselves as having; and that the excitatory effects of exercise were correctly interpreted by the first group but misinterpreted by the second as heightened anger.

This hypothesis was subsequently tested by Cantor, Zillman, and Bryant (1975), who asked subjects to report, at intervals following exercise, whether they still felt its excitatory effects. By measuring the subjects' levels of excitation at the same intervals, these experimenters detected an initial phase during which the effects of exercise continued and were perceived as continuing; a second phase during which the effects of exercise continued but were not perceived as such; and a third phase during which these effects had disappeared both objectively and subjectively. During each of these phases, erotic materials were shown to one third of the subjects, who were asked to report their degree of sexual arousal. Subjects exposed to erotica during the first phase reported no greater arousal than those exposed during the third phase; but those exposed during the second phase reported greater arousal than the others. Thus, arousal that was not attributed to exercise appears to have been misattributed to the erotica, supporting the hypothesis of a similar misattribution in the previous experiment.

Zillman (1978) therefore concludes that what led the previous subjects to behave angrily was a self-attribution of anger.[43] These experiments suggest that people tend to manifest not only what they're feeling but also what they think they're feeling. Note that there is no competing explanation of this tendency in terms of self-enhancement, since people are unlikely to regard anger as a self-enhancing attribute. The most likely explanation is that people tend to behave consistently with their self-attributions, being true to themselves in precisely the manner envisioned by Lecky.

Summary

This review of dissonance and attribution research has yielded two tentative conclusions. The research appears to show, first, that we tend to act in accordance with the motives and traits of character that we conceive of ourselves as having. The research is also consistent with a second conclusion, that this tendency is due to a cognitive motive, to find ourselves explicable and predictable.

In the past I have argued that creatures endowed with such a motive would satisfy our ordinary concept of an agent in the respects that often seem to make that concept seem unsatisfiable. Creatures so motivated would have futures that were open in a sense sufficient to afford them choices or decisions;[44] they would be the causes rather than the mere vehicles of behavior;[45] they would be guided by the normative force of reasons for acting;[46] and they would find such force in principles requiring them to be moral.[47]

I will not repeat these arguments here. What I'll attempt instead is to highlight pieces of the psychological literature that already point the way toward the philosophy of action. This work by psychologists tends to support a philosophical theory like mine.

Philosophical Implications

Some psychologists have gestured toward the philosophy of action in the course of discussing self-consistency motivation. Zillman, for example, having concluded that self-attributions of emotion can influence behavior, goes on to speculate that their influence makes for the difference between automatic manifestations of emotion and emotional actions that are under voluntary control. In Zillman's view, an emotion involves some basic motor responses, which can be reinforced, suppressed, or redirected by the subject's interpretation of them. The basic motor responses belong to "the primitive heritage of man," which we share with the lower animals, and they are not under voluntary control; their modulation by the subject's self-interpretation manifests his "rational capabilities," by which he controls his behavioral response.[48]

Berkowitz draws a similar distinction between impulsive and purposive aggression. In collaboration with Turner (1974), he manipulated the degree of anger that subjects attributed to themselves toward a particular person, thereby modifying the intensity of the "punishment" that they inflicted on that person, though not their aggression toward a third party. Berkowitz emphasizes that the attribution-governed aggression observed in this experiment was purposive rather impulsive. "[I]mpulsive acts," he says, "are automatic, stimulus-elicited responses to the external situation governed primarily by associative factors and relatively unaffected by cognitive processes."[49] By contrast, purposive aggression is subject to cognitive governance:[50]

> The present results generally support [my] cognitive analysis of purposive aggression. Emotionally aroused people seek to attack a particular target when (a) they interpret their internal sensations as "anger," and (b) they believe this specific target had been the cause of their feelings. As indicated in this study, the intensity of

the subjects' desire to hurt a particular person, reflected in the intensity of the punishment given him, arose from their perceptions of the strength of their anger and their belief that this person had been the one who had provoked them.

Berkowitz goes on to explain this mechanism in terms of a cognitive motive toward self-consistency:[51]

> Looked at from a larger perspective, the findings also provide yet another demonstration of the search for cognitive consistency. We want our actions to be in accord with our emotions, as we understand them, and apparently we are also disturbed if these feelings do not seem to be warranted by the causal incident. The emotion as well as the behavior must be consistent with our other cognitions.

The idea that behavior becomes purposive or intentional when it is regulated for self-consistency can be traced back to the early days of self-consistency theory. Six years after the publication of Lecky's treatise, Carl Rogers published "A Theory of Personality and Behavior" offering a similar postulate:[52]

> *Most of the ways of behaving which are adopted by the organism are those which are consistent with the concept of self.* ... As the organism strives to meet its needs in the world as it is experienced, the form which the striving takes must be a form consistent with the concept of self. ... The person who regards himself as having no aggressive feelings cannot satisfy a need for aggression in any direct fashion. The only channels by which needs may be satisfied are those which are consistent with the organized concept of self.

To this Leckian postulate, Rogers added the following piece of action theory:[53]

> *Behavior may, in some instances, be brought about by organic experiences and needs which have not been symbolized. Such behavior may be inconsistent with the structure of the self, but in such instances the behavior is not "owned" by the individual.* ...In such instances the individual feels "I didn't know what I was doing," "I really wasn't responsible for what I was doing." The conscious self feels no degree of government over the actions which took place.

According to Rogers, then, only behavior that is regulated for self-consistency is experienced as intentional action, for which the subject takes responsibility. Hence the difference between mere behavior and intentional action—the difference, as Wittgenstein put it, between my arm's rising and my raising it—may be due to the intervention of a self-consistency motive.

Carrying out an intention

Other psychologists have filled in the self-verification process with steps that correspond to steps in the production of intentional action, as it is ordinarily understood. They have pointed out that people must have not only a conception of their motives but also a conception of what they are doing out of those motives—for example, that they are "retaliating" against someone, or that they are "donating" to the poor. There is evidence that the latter conception also tends to influence their behavior, thereby playing the role of an intention to act.

Wegner, Vallacher, and colleagues (1986) led subjects through a sham experiment involving a clerical task, and then asked them to complete a questionnaire about the degree to which various descriptions applied to the activity in which they had just participated. Some of the suggested descriptions were designed to test whether the subjects conceived of the activity in low-level, mechanical terms, such as "making marks on paper," or high-level, explanatory terms, such as "participating in an experiment." The last seven items were designed to suggest either altruistic descriptions ("helping people study psychology," "aiding the experimenter") or egoistic descriptions ("getting a better grade in psychology," "earning extra credit"). The experimenters then left the room, to allow the subject-pool coordinator to distribute a questionnaire about the subjects' preferences among future opportunities to participate in research. Among the opportunities offered, one was described in altruistic terms, and another in egoistic terms.

The experimenters found that subjects who initially conceived of the prior activity in low-level terms were more likely to adopt the suggested high-level descriptions and also expressed a higher preference for future opportunities described in similar terms. In other words, subjects who could be induced to think of their current participation as "helping" were more inclined to "help" in the future, whereas subjects who could be induced to think of their current participation as "getting ahead" were more inclined toward future opportunities to "get ahead."

This experiment can be interpreted as a demonstrating a "foot-in-the-door" effect; but in this case the effect appears to be mediated by act-descriptions rather that trait- or motive-attributions. The experimenters got their foot in the door by enlisting a subject's participation in one experiment, and they were then able to elicit his willingness to participate in another, but only by getting him to conceive of the second under the same description as the first.[54] This dependence was the same for egoistic as for altruistic actions. Vallacher and Wegner (1985) therefore remark, "although egoism and altruism can represent opposing forces in everyday life, they arise from similar action identification processes."[55]

On the basis of this and related experiments, Wegner and Vallacher have proposed a theory of action identification. The first principle of their theory is "that people do what they think they are doing," by selecting a "prepotent act identity," or act description, and then instantiating it in their behavior.[56] The result, according to Wegner and Vallacher, is that people usually *know* what they're doing, because they are doing what they think.[57]

This principle can readily be interpreted as describing an intermediate step in the self-verification process described above.[58] We can imagine, first, that the cognitively motivated agent selects a "prepotent act identity" consistent with the motives and other dispositions that he conceives himself to have. Conceiving of himself as angry, he thinks of doing something consistent with anger, such as retaliating; conceiving of himself as generous, he thinks of doing something consistent with generosity, such as making a donation. He thereby maintains the coherence of his self-conception. When he goes on to do what he is thinking, we can regard him as taking the next step in the same process. For we can imagine that he does what he's thinking *in order to* know what he's doing, given that whatever he thinks he's about to do is the thing that he would consequently know about, if he did it. The agent thinks of doing something that fits his self-attributed motive, and then he does what fits this self-attribution of action, so that his self-conception is consistent with itself and with his actual behavior.

Wegner and Vallacher suggest that the agent's "prepotent act identity" is in fact an intention to act: in doing what he thinks, the agent is carrying out an intention.[59] This suggestion enables us to map the self-verification process, as now elaborated, onto the process of intentional action as ordinarily understood. Described in theoretical terms, the process goes like this: first something arouses the agent's anger, which already involves some behavioral dispositions; then the agent interprets his arousal *as* anger and thinks of what, in light of it, would make sense for him to do; finally, the agent's anger and his thought of behaving angrily jointly cause the corresponding behavior—the behavioral impetus of the one being regulated for consistency with the other by the agent's motive for making sense. But now we can redescribe the same process in ordinary language, by attaching the term 'motive' to the agent's anger and the term 'intention' to his thought of behaving angrily. Thus redescribed, the process goes like this: the agent forms an intention that's consistent with his motive; and then he acts, under the impetus of his motive, as regulated for consistency with his intention. The theory of self-verification can thus be seen to coincide with our ordinary understanding of intentional action.

Acting for reasons

If the agent's doing what he is thinking constitutes the carrying out of an intention, then what about the preceding step, in which he thinks of doing what would make the most sense? To which phase or aspect of an action, as ordinarily understood, does that earlier part of the self-consistency process correspond?

Wegner and Vallacher allude to this step in a further principle, which says that people ordinarily seek to identify their behavior at a "high" or "comprehensive" level, representing their underlying motives and ultimate goals. Wegner and Vallacher describe this tendency as a "search for meaning in action"[60] or "a human inclination to be informed of what we are doing in the most inte-grative and general way available."[61] An act-description will be "integrative," of course, insofar as it incorporates the motives and traits that the act expresses and in light of which it will make sense. Hence the "search for meaning" pos-ited by Wegner and Vallacher coincides with the agent's search for an act-description that makes sense light of his self-conception.

The process of adopting and then instantiating integrative act-descriptions resembles—or, in fact, may just *be*—a process of enacting a coherent narra-tive.[62] Consider Trzebinski's (1995) discussion of self-narratives, which makes them sound like Wegner and Vallacher's act identities:

> Constructing self-narratives is the mode of searching for a meaning. ... To find mean-ing, and more often just to maintain meaning and avoid disruption of the ordered world, an individual has to move in a specified way within the narrated events. In this way the active schema...not only directs the individual's interpretations of on-going and foreseen events, but also pushes him toward specific aspirations, deci-sions, and actions. By particular moves within the events an individual elaborates, fulfils, and closes important episodes in the developing self-narrative. Personal de-cisions and actions are inspired by, and take strength from self-narratives—devices for meaning searching.

A self-narrative can thus provide the meaningful act descriptions that enable the agent to understand what he's doing. When he instantiates one of these nar-rative act descriptions, he performs an action that "elaborates, fulfils, and closes" an episode in his self-narrative, so that his behavior is intelligible as part of the story.

I suggest that the narrative background on which the agent draws, in order to fashion an integrative act description, is material that would ordinarily be called his reasons for acting—the circumstances, motives, and other consider-ations that make one action rather than another the sensible thing to do. I there-fore suggest that adopting an integrative act description amounts to forming an intention on the basis of a reason, and that enacting such a description amounts to acting for the reason on which the intention was based.

Philosophers have long noted a distinction between doing something that one has reason to do, on the one hand, and doing it *for* that reason, on the other.[63] One can do something that one has reason to do without necessarily doing it *for* that reason, because one can fail to be appropriately influenced by the reason that one has. Philosophers have therefore sought to analyze the in-fluence that a reason exerts when one acts for that reason.

The traditional assumption among philosophers is that a reason for acting must include the expectation of a desired outcome, and that this expectation influences the agent by appealing to his desire for the outcome expected. Else-where I have argued that the influence exerted by an agent's expectation of a desired outcome does not satisfy our concept of the influence exerted by a reason.[64] Indeed, the assumption that expectations of desire- or preference-satisfaction have the normative force of reasons is itself in need of justification.[65]

In my view, an agent is influenced by a reason, and his action is consequently performed *for* that reason, when he is influenced by a representation of the action that makes it intelligible to him. Naturally, this representation may make the action intelligible precisely by setting it in the context of his desires and expectations, but his reason for the action consists in this cognitively attractive representation of it rather than in the desires and expectations to which it alludes. A reason is a *rationale*, in light of which an action makes sense to the agent, and promoting a desired outcome is one such rationale.

If I am right, then the search for an integrative act description to instantiate, or a meaningful story to enact, is in fact a search for an action supported by reasons. And an act identity has "pre-potency" insofar as it satisfies this search, by serving as a rationale. When the agent does what he is thinking under an integrative act description, or "fulfills and closes" an episode in his self-narrative, he is doing what philosophers call acting for reasons. The upshot is that the steps of finding and acting for reasons correspond to successive steps in the self-verification process, the process of being true to oneself.

Conclusion

Nuttin has illustrated the resulting theory of practical reasoning as follows:[66]

> Consider a son who is tempted to lie to his parents in order to be able to accompany his friends on a vacation despite the anticipated opposition of his father. The son must evaluate and determine the extent to which he is able to integrate within one structure the two conflicting components: his image of himself and the lie to his parents as he perceives it in the present behavioral context. Is he able to take up, subsume, or accept that concrete type of lying within his dynamic self-concept? The strength of the tendency to accompany his friends will be one of the factors determining the degree of distortion of the self-image that can be tolerated by the personality. The degree of inner consistency within the subject's personality will be another factor. In some people, there will be no difficulty at all in subsuming the lying behavior in the self-concept; in other people, accepting such a lie within their own personality functioning will not be possible. In the latter case, the subject is not "willing" to lie in the present behavioral context.

In my view, the conflict between the boy's desire to accompany his friends, on the one hand, and his need for a coherent self-conception, on the other, is a conflict between inclination and practical reason. If the boy finds a way to reconcile the lie with his self-conception—a story to tell himself about telling the lie, which would amount to a rationale for telling it—then his practical reason condones telling the lie, and he is consequently "willing" to tell it. But if he cannot reconcile telling a lie with his self-conception, then his need for self-understanding opposes his telling it, and this opposition embodies the restraint that practical reason places on his inclination to lie.

As Vallacher and Wegner point out,[67] this same process can lead to immoral as well as moral behavior. Or, as Lecky suggested, it can lead to bad spelling. What a Leckian moral philosophy will need, then, is an account of why a conception of oneself as honest is more rational than a conception of oneself as dishonest; or, for that matter, why a conception of oneself as a good speller is more rational than a conception of oneself as a poor one, given that one will do as one conceives. I have attempted such an account elsewhere.[68] Here I have tried to connect the underlying moral philosophy to an empirical basis in the psychological research that Lecky inspired.

Notes

1. Work on this paper was supported by a fellowship from the John Simon Guggenheim Memorial Foundation, and by a matching leave funded by the Philosophy Department and the College of Literature, Science, and the Arts, University of Michigan. For comments on an earlier draft of the paper, I am grateful to Elizabeth Anderson, Elliot Aronson, Don Herzog, Richard Nisbett, Bill Swann, and Dan Wegner.
2. See the "Biographical Sketch" in the 1961 edition of Lecky's book. At the time of his death, Lecky was employed as an instructor in the Extension Division of Columbia University, having been fired seven years earlier from a faculty position at Columbia College for failing to complete his Ph.D. dissertation.
3. Lecky (1945), 82.
4. "One source of motivation only, the necessity to maintain the unity of the system, must serve as the universal dynamic principle" (81). "By interpreting all behavior as motivated by the need for unity, we understand particular motives or tendencies simply as expressions of the main motive, pursuing different immediate goals as necessary means to that end" (82).
5. *Ibid.*, 50.
6. *Ibid.*, 85. See also 90.
7. *Ibid.*, 86.
8. *Ibid.*, 136.
9. *Ibid.*, 103–04.
10. For recent research on this topic, see Jussim, Eccles, & Madon (1996).
11. Velleman (1989), (1993), and the Introduction to Velleman (in press).
12. See the Introduction to Velleman (1989).
13. For recent contributions to the dissonance debate, see Harmon-Jones & Mills (1999).
14. See also Aronson (1969); Thibodeau & Aronson (1992).
15. On this point, see also Nisbett & Valins (1972).
16. See Sherman (1980), in which subjects greatly under-predicted their compliance with a typical dissonance protocol.
17. See also Nisbett & Wilson (1977).
18. *Ibid.*, p. 68.
19. Zanna & Cooper (1974); Zanna, Higgins, & Taves (1976); Cooper, Zanna, & Taves (1978); Higgins, Rhodewalt, & Zanna (1979); Elliott & Devine (1994).
20. See Fazio, Zanna, & Cooper (1977).
21. These phrases are drawn from the quotations on p. 1, above.

22. There may be one other point of disagreement, but it is too small to worry about. Aronson tends to describe the subject as changing his belief about the experimental task; Bem tends to describe him as attributing such a belief to his earlier self. As I have explained, Aronson's version requires the assumption that the subject not only forms the belief in the present but also projects it back into the past, thus arriving at the same attribution as in Bem's version. But Bem's version says only that the subject attributes the belief to his earlier self—which, in principle, he could do without forming the belief in the present. Bem doesn't say that the subject now believes the task to have been enjoyable; what Bem says is that the subject believes himself to have believed what he was saying when he said that the task was enjoyable.

    But this in-principle difference between Bem and Aronson makes no difference in practice. Surely, if someone believes that shortly after finishing a task, he believed it to have been enjoyable, then he is likely to believe, in the present, that the task was enjoyable, unless he has some reason for doubting the truth of his earlier belief. In the absence of such a reason, he will probably be unable to attribute the belief to his former self without adopting it. Bem and Aronson agree that what the subject wants is to attribute the belief to his former self, so as to account for his behavior. Bem doesn't mention that the subject will probably have to adopt the belief in order to attribute it to his former self, in the absence of reasons for doubting it. But this omission hardly constitutes an important difference of opinion with Aronson.

23. In a paper presented to the 1967 Nebraska Symposium on Motivation, Harold Kelley connected dissonance theory and self-perception theory by way of attribution theory, which he presented as containing a "broad motivational assumption," to the effect that attributional processes "operate *as if* the individual were motivated to attain a cognitive mastery of the causal structure of his environment." Commenting on the passage in which this statement occurred, Bem says: "It is an admirable attempt, but the strongest motivation to emerge from this quotation appears to be Kelley's need to understand why he was there" (Bem [1972], p. 45).

    This remark is wonderfully self-refuting. Bem claims that the processes discussed by Kelley involve no motivation, despite Kelley's assertions to the contrary. Yet Bem's attempt to discredit the latter assertions ends up confirming them instead. Bem suggests that we shouldn't credit Kelley's assertions about motivation because he made them only in order to satisfy his need to understand why he was addressing a symposium on motivation. The psychological process to which Bem thus attributes Kelley's assertions is one of the very processes whose existence Kelley was asserting—a process driven by the need for self-understanding. What better reason could we have for accepting Kelley's assertions as true than his having made them out of a need to understand himself?

24. See Bem (1972); Nisbett & Valins (1972).

25. This view of the debate is suggested by Aronson (1992).

26. Discussed by Bem (1972), 31–33.

27. For ease of exposition, I speak here as if Snyder & Ebbesen applied their modifications to the dissonance experiment of Festinger & Carlsmith (1959). In fact, they modified a different dissonance experiment, but the differences aren't relevant in this context.

28. See, e.g., Steele & Liu (1983). Aronson (1968) rightly points out that this self-enhancement hypothesis can be subsumed under the hypothesis of cognitive dissonance. People tend to conceive of themselves as rational agents, and their perception

of having acted with insufficient justification will be inconsistent with this self-conception, producing a higher-order dissonance that is cognitive. Yet there is a difference between a desire to avoid seeming irrational and a desire to avoid the inconsistency of believing that one is rational while also believing that one has behaved irrationally.

29. See, e.g., Prislin & Pool (1996); Stone, Cooper, Wiegand, & Aronson (1997).
30. For reviews of Swann's research, see: Swann (1983); Swann (1985); Swann and Brown (1990); McNulty and Swann (1991); Swann (1996).
31. Swann, De La Ronde, and Hixon (1992); Swann, De La Ronde, and Hixon, (1994); Swann, Pelham, and Krull (1989), Study 3. See also Swann and Predmore (1985) and the research by Swann and B.W. Pelham reported in Swann (1986), pp. 419–20.
32. Swann and Read (1981a), Investigation II; Swann and Hill (1982).
33. Swann and Read (1981a), Investigation III.
34. See Swann (1986); Swann, Pelham, and Krull (1989); Swann, Hixon, Stein-Seroussi, and Gilbert (1990); Swann, Stein-Seroussi, and Giesler (1992); Jussim, Yen, and Aiello (1995).
35. On a later occasion, the 8-year-olds were induced to help a different experimenter prepare materials for building toy houses, and they were again given praise, an attribution of helpfulness, or no feedback. They were then left alone and allowed to choose between playing with a toy or continuing with the helpful task, while an experimenter observed through a one-way mirror. Only attribution showed an effect on their tendency to help. One or two weeks later, these children were given an opportunity to donate drawings and craft materials to hospitalized children. Although total donations were too few for a full statistical analysis, more donations were received from the attribution group than from either of the others.
36. For research connecting the foot-in-the-door effect to self-consistency motivation in adults, see Kraut (1973) and Goldman, Seever, & Seever (1982). For contrary findings, see Gorassini & Olson (1995). For other experiments in which children show a tendency to verify attributions, see Jensen & Moore (1977), Toner, Moore, & Emmons (1980), Biddle *et al.* (1985), and McGrath, Wilson, & Frassetto (1995).
37. The same is true of Jensen and Moore (1977); Toner, Moore, & Emmons (1980); Goldman, Seever, & Seever (1982); and Kraut (1973).
38. See the review in Dipboye (1977).
39. Swann & Ely (1984); Maracek & Mettee (1972); see also Setterlund & Niedenthal (1993).
40. Maracek & Mettee (1972).
41. Actually, Schachter's (1964) theory of emotion implies that people actually *have* the emotions that they believe themselves to have, provided that they are in fact aroused or excited. This feature of Schachter's theory is philosophically problematic, but I won't discuss it here.
42. Most recently by Messacappa, Katkin, & Palmer (1999).
43. For related experiments, see Brodt & Zimbardo (1981); Olson (1990); and the research of Berkowitz, discussed below.

    Bem (1972) points out that experiments of this form often show more effect on the subjects' behavior than on their reported attitudes. In the Schachter-Singer study, for example, the misattribution condition was more strongly correlated with a tendency to join in the angry or giddy behavior of a fellow subject than with a tendency to report anger or giddiness. Bem argues that if the behavior was caused, as hypothesized, by the subjects' self-attributions, then the self-attributions ought to have been more strongly correlated with the experimental manipulations, not less. Bem therefore concludes that such experiments support self-perception theory, according to which the subjects' self-attributions were based on their behavior rather than vice versa.

Yet there are many ways of accounting for the weaker effect on attitudes than on behavior, even under the hypothesis that the attitudes came first in the order of causation. After all, the problematic correlations were observed, not with the attitudes themselves, but rather with the subjects' reports of those attitudes. Any gaps in the process of articulating self-attributions could therefore account for the results. Suppose, for example, that the subjects attributed anger or euphoria to themselves but not in so many words, or not in words at all. Perhaps they had mental images of those emotions (say, images of facial expressions or bodily postures), which they immediately associated with particular kinds of behavior, but to which they were not equally quick to attach names. Their self-attributions would then have been less reliable in prompting self-reports than in prompting behavior.

Even if we grant that Bem is right about the order of causation, his interpretation of the results would still support the hypothesis of cognitive motivation. A plausible explanation of the results, even as interpreted by Bem, is that the subjects behaved emotionally in order to facilitate the emotional attributions that would render their feelings intelligible. Feeling aroused, they sought a self-conception that would explain why, and they consequently behaved in ways that would make such a self-conception applicable to them. If their behavior was thus designed to facilitate the attribution, then it preceded the attribution in the order of causation; but it would still have been motivated by a cognitive interest in the self-understanding that the attribution would provide.

44. Velleman (1989a)
45. Velleman (1992a) and Introduction to (in press).
46. Velleman (1996) and Introduction to (in press).
47. Velleman (1989b), Part Four.
48. Zillman (1978), pp. 356–57. See also Cross & Markus (1990); Wegner & Bargh (1998).
49. *Ibid.*, p. 176.
50. *Ibid.*, pp. 186–87. See also Berkowitz (1987).
51. *Ibid.* See also Berkowitz (1987).
52. *Client-Centered Therapy: It's Current Practice, Implications, and Theory* (Boston: Houghton Mifflin, 1951), Chapter 11, 507–08. For other theories in the Leckian tradition, see Snygg & Combs (1959); Kelley (1967); Korman (1970); Epstein (1973), (1981); Andrews (1991); Nuttin (1984).
53. *Ibid.* p. 509. In this quotation, philosophers of action will detect a resemblance to Harry Frankfurt's theory of autonomy (1987, 1999). Like Frankfurt, Rogers believed that whether behavior amounts to an autonomous action depends on its relation to the self. But if Rogers had expressed his view in these terms, he would have been using the psychologist's sense of 'self', which refers to the self-conception; whereas Frankfurt uses the term in a philosophical sense referring to the core or essence of the person. Rogers thus resembles Frankfurt partly by courtesy of ambiguity. (For psychologists who prefer a Frankfurtian conception of the self, see Deci & Ryan [1991].)
54. Kraut (1973) links the foot-in-the-door effect to the attribution of traits, such as "charitable" and "uncharitable," rather than to act-descriptions. But my view is that

attributions of traits, motives, and acts are themselves linked, under the principle of self-consistency. That is, someone who conceives of himself as angry finds it consistent to conceive of himself as retaliating; someone who conceives of himself as uncharitable finds it inconsistent to conceive of himself as donating to charity; and so on.

55. P. 143.
56. Wegner & Vallacher (1986), p. 552
57. *Ibid.*, p. 568. See also Velleman (1989), Chapters 1 and 2.
58. See also Aronson, 1992, p. 307.
59. Vallacher & Wegner (1985), pp. 6–11.
60. Wegner & Vallacher (1986), pp. 555–56.
61. Vallacher & Wegner (1985), p. 26.
62. See Velleman (1993).
63. E.g., Davidson (1980).
64. Velleman (1992a), (1992b), (1996); "Introduction" to Velleman (in press).
65. Velleman (1993); Korsgaard (1997).
66. Nuttin (1984), p. 187.
67. Quoted above at note 55.
68. See Velleman (1989a), Part III.

References

Andrews, J.D.W., *The Active Self in Psychotherapy: An Integration of Therapeutic Styles* (Boston: Allyn & Bacon, 1991).

Aronson, E., "Dissonance theory: Progress and problems," in *Theories of Cognitive Consistency: A Sourcebook*, ed. Robert P. Ableson, Elliot Aronson, William J. McGuire, Theodore M. Newcomb, Milton J. Rosenberg, Percy H. Tannenbaum (Chicago: Rand McNally, 1968), 5–27.

Aronson, E., "The Theory of Cognitive Dissonance: a Current Perspective, *Advances in Experimental Social Psychology* 4 (1969):1–34.

Aronson, E., "The Return of the Repressed: Dissonance Theory Makes a Comeback," *Psychological Inquiry* 3 (1992): 303–311.

Aronson, E., and Carlsmith, J.M., "Performance expectancy as a determinant of actual performance," *Journal of Abnormal and Social Psychology* 65 (1962): 178–82.

Bem, D.J., "Self-perception theory," in *Advances in Experimental Social Psychology*, Vol. 6, ed. Leonard Berkowitz (New York: Academic Press, 1972), 1–62.

Berkowitz, L., "Mood, self-awareness, and willingness to help," *Journal of Personality and Social Psychology* 52 (1987): 721–29.

Berkowitz, L., & Turner, C., "Perceived anger level, instigating agent, and aggression," in *Cognitive Alteration of Feeling States*, ed. H. London & R.E. Nisbett (Chicago: Aldine, 1972), 174–89.

Brodt, S.E., & Zimbardo, P.G., "Modifying shyness-related social behavior through symptom misattribution," *Journal of Personality and Social Psychology* 41 (1981): 437–49.

Cantor, J.R., Zillman, D., & Bryant, J., "Enhancement of experienced sexual arousal in response to erotic stimuli through misattribution of unrelated residual excitation," *Journal of Personality and Social Psychology*, 32 (1975): 69–75.

Cooper, J., Zanna, M.P., & Taves, P.A., Arousal as a necessary condition for attitude change following induced compliance," *Journal of Personality & Social Psychology* 36 (1978): 1101–1106.

Cross, S.E., & Markus, H.R., "The Willful Self," *Personality and Social Psychology Bulletin* 16 (1990): 726–42.

Davidson, D., *Essays on Actions and Events* (Oxford: Clarendon Press, 1980).

Deci, E.L., & Ryan, R.M., "A motivational approach to self: Integration in Personality," *Perspectives on Motivation, Nebraska Symposium on Motivation 1990*, ed. Rtichard Dienstbier (Lincoln: University of Nebraska Press, 1991), 237–88.

Dipboye, R.L., "A critical review of Korman's self-consistency theory of work motivation and occupational choice," *Organizational Behavior and Human Performance* 18 (1977): 108–26.

Eisenberg, N., Cialdini, R.B., McCreath, H, and Shell, R, "Consistency-based compliance: When and why do children become vulnerable?" *Journal of Personality and Social Psychology* 52 (1987): 1174–81.

Eisenberg, N., Cialdini, R.B., McCreath, H., and Shell, R., "Consistency-based compliance in children: When and why do consistency procedures have immediate effects?", *International Journal of Behavioural Development* 12 (1989): 351–67.

Elliot, A.J., & Devine, P.G., "On the motivational nature of cognitive dissonance: Dissonance as psychological discomfort," *Journal of Personality and Social Psychology* 67 (1994): 382–94.

Epstein, S., "The Self-Concept Revisited; Or a Theory of a Theory," *American Psychologist* 28 (1973): 404–416.

Epstein, S., "The Unity Principle Versus the Reality and Pleasure Principles, *Or* the Tale of the Scorpion and the Frog," in *Self-Concept: Advances in Theory and Research*, ed. M.D. Lynch, A.A. Norem-Hebeisen, & K.J. Gergen (Cambridge, MA: Ballinger, 1981).

Fazio, R.H., Zanna, M.P., & Cooper, J., "Dissonance and self-perception: An integrative view of each theory's proper domain of application," *Journal of Experimental Social Psychology* 13 (1977): 464–479.

Festinger, L., & Carlsmith, J.M., "Cognitive Consequences of Forced Compliance," *Journal of Abnormal and Social Psychology* 58 (1959), 203–11.

Frankfurt, Harry, *The Importance of What We Care About* (Cambridge: Cambridge University Press, 1987).

Frankfurt, Harry, *Necessity, Volition, and Love* (Cambridge, Cambridge University Press, 1999).

Freedman, J.L., & Fraser, S.C., "Compliance without pressure: The foot-in-the-door technique," *Journal of Personality and Social Psychology* 4 (1966): 195–202.

Goldman, M., Seever, M., and Seever, M., "Social labeling and the foot-in-the-door effect," *The Journal of Social Psychology* 117 (1982): 19–23.

Gorasini, D.R., and Olson, J.M., "Does self-perception change explain the foot-in-the-door effect?" *Journal of Personality and Social Psychology* 69 (1995): 91–105.

Grusec, J.E., & Redler, E., "Attribution, reinforcement, and altruism: A developmental analysis," *Developmental Psychology* 16 (1980): 525–34.

Harmon-Jones, E., & Mills, J., (eds.), *Cognitive Dissonance: Progress on a Pivotal Theory in Social Psychology* (Washington, DC: American Psychological Association, 1999).

Higgins, E.T., Rhodewalt, F., Zanna, M.P., "Dissonance motivation: Its nature, persistence, and reinstatement," *Journal of Experimental Social Psychology* 15 (1979): 16–34.

Jensen, R.E., & Moore, S.G., "The effect of attribute statements on cooperativeness and competitiveness in school-age boys," *Child Development* 48 (1977): 305–07.

Jussim, L. , Eccles, J., & Madon, S., "Social perception, social stereotypes, and teacher expectations: Accuracy and the quest for the powerful self-fulfilling prophecy," in *Advances in Experimental Social Psychology*, Vol 28, ed. M.P. Zanna (New York: Academic Press, 1996), 281–388.

Jussim, L., Yen, H.J., Aiello, J.R., "Self-consistency, self-enhancement, and accuracy in reactions to feeback," *Journal of Experimental and Social Psychology* 31 (1995): 322–56.

Kelley, H.H., "Attribution theory in social psychology," in *Nebraska Symposium on Motivation, 1967*, Vol. 15 of *Current Theory and Research in Motivation*, ed. David Levine (Lincoln: University of Nebraska Press, 1967), 192–238.

Korman, A.K., "Toward an Hypothesis of Work Behavior," 54 *Journal of Applied Psychology* 54 (1970): 31–41.

Korsgaard, Christine, "The Normativity of Instrumental Reason, in *Ethics and Practical Reason*, ed. Garrett Cullity & Berys Gaut (Oxford: Oxford University Press, 1997), 213–54.

Kraut, R.E., "Effects of social labeling on giving to charity," *Journal of Experimental Social Psychology* (1973): 551–62.

Lecky, P., *Self-Consistency: A Theory of Personality* (New York: Island Press, 1945).

Maracek, J., & Mettee, D.R., "Avoidance of continued success as a function of self-esteem, level of esteem certainty, and responsibility for success," *Journal of Personality and Social Psychology* 22 (1972): 98–107.

Mezzacappa, E.S., Katkin, E.S., & Palmer, S.N., "Epinephrine, arousal, and emotion: A new look at two-factor theory," *Cognition and Emotion* 13 (1999): 181–99.

McNulty, S.E., & Swann, W.B., Jr., "Psychotherapy, Self-Concept Change, and Self-Verification," in *The Relational Self; Theoretical Convergences in Psychoanalysis and Social Psychology*, ed. Rebecca C. Curtis (New York: Guildford Press, 1991), 213–37.

Miller, R.L, Brickman, P., & Bolen, D., "Attribution Versus Persuasion as a Means for Modifying Behavior," *Journal of Personality and Social Psychology* 31 (1975): 430–41.

Nisbett, R.E., & Valins, S., "Perceiving the causes of one's own behavior," in *Attribution: Perceiving the Causes of Behavior*, ed. Edward E. Jones, David E. Kanouse, Harold H. Kelley, Richard E. Nisbett, Stuart Valins, & Bernard Weiner (Morristown, NJ: General Learning, 1972).

Nisbett, R.E., & Wilson, T.D., "Telling more than we can know: Verbal reports of mental processes," *Psychological Review* 84 (1977), 231–59.

Nuttin, Joseph, *Motivation, Planning, and Action; a Relational Theory of Behavior Dynamics*, trans. Raymond P. Lorion & Jean E. Dumas (Hillsdale, NJ: Erlbaum, 1984).

Olson, J.M., "Self-inference processes in emotion," in *Self-Inference Processes: The Ontario Symposium*, Vol. 6, ed. James M. Olson and Mark P. Zanna (Hillsdale, NJ: Erlbaum, 1990), 17–41.

Prislin, R., & Pool, G.J., "Behavior, consequences, and the self: Is all well that ends well?" *Personality and Social Psychology Bulletin* 22 (1996): 933–48.

Rogers, C.R., *Client-Centered Therapy; It's Current Practice, Implications, and Theory* (New York: Houghton Mifflin, 1951).

Schachter, S., "The interaction of cognitive and physiological determinants of emotional state," *Advances in Experimental Social Psychology*, Vol. 1, ed. Leonard Berkowitz (New York: Academic Press, 1964).

Schachter, S., & Singer, J.E., "Cognitive, social and physiological determinants of emotional state," *Psychological Review* 69 (1962): 379–99.

Setterlund, M.B., & Niedenthal, P.M., "'Who am I? Why am I here?': Self-esteem, Self-clarity, and prototype matching," *Journal of Personality and Social Psychology* 65 (1993): 769–80.

Sherman, S.J., "On the self-erasing nature of errors of prediction," *Journal of Personality and Social Psychology* 39 (1980): 211–21.

Snyder, M., & Ebbesen, E.B., "Dissonance awareness: A test of dissonance theory versus self-perception theory," *Journal of Experimental Social Psychology* 8 (1972): 502–17.

Snygg, D., & Combs, A.W., *Individual Behavior: A Perceptual Approach to Behavior* (New York: Harper & Brothers, 1959).

Steele, C.M., & Liu, T.J., "Dissonance processes as self-affirmation," *Journal of Personality and Social Psychology* 45 (1983): 5–19.

Stone, J., Cooper, J., Wiegand, A.W., & Aronson, E., "When exemplification fails: Hypocrisy and the motive for self-integrity," *Journal of Personality and Social Psychology* 72 (1997): 54–65.

Swann, W.B., Jr., "Self-Verification: Bringing Social Reality into Harmony with the Self," in *Psychological Perspectives on the Self*, Vol. 2, ed. J. Suls & A.G. Greenwald (Hillsdale, NJ: Erlbaum, 1983), 33–66.

Swann, W.B., Jr., "The Self as Architect of Social Reality," in *The Self and Social Life*, ed. Barry R. Schlenker (New York: McGraw-Hill, 1985), 100–25.

Swann, W.B., Jr., "To be adored or to be known? The interplay of self-enhancement and self-verification," in *Handbook of Motivation and Cognition: Foundations of Social Behavior*, Vol. 2, ed. E.T. Higgins and R.M. Sorrentino (New York: Guilford Press, 1986), 408–48.

Swann, W.B., Jr., *Self-Traps; The Elusive Quest for Higher Self-Esteem* (New York: W.H. Freeman, 1996).

Swann, W.B., Jr., & Brown, J.D., "From Self to health: Self-verification and identity disruption," in *Social Support: An Interactional View*, ed. Barbara R. Sarason, Irwin G. Sarason, & Gregory R. Pierce (New York: Wiley-Interscience, 1990), 150–72.

Swann, W.B., Jr., De La Ronde, C., & Hixon, G., "Embracing the bitter 'truth': Negative self-concepts and marital commitment," *Psychological Science* 3 (1992), 383–86.

Swann, W.B., Jr., De La Ronde, C., & Hixon, G., "Authenticity and positivity strivings in marriage and courtship," *Journal of Personality and Social Psychology* 66 (1994): 857–69.

Swann, W.B., Jr., & Ely, R.J., "A Battle of Wills: Self-Verification Versus Behavioral Confirmation," *Journal of Personality and Social Psychology* 46 (1984): 1287–1302.

Swann, W.B., Jr., & Hill, C.A., "When Our Identities are mistaken: Reaffirming self-conceptions through social interaction," *Journal of Personality and Social Psychology*, 43 (1982): 59–66.

Swann, W.B., Jr., Hixon, G., Stein-Seroussi, A., & Gilbert, D.T., "The fleeting gleam of praise: Cognitive Processes underlying behavioral reactions to self-relevant feedback," *Journal of Personality and Social Psychology* 59 (1990): 17–26.

Swann, W.B., Jr., & Predmore, S.C., "Intimates as agents of social support: Sources of consolation or despair?" *Journal of Personality and Social Psychology* 49 (1985): 1609–17.

Swann, W.B., Jr., Pelham, B.W., & Krull, D.S., "Agreeable Fancy or disagreeable truth? Reconciling self-enhancement and self-verification," *Journal of Personality and Social Psychology* 57 (1989): 782–91.

Swann, W.B., Jr., & Read, S.J., "Self-Verification Processes: How We Sustain Our Self-Conceptions," *Journal of Experimental Social Psychology* 17 (1981a): 351–72.

Swann, W.B., Jr., & Read, S.J., "Acquiring Self-Knowledge: The Search for Feedback that Fits," *Journal of Personality and Social Psychology* 41 (1981b): 1119–1128.

Swann, W.B., Jr., Stein-Seroussi, A., & Giesler, R.B., "Why people self-verify," *Journal of Personality and Social Psychology* 62 (1992): 392–401.

Thibodeau, R., & Aronson, E., "Taking a Closer Look: Reasserting the Role of the Self-Concept in Dissonance Theory," *Personality and Social Psychology Bulletin* 18 (1992): 91–602.

Toner, I.J., Moore, L.P., & Emmons, B.A., "The effects of being labeled on subsequent self-control in children," *Child Development* 51 (1980): 618–21.

Trzebinski, J., "Narrative Self, Understanding, and Action," in *The Self in European and North American Culture: Development and Processes*, ed. A. Oosterwegel and R.A. Wicklund (Dordrecht: Kluwer, 1995), 73–88.

Vallacher, R.R., & Wegner, D.M., *A Theory of Action Identification* (Hillsdale, NJ: Erlbaum, 1985).

Vallacher, R.R., & Wegner, D.M., "What Do People Think They're Doing? Action Identification and Human Behavior," *Psychological Review* 94 (1987): 3–15.

Velleman, J. David, "Epistemic Freedom," *Pacific Philosophical Quarterly* 70 (1989a): 73–97.

Velleman, J. David, *Practical Reflection* (Princeton: Princeton University Press, 1989b); reprinted at http://www-personal.umich.edu/~velleman/Practical_Reflection.

Velleman, J. David, "The Story of Rational Action," *Philosophical Topics* 21(1993): 229–53 (1993); to be reprinted in Velleman (in press).

Velleman, J. David, What Happens When Someone Acts?" *Mind* 101 (1992a): 461–81; to be reprinted in Velleman (in press).

Velleman, J. David, "The Guise of the Good" *Nous* 26 (1992b): 3–26; to be reprinted in Velleman (in press).

Velleman, J. David, "The Possibility of Practical Reason," *Ethics* 106 (1996): 694–726; to be reprinted in Velleman (in press).

Velleman, J. David, *The Possibility of Practical Reason* (Oxford: Oxford University Press, in press).

Wegner, D.M., & Bargh. J.A., "Control and Automaticity in Social Life," in *The Handbook of Social Psychology*, 4th ed., Vol. 1, ed. Daniel T. Gilbert, Susan T. Fiske, and Gardner Lindzey (Boston: McGraw-Hill, 1998), 446–96.

Wegner, D.M., & Vallacher, R.R., "Action Identification," in *Handbook of Motivation and Cognition*, ed. Richard M. Sorrentino & E. Tory Higgins (New York: Guilford Press, 1986), 550–82.

Wegner, D.M., Vallacher, R.R., Kiersted, G.W., & Dizadji, D., "Action Identification in the Emergence of Social Behavior," *Social Cognition* 4 (1986): 18–38.

Zanna, M.P., & Cooper, J., "Dissonance and the pill: An attribution approach to studying the arousal properties of dissonance," *Journal of Personality & Social Psychology* 29 (1974): 703–709.

Zanna, M.P., Higgins, E.T., & Taves, P.A., "Is dissonance phenomenologically aversive?" *Journal of Experimental Social Psychology* 12 (1976): 530–538.

Zillman, D., "Attribution and misattribution of excitatory reactions," *New Directions in Attribution Research*, Vol. 2, ed. John H. Harvey, William Ickes, & Robert F. Kidd (Hillsdale, NJ: Erlbaum, 1978), 335–68.

Zillman, E., Johnson. R.C., & Day, K.D., "Attribution of apparent arousal and proficiency of recovery for sympathetic activation affecting excitation transfer to aggressive behavior," *Journal of Experimental Social Psychology* 10 (1974): 503–15.